D0909432

UN

University of Pennsylvania Library
Circulation Department

Please ... on as you have
finishe ... a fine it must

BURT FRANKLIN: RESEARCH & SOURCE WORKS SERIES 681
Philosophy Monograph Series 45

PHILOSOPHICAL DISCUSSIONS

PHILOSOPHICAL DISCUSSIONS

BY

CHAUNCEY WRIGHT

WITH A BIOGRAPHICAL SKETCH OF THE AUTHOR

BY

CHARLES ELIOT NORTON

WITHDRAWN
FROM
UNIVERSITY OF PENNSYLVANIA
LIBRARIES

BURT FRANKLIN
NEW YORK

B
945
W73
P5
1971

WITHDRAWN
FROM
UNIVERSITY OF PENNSYLVANIA
LIBRARIES

Published by LENOX HILL Pub. & Dist. Co. (Burt Franklin)
235 East 44th St., New York, N.Y. 10017
Originally Published: 1877
Reprinted: 1971
Printed in the U.S.A.

S.B.N.: 8337-3895X
Library of Congress Card Catalog No.: 78-131415
Burt Franklin: Research and Source Works Series 681
Philosophy Monograph Series 45

Reprinted from the original edition in the Wesleyan University
Library.

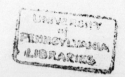

CONTENTS

BIOGRAPHICAL SKETCH OF CHAUNCEY WRIGHT.

BY CHARLES ELIOT NORTON.

CHAUNCEY WRIGHT died in Cambridge, Massachusetts, on the 12th of September, 1875, aged forty-five years.

His name was not widely known. He had written comparatively little. A few essays by him on scientific subjects had appeared in."The Mathematical Monthly," and the "Memoirs" and "Proceedings of the American Academy of Arts and Sciences"; he had contributed several articles, mostly upon philosophical topics, to the "North American Review," and he had printed numerous briefer papers in "The Nation." His work gave evidence not only of a mind of rare power and unusual balance, but also of wide acquisitions and thorough intellectual discipline, and he had won recognition from competent judges as a philosophical thinker of a high order, from whom much was to be expected.

To collect his principal writings, and to present them in a form accessible to students was a duty to his memory, and in the interest of philosophy. Fragmentary, as of necessity such a collection must be, and but imperfectly representative of the scope of the author's mind, the general character of his philosophical opinions and method may clearly enough be learned from it.

It seemed desirable to prefix to this selection from his writings an account of the author, not merely to gratify the natural desire of his readers to know something of the man to whom they might owe the incitement of thought, but still more because the character of Chauncey Wright was no less remarkable than his intelligence, and was of such uncommon and admirable quality that upon those who knew him intimately his death fell as a great misfortune, and has left a void in their lives that can never be filled.

The task of preparing this account has been assigned to me as one who knew him well, especially during the last fifteen years of his life, and who had enjoyed the happiness of his close and helpful friendship. The external events of his life were not striking, and all that need be told of them can be said in a few words.

Chauncey Wright was born in Northampton, in the year 1830. His father and mother were of old New England stock, with such characters and habits as were the results of a long succession of generations who had lived simply and seriously, transmitting from one to another the traditions of labor, frugality, domestic comfort, and intelligence. His father was an active man in his town, carrying on a successful country trade, and occupied with the various duties of the office of a deputy-sheriff of the county, a post which he filled for many years. Wright's boyhood was fortunate in the advantages common to New England country boys at a time when the conditions which have, during the present generation, wrought so rapid and great a change in American society, had hardly begun to manifest themselves. The circumstances of his life were eminently wholesome. He was an affectionate, reserved, and thoughtful boy, fond of animals and plants, observant of their habits, and in general more interested in outdoor than indoor pursuits. He did not especially distinguish himself at school, except, perhaps, in mathematics and in the writing of compositions, which he often preferred to write in verse rather than in prose. No strong personal influence seems to have affected the natural development of his intelligence; and, though neither solitary nor unsocial, he worked out much by himself the problems and devices of his youth, and early displayed the solid independence of his mind and character. He had a serious disposition, and even in early years he, at times, suffered from a tendency toward melancholy. He entered Harvard College in 1848. His classical attainments were slight, and he took little interest in the study either of languages or of literature. The bent of his mind was strong toward abstract pursuits, and he applied himself chiefly to mathematics and philosophy, displaying the acuteness and originality of his intelligence in his themes and other written exercises. He had a certain inertness of temperament which caused the action of his mind to appear slow and difficult. But often when he seemed least active, he was engaged in reflection, and the want of brilliancy or vivacity of power was more than compensated for by solidity of acquisition, as well as by the assimilation of his knowledge with his thought. He learned slowly, but he knew whatever he learned. His memory was retentive, and well disciplined, so that its stores not only became abundant, but were also held in good order for service. One of the most marked features of his intellectual nature, even at this comparatively early date, was the steadiness and consistency of its growth. There was nothing desultory in the pursuit of his aims; and, though his efforts were often intermittent, they were not dispersed.

His modesty and reserve combined with the nature of his interests to prevent him from being well known by any large circle of acquaintances; but the disinterestedness of his disposition and the amiability of his temper endeared him to a few intimate friends, while his classmates generally felt for him more than ordinary regard and respect.

Soon after leaving college, in 1852, he was appointed one of the computers for the recently established "American Ephemeris and Nautical Almanac." By occasional contributions to the "Mathematical Monthly" and other journals, he gradually won repute as a mathematician and physicist of distinguished ability and accomplishment. In 1863 he was made Recording Secretary of the American Academy of Arts and Sciences, a place which he held for seven years, and which gave opportunity not only for the exercise of his sound judgment in practical questions, but for the exhibition of critical discrimination in the editing of the Academy's "Proceedings."

His attention gradually became more and more fixed upon the questions in metaphysics and philosophy presented in their latest form in the works of Mill, Darwin, Bain, Spencer, and others, and in 1864 he published in the "North American Review," then under my charge, the first of a series of philosophical essays, of which the last appeared only two months before his death, and of which it is not too much to say that they form the most important contribution made in America to the discussion and investigation of the questions which now chiefly engage the attention of the students of philosophy.

From the time of his leaving college to his death, he resided, with brief intervals of absence, in Cambridge. In 1872, he spent a few months in Europe. In 1870 he delivered a course of University Lectures in Harvard College on the principles of Psychology. In 1874–75, he was instructor in Harvard College in Mathematical Physics.

He lived all his life simply, frugally, and modestly. He had few wants, and he used a considerable part of his somewhat scanty means to add to the comfort of those who were dear to

·him. He had what may be truly called an elevated nature, not remote from human interests, but above all selfishness or meanness. The motives by which the lives of common men are determined had little influence with him. He did not feel the spur of ambition, or the sting of vanity. No thought of personal advantage, no jealousy of others, affected his judgment or his conduct. His principles were so firmly established that his moral superiority seemed not so much the result of effort as the expression of what was natural to him. His sympathies were not stimulated by his mode of life, but they were keen, and so interpenetrated by his intelligence.that in cases of need they made him one of the most helpful of men. He was, for instance, admirable as a nurse by the sick-bed, alike tender and firm; and while the touch of his hand and the modulation of his voice afforded the invalid unwonted comfort and repose, the steadiness of his judgment gave the supporting tone so often wanting in the sick-room. The same qualities brought him frequently into happy relations with children and with old people. If his imagination once felt the appeal, his adaptation of his strength to their weakness, of his multiplicity of resource to their need of entertainment, was so complete as to win for him the love of young and old. He was fond of games with children, and would devote himself to their amusement with unwearied patience and spirit. He had great skill in sleight-of-hand, and frequently amused himself with finding out and reproducing the tricks of the most renowned jugglers. He would hardly have been suspected by a casual acquaintance to be a master in legerdemain; for his massive build and heavy proportions, and the absence of agility in his common movements, seemed to unfit him for performances of this sort. But, after seeing him display his dexterity, it was easily recognized as the outgrowth and indication of faculties already exercised in higher fields. The same fine touch and precise and delicate movement which were shown in his nursing, the same quick and exact vision which distinguished his observation as a physicist were exhibited in his feats of parlor magic. He brought his keen analytical powers to bear on the seemingly mysterious processes of jugglers or of spiritualists; he used his knowledge of mechanics in the construction of toys, and applied his mathematical genius to the invention and performance of marvelous games and puzzles of cards.

I dwell thus at length on what might seem a mere trivial accomplishment, not only because it affords a vivid illustration of marked personal traits, but more because it was the means by which he gave concrete and visible expression to certain mental qualities trained to rare perfection in higher fields of exertion.

His temper was naturally calm, and he early attained a degree of self-discipline that enabled him to keep it under complete control. He was fond of debate and argument, and the full force of his mind was brought out through the animation of talk, more than in the solitary exercise of writing. Yet he was seldom ruffled by controversy, and never made ungenerous use of his strength, or forced his opponent to pass through the Caudine Forks of unwilling concession and acknowledgment of defeat. This control of his own temper secured that of his adversary. To argue with him was a moral no less than an intellectual discipline. The words he used of Mill apply with equal fitness to himself. " He sincerely welcomed intelligent and earnest opposition with a deference due to truth itself, and to a just regard of the diversities in men's minds from differences of education and natural dispositions. These diversities even appeared to him essential to the completeness of the examination which the evidences of truth demand. Opinions positively erroneous, if intelligent and honest, are not without their value, since the progress of truth is a succession of mistakes and corrections. Truth itself, unassailed by erroneous opinion, would soon degenerate into narrowness and error. The errors incident to individuality of mind and character are means, in the attrition of discussion, of keeping the truth bright and untarnished, and even of bringing its purity to light."

It was in this spirit that Wright himself carried on the discussions in which he engaged. He early learned that truth is a double question; and in the pursuit of truth, which was the controlling motive of his life, he disciplined himself by the study of opposing opinions. As he himself said, " Men are born either Platonists or Aristotelians; but by their education through a more and more free and enlightened discussion, and by progress in the sciences, they are restrained more and more from going to extremes in the directions of their native biases." And this general remark may be applied with fitness to himself. For while his intellectual operations were directed by a spirit of observation and experiment, which, though training the judgment and imagination in habits of accuracy, might also have a tendency to direct the attention to exclusive views of truth, he was on the other hand in all matters of speculation, to use a phrase of Mr. Mill's, essentially a seeker, testing every opinion, and recognizing the difficulties which adhere to them all. He exhibited that union of science and of philosophy which is the highest distinction of the leading thinkers of our time, and which hereafter will be indispensable for all who may succeed in deepening the current of thought or in opening for it new channels.

It was a marked quality of his genius as a thinker, that its springs were mainly fed from other sources than those of books. He was no wide reader; but, making himself master of a few comprehensive books, he gained from them, by reflection upon them, much more than their mere contents. He was never a persistent and systematic student; but he was essentially a persistent and systematic thinker.

During his college life he had been a judicious reader of Emerson and of Lord Bacon, but in the years of his early manhood, while he was accumulating large stores of observation and reflection, two or three books, similar in interest, but widely different in spirit and in method, were of special interest and importance to him,—chiefly Sir William Hamilton's Dissertations and Lectures, and Mill's Political Economy and his System of Logic. The repute and influence of Hamilton as a metaphysician and psychologist have undoubtedly declined since the publication, in 1865, of Mill's Examination of his Philosophy,—a philosophy, which professed to combine in an original form the German and French developments of the earlier Scotch reaction against Locke and Hume, with the demonstrations of modern science in respect to the necessary limits of knowledge. Hamilton had, however, succeeded previously not only in re-awakening among English students a fresh interest in metaphysics, but also in exercising a strong influence upon the general current of philosophical opinion. It was his great service, and one which will always deserve recognition, whatever be the ultimate verdict upon his special doctrines, that he produced a real revival of interest in a subject of fundamental importance which for a generation at least had ceased to receive due attention, and that he forced once more upon the consciousness of his generation the conviction that a true Psychology is, in the words of Mr. Mill, "the indispensable scientific basis of Morals, of Politics, and of the science and art of Education," and that upon the resolution of the difficulties of metaphysics, using the word in its proper sense, depends the assurance of the solid foundation of all knowledge. For this stimulus, and for this conviction, Wright, like many others, was indebted to his early studies of Hamilton. But he had studied Hamilton too thoroughly, and with too much clearness of mind, not to have become aware, even before Mill's exposure of them, of some at least of the weak points and inconclusive determinations of his system.

But Mill's work was much more than a simple refutation of the errors of Hamilton. In accomplishing this, he did much to re-establish, and upon more solid foundations than before, certain principles in philosophy of which the validity had seemed to be shaken. He showed that the determination of the vexed problems of metaphysics was to be sought in a properly scientific, and not in an *a priori*, or spiritualist psychology. His work went far to determine the mutual dependence of mental philosophy and of experimental science, the general recognition of which has already become effective in determining their respective courses of advance. The doctrine of experience may not yet be the dominant doctrine of the English school of psychologists; but the fact is obvious, that the recent independent investigations of science, and the rapid and unforeseen developments of knowledge, have tended to confirm its main propositions, and to strengthen its claim to acceptance. With this doctrine in psychology, the ill-named but generally well-understood doctrine of utilitarianism in morals is closely associated, so closely indeed that one may be said to be in great measure dependent on the other. Whatever contributes to the support of either, contributes more or less directly to the support of both. It may not be correct to assert, that if either be overthrown the other must fall with it; but it is at least certain, that the validity of a great part of each depends on evidence common to both.   The consistency among the postulates of psychology, and morals, has never been so clearly manifest, and has never received such valuable exposition, as during the last twenty years, mainly through the efforts of English investigators and thinkers, with Mill and Darwin at their head.

The effect of Mill's doctrine upon the direction of Wright's thought was confirmed by that of Darwin's work on The Origin of Species by means of Natural Selection.   The strong moral element in the works of both writers found a warm response in his own nature.   The entire candor, the love of truth, the disinterested search for it, the patience of investigation, the accuracy of statement, the modesty of assertion, characteristic of both these masters, were in entire harmony with his own mental traits.   The conclusions and the theories of Mill and Darwin may be disputed, may be overthrown, but their respective methods of investigation and of statement are of such excellence, and their desire for truth so sincere and impersonal, that their works would remain as models of scientific investigation and philosophic inquiry even though they should lose their doctrinal authority.

The questions opened and partially solved by these authors were those which chiefly occupied Wright during the last ten years of his life.   The rare combination in him of a genius for reflection, disciplined by long exercise, with great natural powers of observation, and with unusually wide and accurate scientific attainments, fitted him to deal with them not merely as a reporter of other men's thought, but as an original investigator, capable himself of making additions to the sum of knowledge. The position which he occupied as a philosopher is the standpoint common to one of the two fundamental divisions of the philosophic world; namely, that of the assumption of the universality of physical causation. It cannot be stated better than in his own words. "The very hope of experimental philosophy," he says, "its expectation of constructing the sciences into a true philosophy of nature, is based on the induction, or, if you please, the *a priori* presumption, that physical causation is universal; that the constitution of nature is written in its actual manifestations, and needs only to be•deciphered by experimental and inductive research; that it is not a latent invisible writing, to be brought out by the magic of mental anticipation or metaphysical meditation. Or, as Bacon said, it is not by the 'anticipations of the mind,' but by the 'interpretation of nature,' that natural philosophy is to be constituted; and this is to presume that the order of nature is decipherable, or that causation is everywhere either manifest or hidden, but never absent." The methods of this interpretation of nature or, in other words, of this discovery of truth, he regarded as those of all true knowledge; namely, the methods of induction from the facts of particular observation. This was his position in respect to the much-debated problem of metaphysical causation, or the question of what are called "*real* connections between phenomena as causes and effects, which are independent of our experiences, and the invariable and unconditional sequences among them." "To those," I cite his own words, "who have reached the positive mode of thought, the word 'cause' simply signifies the phenomena, or the state of facts, which precede the event to be explained, which make it exist, in the only sense in which it can clearly be supposed to be made to exist; namely, by affording the conditions of the rule of its occurrence. But with those," he adds, "who have not yet attained to this clear and simple conception of cause, a vague but familiar feeling prevails, which makes this conception seem very inadequate to express their idea of the reality of causation.

Such thinkers feel that they know something more in causation than the mere succession, however simple and invariable this may be. The *real* efficiency of a cause, that which makes its effect to exist absolutely, seems, at least in regard to their own volitions, to be known to them immediately." "But," he goes on, after an interval, "that certain mental states of which we are conscious are followed by certain external effects which we observe is to the sceptical schools a simple fact of observation. These thinkers extend the method of the more precisely known to the interpretation of what is less precisely known, interpreting the phenomena of self-consciousness by the methods of physical science, instead of interpreting physical phenomena by the crudities of the least perfect though most familiar of all observations, the phenomena of volition."*

It is not to be assumed, from the phrase in the preceding extract concerning those "who have reached the positive mode of thought," that Wright classed himself with any specific school of so-called Positivists. He used the term *positive*, as it is now commonly employed, as a general appellation to designate the whole body of thinkers who in the investigation of nature hold to the methods of induction from the facts of observation, as distinguished from the *a priori* school, who seek in the constitution of the mind the key to the interpretation of the external world. It was only in this sense that he himself was a positivist. So too with regard to his use of the word "sceptical." In his employment of it, it had no direct theological significance. It meant with him the temper of mind which puts no confidence in assertion unsupported by the evidence of experience; it meant the temper of questioning and investigation as opposed to that of concluded opinion;

---

*North American Review, 106, p. 286, notice of Peabody's Positive Philosophy, January, 1868.

the temper in which the unknown remains matter of inquiry, not of dogmatism, and to which the unknowable, or that which lies plainly outside the range of human faculties, is of no concern save as matter of sentiment. To the quality of this sentiment he gave great weight as a test of the worth of individual character. His scepticism rested upon the proposition, that the highest generality, or universality, in the elements, or connections of elements, in phenomena, is the utmost reach both in the power and the desire of the scientific intellect. There was nothing aggressive in such scepticism as this, except so far as it led him to expose the fallacious arguments of the supporters of the orthodox metaphysics. The sympathetic quality of his nature showed itself in his respect for individual beliefs sincerely held. He felt, to use his own words, "that the subordinate, almost incidental value that some traditional metaphysical issues, like the ultimate nature of the connection of mind and matter, and of cause and effect, and the dependence of life on matter, have in the view of the scientific psychologist, is with difficulty comprehended by those who approach the subject from a religious point of view." He had no liking for the iconoclasts who would destroy ancient faiths in the hearts of those who are incapable of substituting, with good effect on their lives, rational convictions in the place of sentimental beliefs. He had confidence in the constant and progressive extension of the field of knowledge; but he did not believe that the question of the origin and destiny of things would ever be included within its limits. If asked for his speculations on these topics, that so greatly exercise the curiosity of the race, he would have been very likely to reply with the words of Newton, which were among his favorite apothegms, "*Hypotheses non fingo.*"

In the year 1870, Mr. Wright published the first of a series of papers, of which the last appeared but a short time before his death, expository of the true nature of the doctrine of Natural Selection, of its various applications, and of its relations to common metaphysical speculations. In the first of these articles, which had the form of a review of Mr. Wallace's contributions to the Theory of Natural Selection, Mr. Wright touches upon the application of the principles involved in the doctrine of Natural Selection to the development of the mental powers of man. The full importance of the topic did not, however, appear till the publication, more than two years afterward, of his most considerable contribution to philosophy, his essay on the Evolution of Self-Consciousness, in which a natural explanation is given of the chief phenomena of human consciousness, involving the refutation of many of the main propositions of mystical metaphysics or idealism. In 1871, he published a paper on the Genesis of Species, in reply to Mr. St. George Mivart's attack on the theory of Natural Selection. The vigor and effectiveness of his defense of the theory led to the republication of this essay in England, at Mr. Darwin's instance, and compelled Mr. Mivart to attempt to make good his position in a communication to the "North American Review," the journal in which Mr. Wright's article originally appeared. To this reply Mr. Wright rejoined in the succeeding number of the "Review," July, 1872.*

In these discussions of the problems of modern research, and other shorter papers on similar topics, published for the most part in "The Nation," Mr. Wright showed the wide reach of his thought, his powers of keen analysis, and the large store of his acquirements. His training in the sound scientific method of investigation gave precision to his statement of the

---

* In his recently published work, entitled "Lessons from Nature as manifested in Mind and Matter," Mr. Mivart reprints his reply to Mr. Wright's criticisms, but fails to notice Mr. Wright's rejoinder.

inductions of philosophic thought. He carried the scientific method into the region of reflection. In respect to all matters concerning which the facts necessary for the formation of opinion were not known, or had been but insufficiently observed, he held a suspended judgment. He never seemed to have a prepossession in favor of or against any opinion, concerning which the testimony of experience was doubtful, and the evidence of fact apparently inconsistent.

But his thought was by no means limited to the topics which philosophy derives from the exact or the natural sciences. The main attraction of science and philosophy to him was not on the side of abstract truth, but much more on the application of truth to the life and conduct of man. The questions of morality, of politics, of jurisprudence, of education, in the light thrown on them by psychology and by experience, were those which in his later years were continually assuming an increasing share of his attention. And in his treatment of these questions he displayed the most eminent trait of his genius, and the highest result of the discipline of his philosophic powers,—I mean a good practical judgment, or the quality of wisdom. Chauncey Wright was in the true sense a wise man. I do not assert, that, in the ordering of his own life, he was always guided by the considerations of wisdom. In some important respects his self-control was greatly deficient in steadiness. Few, indeed, of the wisest men have succeeded in conforming their lives in all respects to their principles. Wisdom more frequently manifests itself in objective relations, than in the complete mastery of personal dispositions, and a consistently judicious regulation of conduct. And, in all matters in which the interests of others were involved, Mr. Wright's judgment was one of the most trustworthy. His sympathetic nature gave him the power to enter into moods of character and conditions of feeling widely diverse from his own, while his judgment in each particular instance was the result of inductions of large experience and careful reflection. Instant as the expression of his opinions might be, there was nothing of haste in their formation. Emotion, sentiment, opinion, all rested with him on a rational foundation. I should give a false image, if, in thus speaking, I were to convey the impression of anything dry or formally deliberate in his intercourse with others. He was, especially in his later years, always ready and fluent in talk, easily animated, accessible to the ideas of others, neither preoccupied with his own reflections to the exclusion of external suggestions, nor using the predominant weight of his own intelligence to crush the slighter fabric of the thought of his companions. He had the modesty of the philosopher in happy combination with his just self-confidence, and the vigor of his moral sentiment was as evident in the manner as in the substance of his discourse. I have referred to his tendency in early life to melancholy. He was never wholly free from occasional periods in which some defect of physical organization or constitution showed itself in uncontrollable mental depression. But he was for the most part cheerful, and often gay. He was an easy and equable companion, and the lighter regions of life and thought were as open and accessible to him, as the grave solitudes in which he habitually dwelt.

Those who knew him best will most clearly discern the fact that his published writings, able as they are, and deserving of the respect due to high qualities of thought, fall short of being a satisfactory expression, even of the purely intellectual part of his nature. The action of his mind in composition was laborious, and his style was often too compact of thought, and not sufficiently relieved by the lighter graces of expression. His writings and his oral lectures sometimes required closer attention on the part of readers or hearers than it would have been well to demand of them. His thought, indeed, was never obscure; but it was too condensed, and at times too profound to be readily followed. His own ability misled him, and he did not always estimate aright the average incapacity of untrained intelligence to follow a process of exact reasoning. But nothing of this defect was to be found in his conversation, which was constantly lighted up by the pleasant play of a suggestive humor, that often added a happy and unexpected stroke wherewith to clinch the point of argument. In talk, the readiness of his intelligence was not less remarkable than its force; and the abundance and variety of his resources not less surprising than their accuracy. Whatever he knew was at his command, and his knowledge extended over many fields with which he might not have been supposed to be familiar. One could hardly turn to him with a question on any topic, however remote from his ordinary studies, without receiving from him an answer that seemed as if he already had devoted special attention to the subject now for the first time presented. The method of his thought was so excellent that new topics fell naturally into their right positions, and received immediate illustration from previous acquisitions, made originally without reference to any such application. With such capacities as his, and with such training as he had given them, the growth of his mind was constant. There was no period to his progress, and what he had done seemed but the beginning and assurance of the greater things of which he was capable. His sudden death in the fullness of power was a loss to be mourned by all who have at heart the interests of philosophy; that is, by all to whom the highest interests of man are of concern.

PHILOSOPHICAL DISCUSSIONS.

A PHYSICAL THEORY OF THE UNIVERSE.*

In 1811 Sir William Herschel communicated to the Royal Society a paper in which he gave an exposition of his famous hypothesis of the transformation of nebulæ into stars. "Assuming a self-luminous substance of a highly attenuated nature to be distributed through the celestial regions, he endeavored to show that, by the mutual attraction of its constituent parts, it would have a tendency to form itself into distinct aggregations of nebulous matter, which in each case would gradually condense from the continued action of the attractive forces, until the resulting mass finally acquired the consistency of a solid body, and became a star. In those instances wherein the collection of nebulous matter was very extensive, subordinate centres of attraction could not fail to be established, around which the adjacent particles would arrange themselves; and thus the whole mass would in process of time be transformed into a determinate number of discrete bodies, which would ultimately assume the condition of a cluster of stars. Herschel pointed out various circumstances which appeared to him to afford just grounds for believing that such a nebulous substance existed independently in space. He maintained that the phenomena of nebulous stars, and the changes observable in the great nebula of Orion, could not be satisfactorily accounted for by any other hypothesis. Admitting, then, the existence of a nebulous substance, he concluded, from indications of milky nebulosity which he encountered in the course of his observations, that it was distributed in great abundance throughout the celestial regions. The vast collections of neb-

* From the North American Review, July, 1864.

ulæ which he had observed, of every variety of structure and in every stage of condensation, were employed by him with admirable address in illustrating the *modus operandi* of his hypothesis." *

Laplace, in his *Système du Monde*, applied this hypothesis, by an ingenious but simple use of mechanical principles, to the explanation of the origin of the planetary bodies, and of the general features of their movements in the solar system. Supposing the original nebulous mass to receive a rotatory motion by its aggregation, he showed that this motion would be quickened by a further contraction of the mass, until the centrifugal force of its equatorial regions would be sufficient to balance their gravitation, and to suspend them in the form of a vaporous ring. Again, supposing this revolving ring to be broken, and finally collected by a further aggregation into a spherical nebulous mass, he showed, in the same way, how the body of a planet, with its system of satellites, might be formed. The material and the original motions of the planets and their satellites could thus, he supposed, be successively produced, as the nebula gradually contracted to the dimensions of the sun.

No scientific theory has received a fairer treatment than the nebular hypothesis. Arising as it did as a speculative conclusion from one of the grandest inductions in the whole range of physical inquiry,—connecting as it does so many facts, though vaguely and inconclusively, into one system,—it possesses, what is rare in so bold and heterodox a view, a verisimilitude quite disproportionate to the real evidence which can be adduced in its support. The difficulties which ordinarily attend the reception of new ideas, were in this case removed beforehand. The hypothesis violated no habitual association of ideas, at least among those who were at all competent to comprehend its import. Though resting on a much feebler support of direct evidence than the astronomical theories of Copernicus, Galileo, and Kepler, it met with a cordial reception from its apparent accordance with certain preconceptions, of the same kind as those, which, though extrinsic and irrele-

---

* Grant's History of Physical Astronomy.

vant to scientific inquiry, were able to oppose themselves suc-cessfully for a long time to the ascertained truths of modern astronomy.

The test of conceivableness, the receptivity of the imagina-tion, is a condition, if not of truth itself, at least of belief in the truth; and in this respect the nebular hypothesis was well founded. It belonged to that class of theories of which it is sometimes said, "that, if they are not true, they *deserve* to be true." A place was already prepared for it in the imaginations and the speculative interests of the scientific world.

We propose to review briefly some of the conditions which have given so great a plausibility to this hypothesis. In the first place, on purely speculative grounds, this hypothesis, as a cosmological theory, happily combines the excellences of the two principal doctrines on the origin of the world that were held by the ancients, and which modern theorists have discussed as views which, though neither can be established scientifically, have no less interest from a theological point of view;—namely, first, the materialistic doctrine, that the world, though finite in the duration of its orderly successions and changes, is infinite in the duration of its material substance; and, secondly, the spiritualistic doctrine, that matter and form are equally the effects, finite in duration, of a spiritual and eternal cause.

At first sight the nebular hypothesis seems to agree most nearly with the materialistic cosmology, as taught by the greater number of the ancient philosophers; but the resem-blance is only superficial, and, though the hypothesis possesses those qualities by which the ancient doctrine was suited to the limitations and requirements of the poetical imagination, yet it does not involve that element of fortuitous causation which gave to the ancient doctrine its atheistic character. In the nebular hypothesis the act of creation, though reduced to its simplest form, is still essentially the same as that which a spir-itualistic cosmology requires. The first created matter filling the universe is devoid only of outward and developed forms, but contains created within it the forces which shall determine every change and circumstance of its subsequent history.

The hypothesis being thus at once simple and theistic appeals to imagination and feeling as one which at least ought to be true.

Such considerations as these doubtless determined the fate of another ancient cosmological doctrine, which, though adopted by Aristotle, was regarded with little favor by ancient philosophers generally. For there could be but little support, either from poetry or religion, to the doctrine which denied creation, and held that the order of nature is not, in its cosmical relations, a progression toward an end, or a development, but is rather an endless succession of changes, simple and constant in their elements, though infinite in their combinations, which constitute an order without beginning and without termination.

While this latter doctrine was not necessarily materialistic, like that which has been so termed, and which was more generally received among the ancients, and though it has the greater scientific simplicity, yet it fails on a point of prime importance, so far as its general acceptance is concerned, in that it ignores the main interest which commonly attaches to the problem. Cosmological speculations are, indeed, properly concerned with the mode or order of the creation, and not with the fact of the creation itself. But that the first cosmogonies were written in verse shows the almost dramatic interest which their themes inspired. "In the beginning" has never ceased to charm the imagination; and these are almost the only words in our own sacred cosmogony to which the modern geologist has not been compelled to give some ingenious interpretation. That there was a beginning of the order of natural events and successions may be said to be the almost universal faith of Christendom.

The nebular hypothesis, conforming to this preconception and to the greatest poetic simplicity, passed the ordeal of unscientific criticism with remarkable success. Not less was its success under a general scientific review. A large number of facts and relations, otherwise unaccounted for, become explicable as at least very probable consequences of its assumptions; and these assumptions were not, at first, without that independent probability which a true scientific theory requires. The existence of the so-called nebulous matter was rendered very probable by the earlier revelations of the telescope ; and, though subsequent researches in stellar astronomy have rather diminished than increased the antecedent probability of the theory, by successively resolving the nebulæ into clusters of star-like constituents,—suggesting that all nebulosity may arise from deficiency in the optical powers of the astronomer rather than inhere in the constitution of the nebulæ themselves,—and thereby invalidating the scientific completeness of the theory, yet the plausible explanations which it still affords of the constitution of the solar system have saved it from condemnation with a considerable number of ingenious thinkers. With astronomers generally, however, it has gradually fallen in esteem. It retains too much of its original character of a happy guess, and has received too little confirmation of a precise and definite kind, to entitle it to rank highly as a physical theory.

But there are two principal grounds on which it will doubtless retain its claim to credibility, till its place is supplied, if this ever happens, by some more satisfactory account of cosmical phenomena. To one of these grounds we have just alluded. The details of the constitution of the solar system present, as we have said, many features which suggest a physical origin, directing inquiry as to how they were produced, rather than as to why they exist,—an inquiry into physical, rather than final causes; features of the same mixed character of regularity and apparent accident which are seen in the details of geological or biological phenomena; features not sufficiently regular to indicate a simple primary law, either physical or teleological, nor yet sufficiently irregular to show an absence of law and relation in their production.

The approximation of the orbits of the planets to a common plane, the common direction of their motions around the sun, the approximation of the planes and the directions of their rotations to the planes of their orbits and the directions of their revolutions, the approximatively regular distribution of their distances from the sun, the relations of their satellites to the general features of the primary system,—these are some of the facts requiring explanations of the kind which a geologist or a naturalist would give of the distribution of minerals, or stratifications in the crust of the earth, or of the distribution of plants and animals upon its surface,—phenomena indicating complex antecedent conditions, in which the evidence of law is more or less distinct. The absence of that perfection in the solar system, of that unblemished completeness, which the ancient astronomy assumed and taught, and the presence, at the same time, of an apparently imperfect regularity, compel us to regard the constitution of the solar system as a secondary and derived product of complicated operations, instead of an archetypal and pure creation.

Such is one of the grounds on which the nebular hypothesis rests. The other is of a more general character. The antecedent probability which the theory lacks, from its inability to prove by independent evidence the fundamental assumption of a nebulous matter, is partially supplied by a still more general hypothesis, to which this theory may be regarded as in some sort a corollary. We refer to the "development hypothesis," or "theory of evolution,"—a generalization from certain biological phenomena, which has latterly attracted great attention from speculative naturalists. This hypothesis has been less fortunate in its history than that of the astronomical one. Inveterate prejudices, insoluble associations of ideas, a want of preparation in the habits of the imagination, were the unscientific obstacles to a general and ready acceptance of this hypothesis at its first promulgation. Though in one of its applications it is identical with the nebular hypothesis, yet, in more direct application to the phenomena of the general life on the earth's surface, it appears so improbable, that it has hitherto failed to gain the favor which the nebular hypothesis enjoys. Nevertheless, as a general conception, and independently of its specific use in scientific theories, it has much to recommend it to the speculative mind. It is, as it were, an abstract statement of the order which the intellect expects to find in the phenomena of nature. "Evolution," or the progress "from the homogeneous to the heterogeneous, and from the simple to the complex," is the order of the progress of knowledge itself, and is, therefore, naturally enough, sought for as the order in time of all natural phenomena. The specific natural phenomena in which the law of "evolution" is determined by observation as a real and established law, are the phenomena of the growth of the individual organism, animal or plant. As a law of psychological phenomena, and even of certain elements of social and historical phenomena, it is also well established. Its extension to the phenomena of the life of the races of organized beings, and to the successions of life on the surface of the earth, is still a speculative conclusion, with about the same degree of scientific probability that the nebular hypothesis possesses. And lastly, in the form of the nebular hypothesis itself, it is extended so as to include the whole series of the phenomena of the universe, and is thus in generality, if accepted as a law of nature, superior to any other generalization in the history of philosophy.

As included in this grander generalization, the nebular hypothesis receives a very important accession of probability, provided that this generalization can be regarded as otherwise well founded. As a part of the induction by which this generalization must be established, if it be capable of proof, the nebular hypothesis acquires a new and important interest.

We are far from being convinced, however, that further inquiry will succeed in establishing so interesting a conclusion. We strongly suspect that the law of "evolution" will fail to appear in phenomena not connected, either directly or remotely, with the life of the individual organism, of the growth of which this law is an abstract description. And, heterodox though the opinion be, we are inclined to accept as the soundest and most catholic assumption, on grounds of scientific method, the too little regarded doctrine of Aristotle, which banishes cosmology from the realm of scientific inquiry, reducing natural phenomena in their cosmical relations to an infinite variety of manifestations (without a discoverable tendency on the whole) of causes and laws which are simple and constant in their ultimate elements.*

---

* The laws or archetypes of nature are properly the laws of invariable or unconditional sequence in natural operations. And it is only with the objective relations of these laws,

In rejecting the essential doctrine of "the theory of evolution" or "the development hypothesis," we must reserve an important conclusion implied in the doctrine, which we think is its strongest point. There are several large classes of facts, apparently ultimate and unaccountable, which still bear the marks of being the consequences of the operations of so-called secondary causes,—in other words, have the same general character as phenomena which are known to be the results of mixed and conflicting causes, or exhibit at the same time evidence of law and appearance of accident. That such facts should be regarded as evidence of natural operations still unknown, and perhaps unsuspected, is, we think, a legitimate conclusion, and one which is presupposed in "the theory of evolution," and in the nebular hypothesis, but does not necessitate the characteristic assumptions of these speculations. An extension of the sphere of secondary causes, even to the explanation of all the forms of the universe as it now exists, or of all the forms which we may conceive ever to have existed, is a very different thing from adopting the cosmological doctrine of the "development theory." Naturalists who have recently become convinced of the necessity of extending natural explanations to facts in biology hitherto regarded as ultimate and inexplicable, but who are unwilling to adopt the cosmological view implied in the "development theory," have adopted a new name to designate their views. "The derivative theory," or "derivative hypothesis," implies only continuity, not growth or progress, in the succession of races on the surface of the earth. Progress may have been made, as a matter of fact, and the evidence of it may be very conclusive in the geological record; but the fact may still be of secondary importance in the cosmological relations of the phenomena, and the theory ought not, therefore, to give the fact too prominent a place in its nomenclature.

---

as constituting the order of nature, that natural science is concerned. Their subjective relations, origin, and essential being belong to the province of transcendental metaphysics, and to a philosophy of faith. According to this division, there can never arise any conflict between science and faith; for what the one is competent to declare, the other is incompetent to dispute. Science should be free to determine what the order of nature is, and faith equally free to declare the essential nature of causation or creation.

That the constitution of the solar system is not archetypal, as the ancients supposed, but the same corrupt mixture of law and apparent accident that the phenomena of the earth's sur- face exhibit, is evidence enough that this system is a natural product;* and the nebular hypothesis, so far as it is concerned with the explanation simply of the production of this system, and independently of its cosmological import, may be regarded as a legitimate theory, even on the ground we have assumed, though on this ground the most probable hypothesis would assimilate the causes which produced the solar system more nearly to the character of ordinary natural operations than the nebular hypothesis does.   With a view to such assimilation, and in opposition to "the theory of evolution" as a general- ization from the phenomena of growth, we will now propose another generalization, which we cannot but regard as better founded in the laws of nature.   We may call it the principle of *counter-movements*,—a principle in accordance with which there is no action in nature to which there is not some counter- action, and no production in nature from which in infinite ages there can result an infinite product.   In biological phenomena this principle is familiarly illustrated by the counter-play of the forces of life and death, of nutrition and waste, of growth and degeneration, and of similar opposite effects.   In geology the movements of the materials of the earth's crust through the counteractions of the forces by which the strata are elevated

---

* This argument for physical causes is apparently the reverse of that which Laplace derived from the regularities of the solar system and the theory of probabilities; but in reality the objects of the two arguments are distinct.   For the legitimate conclusion from Laplace's computation is, not that the solar system is simply a physical product, but that the causes of its production could not have been irregular.   The result of this computation was a probability of two hundred thousand billions to one that the regular- ities of the solar system are not the effects of chance or irregular causes.

The gist of this argument is to prove simplicity in the antecedents of the solar sys- tem; and, had the proportion been still greater, or infinity to one, the argument might have proved a primitive or archetypal character in the movements of this system.   It is therefore in the limitations, and not in the magnitude, of this proportion, that there is any tendency to show physical antecedence.   Hence it is not from the regularities of the solar system, but from its complexity, that its physical origin is justly inferred.

Regarding the *law of causation* as universal, since, if not implied in the very search for causes, it is at least the broadest and the best established induction from natural phenomena, we conclude that the appearance of accident among the manifestations of law is proof of the existence of complex antecedent conditions and of physical causa- tion, and that the absence of this appearance is proof of simple and primitive law.

and denuded, depressed and deposited, ground to mud or hardened to rock, are all of the compensative sort; and the movements of the gaseous and liquid oceans which surround the earth manifest still more markedly the principle of counter-movements in the familiar phenomena of the weather.

Of what we may call cosmical weather, in the interstellar spaces, little is known. Of the general cosmical effects of the opposing actions of heat and gravitation, the great dispersive and concentrative principles of the universe, we can at present only form vague conjectures; but that these two principles are the agents of vast counter-movements in the formation and destruction of systems of worlds, always operative in never-ending cycles and in infinite time, seems to us to be by far the most rational supposition which we can form concerning the matter. And indeed, in one form or another, the agencies of heat and gravitation must furnish the explanations of the circumstances and the peculiarities of solar and sidereal systems. These are the agents which the nebular hypothesis supposes; but by this hypothesis they are supposed to act under conditions opposed to that general analogy of natural operations expressed by the law of counter-movements. Their relative actions are regarded as directed, under certain conditions, toward a certain definite result; and this being attained, their formative agency is supposed to cease, the system to be finished, and the creation, though a continuous process, to be a limited one.

It should be noticed, however, in favor of the nebular hypothesis, that its assumptions are made, not arbitrarily, in opposition to the general analogy of natural operations, but because they furnish at once and very simply certain mechanical conditions from which systems analogous to the solar system may be shown to be derivable. The dispersive agency of heat is supposed to furnish the primordial conditions, upon which, as the heat is gradually lost from the clouds of nebulous matter, the agency of gravitation produces the condensations, the motions, and the disruptions of the masses which subsequently become suns and planets and satellites. And if the mechanical conditions assumed in this hypothesis could be shown to be the only ones by which similar effects could be produced, the hypothesis would, without doubt, acquire a degree of probability amounting almost to certainty, even in spite of the absence of independent proof that matter has ever existed in the nebulous form.

But the mechanical conditions of the problem have never been determined in this exhaustive manner, nor are the conditions assumed in the nebular hypothesis able to determine any other than the general circumstances of the solar system, such as it is supposed to have in common with similar systems among the stars. A more detailed deduction would probably require as many separate, arbitrary, and additional hypotheses as there are special circumstances to be accounted for. Until, therefore, it can be shown that the nebular hypothesis is the only one which can account mechanically for the agency of heat and gravitation in the formation of special systems of worlds, like the solar system, its special cosmological and mechanical features ought to be regarded with suspicions, as opposed to the general analogy of natural operations.

We propose to criticise this hypothesis more in detail, and to indicate briefly the direction in which we believe a better solution of the problem of the construction of the solar system will be found. But before proceeding, we must notice an able Essay, by Mr. Herbert Spencer, the first in his Second Series of "Essays: Scientific, Political, and Speculative."

In this essay on the "Nebular Hypothesis," and in the following one on "Illogical Geology," Mr. Spencer has attempted the beginning of that inductive proof of the general theory of "evolution" to which we have referred. Undoubtedly the clearest and the ablest of the champions and expounders of this theory, he brings to its illustration and defense an extraordinary sagacity, and an aptitude for dealing with scientific facts at second hand, and in their broad general relations, such as few discoverers and adepts in natural science have ever exhibited. For dealing with facts which are matters of common observation, his powers are those of true genius. In the essays following those with which we are immediately interested, and particularly in the essay on "The Physiology of Laughter," and in the review of Mr. Bain's work on "The Emotions and the Will," he displays the true scope of his genius. In psychology, and in the physiology of familiar facts, we regard his contributions to philosophy as of real and lasting value. He is deficient, however, in that technical knowledge which is necessary to a correct apprehension of the obscure facts of science; and his generalizations upon them do not impress us as so well founded as they are ingenious.

In his *résumé* of the facts favorable to the nebular hypothesis, he has committed sundry errors of minor importance, which do not in themselves materially affect the credibility of the hypothesis, but illustrate the extremely loose and uncertain character of the general arguments in its support. A singular use is made of a table, compiled by Arago, of the inclinations of the planes of the orbits of the comets. The legitimate inference from this table is, that there is a well-marked accumulation of the planes of these orbits at small inclinations to the plane of the ecliptic. In considering the directions of the poles of these planes, we ought to find them equally distributed to all parts of the heavens, in case the orbits of the comets bear no relation to those of the planets or to each other. Instead of this, we find a marked concentration of these poles about the pole of the ecliptic, showing that their planes tend decidedly to coincide with the ecliptic. But Mr. Spencer has drawn from this table a conclusion directly the reverse of this. Assuming, as we cannot but believe on insufficient evidence, that the directions of the major axes of the orbits of those comets whose planes are greatly inclined to the ecliptic have nearly as great an inclination as they can have, or that they are nearly as much inclined to the ecliptic as the planes of the orbits themselves, he regards the table of the inclinations of the planes of the orbits as indicating, at least for such comets, the directions of their *axes*, and draws thence the conclusion, that there is a well-marked concentration about the pole of the directions of the *axes* of the cometary orbits, and hence, that the regions in which the *aphelia* of comets are most numerous are above and below the sun, in directions nearly perpendicular to the ecliptic. This conclusion, though the reverse of that which is legitimately drawn from Arago's table, is not inconsistent with it; and if Mr. Spencer were correct in his assumption concerning the directions of the axes of highly inclined orbits, the table would show that there are really *two* well-distinguished systems of comets, the one belonging to the general planetary system, and the other, Mr. Spencer's, forming a system by itself,—an axial one, at right angles with the general system.

But either conclusion serves the purpose of the discussion equally well. For what Mr. Spencer wished to show was, that the relations of the comets to the solar system are not utterly fortuitous and irregular, but such as indicate a systematic connection; and this is undoubtedly true, since the connection of the planetary and cometary orbits is even more direct and intimate than Mr. Spencer has suspected. The inference which Arago's table warrants is, then, another in that interesting series of facts which some physical theory, whether nebular or not, by "evolution" or by involution, may some day explain.

The greater number of the arguments, old and new, which Mr. Spencer adduces in support of his thesis, do not apply specifically to the nebular hypothesis in particular, but are simply an enumeration of the facts which go to show the existence of physical connections, of an unknown origin and species, in the solar system. In his handling of the mechanical problems of the nebular genesis, Mr. Spencer has succeeded no better than his predecessors. In attempting to account for the exceptions to a general law which the rotations of the outer planets, Uranus and Neptune, and the revolutions of their satellites, exhibit,—the great inclinations of the planes of these rotations and revolutions to the planes of the orbits of the primaries,—Mr. Spencer makes what appears to us a very erroneous assumption, and one from which the conclusion he wishes to draw by no means inevitably follows.

It is one of the few successes of the nebular hypothesis, that it accounts in a general way for the fact that the planes and directions of the rotations of the planets, and the revolutions of their satellites, nearly coincide with the planes and directions of their own orbital motions. A ring of nebulous matter, detached by its centrifugal force from the revolving mass of the nebula, contains within it the conditions by which the direction, and even the amount, of the rotation of the resulting planet is determined; and this direction is the same as that of the revolution of the ring. The ring must originally be of a very thin, quoit-shaped form, even if it be composed of separate, independently moving parts; otherwise the planes of the orbits of the several parts would not pass through or near to the centre of attraction in the central nebula, and the parts must either pass through each other from one to the other surface of the ring, which would tend, along with other forces, to flatten it to the requisite thinness. Hence, a hoop-shaped fluid ring, or one thinner in the directions of its radii than in a direction perpendicular to its general plane, could not exist. Much less could such a ring be detached by its self-sustaining centrifugal force from the body of the nebula. The nebula must necessarily be flattened in its equatorial regions to a sharp, thin edge by the centrifugal force of its revolution, before those regions could be separated to form a ring. The supposition, therefore, which Mr. Spencer's ingenuity has devised to account for the anomalies presented in the rotations and the secondary systems of Uranus and Neptune,—a hoop-shaped ring, with a less determinate tendency to rotation in forming a planet,—is untenable. But this is not all. Supposing such a form possible, and even if the parts of the ring did not move among themselves, or press upon one another so as to flatten the ring, yet the direction of its tendency to rotation in contracting to a planet is just as determinate as in the quoit-shaped ring.

We have gone thus into detail, to show the vague and uncertain character of the mechanical arguments of the nebular hypothesis when they deal with details in the constitution of the solar system. In his treatment of recent discoveries and views in stellar astronomy, we think Mr. Spencer more fortunate. We agree with him in believing the current opinion to be an error, which represents the nebulæ as isolated sidereal systems, inconceivably remote, and with magnitudes commensurate with the Galactic system itself. There are many reasons for believing that the nebulæ belong to this system, and that they are, in general, at no greater distance from us than the stars themselves. We think, also, with him, that the actual magnitudes of the stars are probably of all degrees, and that their apparent magnitudes do not generally indicate their relative distances from us. We would even go further, and maintain, as both *a priori* most probable, and most in accordance with observation, that the free bodies of the universe range in size from a grain of dust to masses many times larger than the sun, and that the number of bodies of any magnitude is likely to bear some simple proportion to the smallness of this magnitude itself. Star-dust is not at all distasteful to us, except in the form of nebular boluses. For reasons which will appear hereafter, the smaller bodies are not likely to be self-luminous; and star-dust is probably the cause of more obscuration than light in the stellar universe. That gaseous and liquid masses also exist with all degrees of rarefaction or density, dependent on the actions of heat and gravitation, is also, we think, very probable; and the three states of aggregation in matter doubtless play important parts in the cosmical economy.

Before leaving Mr. Spencer, to attend more immediately to the merits of the nebular hypothesis, we wish to adopt from him an estimate of the value of certain ideas in geology, the bearing of which on our subject is not so remote as it may at first sight appear to be.

Geology has not yet so far detached itself from cosmological speculations as to be entitled to the rank of a strictly positive science. The influence of such speculations upon its terminology, and upon the forms of the questions and the directions of the researches of its cultivators, is still very noticeable, and shows how difficult it is to start anew in the prosecution of physical inquiries, or completely to discard unfounded opinions which have for a long time prevailed. Greater sagacity is sometimes required to frame wise questions, than to find their answers. Geologists still continue to collate remote stratifications as to their stratigraphical order, mineral composition, and fossil remains, as if these were still expected to disclose a comparatively simple history—simple at least in its outlines —of the changes which the life of our globe has undergone. A story, dramatically complete from prologue to epilogue, was demanded in the cosmological childhood of the science, and its manhood still searches in the fragmentary and mutilated records for the history of the creation. But doubtless the story is as deficient in the dramatic unities, as the record itself is in continuity or completeness. Referring to Mr. Spencer's admirable essay on "Illogical Geology" for our reasons, we will simply state our belief that nothing in the form of a complete or connected history will ever be deciphered from the geological record.

"Only the last chapter of the earth's history has come down to us. The many previous chapters, stretching back to a time immeasurably remote, have been burnt, and with them all the records of life we may presume they contained. The greater part of the evidence which might have served to settle the development controversy is forever lost; and on neither side can the arguments derived from geology be conclusive."

We must not ascribe to Mr. Spencer, however, our opinion, that, even if this record were more complete, we should not necessarily be the wiser for it. According to Mr. Spencer's views, the first strata, had they been preserved, would have contained the remains of protozoa and protophytes; but, for aught we dare guess, they might have contained the footprints of archangels.

Evidence of progress in life through any ever so considerable portion of the earth's stratified materials would not, in our opinion, warrant us in drawing universal cosmical conclusions therefrom. Alternations of progress and regress relatively to any standard of ends or excellence which we might apply, is to us the most probable hypothesis that the general analogy of natural operations warrants. Nevertheless, as we have already intimated, we accept the purely physical portion of the "development hypothesis," both in its astronomical and biological applications, but would much prefer to designate the doctrine in both its applications by the name we have already quoted. This name, "the derivative hypothesis," simply connotes the fact that, in several classes of phenomena hitherto regarded as ultimate and inexplicable, physical explanations are probable and legitimate. But it makes no claim to rank with the names of the Muses as a revealer of the cosmical order and the beginning of things.

We are aware that in thus summarily rejecting the cosmological import of the nebular hypothesis, along with its special physical assumptions, and retaining only its fundamental assumption, that the solar system is a natural product, we leave no provision to meet a demand which we allow, and we ought to justify this insolvency by proving the bankruptcy of the hypothesis whose debts we thus assume. It would be difficult, however, to prove that this hypothesis cannot fulfill the promise it has so long held out. Much more difficult would it be to supply its place with an equally plausible theory. But our object should not be to satisfy the imagination with plausibility. If we succeed in satisfying our understanding with the outlines of a theory sufficiently probable, we shall have done all that in the present state of our knowledge can reasonably be demanded.

The agencies of heat and gravitation acting, however slowly, through the ages of limitless time, and according to the law of counter-movements, or according to the analogy of the weather, constitute the means and the general mode of operation from which we anticipate an explanation of the general constitutions of solar and sidereal systems.

There comes to our aid a remarkable series of speculations and experiments recently promulgated upon the general subject of the nature and origin of heat, and under the general name of " The Dynamical Theory of Heat," the principles of which we shall endeavor briefly to explain. It is a fundamental theorem in mechanical philosophy, that no motion can be destroyed, except by the production of other equivalent motions, or by an equivalent change in the antecedent conditions of motion. If we launch a projectile upward, the motion which we impart to it is not a new creation, but is derived from forces or antecedent conditions of motion of a very complicated character in our muscular organism. It would be confusing to consider these at the outset; but if we look simply to the motion thus produced in the projectile itself, we shall gain the best preliminary notions as to the character of the phenomena of motion in general. The projectile rises to a certain height and comes to rest, and then, unless caught upon some elevated support, like the roof of a house, it returns to the ground with constantly accelerated motion, till it is suddenly brought to rest by collision with the earth. In this series of phenomena we have in reality only a series of commutations of motions and conditions of motion. The projectile is brought to rest at its greatest elevation by two forms of commutation. A small part of its motion is given to the air, and the remainder is transformed into the new condition of motion represented by its elevated position. The latter may remain for a long time permanent in case the projectile is caught at its greatest elevation upon some support. But a small auxiliary movement dislodging the projectile may at any time develop this condition of motion into a movement nearly equal to that which the projectile first received from our muscles. The small part that is lost in the air or other obstacles still exists, either in some form of motion or in some new conditions of motion, and the much greater part which disappears in the collision of the projectile with the earth is converted into several kinds of vibratory molecular movements in the earth, in the air, and in the projectile itself; and perhaps in part also in various new molecular conditions of motion.

If we designate by the word "power" that in which all forms of motion or antecedent conditions of motion are equivalent, we find that in the operations of nature no "power" is ever lost. Nor is there any evidence that any new "power" is ever created. It would be foreign to our purpose to follow into their ramifications the speculations by which this interesting theorem has been illustrated in many branches of physical inquiry. We are immediately interested only in the three principal and most general manifestations of "power" in the universe, namely, the movements *of* bodies, the movements *in* bodies, and the general antecedent conditions of both.

The proposition that the principal molecular motions in bodies are the cause which produces in our nerves the sensations of heat, or that they are what we denominate "the substance of heat,"—the objective cause of these sensations,—has long been held as a very probable hypothesis; and has latterly received experimental confirmations amounting to complete proof. The three principal manifestations of "power" in the universe are then, more specifically, the massive motions of bodies in translation and rotation, their molecular motions, or heat; and the principal antecedent condition of both, or gravitation.

In comparing these as to their equivalence we obtain a sum of "power," which remains invariable and indestructible by the operations of nature. It remains to determine the precise relations of their equivalence, and what the operations are by which they are converted into each other.

The mechanical equivalent of heat is a quantity which has been very accurately determined by experiment. By means of it we may very readily compute what amount of heat would be produced if a given amount of massive motion were converted into heat by friction or otherwise; or conversely, what amount of massive motion could be produced by the conversion of a given amount of heat into mechanical effect; but it is unnecessary to our purpose to give the precise method of this computation.

The mechanical equivalent of gravitation is another quantity or relation depending on the changes of what is called the "potential" of gravitation, or the sum of the ratios of the masses to the distances apart of the gravitating bodies. The "power" of motion is a relation or quantity, commonly called the "living force" of motion, and depends on the mass and on the square of the velocity of the moving body.

The living forces of all moving bodies, *minus* the potentials of their forces of gravitation, *plus* the mechanical values of their heat, *equal* to a constant quantity,—is the precise formula to which our cosmical speculations should conform. It will be impossible, however, to make any other than a very general use of this precise law. What concerns us more nearly is the consideration of the natural operations by which these manifestations of "power" are converted into each other.

The origin of the sun's light and heat is a problem upon which speculative ingenuity has long been expended in vain. The metaphysical conclusion, that the sun is composed of pure fire, or of fire *per se*, the very essence of fire, is one of many illustrations of the ingenious way in which speculation covers its nakedness with words, and can really mean, we imagine, only that the sun is very hot. That the sun, like any other body, must grow cooler by the expenditure of heat, is without doubt an indisputable proposition; and the question, how this heat is restored to it, is thus a legitimate one. The nebular hypothesis explains how the primitive heat in the sun and in other bodies could be generated by the condensation of the original nebulous mass, in which the heat is supposed to have been originally diffused; but it affords no explanation of the manner in which this heat could be sustained through the ages that must have elapsed since the nebular genesis must have been completed.

There are no precise means of estimating the amount of heat contained in the sun, since the capacity for heat of the materials which compose it are unknown; but from general analogy it may safely be assumed that the sun must grow cooler at a sensible rate, unless its heat is in some way renewed. Concerning the rate of its expenditure of heat, and the means which the dynamical theory of heat proposes to supply the loss, we will quote from the interesting lectures of Professor Tyndall, "On Heat considered as a Mode of Motion."

"The researches of Sir J. Herschel and M. Pouillet have informed us of the annual expenditure of the sun as regards heat, and by an easy calculation we ascertain the precise amount of the expenditure which falls to the share of our planet. Out of 2,300 million parts of light and heat the earth receives one. The whole heat emitted by the sun in a minute would be competent to boil 12,000 millions of cubic miles of ice-cold water. How is this enormous loss made good? Whence is the sun's heat derived, and by what means is it maintained? No combustion, no chemical affinity with which we are acquainted, would be competent to produce the temperature of the sun's surface. Besides, were the sun a burning body merely, its light and heat would assuredly speedily come to an end. Supposing it to be a solid globe of coal, its combustion would only cover 4,600 years of expenditure. In this short time it would burn itself out. What agency, then, can produce the temperature and maintain the outlay? We have already regarded the case of a body falling from a great distance towards the earth, and found that the heat generated by its collision would be twice that produced by the combustion of an equal weight of coal. How much greater must be the heat developed by a body falling towards the sun! The maximum velocity with which a body can strike the earth [arising from the earth's attraction] is about 7 miles a second; the maximum velocity with which it can strike the sun is 390 miles a second. And as the heat developed by the collision is proportional to the square of the velocity destroyed, an asteroid falling into the sun with the above velocity would generate about 10,000 times the quantity of heat generated by the combustion of an asteroid of coal of the same weight.

"Have we any reason to believe that such bodies exist in space, and that they may be rained down upon the sun? The meteorites flashing through our air are small planetary bodies, drawn by the earth's attraction, and entering our atmosphere with planetary velocity. By friction against the air they are raised to incandescence, and caused to emit light and heat. At certain seasons of the year they shower down upon us in great numbers. In Boston [England] 240,000 of them were observed in nine hours. There is no reason to suppose that the planetary system is limited to vast masses of enormous weight; there is every reason to believe that space is stocked with smaller masses, which obey the same laws as the large ones. That lenticular envelope which surrounds the sun, and which is known to astronomers as the zodiacal light, is probably a crowd of meteors; and, moving as they do in a resisting medium, they must continually approach the sun. Falling into it, they would be competent to produce the heat observed, and this would constitute a source from which the annual loss of heat would be made good. The sun, according to this hypothesis, would be continually growing larger; but how much larger? Were our moon to fall into the sun, it would develop an amount of heat sufficient to cover one or two years' loss; and were our earth to fall into the sun, a century's loss would be made good. Still, our moon and our earth, if distributed over the surface of the sun, would utterly vanish from perception. Indeed, the quantity of matter competent to produce the necessary effect would, during the range of history, produce no appreciable augmentation of the sun's magnitude. The augmentation of the sun's attractive force would be more appreciable. However this hypothesis may fare as a representant of what is going on in nature, it certainly shows how a sun might be formed and maintained by the application of known thermo-dynamic principles." *

---

* Appendix to Lecture XII. p. 455.

This part of our inquiry—how gravitation and motion are converted into heat—is receiving the amplest illustration and discussion from physicists at the present time; and, though the somewhat startling conclusions we have quoted are still too new to be generally credited, they are too well founded in experiment and the general analogies of natural phenomena to be passed lightly by.

The second part of our inquiry—how heat is refunded, in the eternal round of cosmical phenomena, into the antecedent conditions of motion, or to the conditions which preceded the production of the motions that are converted into heat—is a subject to which physicists have given little attention. Indeed, the cosmological ideas which prevail in geological inquiries beset this subject also, and impede inquiry. The order of nature is almost universally regarded as a progression from a determinate beginning to a determinate conclusion. The dynamical theory of heat lengthens out the process better, perhaps, than the nebular hypothesis alone; but both leave the universe at length in a hopeless chaos of huge, dark masses,—ruined suns wandering in eternal night.

It seems not to have occurred to physicists to inquire what becomes of the heat the generation of which requires so great an expenditure of motion. The heat is, in another form, the same motion as that which is lost by the fallen bodies. It is radiated into space, while the bodies remain in the sun; but this radiation is still the same motion in other bodies, in the luminiferous ether, or in the diffused matters of space. It cannot be lost from the universe, and must either accumulate in diffused materials or be converted into other motions or into new conditions of motion. But if the solid bodies of the universe are gradually collected at certain centres, and their motions are diffused in the form of heat throughout the gaseous materials of space, what do we gain? How do we by such a conclusion avoid the ultimate catastrophe which we regard as the *reductio ad absurdum* of a scientific theory? How do we thereby constitute that cycle of movements which we regard as characteristic of all natural phenomena? Perhaps we have been somewhat too hasty in adopting the conclusion that the

fallen bodies must necessarily remain in the sun, and grad
ually augment its mass. Let us, therefore, examine this point
more closely.

The principles of the steam-engine afford a clew to the
converse process we are in search of, by which heat may be
refunded into mechanical effects and conditions. The mechanical effects of the expanding power of steam are only partially
developed in the work which the engine performs. This work,
converted back to heat by friction or otherwise, would be insufficient to reproduce the same effects in the form of steam.
The remaining power consists in the motions and the power
of expansion with which the steam escapes from the engine.
This is lost power; but if it should be allowed to develop itself
by an expansion of the steam into an indefinitely extended
vacuum, the molecular motions of the particles of the steam
would gradually, and on the outside of the expanding vaporous mass, be converted into velocities or massive motions; the
vapor itself would be converted back into water, or even be
frozen into snow, and the particles of this water or snow would,
at the top of the expanding cloud, finally come to rest by the
force of gravitation. A part, therefore, of the lost power of
the heat which escaped in steam would be converted into that
antecedent condition of motion represented by elevation above
the attracting mass of the earth or by gravitation; a part would
continue to manifest itself as velocity or massive motion; and
the remainder would still continue to exert an outward pressure in the form of heat in vapor. This development would
continue so long as the steam continued to discharge itself into
the indefinitely extended vacuum we have supposed. The
rain or snow falling from the top of the cloud would convert
its gravitative power back again into motion, which, again
arrested by collision with the earth, would suffer other transformations in the endless round. In the actual case, where
the steam escapes into the air instead of a vacuum, the phenomena would be less simple. The history of its heat would
become involved with the grander phenomena of the weather,
—phenomena that may be regarded as typical of that cosmical
weather, concerning the laws of which we must inquire in considering what becomes of the sun's heat.

This heat is capable, provided it could all be so expended, of lifting the amount of matter which, by falling into the sun, is supposed to produce it, to the same height from the sun as that from which the fallen bodies may be supposed to have descended. This follows from the general mechanical principles we have stated. But how is this lifting effected ? What is the Titanic machinery by which the sun performs this labor ? The velocity with which a body falling from the interstellar spaces enters the body of the sun is sufficient, when converted to heat by friction and the shock, to convert the body itself into vapor, even if the body be composed of the least fusible of materials. The heat thus produced is not, however, confined to the fallen matter. A large portion is imparted to the matter already in the sun; but parts, no doubt, both of the projectile and of the resisting material are vaporized. The atmosphere immediately surrounding the sun contains the vapors of many of the most refractory metals that are known, as we learn from that wonderful instrument, the spectroscope. And this is made evident by the absorption from the sun's luminous rays of certain portions characteristic of these metals. Doubtless, in absorbing their characteristic vibrations, these metals are further heated and expanded, and gradually lifted from the surface of the sun ; and the vibrations of light and heat that pass through them and escape are probably all ultimately absorbed in the same or some similar way in the diffused materials of space. The speculations of the elder Struve on the extinction of light in its passage through space—conclusions founded on Sir William Herschel's observations of the Milky-Way—afford a happy and independent confirmation of these views. Moreover, the spectroscopic analyses of the light of the stars show broad dark bands, indicative of great extinctions of light. And we may add, that many gases and vapors which are transparent to luminous rays are found to absorb the obscure rays of heat.

Such is the kind of evidence we have of what becomes of the light and heat, and a portion, at least, of the material of the sun. The heat which is not expended immediately in vaporizing these materials is ultimately extinguished in further heat-

ing, expanding, and thus lifting the materials (may we not believe?) which have already been partially raised to the height,
whence perhaps, in former ages, they in their turn were rained
down as meteors upon the sun. In these suppositions we have
exactly reversed the nebular hypothesis. Instead of, in former
ages, a huge gaseous globe contracted by cooling and by gravitation, and consolidated at its centre, we have supposed one
now existing, and filling that portion of the interstellar spaces
over which the sun's attraction predominates,—a highly rarefied
continuous gaseous mass, constantly evaporated and expanded
from its solid centre, but constantly condensed and consolidated near its outer limits,—constantly heated at its centre
by the fall of solid bodies from its outer limits, and constantly
cooled and condensed at these limits by the conversion of heat
into motion and the arrest of this motion by gravitation.

There are certain chemical objections which apply equally
to the views here advanced and to the nebular hypothesis.
But these must necessarily arise from the limits to the knowledge we can gain of the whole range of chemical phenomena.
For what takes place in the chemist's laboratory, under the
very limited conditions of temperature and pressure he can
command, ought not to be regarded as determining the possibilities, or even the probabilities, of that cosmical chemistry of
which we can hardly be supposed to know even the rudiments.
We shall consider this subject, however, more particularly,
after attending to what is now of more immediate interest,
namely, the secondary mechanical conditions and phenomena
that result from the suppositions we have made; and particularly the question, how the systems of the planets and their
satellites stand related to the round of changes we have considered.

The fundamental and most important motions of the solar
system are, as we suppose, the radial movements of solid bodies
inward and of gaseous bodies outward, arising from the counteractions of gravitation and heat. But these radial movements must assume a vortical form, if one does not already
exist, such as is constantly exhibited by movements in the air
and in water. The rotation of the sun, imparted to the mate-

rials which rise in vapor from its surface, continues in them as they rise higher and higher, and though exhibited in a constantly diminishing tangential motion, remains in reality constant, as measured by what mechanicians term "rotation area." Or, rather, it is slowly increased by the mutual resistances of contiguous strata in the expanding gases, so that when this matter falls again towards the sun in the form of solid bodies, it falls in spiral trajectories, and only reaches the sun after perhaps many revolutions, or not at all, unless its motions be rapidly diminished by the resisting medium. If the resistance of the medium is not sufficient to convert the path of a falling meteor into a spiral, the meteor will mount again, and continue to move perhaps for a long time in an eccentric orbit, like a comet. When, however, the meteor at length, in any way, reaches the sun, a part of its motion is expended in increasing the sun's rotation, and thus compensating the loss of motion continually sustained by the sun in the evaporation of its material. The denser the resisting medium is in any system, the greater will be the revolution of its outer parts, and the larger will be the spiral trajectories which its falling bodies will describe. Such spiral or vortical motions as would thus be produced, or rather sustained, in the matter surrounding the sun, is exhibited by the most powerful telescopes, in the forms of the appendages to certain nebulous stars, and in the structure of the so-called Spiral Nebulæ. Perhaps the bodies which are supposed to give rise to the appearance of the zodiacal light would exhibit some such spiral arrangement, if seen from a point far above or below the ecliptic.

It follows from this vortical motion, that the form which the diffused materials of the solar system would assume, or rather maintain, would be that of an oblate ellipsoid or of a flattened lenticular body. The height to which the matter would rise in the plane of the sun's equator before its massive and molecular motions would be arrested by gravitation, would be much greater than in the directions of the sun's axis of rotation. The degree of oblateness which such a system of diffused matter will maintain depends on the frictions or resistances that successive strata exert on each other. It should be borne in mind in this connection that friction is not a loss of force, where all kinds of force are taken into account. Friction or resistance can only effect a conversion of massive into molecular motions, or the motion of velocity into the motion of heat. Hence, whatever velocity is lost by interior strata in the gaseous materials of the solar system, and is not gained by those exterior to them, must yet be ultimately restored; for the stability of such a system is no longer a question; this is insured in the fundamental mechanical law on which our speculations are founded.

It may still be a question, however, whether the planetary bodies of such a system are successively produced and destroyed, like generations of animals and plants, or whether they are permanent elements in a system of balanced forces and operations. So far as the effects of mutual perturbation are concerned, and independently of a resisting medium, astronomers have shown that the latter supposition is the more probable one; but there are several other considerations which point to a different conclusion. In the first place, the considerations already mentioned. The existence of systematic relations in the structure of the solar system, some of which are independent of its stability under the law of gravity, indicate the operations of causes other than the simple ones on which this stability depends,—such causes as the nebular hypothesis endeavored to define, but which we, in rejecting this hypothesis, have still to search for.

It has undoubtedly occurred to our readers to ask how the planets stand related to the meteoric system, and in what manner, if at all, their motions and masses are affected by this perpetual shower of matter. As out of every two thousand million parts of the light and heat of the sun's radiation the earth receives one part, so out of the two thousand million meteors sent back in return the earth will receive one, or perhaps a somewhat larger proportion, since the meteors are supposed to fall most thickly near the plane of the sun's equator. If we multiply this proportion by ten, as we probably may, it is still a very small quantity; but if we are permitted to multiply it by a factor of time as great as we please, this insignificance will disappear, and in its place we shall have a cosmical cause of the greatest moment in the history of the solar system. Two hundred million years is but a day in the cosmical eras, yet in that time the earth could receive as many bodies as fall to the sun in a year, or a hundredth part of the mass of the earth itself. In a hundred such days, then, the earth might be built up by the aggregation of meteors, provided it should lose none of the material thus collected, as the sun probably does. But this calculation proceeds on the supposition that the earth would have caught as many meteors when it was smaller, as it probably does now. A correction is therefore required which lengthens the period to three hundred such days, or to about a cosmical year, if we may so estimate times which are without limits or measure. In sixty thousand million years, then, the earth could have been made by the aggregation of meteors.* In this time the sun itself would have received and evaporated fifteen hundred times the amount of its present mass, provided a permanent amount of matter and heat should have been maintained in it during so long a period. In these estimates no account is taken of the heat immediately absorbed in evaporation, or absorbed in the space included within the earth's orbit. This heat would probably require a still greater expenditure of motion, and the fall of a still greater number of bodies. Hence the period required to build up the earth's mass might be materially shortened.

Such a method of inquiry, however, violates the canon we have laid down for our guidance in physical speculation. We must not suppose any action in nature to which there is not some counteraction, and no mode of production, however slow, from which in infinite time there could result an infinite

---

* Most of the materials which fall to the earth are probably in the form of very small bodies, which must be disintegrated by heat in their passage through the atmosphere, and must consequently reach the earth's surface in the form of fine dust. At the rate of accumulation estimated above, this dust, when reduced to the mean density of the earth's materials, would add one foot to the thickness of its crust in about three thousand years. In the loose form of dust or mud this accumulation would amount to about a hundredth of an inch in a year. The materials which have accumulated within historical periods over the ruins of ancient cities may thus in great part have been collected from the sky. The agencies of the winds and of flowing water in transporting and depositing the loose materials of the earth's surface would distribute this star-dust in deposits at the bottom of the sea, and in hills and mounds on the land.

product. We must, therefore, conclude that the planets either ultimately fall into the sun, and make a restitution of their peculations, or that heat and gravitation preserve in them also the balance of nature and the golden mean of virtue. The existence of a resisting medium favors the first supposition, unless it can be rendered probable that this medium revolves with velocities equal to those of the planets at the same distances from the sun. There is also another cause affecting the mean distances of the planets. An increase of mass in the sun will diminish the size of the planetary orbits, and conversely a diminution of this mass will increase the size of these orbits. The rate of change in the mass of the sun, whether to increase or to decrease, must depend on the relative rates of cooling by radiation and by evaporation. As the sun grows cooler by excessive radiation, its mass must be increased by the fall of meteors, and the planets will draw nearer to the sun; but if its radiation be diminished, and a larger proportion of the heat be expended in evaporation, then the planets will withdraw from the sun. Such are the causes which may affect the mean distances of the planets.

If on such grounds we may adopt the first of our suppositions, that the planets are successively formed and finally lost in the sun, like the meteors, the most probable hypothesis we can make concerning their origin is, that they are formed by the aggregation of meteors. Certain conditions, which, in the present state of our knowledge, it would perhaps be impossible to define, must determine the distances from the sun where these aggregations will begin; but the body and the attraction of the planet, when once begun, will determine further aggregation until the planet either falls into the sun, or approaches to such a distance that the evaporation of its material keeps pace with the fall of matter upon it. The size to which a planet could attain would thus be determined by the distance from the sun at which it begins to grow. A nearly circular orbit, and a small inclination of its plane to the plane of the sun's equator, would result from the circumstances attending the fall of the meteors,—their approach to the sun from every direction near the plane of the sun's equator.* A vortical motion and a rotation of the planet might result from such aggregations, which would be analogous to those of the sun and the general system. A more rigorous and comprehensive discussion of such problems than has yet been attempted is required before trustworthy conclusions can be formed.

The following considerations may materially affect the conclusions we have drawn from the existence of a resisting medium. The gaseous medium of the solar system might receive from the sun's rotation, and by the mutual friction of its own materials, greater velocities in its interior parts than the planets could have at the same distances from the sun, provided the exterior parts should move with less than planetary velocities, and should press with a portion of their weight upon the parts below them. For the centrifugal forces of the interior parts might thus be balanced, not merely by their own gravitation, but by a portion also of the weight of the superincumbent masses. At a distance from the sun less than half the mean distance of the planet Mercury, a period of revolution equal to that of the sun would produce a planetary velocity. At a greater distance, the medium might revolve more rapidly than the planets. But there must be a limit where the revolutions would be simply self-sustaining, and beyond this the medium would move less rapidly than the planets. So far, therefore, as a resisting medium could affect the motions of the planetary bodies, it might tend to increase the dimensions of the interior orbits, and to diminish those of the exterior ones; and it would thus tend to concentrate the planets, not in the sun, but at this limiting distance, where the medium would neither accelerate nor retard their motions. The motions of the medium would produce the greatest effect upon the smaller bodies of the solar system, which would, therefore, approach most rapidly to this limiting distance. That region in the solar system, about half the distance from the sun to the orbit of Jupiter, which is so thickly crowded with small planetary bodies or asteroids, may

---

* The rare occurrence of spots on the sun beyond thirty degrees either side of its equator may indicate some connection between these spots and the fall of meteors and serve to determine the limits of the meteoric system.

be regarded, on this hypothesis, as the region in which the gaseous medium now revolves with planetary velocity. Could this limiting distance remain fixed for a very long period, most of the planetary masses of the solar system might accumulate there, and be concentrated into one huge planet or secondary sun, and the solar system would thus be converted into a binary system, like those observed among the stars. But from the small amount of matter probably contained in the asteroid system, we ought to conclude that this limiting distance changes from time to time, as the medium grows denser or rarer.

The planets are not the only aggregations of meteoric bodies which we have to account for. Besides the comets, there are probably streams of meteors falling to or circulating around the sun. This is rendered very probable by the phenomena of the showers of these bodies which fall into our atmosphere at certain seasons of the year, or at certain positions in the earth's orbit.* And further, the rings of Saturn are probably examples of the same kind of meteoric aggregation. For of the three hypotheses in regard to the constitution of these rings which have been submitted to rigorous mathematical examination,— namely, first, that they are solid, secondly, that they are fluid, and, thirdly, that they are composed of distinct bodies or me- teors,—the latter is the only one which has been found to afford the conditions of stability which are implied in their continued existence. It is unnecessary to add the physical reasons which render this hypothesis still more probable.

We have no space to consider the many interesting geological

---

* There is a period of about eleven years in the numbers of spots that appear on the surface of the sun, a period coincident with that of the amount of diurnal variations in terrestrial magnetism,—an amount undoubtedly due to the influence of the sun. This period also coincides nearly with the period of the revolution of Jupiter, the largest planet in our system. If, then, we may suppose that the sun's spots are occasioned by the fall of large meteors, the courses of which lie near to the orbit of Jupiter, the attrac- tions of this planet, alternately turning such a stream of bodies upon and away from the surface of the sun, would connect these three nearly coincident periods by a common physical cause.

The phenomena of magnetism and electricity, as subordinate manifestations of motion and conditions of motion, have not been included in our speculations on the commuta- tions of "power," on account of their insignificant values as compared with the three principal forms of "power." For the same reason, we omit any consideration of the numerous but minute modifications of "power" which are manifested by the forces of vital phenomena on the surface of the earth.

consequences which follow from our hypothesis. Let it suffice to remark, that the formation of the earth's mass by meteoric aggregation precludes the hypothesis, otherwise improbable, that the core of the earth is a molten mass. The occurrence of volcanoes in local systems, distinct from each other, points to local causes of an unknown chemical character as the true sources of these phenomena. The heterogeneous character of the materials of the earth's crust, in which are mingled, in the most intimate manner, all kinds of substances, irrespectively of their chemical affinities, and in opposition to their chemical forces of aggression, could hardly be the results of the actions of heat and aqueous solution, both of which afford conditions favorable to chemical aggregation. Indeed, in most cases in which such aggregation occurs, where homogeneous and chemically simple substances are found in considerable quantities, the agency either of heat or aqueous solution is evident. It is hardly necessary to add, that the theory of meteoric aggregation is the one which would most readily explain these facts.

But we must here leave the consideration of these interesting problems, and return to a topic much more obscure, to which we called attention a few pages back.

The dynamical theory of heat has not only suggested new and interesting inquiries concerning the constitution of the universe, but it throws new light in the philosophy of chemical phenomena on such problems as the origin of the three states of aggregation in matter, and on the character of the changes which may take place under circumstances beyond the reach of chemical experiments and observation.

That the dreams of the alchemists were at fault rather in point of method than of doctrine, is a confession which the modern chemist must make, when he compares the slight resources of experiment at his command with the possibilities of nature. If, as has been surmised, the characteristic properties of different kinds of matter consist in characteristic internal or molecular motions (and molecular conditions of motion), a complete destruction of such motions would obliterate all the characteristic differences of matter, and such a result might be attained by the production of absolute cold. In respect to the motions of light and heat, however, the universe, so far as we know it, and even so far as we could know it, is a perfectly continuous body. In no corner or recess of its unfathomable depths to which the feeblest light of a single star could find its way, can there be an absence of the motions of light and heat. Nothing can set bounds to the all-pervading reach of these motions except limits to that medium of motion, the luminiferous ether; and these, so far as all cognizable physical conditions are concerned, would be limits to space itself. That potent sidereal influence, the absolute cold, transmuting all substances into one, could only arise momentarily, in nodal points or lines or surfaces, but could not be extended discontinuously into space of three dimensions. What may happen at such times and limits, where matter, expiring from one form of chemical life, may be awakened to another, according to the kind of molecular agitation which may next overtake it, and determine its history, perhaps for myriads of years, is what the chemist cannot tell us, and only the alchemist can dream. It suffices for our instruction, that the chemistry of absolute cold has possibilities of which experimental chemistry affords no criterion, and may play a part in the economy of nature not inferior to that of gravitation or heat.

But it may be objected, on grounds of experimental chemistry, "that the sun's heat, though sufficient to volatize the least fusible materials, could not keep them in the form of vapor at the heights and in the temperature of the interplanetary spaces, much less lift them in the form of vapor to the heights of the interstellar regions whence the meteors are supposed to fall. For most bodies which are solid at ordinary terrestrial temperatures tend, upon cooling, to crystallize with such energy that they would soon be precipitated from the vaporous form." But this objection takes no account of those effects of diffusion, expansion, and commingling of heterogeneous materials, which must remove the parts of a volatilized body to such hopeless distances from each other that the forces of chemical aggregation might require ages to collect what is thus dispersed. Nor can any account be taken of such unknown laws of chemical affinity and aggregation as are possible under the circumstances we are considering. The known laws of chemical action should, then, be ranked with those laws of life, exhibited in the phenomena of growth, which were too hastily generalized and applied, in "the theory of evolution," to the interpretation of the riddles and the explication of the order of the System of the World.

NATURAL THEOLOGY AS A POSITIVE SCIENCE.*

Natural history and anatomy have hitherto furnished the principal grounds to the theologian for the speculation of final causes, since these sciences exhibit many instances of a complex combination of causes in the structures and habits of organic bodies, and at the same time a distinct and peculiar class of effects, namely, those which constitute the well-being and perfection of organic life; and from these causes and effects, regarded as means and ends in the order of nature, the arguments and illustrations of natural theology have been chiefly drawn. The facts of these sciences are not merely the most useful to the theologian; they are indeed indispensable, and occupy a peculiar position in his argument, since they alone afford the class of effects on which, assumed as ends, the speculation of final causes ultimately rests.

It is only by assuming human welfare, or with this the welfare also of other sentient beings, as the end for which the universe exists, that the doctrine of final causes has hitherto found any support in natural science.

Though it is still maintained by theologians that the arguments for design are properly inductive arguments, yet the physical proofs of natural theology are not regarded by many modern writers as having any independent weight; and it is in mental and moral science that the facts are sought which will warrant the induction of design from the general phenomena of nature. It is hardly considered logical, even by the theological writers of our day, to conclude, with Paley, "that

* From the North American Review, for January, 1865.

the works of nature proceed from intelligence and design ; because, in the properties of relation to a purpose, subserviency to a use, they resemble what intelligence and design are constantly producing, and what nothing [which we know] except intelligence and design ever produce at all." For it is denied by the physical philosopher that causes and effects in natural phenomena can be interpreted into the terms of natural theology by any key which science itself affords. By what criterion, he would ask, can we distinguish among the numberless effects, that are also causes, and among the causes that may, for aught we can know, be also effects,—how can we distinguish which are the means and which are the ends ? What effects are we warranted by observation in calling final, or final causes, or the ends for which the others exist ? The belief on other grounds that there *are* final causes, that the universe exists for some purpose, is one thing ; but the belief that science discloses, or even that science can disclose, what this purpose is, is quite a different thing. The designation of those effects as final in nature which contribute to human desires or human welfare, or even to the welfare of all sentient beings, cannot be legitimately made for the purpose of this argument, since human and other sentient beings are not the agents by which these supposed ends are attained; neither can the causes which bring these effects to pass be regarded as servants obedient to the commands of the agents to whom these effects are desirable. The analogy of natural production to human contrivance fails them at the very outset; and the interpretation of natural causes and effects as means and ends, virtually assumes the conclusion of the argument, and is not founded on any natural evidence. These considerations are overlooked by most writers on this subject, who, in addition to a legitimate faith in final causes, assume the dogma that these causes are manifest or discoverable. They begin with the definition, sometimes called an argument, "that a combination of means conspiring to a particular end implies intelligence," and they then assume that the causes which science discovers are means, or exist for the sake of the effects which science accounts for; and from the relation of means to ends, thus assumed, they infer intelligence.

The definition we have quoted contains, however, more than is really implied in this argument, since the relation of means to ends in itself, and without further qualification, implies intelligence, while a combination of means conspiring to a particular end implies a high degree of intelligence; and it is with this, the degree of intelligence manifested in the phenomena of nature, that scientific discourses on the natural evidences are really dealing, though sometimes unconsciously. These discourses really aim, not so much to prove the existence of design in the universe, as to show the wisdom of certain designs which are assumed to be manifest. But for this purpose it is requisite to translate the facts of science, and those combinations of causes which are discovered to be the conditions of particular effects, into the terms of the argument, and to show that these combinations are means, or exist for the sake of particular effects, for which, as ends, the universe itself must be shown to exist,—a task for which science is obviously incompetent.

Waiving these fundamental objections to the argument for design, which, let us repeat, are not objections to the spiritual doctrine of final causes, or to the belief that final causes exist, we will turn to the objections which modern writers of natural theology themselves allow.

It is essential to the validity of Paley's argument, that "design," or the determination of effects by the intelligence of an agent, be shown to be not merely the only known cause of such effects, but also to be a real cause, or an independent determination by an efficient agent. If intelligence itself be a product, if the human powers of contrivance are themselves effects, it follows that designed effects should be ascribed, not to intelligence, but to the causes of intelligence; and the same objection will hold against the theologian's use of the word "design," which he urges against the physicist's use of the word "law." "It is a perversion of language," says Paley, "to assign any law as the efficient operative cause of anything. A law presupposes an agent, for it only is the mode according to which the agent proceeds; it implies a power, for it is the order according to which this power acts. Without this agent, without this power, which are both distinct from itself, the 'law' does nothing, is nothing." By substituting the word "design" for the word "law" in this quotation, we have the materialist's objection to the theologian's perversion of language. This objection was entirely overlooked by Paley, who seems to have thought it sufficient for the purposes of his argument to consider only the phenomena of the visible material universe. But later writers have seen the necessity of basing the argument for design on the psychological doctrine that intelligence is a free, undetermined power, and that design is the free, undetermined act of this power. Without this assumption, which indeed Paley himself virtually makes, it would be as unphilosophical to refer the course of nature to the determination of intelligence, as it is to refer it to the determination of the abstraction which the materialist prefers, or to the "agency of law."

"That intelligence stands first in the absolute order of existence,—in other words, that final preceded efficient causes,—and that the universe is governed by moral laws," are the two propositions, the proof of which, says Sir William Hamilton, is the proof of a God; and this proof "establishes its foundation exclusively on the phenomena of mind." Without this psychological proof, the order of adaptation cannot be logically referred to the order of design; and the resemblance of human contrivances to the adaptations of nature can only warrant the conclusion that both proceed from similar conditions, and by a power of whose efficiency human intelligence and physical laws are alike manifestations, but whose nature neither human intelligence comprehends nor physical laws can disclose.

Even such a result, which is all that the unaided physical sciences can compass, is not altogether barren of religious interest, though it is made so by the materialist's attempt to define the nature of power by assigning to physical forces an absolute efficiency. The spiritualist, on the other hand, if we allow his psychological proof that intelligence stands first in the absolute order of existence, and is a free, undetermined power, is logically competent to interpret the order of nature as a designed order. Yet to him physical proofs of design have little or no value, and can only serve as obscure and enigmatical illustrations of what is far more clearly apparent in the study of mind. And though logically competent to interpret the order of design, if his spiritual doctrine be true, yet the difficulties which we first mentioned, and waived for the nonce, are difficulties as insuperable to the psychologist as to the physicist. He gains no criterion from his studies by which to distinguish, in the order of natural phenomena, which are the means and which are the ends, or where the relation of means to ends is to be found, among the infinite successions of effects which are also causes, and of causes which may, for aught he can know, be also effects. His faith in final causes is not a guide by which he can determine what the final causes are by which he believes the order of nature to be determined.

These theoretical objections to a philosophy, which assigns physical reasons for a faith in final causes, are by no means the most important objections. The practical influences and effects of such philosophizing are, we believe, more obnoxious to the true interests of religion than its methods are to the true principles of philosophy, and fully justify an examination of its arguments. For bad arguments may go for nothing, while good ones necessitate their conclusions; and we think it fortunate for the purity of religious truth that theologians have succeeded no better in this direction.

Not only do the peculiar doctrines of natural theology add nothing to the grounds of a faith in final causes; they, in effect, narrow this faith to ideas which scarcely rise in dignity above the rank of superstitions. If to believe that God is what we can think him to be is blasphemy, what shall we call the attempt to discover his intentions and to interpret his plans in nature? If science were able to discover a much closer analogy than it does between the adaptations of nature and the designs of human contrivance, would it be any less derogatory to the dignity of the Divine nature to attempt by such analogies to fathom his designs and plans, or to suppose that what appears as a designed order is really any clew to the purposes of the Almighty? And when, even transcending this degree of presumption, theology would fix a limit to the researches and

hypotheses of science, on the ground that they tend to subvert
religious doctrines, or the assumed results of a religious philosophy, we are warranted—nay, constrained, from practical
considerations—to question the grounds of its pretensions, to
allow it no longer to shield its falseness and weakness behind
the dignity and worth of the interests to which it is falsely
dedicated. It is from the illegitimate pretensions of natural
theology that the figment of a conflict between science and religion has arisen; and the efforts of religious thinkers to coun-
teract the supposed atheistical tendencies of science, and to
give a religious interpretation to its facts, have only served to
deepen the false impression that such a conflict actually exists, so that revolutions in scientific theories have been made to
appear in the character of refutations of religious doctrines.

That there is a fundamental distinction between the natures
of scientific and religious ideas ought never to be doubted;
but that contradiction can arise, except between religious and
superstitious ideas, ought not for a moment to be admitted.
Progress in science is really a progress in religious truth, not
because any new reasons are discovered for the doctrines of
religion, but because advancement in knowledge frees us from
the errors both of ignorance and of superstition, exposing the
mistakes of a false religious philosophy, as well as those of a
false science. If the teachings of natural theology are liable
to be refuted or corrected by progress in knowledge, it is legitimate to suppose, not that science is irreligious, but that these
teachings are superstitious; and whatever evils result from the
discoveries of science are attributable to the rashness of the theologian, and not to the supposed irreligious tendencies of science.
When a proof of special design is invalidated by the discovery
that a particular effect in the operations of nature, which previously appeared to result from a special constitution and ad-
justment of certain forces, is really a consequent of the general
properties of matter,—when, for example, the laws of planetary motion were shown to result from the law of universal
gravitation, and the mathematical plan of the solar system was
seen to be a consequent of a single universal principle,—the
harm, if there be any, results from the theologian's mistakes,

and not from the corrections of science. He should refrain from attributing any special plan or purpose to the creation, if he would find in science a constant support to religious truth. But this abstinence does not involve a withdrawal of the mind from the proper religious interests of natural science, nor weaken a legitimate faith in final causes. Even the Newtonian mechanism of the heavens, simple, primordial, and necessary as it seems, still discloses to the devout mind evidence of a wisdom unfathomable, and of a design which transcends interpretation; and when, in the more complicated order of organic life, surprising and beautiful adaptations inspire in the naturalist the conviction that purpose and intelligence are manifested in them,—that they spring from a nature akin to the devising power of his own mind,—there is nothing in science or philosophy which can legitimately rebuke his enthusiasm,—nothing, unless it be the dogmatism which would presumptuously interpret as science what is only manifest to faith, or would require of faith that it shall justify itself by proofs.

The progress of science has indeed been a progress in religious truth, but in spite of false theology, and in a way which narrow theologians have constantly opposed. It has defined with greater and greater distinctness the boundary between what can be discovered and what cannot. It has purified religious truth by turning back the moral consciousness to discover clearly in itself what it had obscurely divined from its own interpretations of nature. It has impressed on the mind of the cautious inquirer the futility, as well as the irreverence, of attempting a philosophy which can at best be but a finer sort of superstition, a real limitation to our conceptions of final causes, while apparently an extension of them.

But instead of learning these lessons from the experience of repeated failures, theologians have constantly opposed new hypotheses in science, until proof has compelled a tardy assent, and even then they have retreated to other regions of science, as if these were the only refuge of a persecuted faith.

Humility and cautiousness, and that suspension of judgment in matters about which we really know so little, which a recent theological writer has recommended, in view of the pending controversy on the origin of organic species and adaptations, are virtues, which, had they been generally cultivated by theologians, would have rendered this controversy harmless at least, if not unnecessary.

THE PHILOSOPHY OF HERBERT SPENCER.*

Why the inductive and mathematical sciences, after their
first rapid development at the culmination of Greek civilization, advanced so slowly for two thousand years,—and why in
the following two hundred years a knowledge of natural and
mathematical science has accumulated, which so vastly exceeds
all that was previously known that these sciences may be justly
regarded as the products of our own times,—are questions
which have interested the modern philosopher not less than
the objects with which these sciences are more immediately
conversant. Was it in the employment of a new method of
research, or in the exercise of greater virtue in the use of old
methods, that this singular modern phenomenon had its origin ? Was the long period one of arrested development, and
is the modern era one of a normal growth ? or should we ascribe the characteristics of both periods to so-called historical
accidents,—to the influence of conjunctions in circumstances
of which no explanation is possible, save in the omnipotence
and wisdom of a guiding Providence ?

The explanation which has become commonplace, that the
ancients employed deduction chiefly in their scientific inquiries, while the moderns employ induction, proves to be too
narrow, and fails upon close examination to point with sufficient distinctness the contrast that is evident between ancient
and modern scientific doctrines and inquiries. For all knowledge is founded on observation, and proceeds from this by analysis and synthesis, by synthesis and analysis, by induction and
deduction, and if possible by verification, or by new appeals to

---

* From the North American Review, April, 1865.

observation under the guidance of deduction,—by steps which are indeed correlative parts of one method; and the ancient sciences afford examples of every one of these methods, or parts of the one complete method, which have been generalized from the examples of science.

A failure to employ or to employ adequately any one of these partial methods, an imperfection in the arts and re-sources of observation and experiment, carelessness in observa-tion, neglect of relevant facts, vagueness and carelessness in reasoning, and the failure to draw the consequences of theory and test them by appeal to experiment and observation,—these are the faults which cause all failures to ascertain truth, whether among the ancients or the moderns; but this statement does not explain why the modern is possessed of a greater virtue, and by what means he attained to his superiority. Much less does it explain the sudden growth of science in recent times.

The attempt to discover the explanation of this phenome-non in the antithesis of " facts" and "theories" or "facts" and "ideas,"—in the neglect among the ancients of the former, and their too exclusive attention to the latter,—proves also to be too narrow, as well as open to the charge of vagueness. For, in the first place, the antithesis is not complete. Facts and the-ories are not co-ordinate species. Theories, if true, are facts,— a particular class of facts indeed, generally complex ones, but still facts. Facts, on the other hand, even in the narrowest signification of the word, if they be at all complex, and if a logical connection subsists between their constituents, have all the positive attributes of theories.

Nevertheless, this distinction, however inadequate it may be to explain the source of true method in science, is well found-ed, and connotes an important character in true method. A fact is a proposition of which the verification by an appeal to the primary sources of our knowledge or to experience is direct and simple. A theory, on the other hand, if true, has all the characteristics of a fact, except that its verification is possible only by indirect, remote, and difficult means. To con-vert theories into facts is to add *simple verification*, and the theory thus acquires the full characteristics of a fact. When Pascal caused the Torricellian tube to be carried up the Puy de Dôme, and thus showed that the mercurial column was sustained by the weight of the atmosphere, he brought the theory of atmospheric pressure nearly down to the level of a fact of observation. But even in this most remarkable instance of scientific discovery theory was not wholly reduced to fact, since the verification, though easy, was not entirely simple, and was incomplete until further observations showed that the quantity of the fall in the Torricellian tube agreed with deductions from the combined theories of atmospherical pressure and elasticity. In the same way the theory of universal gravitation fails to become a fact in the proper sense of this word, however complete its verification, because this verification is not simple and direct, or through the immediate activity of our perceptive powers.

Modern science deals then no less with theories than with facts, but always as much as possible with the verification of theories,—if not to make them facts by simple verification through experiment and observation, at least to prove their truth by indirect verification.

The distinction of fact and theory thus yields an important principle, of which M. Comte and his followers have made much account. It is in the employment of verification, they say, and in the possibility of it, that the superiority of modern inductive research consists; and it is because the ancients did not, or could not, verify their theories, that they made such insignificant progress in science. It is indisputable that verification is essential to the completeness of scientific method; but there is still room for debate as to what constitutes verification in the various departments of philosophical inquiry. So long as the philosophy of method fails to give a complete inventory of our primary sources of knowledge, and cannot decide authoritatively what are the origins of first truths, or the truths of observation, so long will it remain uncertain what is a legitimate appeal to observation, or what is a real verification. The Platonists or the rationalists may equally with the empiricists claim verification for their theories; for do they not appeal to the reason for confirmation of deductions from their theories, which they regard as founded on observation of what the reason reveals to them?

The positivists' principle of verification comes, then, only to this,—that, inasmuch as mankind are nearly unanimous about the testimony and trustworthiness of their senses, but are divided about the validity of all other kinds of authority, which they in a word call the reason, or internal sense, therefore verification by the senses produces absolute conviction, while verification by the reason settles nothing, but is liable to the same uncertainty which attends the primary appeals to this authority for the data of speculative knowledge.

But not only does the so-called metaphysical philosophy employ a species of verification by appealing to the testimony of reason, consciousness, or internal sense; but the ancient physical sciences afford examples of the confirmation of theory by observation proper. The Ptolemaic system of astronomy was an instance of the employment of every one of the partial steps of true method; and the theory of epicycles not only sought to represent the facts of observation, but also by the prediction of astronomical phenomena to verify the truth of its representation. Modern astronomy does not proceed otherwise, except that its theories represent a much greater number of facts of observation, and are confirmed by much more efficient experimental tests.

The difference, then, between ancient and modern science is not truly characterized by any of the several explanations which have been proposed. The explanation, however, which, in our opinion, comes nearest to the true solution, and yet fails to designate the real point of difference, is that which the positivists find in the distinction between "objective method" and "subjective method." The objective method is verification by sensuous tests, tests of sensible experience,—a deduction from theory of consequences, of which we may have sensible experiences if they be true. The subjective method, on the other hand, appeals to the tests of internal evidence, tests of reason, and the data of self-consciousness. But whatever be the origin of the theories of science, whether from a systematic examination of empirical facts by conscious induction, or from the natural biases of the mind, the so-called intuitions of reason, in other words what seems probable without a distinct survey of our experiences,—whatever the origin, real or ideal, the *value* of these theories can only be tested, say the positivists, by an appeal to sensible experience, by deductions from them of consequences which we can confirm by the undoubted testimony of the senses. Thus, while ideal or transcendental elements are admitted into scientific researches, though in themselves insusceptible of simple verification, they must still show credentials from the senses, either by affording from themselves consequences capable of sensuous verification, or by yielding such consequences in conjunction with ideas which by themselves are verifiable.

It is undoubtedly true, that one of the leading traits of modern scientific research is this reduction of ideas to the tests of experience. The systematic development of ideas through induction from the first and simplest facts of observation, is by no means so obvious a characteristic. Inductions are still performed for the most part unconsciously and unsystematically. Ideas are developed by the sagacity of the expert, rather than by the systematic procedures of the philosopher. But when and however ideas are developed science cares nothing, for it is only by subsequent tests of sensible experience that ideas are admitted into the pandects of science.

It is of no consequence to scientific astronomy whence the theory of gravitation arose; whether as an induction from the theories of attractions and the law of radiations, or from the rational simplicity of this law itself, as the most natural supposition which could be made. Science asks no questions about the ontological pedigree or *a priori* character of a theory, but is content to judge it by its performance; and it is thus that a knowledge of nature, having all the certainty which the senses are competent to inspire, has been attained,—a knowledge which maintains a strict neutrality toward all philosophical systems, and concerns itself not at all with the genesis or *a priori* grounds of ideas.

This mode of philosophizing is not, however, exclusively found in modern scientific research. Ptolemy claimed for his epicycles only that "they saved the appearances;" and he might have said, with as much propriety as Newton, "*Hypotheses non fingo*," for it was the aim of his research to represent abstractly, and by the most general formulas, the characteristics of the movements of the planets,—an aim which modern astronomy, with a much simpler hypothesis, and with immensely increased facilities, still pursues.

We find, therefore, that while moderns follow a true method of investigation with greater facilities and greater fidelity than the ancients, and with a clearer apprehension of its elements and conditions, yet that no new discoveries in method have been made, and no general sources of truth have been pointed out, which were not patent and known to the ancients; and we have so far failed to discover any solution to the problem with which we began. We have seen that it was not by the employment of a new method of research, but in the exercise of greater virtue in the use of old methods, that modern scientific researches have succeeded. But whence this greater virtue? What vivifying, energizing influence awakened the sixteenth century to the movement, which has continued down to the present day to engross, and even to create, the energies of philosophic thought in the study of natural phenomena? Obviously some interest was awakened, which had before been powerless, or had influenced only men of rare and extraordinary genius, or else some opposing interest had ceased to exercise a preponderating influence.

We have now arrived at a new order of inquiries. We ask no longer what are the differences of *method* between ancient and modern scientific researches, but we seek the difference in the *motives* which actuated the philosophic inquiries of the two periods. We seek for the interests which in modern times have so powerfully drawn men of all orders of intelligence to the pursuit of science, and to an observance of the conditions requisite for its successful prosecution. We do not inquire what course has led to successful answers in science, but what motives have prompted the pertinent questions.

In place of the positivists' phraseology, that the ancients followed "the subjective method," or appealed for the verification of their theories to natural beliefs, while the moderns follow, "the objective method," or appeal to new and independent experimental evidence,—if we substitute the word "motive" for "method," we have the terms of one of the conclusions on which we wish to insist. But these require explanation.

By a subjective motive we mean one having its origin in natural universal human interests and emotions, which existed before philosophy was born, which continue to exist in the maturity of philosophy, and determine the character of an important and by no means defunct order of human speculations. By an objective motive we mean one having an empirical origin, arising in the course of an inquiry; springing from interests which are defined by what we already know, and not by what we have always felt,—interests which depend on acquired knowledge, and not on natural desires and emotions. Among the latter we must include the natural desire for knowledge, or the primitive, undisciplined sentiment of curiosity. This becomes an objective motive when it ceases to be associated with our fears, our respects, our aspirations, —our emotional nature; when it ceases to prompt questions as to what relates to our personal destiny, our ambitions, our moral worth; when it ceases to have man, his personal and social nature, as its central and controlling objects. A curiosity which is determined chiefly or solely by the felt imperfections of knowledge as such, and without reference to the uses this knowledge may subserve, is prompted by what we call an objective motive.

A spirit of inquiry which is freed from the influence of our active powers, and the interests that gave birth to theological and metaphysical philosophies,—which yields passively and easily to the direction of objective motives, to the felt imperfections of knowledge as such,—is necessarily, at all times, a weak feeling; and before a body of systematic, well-digested, and well-ascertained scientific truth had been generated, could hardly have had any persistent influence on the direction of inquiry.

The motives to theological and metaphysical speculation exist from the beginning of civilized human life in the active

emotional nature of man. Curiosity as a love of the marvelous, or as a love of facts,—new facts, prized because they are
new and stimulating,—also dates back of civilized life. These
motives find play in human nature, as it emerges from a semi-
animal state; but they also persist and determine the growth
of the human mind in its most advanced development.

The questions of philosophy proper are human desires and
fears and aspirations—human emotions—taking an intellectual form. Science follows, but does not supersede, this philosophy. The three phases which the positivists assign to the
development of the human mind—the Theological, the Metaphysical, and the Positive or Scientific—are not in reality
successive, except in their beginnings. They co-exist in all the
highest developments of civilization and mental activity. They
co-existed in the golden age of Greek civilization, in the intense mental activity of the Middle Ages. They move on together in this marvelous modern era. But until this latest
epoch positive science was always the inferior philosophy,—
hardly a distinct philosophy at all,—not yet born. But at the
beginning of the modern era its gestation was completed. A
body of knowledge existed, sufficiently extensive, coherent, and
varied, to bear within it a life of its own,—an independent
life,—which was able to collect to itself, by its own determinations, the materials of a continued, new, and ever-increasing
mental activity,—an activity determined solely by an objective
curiosity, or by curiosity in its purest, fullest, and highest energy.

We are probably indebted to the few men of scientific genius
who lived during the slow advancement of modern civilization
for the foundation of this culture,—for the accumulation of
the knowledge requisite for this subsequent growth. These
men were doubtless, for the most part, the products of their
own time and civilization, as indeed all great men have been,
but still originators, by concentrating and making productive
the energies, tendencies, and knowledges which, but for them,
would have remained inert and unfruitful. It is to such men,
born at long intervals in the slow progress of civilization, each
carrying forward a little the work of his predecessor, that we

probably owe our modern science, rather than to the influence of any single mind, like Bacon, who was, like his predecessors, but the lens which collected the light of his times,—who prophesied rather than inaugurated the new era. And we owe science to the combined energies of individual men of genius, rather than to any tendency to progress inherent in civilization.

We find, then, the explanation of the modern development of science in the accumulation of a body of certified knowledge, sufficiently extensive to engage and discipline a rational scientific curiosity, and stimulate it to act independently of other motives. It is doubtless true that other motives have influenced this development, and especially that motives of material utility have had a powerful effect in stimulating inquiry. Ancient schools of philosophy despised narrow material utilities, the servile arts, and sought no instruction in what moderns dignify by the name of useful arts; but modern science finds in the requirements of the material arts the safest guide to exact knowledge. A theory which is utilized receives the highest possible certificate of truth. Navigation by the aid of astronomical tables, the magnetic telegraph, the innumerable utilities of mechanical and chemical science, are constant and perfect tests of scientific theories, and afford the standard of certitude, which science has been able to apply so extensively in its interpretations of natural phenomena.

But the motives proper to science, though purified by their dissociation from the subjective determinations and tendencies, which gave an anthropomorphic and teleological character to ancient views of nature, are not the only legitimate motives to philosophical inquiry. There is another curiosity purified by its association with the nobler sentiments,—with wonder, admiration, veneration,—and with the interests of our moral and æsthetical natures. This curiosity is the motive to philosophy proper. "Wonder is a highly philosophical affection," says Plato's Socrates; "indeed, there is no other principle of philosophy but this."

Curiosity determined by natural sentiments and emotions—subjective curiosity—is the cause of a culture co-extensive with civilization, long preceding the growth of science, and constituting all that is peculiar to civilized life except the material arts. However meanly the conclusions of theological and metaphysical speculations may appear, when tried by the objective standard of science, they too have their superiorities, by the test of which science becomes in turn insignificant. Unverified conclusions, vague ideas, crude fancies, they may be, but they certainly are the products of activities which constitute more of human happiness and human worth than the narrow material standards of science have been able to measure.

Philosophy proper should be classed with the Religions and with the Fine Arts, and estimated rather by the dignity of its motives, and the value it directs us to, than by the value of its own attainments. To condemn this pursuit because it fails to accomplish what science does, would be to condemn that which has formed in human nature habits, ideas, and associations on which all that is best in us depends,—would warrant the condemnation of science itself, since science scarcely existed at all for two thousand years of civilization, and represented as a distinct department during this period only the interests of the servile arts. The objects of Philosophy were those which the religious ideas and emotions of man presented to his speculative curiosity. These motives, though proper to Philosophy, also gave direction to inquiries in Physics and Astronomy. The Fine Arts sprang from the same interests, and persisted through the conservative power of religious interests in a development to which the modern world offers no parallel. We have no styles in Art, no persistently pursued efforts for perfection in beauty, because we are not held to the conditions of this perfection by the religious motives which directed ancient Art. The growth of Theology and Metaphysics is less vigorous now for the same reason. Theology was Philosophy developed in the interests of Religion or of religious feeling, and Metaphysics was cultivated in the interests of Theology. Both aimed at truth; both were determined by the same love of simplicity and unity in knowledge, which determines all search after truth; but neither cared for simple truth alone. When pursued for the truth of fact alone, they both degenerate into affectation and emptiness. We do not omit the sceptical philosophies of antiquity from this description, because they were not held independently of the religious interests of the orthodox philosophy, but in opposition to them or in criticism of them.

Theology and Metaphysics failed to apply a correct method and to arrive at certain results, not because philosophers were ignorant of method, but because the object-matters of their research were not questions of sensible experience,—were not mere questions of facts of which the mind is the passive recipient through the senses. Their aim was to *prove* truth, not to discover it,—to reduce opinions and ideas which had the warrant of religious associations to the simplicity and consistency of truth; and when ideas and opinions have this warrant, it does not require the verification of the senses to make the conclusions of Philosophy acceptable and true to the religious instincts. To educe conclusions acceptable to these instincts and in opposition to no known truth,—in other words, to free religious beliefs from contradictions and to give them consistency,— was the aspiration and the devoted service of Philosophy.

Philosophy has in fact three phases instead of two. For as Theology was a speculation prosecuted in the interest of religious feeling, and Metaphysics a speculation in defense or criticism of the doctrines of Theology, so Criticism or Critical Philosophy is an examination of metaphysical conclusions. But the latter is properly, in its motives, a scientific speculation. Such is the true logical order of Philosophy proper, though all these phases may and do co-exist in history.

It is the opinion of many modern thinkers, besides the so-called Positivists, or avowed followers of M. Comte, that science, as we have defined it, or truth pursued simply in the interests of a rational curiosity, and for the mental discipline and the material utilities of its processes and conclusions, will hereafter occupy more and more the attention of mankind, to the exclusion of the older philosophy. It is also the opinion of these thinkers, that this is not to be regretted, but rather welcomed as a step forward in the advancement of human welfare and civilization; that the pursuit of science and its utilities is capable of inspiring as great and earnest a devotion as those which religious interests have inspired, and which have hitherto determined the destinies of mankind and given form to human thought, and one vastly more beneficent.

Whatever foundations there are for these opinions, it is certain that the claims of science, as a new power in the world, to the regard of thoughtful and earnest men, are receiving a renewed and more candid attention. Through its recent progress, many of the questions which have hitherto remained in the arena of metaphysical disputation are brought forward in new forms and under new auspices. Scientific investigations promise to throw a flood of light on subjects which have interested mankind since the beginning of speculation,—subjects related to universal human interests. History, society, laws, and morality,—all are claimed as topics with which scientific methods are competent to deal. Scientific solutions are proposed to all the questions of philosophy which scientific illumination may not show to have their origin in metaphysical hallucination.

Prominent in the ranks of the new school stands Mr. Herbert Spencer, whose versatility has already given to the world many ingenious and original essays in this new philosophy, and whose aspiring · genius projects many more, which, if his strength does not fail, are to develop the capacities of a scientific method in dealing with all the problems that ought legitimately to interest the human mind.

The programme of his future labors which his publishers have advertised might dispose a prejudiced critic to look with suspicion on what he has already accomplished; but the favorable impression which his works have made, and the plaudits of an admiring public, demand a suspension of judgment; and the extravagance of his pretensions should for the present be credited to the strength of his enthusiasm.

It is through the past labors of an author that we must judge of his qualifications for future work, and the completeness of his preparation. Mr. Spencer's writings evince an extensive knowledge of facts political and scientific, but extensive rather than profound, and mainly at second hand. It is not, of course, to be expected that a philosopher will be an original investigator in all the departments of knowledge with which he is obliged to have dealings. He must take much at second hand. But original investigations in some department of empirical science are a discipline which best tests and develops even a philosopher's powers. He has in this at least an experience of what is requisite to an adequate comprehension of facts. He learns how to make knowledge profitable to the ascertainment of new truths,—an art in which the modern natural philosopher excels. By new truths must be understood such as are not implied in what we already know, or educible from what is patent to common observation. However skillfully the philosopher may apply his analytical processes to the abstraction of the truths involved in patent facts, the utility of his results will depend not so much on their value and extent as mere abstractions, as on their capacity to enlarge our experience by bringing to notice residual phenomena, and making us observe what we have entirely overlooked, or search out what has eluded our observation. Such is the character of the principles of modern natural philosophy, both mathematical and physical. They are rather the eyes with which nature is seen, than the elements and constituents of the objects discovered. It was in a clear apprehension of this value in the principles of mathematical and experimental science, that the excellence of Newton's genius consisted; and it is this value which the Positive Philosophy most prizes. But this is not the value which we find in Mr. Spencer's speculations.

Mr. Spencer is not a positivist, though that was not a very culpable mistake which confounded his speculations with the writings of this school. For however much he differs from the positivists in his methods and opinions, he is actuated by the same confidence in the capacities of a scientific method, and by the same disrespect for the older philosophies. Mr. Spencer applies a method for the ascertainment of ultimate truths, which a positivist would regard as correct only on the supposition that the materials of truth have all been collected, and that the research of science is no longer for the enlargement of our experience or for the informing of the mind. Until these conditions be realized, the positivist regards such attempts as Mr. Spencer's as not only faulty, but positively pernicious and misleading. Nothing justifies the development of abstract principles in science but their utility in enlarging our concrete knowledge of nature. The ideas on which mathematical Mechanics and the Calculus are founded, the morphological ideas of Natural History, and the theories of Chemistry are such working ideas,—finders, not merely summaries of truth.

But before examining more in detail Mr. Spencer's method of philosophizing, it will be useful to consider his career and character as a thinker and writer. Born in Derby in 1820, he was educated by his father, who was a school-teacher in that town, and by his uncle, a clergyman of the Established Church. At the age of seventeen he entered on the profession of civil engineering, which he followed for eight years. He then abandoned this pursuit for a literary career. He had already published in a scientific journal several papers on professional subjects, and at the age of twenty-two gave an earnest of his tastes for political speculation in a newspaper article on "The Proper Sphere of Government." He afterwards became a writer in the Economist, and in 1851 published his "Social Statics, or the Conditions essential to Human Happiness specified, and the First of them developed." By this work he became first generally known to the reading public in America. This work exhibits the traits which characterize all Mr. Spencer's subsequent writings. A constant and close student of facts both political and scientific, with the practical bent of the English radical and idealist, he is none the less strongly attracted to the abstractions of speculative thought. He aims at the same time at system and at effect. No distract idealist, though always actuated by that uncontent which moves revolutions and reforms, he uses abstractions and abstract modes of thought for moral ends. His allegiance to his speculative and his practical aims seems sometimes divided, and then he shows a tendency to follow out the consequences of theory, and to trust the welfare of mankind to its omnipotent care. He has great faith in the self-sufficingness of things. The very elements have in them the seeds of moral perfectibility. But he would leave out of the category of natural agencies in politics the paternal care of the rulers of mankind. He regards with lofty scorn that presumption in the governing classes which pretends to comprehend and help forward the inherent progressiveness of the world. Moral idealism colors all Mr. Spencer's views, both in science and politics. This gains him a popular hearing, especially with the youth of democratic America. But American democracy itself sympathizes with English radicalism only as the rich and benevolent sympathize with the poor. We wish them the good of universal suffrage. We are studying how to remedy the evils of it. To us this boon is a present fate, mixed of good and evil,—a thing neither to seek nor to avoid, but of which we must make the best. We suffer our legislators to exercise that absolute tyranny which Mr. Spencer proves to be an absolute immorality,—a compulsory universal common-school education,—without a murmur. We have not even suspected its immorality. Some of us regard it as a little overdone; but few or none have found that the system is radically faulty, though it be at variance with Mr. Spencer's moral premises. But we must defer the consideration of the arguments of this work, for we are at present only concerned with the characteristics of the writer.

The strong tendency to speculative and abstract modes of thought which his first work evinces found a more distinct utterance in the author's "Principles of Psychology," published four years later, in 1855. The choice of this subject seems to have been determined by the author's genius for the kind of thinking to which this subject is adapted, rather than by any special training in its literature. Indeed, this work, like the "Social Statics," is characterized by great originality. Constrained by his entire sympathy with modern movements in thought and scientific culture, he is perforce a scientific empiricist, though his peculiar genius would have found a more congenial employment in scholastic philosophy. Mr. Spencer believes in developments. All his writings are developments, and most of them are about developments. He delights in "evolutions from the homogeneous to the heterogeneous,"—in "changes from an indefinite incoherent homogeneity to a definite coherent heterogeneity, through continuous differentiations and integrations." He not only discovers them in all the objects of scientific research, but he rings these changes in all his discourses on them. Analysis is his *forte*, and developments are foibles. But he had not yet in his "Principles of Psychology" fully developed these foibles. He finds, however, in the problems of Psychology scope for his analytical powers. Like all writers who do not speak from the urgency of conviction or dissent, he is an eclectic. He aims to combine in his Psychology what is true in empiricism with what is true in metaphysics; and he had special reasons for this course. Mr. Spencer is here no longer a champion. His moral convictions find their utterance in his political and social essays. In Philosophy he is charmed with ideas, and with his power to unravel them. He is actuated by a simple love of truth, and he is therefore an eclectic. He has no real respect for ideas or for the religious grounds of metaphysics. As between pure empiricism and religious metaphysics his choice would be unhesitating. He would choose empiricism. But ideas are fine things when one has more power to unfold than to find them; and they are still found, as heretofore, by the insights of scientific sagacity rather than by any method. Pure empiricism, however, or Positivism, refuses to Psychology any place in the hierarchy of the sciences. How then can Mr. Spencer get the ideas on which to exercise his powers? There is only one course; he must postulate them. Ideas are all derived from experience, it is true; but we must not seek in actual particular experiences for their validity. These may be, and probably are, beyond the reach of resuscitation. What then is the test of truth or of reality in the grounds of any idea? "The inconceivableness of its negation," says Mr. Spencer; and so he adopted a principle from metaphysics, but with a limitation. This inconceivableness results from the discipline of experience. It does not depend on any plastic power of the mind as an original nature, determining the possibilities of experience and thought, but it is determined in the mind by invariable experiences. Those orders and relationships of events in nature which are present to the mind from its first determinations to thought, those which are never contradicted in experience, determine also the possibilities of thought; and in turn the possibilities of thought are tests of invariable experiences, though the particular experiences are lost in oblivion. In other words, the mind has but one faculty peculiarly its own, and that is memory. The mind is pure memory, but this has various forms. The primordial memory, the intellect, that which is as it were the framework of all the others,—the containing memory,—consists of certain beliefs, the negations of which cannot be conceived, but the particular grounds of which are forgotten. This memory extends back of the individual life, is derived from the experience of the race, and constitutes the innate tendencies and mental powers with which the individual life begins. This sounds like Plato's doctrine, that learning is a kind of reminiscence; but it is in fact pure empiricism. Mind is but a reflex of organism. But the organism has a memory,—a memory of the results of all invariable experiences in the continuous evolutions of the race. No empiricist can find any radical fault with this account of innate ideas.

But Mr. Spencer evolves it in a somewhat different manner. He is seeking for a basis of psychology which shall be consistent with the truth of empiricism, and at the same time with the possibility of psychology as a distinct science. Some first truth or truths peculiarly psychological are wanted, for Mr. Spencer proposes to try his speculative powers in eliciting what has eluded the sagacity of his predecessors in psychology,—in the analysis of ideas. Now, the existence of beliefs, proved to be invariable by the inconceivableness of their negations, is a fundamental fact of consciousness,—the most fundamental fact. Beliefs of all sorts are the constituent elements of consciousness. Every act of the mind involves a judgment, that is, a belief; and the only test, indeed the only meaning, of the *truth* of a belief is its *persistency*. Hence invariableness in a belief, as proved by the inconceivableness of its negation, is the highest possible warrant of truth. Sensible experience can give no higher warrant. The mind, therefore, contains in itself the criterion of truth; and psychology, or a scientific

evolution of the data of consciousness, is a legitimate philosophy. And this is thought to be not inconsistent with the empirical explanation of the origin of invariable beliefs, namely,
the formation of the mind by invariable, often repeated, special
experiences, both in the individual and in the race. But there
is a superfluity somewhere,—too many authorities. Occam's
razor is not too old to apply to this new philosophy. The
characteristic common to particular, real experiences, and to
universal, necessary truths, so called,—namely, that they are
believed, and believed without appeal to anything else,—this
characteristic is either from the same or from different sources.
If from different sources, then empiricism is false, and Psychology is a legitimate philosophy. If from the same source,
namely, particular experiences, then these are a sufficient authority, and indeed the only *final* appeal, though invariable
beliefs, "proved to be invariable by the inconceivableness of
their negations," may be excellent approximate determinations
of what experience certifies. No empiricist will deny this excellence to natural beliefs, but this is not ascribing to them any
proper authority.

In discussing this his criterion or "universal postulate," Mr.
Spencer encounters two of the acutest of modern thinkers,
Mr. Mill and Sir William Hamilton, whose opinions he finds
opposed to his own on opposite grounds. Here is a fine
chance for eclecticism, to combine what is true in both these
philosophies; but first he must refute what is false.

Speaking of the effect of habit in determining the limits of
our conceptive faculty, Mr. Mill says: "There are remarkable
instances of this in the history of science; instances in which
the wisest men rejected as impossible, because inconceivable,
things which their posterity, by earlier practice and longer
perseverance in the attempt, found it quite easy to conceive,
and which everybody now knows to be true." While granting that this evidence is sufficient to disprove the doctrine of
the *a priori* character of our natural beliefs, our author thinks
that "it does not really warrant Mr. Mill's inference, that it
is absurd to reject a proposition as impossible on no other
grounds than its inconceivableness." Further on he says:

"If there be, as Mr. Mill holds, certain absolute uniformities in nature; if these uniformities produce, as they must, absolute uniformities in our experience; and if, as he shows, these absolute uniformities in our experience disable us from conceiving the negations of them,—then, answering to each uniformity in nature which we can cognize, there must exist in us a belief of which the negation is inconceivable, and which is absolutely true. In this wide range of cases subjective inconceivableness must correspond to objective impossibility. Further experience will produce correspondence where it may not yet exist; and we may expect the correspondence to become ultimately complete. In nearly all cases this test of inconceivableness must be valid now; and where it is not, it still expresses the net result of our experience up to the present time; which is the most that any test can do."

True,—the most that any *empirical* test can do; but is not Mr. Spencer's test, "the universal postulate," exempt from this imperfection? If not, how does it warrant rejecting as impossible an inconceivable proposition, *on no other ground* than its inconceivableness? Mr. Spencer's argument, condensed and completed, is this. If there be any such things as universal necessary truths, then invariable beliefs must result from them; but we have invariable beliefs, therefore they must be the tests of truth! If A exists, then B exists; but B exists, therefore— Mr. Spencer must find the conclusion in his own logic: neither *Modus Ponens* nor *Modus Tollens* will serve.

"But," he continues, "the inconsistency into which Mr. Mill has thus fallen is most clearly seen in the second of his two chapters on 'Demonstration and Necessary Truths.' He admits in this the validity of proof by a *reductio ad absurdum*. Now what is a *reductio ad absurdum*, unless a reduction to inconceivableness? And why, if inconceivableness be in other cases an insufficient ground for rejecting a proposition as impossible, is it a sufficient ground in this case?"

After quoting other passages from Mill, Mr. Spencer says of them:

"Here, and throughout the whole of his argument, Mr. Mill assumes that there is something more certain in a demonstration than in anything else,—some necessary truth in the steps of our reasoning which is not possessed by the axioms they start from. How can this assumption be justified? In each successive syllogism, the dependence of the conclusion upon its premises is a truth of which we have no other proof than the inconceivability of the negation. Unless our perception of logical truth is *a priori*, which Mr. Mill will not contend, it too, like our perceptions of mathematical truth, has been gained from experience," etc.

Now all this shows a grand confusion in Mr. Spencer's mind. He bases his postulate, the ultimate test of all truth, on two *hypotheses*,—the existence of universal facts or absolute uniformities in nature, and their effect in producing invariable beliefs in the mind; and because Mr. Mill allows these as *empirical* generalizations, he is regarded as inconsistent in not allowing the character of *necessity* to an imperfect conclusion from them! But Mr. Mill does not deny to natural beliefs a proximate or derivative authority. Both logical axioms and the axioms to which they are applied in reasoning may safely be taken as properly accredited from experience; but their authority is secondary, and such authority is not always to be trusted, as Mr. Mill's historical example shows. The imperfect argument, "If A, then B, but B," proves nothing absolutely, but it may determine a probability. Mr. Mill maintains that there are degrees of trustworthiness in natural beliefs, as well as in the so-called empirical beliefs, and that this trustworthiness depends absolutely, not on the strength of our beliefs, whether this be absolute or not, but on particular experiences, ultimately and absolutely.

Mr. Spencer endeavors to explain away Mill's historical example,—the fact that certain Greek philosophers could not credit the existence of antipodes,—by the consideration that the conception, which seemed impossible to these philosophers, is really a complex one, whereas the truths which are properly attested by the inconceivableness of their negations are simple "undecomposable" ones. He therefore puts a modifying clause into his canon. It is necessary that the ideas so tested be simple. The mind in the confusion of compound ideas may think that it conceives what it really does not conceive, and that it cannot conceive what it really can conceive. The certainty of the application of the test depends on the number of really independent applications which it involves, in each of which the mind is liable to a slip of the attention. Mistakes from a confusion of matters are quite independent of the essential trustworthiness of our primary sources of knowledge. Even the senses may get confused. Why not, then, our invariable ideas? Easily: for does not Mr. Spencer himself confound the *authority* of our natural beliefs with their *utility* in directing us to what our *experiences* certify ?

Mr. Spencer is mistaken in supposing that any middle ground is possible between empiricism and metaphysics, or that the characteristic ideas of these two philosophies can be reconciled by the hypothesis of organized experiences, anterior to the life of the individual mind. In these experiences, as in those of the individual life, particular facts are the real authorities, as is evinced by what Mr. Spencer cannot deny, that such facts are competent to overthrow the most settled beliefs. It avails nothing to say that such facts cannot be experienced, the mind being, *ex hypothesi,* unable to conceive them even if they exist; for this is to convict natural beliefs and the mind itself of incompetency, not to establish these beliefs as competent authorities.

In reviewing previous attempts to find an independent basis for Psychology, Mr. Spencer encounters Sir William Hamilton's philosophy of Common-Sense. After quoting Hamilton's leading maxims, that "Consciousness is to be presumed trustworthy until proved to be mendacious," and that "the mendacity of consciousness is proved, if its data immediately in themselves, or mediately in their necessary consequences, be shown to stand in mutual contradiction," he says:

" Now a sceptic might very properly argue that this test is worthless. For as the steps by which consciousness is tò be proved mendacious are themselves states of consciousness; and as they must be assumed trustworthy in the act of proving that consciousness is not so; the process results in assuming the trustworthiness of particular states of consciousness, to prove the mendacity of consciousness in general. Or to apply the test specifically:—Let it be shown that two data of consciousness stand in contradiction. Then consciousness is mendacious. But if consciousness is mendacious, then the consciousness of this consciousness is mendacious. Then consciousness is trustworthy. And so on forever."

But the condition of vacillation to which Mr. Spencer reduces the sceptic's application of Hamilton's criterion is itself the true condition of scepticism. Mr. Spencer seems to mean by scepticism a dogmatic scepticism,—if we may be allowed the expression,—or a negative dogmatism; whereas Hamilton means by scepticism a negation of all philosophical judgments, the "what do I know?" condition of a mind confused about authorities; and Mr. Spencer has really given an excellent illustration of the application of these maxims, while seeking to depreciate their value. But the condition of scepticism is best illustrated by the original of the sophism to which he reduces Hamilton's maxims. "If you say that you lie, and say so truly, then you do lie; but if you say so falsely, then you speak the truth. In either case, therefore, the same statement is both true and false." To the fearful consequences of such lying is the sceptic reduced who doubts the testimony of consciousness. Mr. Spencer gives to this sophism the more common but inferior form, of which the original is this: "All Cretans are liars. But Epimenides, who says this, is himself a Cretan. Therefore, as he is a liar, this saying is not true. But if the saying is not true, Epimenides may have spoken the truth. Then the saying is true:—and so on as before." In his singular misapprehension of the meaning of the word "scepticism" in philosophy, Mr. Spencer illustrates another trait of his writings. He means by "sceptic" one who doubts the essential doctrines of orthodox philosophy, "natural realism," "personal identity," "the possibility of a science of psychology," and the like; and as he is opposed to such sceptics, he gives the impression to the world that he is ranged on the side of orthodoxy. But it is only with the husks of orthodoxy that he feeds his flock. He does not defend its doctrines as Hamilton did in the interests of dogmatic theology and religion, but simply from the vanity of disputation.

It cannot be said of Hamilton's criterion, that it is of any greater value than Mr. Spencer's, or that it yields anything more as a principle of research, but it at least has the merits of self-consistency and distinctness.

In reviewing the objections to the test of inconceivableness, Mr. Spencer again finds himself opposed to Sir William Hamilton. The doughty knight is encased in a seemingly invulnerable logic, and impedes the progress of truth. After stating certain minor and indecisive objections to the doctrine of the "conditioned," Mr. Spencer waives them.

"Granting all this," he says, "Sir William Hamilton's argument may still be met. He says that inconceivability is no criterion of impossibility. Why? Because of two propositions, one of which must be true; it proves both impossible,—it proves that space cannot have a limit, because a limit is inconceivable, and yet that it has a limit, because unlimited space is inconceivable; it proves, therefore, that space has a limit and has no limit, which is absurd. How absurd? Absurd because 'it is impossible for the same thing to be and not to be.' But how do we *know* that it is impossible for the same thing to be and not to be? What is our criterion of *this* impossibility? Can Sir William Hamilton assign any other than this same inconceivability? If not, his argument is self-destructive; seeing that he assumes the validity of the test in proving its invalidity."

This is the same shaft *ad hominem* which Mr. Spencer leveled at Mill, and it glances for the same reason. He does not precisely apprehend the position of his antagonist. Hamilton's argument is not self-destructive, since it is only designed to prove the incompleteness of the test, which Mr. Spencer has adopted in its baldest and crudest form. What was an obvious *petitio principii* as applied to Mr. Mill, namely, ascribing to him the opinion that logical axioms rest ultimately on the test of the inconceivableness of their negations, is none the less really such as applied to Hamilton's doctrines. Hamilton can and does assign a different criterion. Mr. Mill appeals to particular experiences as the tests, in the proper sense of that word, of all axioms logical or mathematical; while Hamilton admits for them a psychological test, analogous to Mr. Spencer's, yet more complete. "A proposition which can be conceived, but of which the negation cannot be conceived, is true, and its negation is false," is the complete formula.

The conceivable and inconceivable correspond to the possible and impossible only when logically opposed to each other. If two conceivables *could* be logically opposed to each other, we should have scepticism in the philosophical sense of the word, or as Hamilton uses it. If two inconceivables are logically opposed, we have no test of true or false; yet not that vacillation of the mind, that uncertainty, which is the characteristic of scepticism. But we have the feeling that there is truth beyond the power of knowledge, or that "the domain of our knowledge is not co-extensive with the horizon of our faith;" for a principle of truth—the principle of non-contradiction—is seen to extend where sense and imagination and our powers of conception cannot follow. This decides nothing positively. It only shows that unbelief or negative dogmatism is unfounded, and it opens the way for the authority of religious feeling, in whose behalf the contests of philosophy are undertaken by all but such pretended champions as Mr. Spencer. Hamilton went to the extremest verge in the direction of empiricism which it was possible to reach, without renouncing the interests for which philosophy proper has always been cultivated. Empiricism has other interests, worthy interests, but they are not religious.

It was necessary to a philosophical defense of religious doctrines to establish logical axioms on a broader basis than experience can afford, in order to secure a ground for belief in truths which are inconceivable, or truths of which the terms cannot be united in a judgment either by proofs from what is really known or by intuition; and in order also to reason about such truths, and bring the objects of religious feeling, partially at least, within the scope of our thoughts. Such are the motives for metaphysical philosophy, and such indeed are the only grounds for metaphysics. Philosophy converts practical reasons or final causes into theoretical reasons, and postulates a faculty where there is only a feeling. But after all, that which the Best in us most prizes is not so much the service of Philosophy as that for which this service is undertaken.

Mr. Spencer pursues his discussion of this subject in the first part of his recently published work, the "First Principles of a New System of Philosophy," to the consideration of which we shall presently come. Of his further developments in Psychology we can only say that they are very wearisome. He makes little explicit use of his postulate; for this, after all, is only a license to take any ideas one chooses for the bases of science, if one only cannot conceive their negations. It is one of those unproductive principles which Positivism condemns; and he develops others equally useless, except in the mental discipline there may be in following their evolution. One such application of his method is in search of a definition of Life, which after a development in as many pages results in these words: "Life is defined as—The definite combination of heterogeneous changes, both simultaneous and successive, in correspondence with external co-existences and sequences." These words are sufficiently abstract to be of some scientific service, but they only make Life the more perplexing, which had mysteries enough before. But we ought not to prejudge. Perhaps Mr. Spencer will be able, when he comes to treat of Morality in his new philosophy, to apply this definition in elucidating the principles of correct living.

But to return to the argument of his "Social Statics." This is a thorough-going application of one of the conditions of human happiness to all the relations of human life,—namely, the Law of Liberty, or the "Let alone Principle." To warrant the exclusive application of this principle to the deduction of social laws and the limits of state powers, he postulates it as a part or one side of a perfect law, of which we have knowledge through a moral sense. This sense has not an *a priori* character, as the metaphysicians maintain, but is derived from the observation, by the human race as a whole, of the conditions essential to human happiness on the whole, and is developed in our nature with the evolution of civilization, as the instinct which cares for the interests of society, just as the bodily appetites are produced to care for the interests of the individual organism. This doctrine is perfectly analogous to that which he develops more explicitly in the "Principles of Psychology" concerning the origin and character of natural beliefs. He makes the same mistake in basing a criterion on an hypothesis, and he is inconsistent in the same way in ascribing to his "moral sense" an original authority. With the exception of these errors, there is nothing in his doctrine of moral sense with which the utilitarian can find fault. But he develops his ideas in this his earlier work so inexplicitly, that not only Mr. Mill,* but many others, have mistaken him for an opponent of utilitarianism. By ascribing an absolute authority to intellectual and moral ideas, when on his principles he ought only to have ascribed to them a relative and derivative one, he was led into mistakes which have given rise to misinterpretations of his

---

* See Essay on Utilitarianism.

doctrines,—misinterpretations of which he cannot justly complain. But he has also gained a reputation for orthodoxy, which he does not deserve.

Mr. Spencer succeeds better in his shorter essays, many of which for ingenuity, originality, and scientific interest have been rarely surpassed. But judging only by his writing and the general character of his thinking, we should not ascribe to him that precision in the apprehension of scientific facts which comes chiefly from a successful cultivation of experimental and mathematical research in natural history and natural philosophy. To learn only the results of such researches and the general character of their processes is not enough. One must also be qualified to pursue them. The fact that Mr. Spencer was at one time a civil engineer seems to militate against this judgment of his qualifications. But though a marked success and a reputation acquired in this pursuit would be of great weight in determining our judgment, yet, in the absence of any evidence of this kind, we adhere to the opinion we have formed from his writings. We will say nothing of the impossibility of any one man's acquiring adequately all the knowledge requisite for the successful accomplishment of such an undertaking as Mr. Spencer has proposed for himself.

But a part of this work has become an accomplished fact. The "First Principles" of the new system of philosophy has appeared, and a serial publication of parts of another work on the "Principles of Biology" is now in progress. Mr. Spencer modestly omits from his gigantic scheme any special consideration of physics or the principles of inorganic nature ; although his training in mathematics and engineering would seem at first sight to be a preparation best suited to this subject. Perhaps he regards this science as standing in little need of his developments, and besides he has already published some of his views on this subject in his essay on the Nebular Hypothesis, and his "First Principles" involve generalizations from physical theories.

To the positivists the sciences of general physics, that is Astronomy, Mechanical and Chemical Physics, and Chemistry, afford the patterns for all the sciences, and some, like Physiology, are beginning to profit by such examples. But Mr. Spencer does not find in general physics free play for his ideas. It is only in what constitutes the problems and obscurities of these sciences that he finds free exemplifications of his principles. In the nebular hypothesis and in the obscure relations of physical forces to organic life, and in the hypothesis of the development of organic life through successive geological eras, he is at home. He is conscious of the temptation there is to impose teleological interpretations upon the obscurities of science; and he therefore aims to free his speculations as much as possible from these biases, but with as little success as he had in his Psychology in correcting the errors of metaphysics by the light of empirical science.

The idea which has exercised the profoundest influence on the course of Mr. Spencer's thought, as well as on all thought in modern times, and one which appears more or less distinctly in nearly all of Mr. Spencer's writings, is the idea which he elaborates in his "First Principles" as the "Law of Evolution." But what is the origin and value of this idea? Ostensibly it was derived from the investigations of the physiologists in embryology, from Harvey down to the present time. The formula of Von Baer was the first adequate statement of it. This formula Mr. Spencer has elaborated and completed, so as to apply, he thinks, not only to the phenomena of embryology, but to the phenomena of nature generally, and especially, as it appears, to those which we know least about, and to those which we only guess at.

But while this is the ostensible origin and scientific value of this idea, its real origin is a very curious and instructive fact in human nature. Progress is a grand idea,—Universal Progress is a still grander idea. It strikes the key-note of modern civilization. Moral idealism is the religion of our times. What the ideas God, the One and the All, the Infinite First Cause, were to an earlier civilization, such are Progress and Universal Progress to the modern world,—a reflex of its moral ideas and feelings, and not a tradition. Men ever worship the Best, and the consciousness that the Best is attainable is the highest moral

consciousness, the most inspiring of truths. And when indications of that attainment are visible not merely to the eye
of faith, but in sensible progress, scientifically measurable, civilization is inspired with a new devotion. Faith that moral perfectibility is possible, not in remote times and places, not in the
millennium, not in heaven, but in the furtherance of a present
progress, is a faith which to possess in modern times does not
make a man suspected of folly or fanaticism. He may forget
the past, cease to be religious in the conventional sense of the
word, but he is the modern prophet.

When Plato forsook the scientific studies of his youth, and
found the truest interpretations of nature by asking his own
mind what was the best, according to which, he felt sure, the
order and framework of nature must be determined, he did but
illustrate the influence which strongly impressed moral ideas
have on speculative thought at all times; but he did it consciously and avowedly. Modern thinkers may be less conscious
of this influence, may endeavor to suppress what consciousness
they have of it, warned by the history of philosophy that teleological speculations are exploded follies; nevertheless, the influence surrounds and penetrates them like an atmosphere, unless they be moral phlegmatics and mere lookers-on.

It was Mr. Spencer's aim to free the law of evolution from
all teleological implications, and to add such elements and limitations to its definition as should make it universally applicable to the movement of nature. Having done this, as he thinks,
he arrives at the following definition: "Evolution is a change
from an indefinite incoherent homogeneity to a definite coherent
heterogeneity through continuous differentiations and integrations." But teleology is a subtile poison, and lurks where least
suspected. The facts of the sciences which Dr. Whewell calls
palætiological, like the various branches of geology, and every
actual concrete series of events which together form an object
of interest to us, are apt, unless we are fully acquainted with
the actual details through observation or by actual particular
deductions from well-known particular facts and general laws,
to fall into a dramatic procession in our imaginations. The
mythic instinct slips into the place of the chronicles at every

opportunity. All history is written on dramatic principles. All cosmological speculations are strictly teleological. We never can comprehend the whole of a concrete series of events. What arrests our attention in it is what constitutes the parts of an *order* either real or imaginary, and all merely imaginary orders are dramatic, or are determined by interests which are spontaneous in human life. Our speculations about what we have not really observed, to which we supply the order and most of the facts, are necessarily determined by some principle of order in our minds. Now the most general principle which we can have is this : that the concrete series shall be an intelligible series in its entirety ; thus alone can it interest and attract our thoughts and arouse a rational curiosity.

But to suppose that such series exist anywhere but where observation and legitimate particular inferences from observation warrant the supposition, is to commit the same mistake which has given rise to teleological theories of nature. The "law of causation," the postulate of positive science, does not go to this extent. It does not suppose that there are throughout nature unbroken series in causation, forming in their entirety intelligible wholes, determinable in their beginnings, their progressions, and their ends, with a birth, a growth, a maturation, and a decay. It only presumes that the perhaps unintelligible wholes, both in the sequences and the co-existences of natural phenomena, are composed of intelligible elements ; that chaos does not subsist at the heart of things ; that the order in nature which is discernible vaguely even to the unobservant implies at least a precise *elementary* order, or fixed relations of antecedents and consequents in its ultimate parts and constituents ; that the apparently irregular heterogeneous masses, the concrete series of events, are crystalline in their substance.

To discover these elementary fixed relations of antecedents and consequents, is the work of scientific induction ; and the only postulate of science is, that these relations are everywhere to be found. To account, as far as possible, for any concrete order, intelligible as a whole, or regular, like that of life, is the work of scientific explanation, by deductions from the elementary fixed relations which induction may have discovered. But to explain any such order by simply defining it externally in vague, abstract terms, and to postulate such orders as the components of nature and parts of one complete and intelligible order, is to take a step in advance of legitimate speculation, and a step backward in scientific method,—is to commit the mistake of the ancient philosophies of nature.

But Mr. Spencer thinks he has established his "Law of Evolution" by induction. The examples from which he has analyzed his law, the examples of progress in the development of the several elements of civilization, such as languages, laws, fashions, and ideas,—the hypothetical examples of the Nebular Hypothesis and the Development Hypothesis, and the example of embryological development (the only one our conceptions of which are not liable to be tainted by teleological biases),— are examples which, according to Mr. Spencer's philosophy, afford both the definition and its justification. In other words, his definitions are only carefully elaborated general descriptions in abstract terms; or statements of facts which are observed in numerous instances or classes of instances, in terms detached from all objects, in abstract terms, of which the intension is fully known, but of which the extension is unknown except through the descriptions they embody. This, though a useful, is a precarious kind of induction, and is apt to lead to premature and false generalizations, or extensions of descriptions to what is hypothetical or unknown. Such inductions are liable to be mistaken for another sort, and to be regarded as not merely general, but universal descriptions, and as applicable to what they do not really apply to. This liability is strong just in proportion as prominence is given to such definitions in a philosophical system. No convert to Mr. Spencer's philosophy doubts the substantial correctness of the Nebular and Development Hypotheses, though these are only hypothetical examples of Mr. Spencer's law.

The other sort of inductions to which we have referred are peculiar to the exact inductive sciences. Facts which are not merely general, but, from their elementary character and their immediate relations to the orderliness of nature, are presumed to be universal facts, are the sort which the positive philosophy most prizes, and of which the law of gravitation is the typical example. The honor must be conceded to Mr. Spencer of having elaborated a precise and very abstract description of certain phenomena, the number, the other characters, and the extent of which are, however, unknown, but are all the more imposing from this circumstance.

The law of gravity was a key which deciphered a vast body of otherwise obscure phenomena, and (what is more to the purpose) was successfully applied to the solution of all the problems these phenomena presented. It is common to ascribe to Newton the merit of having discovered the law of gravity, in the same sense in which Mr. Spencer may be said to have discovered his law. The justness of this praise may well be doubted; for others had speculated and defined the law of gravity before Newton. What he really discovered was the *universality* of this law, or so nearly discovered it that the astronomers who completed the investigation did not hesitate to concede to him the full honor. He established for it such a degree of probability that his successors pursued the verification with unhesitating confidence, and still pursue it in the fullness of faith.

Mr. Spencer's law is founded on examples, of which only one class, the facts of embryology, are properly scientific. The others are still debated as to their real characters. Theories of society and of the character and origin of social progress, theories on the origins and the changes of organic forms, and theories on the origins and the causes of cosmical bodies and their arrangements, are all liable to the taint of teleological and cosmological conceptions,—to spring from the order which the mind imposes upon what it imperfectly observes, rather than from that which the objects, were they better known, would supply to the mind.

To us Mr. Spencer's speculation seems but the abstract statement of the cosmological conceptions, and that kind of orderliness which the human mind spontaneously supplies in the absence of facts sufficiently numerous and precise to justify sound scientific conclusions. Progress and development, when they mean more than a continuous proceeding, have a meaning suspiciously like what the moral and mythic instincts are inclined to,—something having a beginning, a middle, and an end,—an epic poem, a dramatic representation, a story, a cosmogony. It is not sufficient for the purposes of science that the idea of progress be freed from any reference to human happiness as an end. Teleology does not consist entirely of speculations having happy *dénouements*, save that the perfection or the end to which the progress tends is a happiness to the intellect that contemplates it in its evolution and beauty of orderliness. Plato's astronomical speculations were teleological in this artistic sense.

It is not sufficient for the purposes of science, that the idea of progress be thus purified; and it would be better if science itself were purified of this idea, at least until proof of its extent and reality be borne in upon the mind by the irresistible force of a truly scientific induction. Aristotle exhibited the characteristics of scientific genius in no way more distinctly than in the rejection of this idea, and of all cosmological speculations.

But there is a truth implied in this idea, and an important one,—the truth, namely, that the proper objects of scientific research are all of them processes and the results of processes; not the immutable natures which Plato sought for above a world of confusion and unreality, in the world of his own intelligence, but the immutable elements in the orders of all changes, the permanent relations of co-existences and sequences, which are hidden in the confusions of complex phenomena. Thought itself is a process and the mind a complex series of processes, the immutable elements of which must be discovered, not merely by introspection or by self-consciousness, but by the aid of physiological researches and by indirect observation. Everything out of the mind is a product, the result of some process. Nothing is exempt from change. Worlds are formed and dissipated. Races of organic beings grow up like their constituent individual members, and disappear like these. Nothing shows a trace of an original, immutable nature, except the unchangeable laws of change. These point to no beginning and to no end in time, nor to any bounds in space. All indications to the contrary in the results of physical research are clearly traceable to imperfections in our present knowledge of all the laws of change, and to that disposition to cosmological speculations which still prevails even in science.

We propound these doctrines not as established ones, but as having a warrant from the general results of physical research similar to that which the postulate of science, the law of causation, has in the vaguely discerned order in nature, which forces itself on the attention even of the unobservant. But as a mind unfamiliar with science is easily persuaded that there are phenomena in nature to which the law of causation does not apply, phenomena intrinsically arbitrary and capricious, so even to those most familiar with our present knowledge of physical laws, but who have not attended to the implication of their general characters and relations, the supposition is not incredible that there is a tendency in the forces of nature to a permanent or persistently progressive change in the theatre of their operations, and to an ultimate cessation of all the particular conditions on which their manifestations depend. To show why this is incredible to us would carry us beyond the proper limits of our subject, were it not that our author has speculated in the same direction.

Having developed what he thinks to be the true scientific idea of progress in his "Law of Evolution," Mr. Spencer next considers its relations to ultimate scientific ideas, the ideas of space, time, matter, and force. As evolution is change, and as change, scientifically comprehended, is comprehended in terms of matter, motion, and force, and the conditions necessary to these, or time and space, it is necessary that evolution be further defined in its relations to these ideas. These are only formulating terms, entirely abstract. They imply no ontological theory about the nature of existence of mind or matter; and when Mr. Spencer proposes to formulate the phenomena of mind as well as those of matter in terms of matter, motion, and force, it is because these ideas are the only precise ones in which the phenomena of change can be defined.

Mr. Spencer is not a materialist. Materialism and spiritualism, or psychological idealism, are as dogmatic theories equally self-contradictory and absurd. Mr. Spencer is neither a materialist nor an idealist; neither theist, atheist, nor pantheist. All these doctrines are, he thinks, without sense or reason; and the philosophers who invented them, and the disciples who received and thought they understood them, were deceived. But we are inclined to the opinion that believers, though they may be deceived about their ability to comprehend these theories (for it is easy to mistake meanings), are not deceived about the motives or the spirit which prompts these speculations, and which in fact determines for each his election of what doctrine best suits his character. For within the pale of philosophy, character determines belief, and ideas stand for feelings. We receive the truths of science on compulsion. Nothing but ignorance is able to resist them. In philosophy we are free from every bias, except that of our own characters; and it therefore seems to us becoming in a philosopher, who is solicitous about the moral reputation of his doctrines, and who would avoid classification under disreputable categories, that he teach nothing which he does not know, lest the direction of his inquiries be mistaken for that of his dispositions. The vulgar who use the obnoxious terms, materialism, atheism, pantheism, do not pretend to define them; but they somehow have a very definite idea, or at least a strong feeling, about the dangerous character of such speculations, which appear none the less reprehensible because inconceivable.

But we must defer the considerations of the moral character of Mr. Spencer's speculations, until we have further examined their scientific grounds.

Terms which the real physicist knows how to use as the terms of mathematical formulas, and which were never even suspected of any heterodox tendencies, terms which have been of inestimable service both in formulating and finding out the secrets of nature, are appropriated by Mr. Spencer to the further elaboration of his vague definitions, and to the abstract description of as much in real nature as they may happen to apply to. As if an inventory of the tools of any craft were a proper account of its handiwork! Out of mathematical formulas these terms lose their definiteness and their utility.

They become corrupting and misleading ideas. They are none the less abstract, but they are less clear. They again clothe themselves in circumstance, though vaguely. They appeal to that indefinite consciousness which, as Mr. Spencer says, cannot be formulated, but in which he thinks we have an apprehension of cause and causal agencies.

"Though along with the extension of generalizations, and concomitant integrations of conceived causal agencies," says Mr. Spencer, "the conceptions of causal agencies grow more indefinite; and though as they gradually coalesce into a universal causal agency they cease to be representable in thought, and are no longer supposed to be comprehensible, yet the consciousness of *cause* remains as dominant to the last as it was at first, and can never be got rid of. The consciousness of cause can be abolished only by abolishing consciousness itself."

This is quoted by himself from his "First Principles," as one of his "reasons for dissenting from the philosophy of M. Comte." Though he seems solicitous to avoid all ontological implications in his use of scientific terms, yet we cannot avoid the impression of a vague metaphysical signification in his speculations, as if he were presenting all the parts of a system of materialism except the affirmative and negative copulas. These are withheld, because we cannot be supposed to believe anything inconceivable, as all ontological dogmas are. He seems to lead us on to the point of requiring our assent to a materialistic doctrine, and then lets us off on account of the infirmities of our minds; presenting materialism to our contemplation rather than to our understandings.

Mr. Spencer regards the ultimate ideas of science as unknowable; and in a sense the meanings of the abstractest terms are unknowable, that is, are not referable to any notions more abstract, nor susceptible of sensuous apprehension or representation as such. But the way to know them is to use them in mathematical formulas to express precisely what we do know. It is true that this cannot yet be done, except in the physical sciences proper, and not always with distinctness in these. It is only in astronomy and mechanical physics that these terms are used with mathematical precision. They change their meanings, or at least lose their definiteness, when we come to chemistry and physiology.

"The indestructibility of matter," "the continuity of motion," "the conservation of force," and "the correlation and equivalence of forces," are ideas which mathematical and physical science has rendered familiar. Besides these, Mr. Spencer has analyzed others, descriptive of the general external characteristics of motion; and he continues with a development of what the Law of Evolution implies. To all the ideas which he adopts from science he adds a new sense, or rather a vagueness, so as to make them descriptive of as much as possible. One of these ideas loses in the process so many of its original features, as well as its name, that we should not have recognized it as the same, but for Mr. Spencer's justification of what he regards as a change of nomenclature. He prefers "persistence of force" to "conservation of force," because the latter "implies a conservator and an act of conserving," and because "it does not imply the existence of the force before that particular manifestation of it with which we commence." Science, we are inclined to believe, will not adopt this emendation, because the conservation it refers to is that whereby the special conditions of the production of any mechanical effect in nature are themselves replaced by the changes through which this effect is manifested; so that if this effect ceases to appear as a motion, it nevertheless exists in the altered antecedents of motions, which may subsequently be developed in the course of natural changes. It is this conservation of the conditions of motion by the operations of nature through the strictest observation of certain mathematical laws, that science wishes to express. The objection (if there be any) to this phrase is in the word "force." This word is used in mathematical mechanics in three different senses, but fortunately they are distinct. They are not here fused together, as they are by Mr. Spencer, into one vague expression of what nobody in fact knows anything about. There is no danger of ambiguities arising from this source in mathematics. The ideas expressed by this word are perfectly distinct and definable. The liability to ambiguity is only when we pass from mathematical formulas to sciences, in which the word has more or less of vagueness and an ontological reference. This liability is somewhat diminished, at least so far as distinct mathematical comprehension is concerned, by the use of the phrases, "conservation of mechanical effect" or "the law of power," which are now employed to express the mathematical theorem which has as one of its corollaries the doctrine that "perpetual motion" is impossible in the sense in which practical mechanics use the words. This theorem is deduced from the fundamental laws of motion, or those transcendental ideas and definitions which have received their proof or justification in their ability to clear up the confusions with which the movements of nature fall upon the senses and present themselves to the undisciplined understanding.

The phrase "conservation of force" was adopted from mathematical mechanics into chemical physics, with reference to the question of the possibility of "perpetual motion" by means of those natural forces with which chemistry deals. The impossibility of "perpetual motion," or the fact that "in the series of natural processes there is no circuit to be found by which mechanical force can be gained without a corresponding consumption," had been demonstrated only with reference to the so-called "fixed forces" of nature, or those which depend solely on the relative distances of bodies from each other. Chemical forces are not mathematically comprehended, and are therefore utterly unknown, save in their effects, and their laws are unknown, save in the observed invariable orders of these effects. These forces are merely hypotheses, and hypotheses which include little or nothing that is definite or profitable to research. But mechanical forces suggested to physicists a problem perfectly clear and definite. "Are the laws of chemical forces also inconsistent with 'perpetual motion'?" "Are light, heat, electricity, magnetism, and the force of chemical transformations, correlated with each other, and with mechanical motions and forces, as these are among themselves?" Here is something tangible; and the direction which these questions have given to physical researches in recent times mark out a distinct epoch in scientific progress. Here the answer could not be found *a priori*, as a consequent of any known or presumed universal laws of nature. Experiment must establish these presumptions; and it does so with such an overwhelming amount of evidence, that they are made the grounds of prediction, as the law of gravity was in the discovery of the planet Uranus. Physicists have anticipated, on the ground of the impossibility of perpetual motion, such an apparently remote fact as this, "that the freezing temperature in water depends on the pressure to which the water is subjected." Experiment confirms this anticipation.

The processes of such researches are long and intricate, but they are perfectly precise and definite; and it is thus that the law of the "Conservation of Force" is made of value, and not by such use as Mr. Spencer is able to make of it, if indeed his "Persistence of Force" can be regarded as having any meaning in common with it. His principle seems to us to bear a much closer resemblance to the old metaphysical "Principle of Causality," or the impossibility of any change in the quantity of existence (whatever this may mean); and it also seems to us to be as profitless.

Having developed his Law of Evolution to maturity, he arrives at "Equilibration." All evolutions must have an end, and this end is "Equilibration." Then there is no longer any tendency to "a definite, coherent heterogeneity, through continuous differentiations and integrations." Life is balanced. The worlds are completed.

Throughout this speculation the mechanical arguments of the Nebular Hypothesis have been the guides to Mr. Spencer's abstractions, while the doctrines of embryology have furnished the terminology. Recent developments of this hypothesis in connection with the theory of the correlations of mechanical forces and heat, have afforded him a splendid opportunity to carry out and illustrate his theories, and this opportunity Mr. Spencer has not neglected. Fully convinced of the truth of the Nebular Hypothesis, as well as of the importance of his own Law of Evolution, he reasons with the earnestness of conviction and with the blindness of zeal; and he brings to bear upon his theories the intense interest which the recent developments of physics are calculated to awaken concerning certain problems in astronomy. The source of the sun's heat, the origins of the planets and their motions in the solar system, the past and future histories of the earth and of the universe,— all these topics have an interest outside of science. They appeal to the story-loving, mythic instinct which willingly helps Science over her difficulties and uncertainties. It is desirable on this account to distinguish as far as possible between what is demonstrative or scientifically probable, and what is imaginary or poetically probable, in theories on these subjects. To do this adequately is the work of time, patience, and science, following the methods of experimental philosophy rather than those of Mr. Spencer. We can now present only the elements of these problems, with the impressions which come from an *a priori* distrust of cosmological speculations.

The discovery of the constant relation of mechanical effect and heat, and the determination of the measures by which this relation can be mathematically expressed in an equation, gave at once, by a simple computation with well-known astronomical data, results of the most surprising and interesting character. The mere motions of bodies, such as they have in the spaces of the solar system, and such as the sun is able to produce in bodies falling to it and in the masses of which it is composed through their mutual attractions, were found to represent vastly greater quantities of heat than could be produced by any known chemical agency, like combustion, with the same quantity of matter of whatever kind. Here then was the long sought for origin of the sun's heat. If the motions continually produced and arrested in the contractions of the sun's mass, incident to its cooling, should only amount to what would diminish the sun's diameter by one part in twenty millions in a year, it would be sufficient to produce all the enormous amount of heat which the sun has been proved to radiate in that time. If a body falling from a height not greater than the known limits of the solar system should have the motion it would thus acquire arrested and dissipated in the form of heat in the mass of the sun, it would also produce this amount of heat, provided the mass of the body be to that of the sun only as one to thirty millions. At least one-half of the energy represented by this heat would be acquired in that part of the fall between the surface of the sun and a height not greater than the distance of this surface from the centre; and if the body should have fallen from the greatest supposable height, all but about one in six thousand parts of this energy would have been acquired within the known limits of the solar system, and all but about one in two hundred parts within the limits of the earth's orbit. To explain the origin of the sun's heat, two theories have, therefore, been advanced. One in accordance with the Nebular Hypothesis explains it as arising from the falling in upon itself of the matter which composes the mass of the sun and an arrest of this motion resulting in heat and a continuous contraction of the sun's diameter, but without any change in the sun's mass. The other, on the evidence there is of the existence of innumerable small bodies moving in irregular and eccentric orbits through the spaces of the solar system, supposes the frequent fall of such bodies to the sun, and the arrest of their motions in its mass, as the origin of its heat.

What shall decide between these two theories? At first sight, the fact that the mass of the sun does not change so fast as the second theory appears to require, as is evinced by the fact that there is not a corresponding change in the attractive energy of the sun, and in the resultant periods of revolution in the earth and other planets, seems to refute this theory, and to decide in favor of the first. On the other hand, the second theory appeals to its foundation in independently probable evidence which the first does not possess, and to another theoretical consideration which explains away this difficulty, namely, the consideration that only one-half of the problem has yet been attended to; for on either hypothesis we should explain, not only how the sun's heat is produced, but also what becomes of the mechanical energy which this heat represents.

Dr. Mayer, who advances the second or the meteoric hypothesis, is content to affirm that the matter of the sun is dissipated also, as well as its heat, through the agency of its heat; so that its mass remains sensibly constant. This additional hypothesis has in itself about the same character which the Nebular Hypothesis possesses. So far, therefore, the two explanations are balanced. Both explain the origin of the sun's heat and the constancy of its mass by the union of facts independently probable with an hypothesis made for the purpose of explanation but not inconsistent with observed facts. The one theory adopts the hypothetical contraction of the sun's diameter, which observation has been unable to test, with the observed fact that the sun's mass does not increase so much as the other theory seems to require. And the other theory avoids this requirement by the hypothesis of the dissipation of the matter of the sun, united with the independently probable fact that bodies are continually falling to the sun's surface, just as they are continually falling to that of the earth, only in vastly greater numbers.

It is enough to say of the Nebular Hypothesis, that no physicist of repute regards it as having that degree of independent probability which warrants its use as a ground of probable prediction, or as affording a justification of any new or implied hypothesis. But the uncertainty as to which of the two mechanical theories of the origin of the sun's heat is true, should not for a moment be compared to the uncertainty of the Nebular Hypothesis. For it is almost certain that either one or the other is the true explanation; and, indeed, they are not essentially inconsistent with each other. Both may be true; or rather a third theory, combining both, may have a probability superior to that of either. If it be true that the sun is a body at a minimum of temperature, which on account of its enormous mass and attractive energy is able, through the contractions due to its loss of heat, to make compensation for its radiations at the expense of its dimensions, then it follows that this temperature is also a maximum one, and that an increase of the total heat of the sun by the fall of bodies to it will not increase its temperature, but rather its dimensions; its temperature being kept uniform, much as the energies and impulsions of an engine are reduced to uniformity by the inertia of its fly-wheel and that of the bodies on the resistances of which its energies are expended.

But on what are the energies of the sun expended? What becomes of its radiations? Mr. Spencer speaks in his vague way and in his dialect of the mechanical processes of the solar system as constituting " Evolution where there is a predominant integration of Matter and disintegration of Motion." He regards the laws of change as causes of "Dissolution where there is a predominant integration of Motion and disintegration of Matter." What in the language of physics does all this mean? We suppose it means that the parts of a body or a system of bodies are brought nearer each other on the whole by a loss of internal motions, whether these be in the form of heat or of massive motions; and that a system or a body is expanded on the whole by an addition to its internal motions or the relative motions of its parts. These are important mechanical theorems, but their deduction and extension by generalization necessitates the scholium, that all such "Evolutions" are attended by corresponding "Dissolutions." Motion is the motion of something, though Mr. Spencer seems to speak of it as capable of existing by itself. Motion may grow less or cease in a body or a system without being lost from it, but in this case it is represented by an expansion of the body or the system. The motions of the solar system are continually varying, becoming greater or less according as the bodies of the system are approaching or receding from each other on the whole. But motions really lost from one body or system of bodies are taken up by others, and those which are really gained are acquired from others. This is so universally true, that it includes the motions of living as well as of so-called dead matter. The motions of heat and of mechanical energy in the living body are necessarily derived from the motions and antecedent special conditions of motion which are contained in the sunbeam and in the food through which the living bodies of plants and animals are formed. But while in these bodies, during their growths and throughout their lifetimes, there is a well-marked order and harmony in such changes, the definitions of which are the proper definitions of life, yet such an order is not necessarily implied in the universal laws of change. All that is necessarily implied in these is balance and ultimate compensations,—compensations in times and spaces, which are wholly indefinite, and in concrete series of phenomena, which may or may not be simple orders or intelligible as wholes, but over which it is certain an elementary order reigns supreme.

The principle of the conservation of mechanical energy in and through the operations by which it is manifested, is the expression of this elementary order, from which, however, nothing can be deduced *a priori* in regard to any class or concrete series of phenomena in nature. The positions of the planets are deducible *a posteriori* from a sufficient number of particular facts in *this* concrete series, and by means of elementary laws. But while such successions as life exhibits involve the law of the conservation of force, so far as they involve any changes in matter, yet no characteristic features in such successions are deducible from this law, notwithstanding Mr. Spencer's asserted demonstrations of the contrary. Life must still be studied from without. Its principle is not yet discovered.

Concentration of matter with a transfer of its internal motions to other matter, and separation of matter by motions received from without, are both exemplified in growth. Mr. Spencer calls the first "Evolution," but the growth of plants is really characterized by the second; for though there is a concentration of carbon in the tissues of the plant, yet the mechanical operation by which this is effected is really a separation of the carbon from oxygen by the mechanical energy of the sunbeam, which, coming in from without, overcomes the forces of chemical aggregation in carbonic acid. There is here an aggregation of matter so far as mass or weight is concerned, but none so far as the *chemical* forces are concerned. In respect to these forces, vegetation is a dispersion of matter through an accession of forces; and combustion or consumption as food in animal bodies is a dispersion of forces with a concentration of matter, though so far as mass or weight is concerned this matter is also dispersed in the form of carbonic acid gas.

Dispersion and concentration are not to be mechanically measured by mere distances in space, even in the case of gravitation; for, as we have said, a body falling from the limits of the solar system acquires on reaching the surface of the sun all but one in six thousand parts of the energy which it could acquire in falling from the height of the remotest star. The immense distances by which the stars are separated from each other are not, therefore, the representant of a much greater energy than that which the dimensions of the solar system represent, though these become as nothing in respect to mere distance. Gravitation is a feeble force except in close proximity, and there is some degree of probability in the speculation which regards it as really a resultant of the forces to which it seems to give rise. Whether this speculation be true or not, there is no evidence that the law of gravity is exact, or more than approximately true, or that the force of gravity subsists at all between the remotest stars. That it plays but an insignificant part in determining the distributions and motions of stars and systems of stars is highly probable, since these are but imperfectly accounted for, if at all, by its law. The motions of the closely proximate members of binary stars are in fact the only ones in sidereal astronomy which have been brought under the law of gravity. Still it would be contrary to the postulate of science, or to any sound principle of philosophizing, to regard the distribution of the stars as in any absolute sense fortuitous; for in this also, as in nature generally, there is that vaguely discerned order which warrants the postulate of science, and its efforts to decipher what it has a right to presume, namely, at least an elementary order.

We hold the opinion that the mechanical theory of heat, when it comes to be applied in earnest to the problems of dynamics in sidereal astronomy, will be rewarded with triumphs not inferior to those which the law of gravitation has achieved in the solar system; and that the distribution of the stars will be accounted for, not on the hypothesis of simple attractive or repulsive forces, but by the distributions of matter and heat through the interstellar spaces, and by their actions and reactions, not as centres of simple forces, but as the receptacles of concrete masses and motions, and as the sources of diffused motions and matters, none of which can ever be lost or destroyed; that their motions will be found to result principally from those of the medium of diffused materials, from which they are aggregated precipitates, and into which they are evaporated by heat.

This is at present only an hypothesis, but it is not teleological in any sense of the term. The most obvious objection to it is the theory that there is "a universal tendency in nature to the dissipation of mechanical energy," a theory well founded, nay, demonstrated,* if we only follow this energy as far as the present limits of science extend. But to a true Aristotelian this theory, so far from suggesting a dramatic *dénouement*, such as the ultimate death of nature, only propounds new problems. What becomes of the sun's dynamic energy, and whence do the bodies come which support this wasting power?

The earth is composed of masses mechanically as well as chemically heterogeneous. The forces of chemical aggregation overcome this confusion to a limited extent, through the agency of internal heat and aqueous solution, in the formation of metallic deposits and crystalline segregations, but only to a limited extent. Long persistent mechanical actions of air and water, and vegetable aggregations, produce a similar mechanical homogeneity in geological deposits. Still the materials of the earth's surface exist as if they had been thrown together without any determinable order,—as if the earth and similar bodies had been compounded of the materials of smaller masses falling together, and gradually wrought by geological forces into the little order they present. Materials continue to arrive at the earth's surface,—in how great quantities it is at present impossible to form a trustworthy estimate. Are not all large bodies so formed? But how are the smaller bodies formed? The comets, which are more numerous "in the heavens than fish in the ocean," and the meteors, more numerous than the sands of the desert,—how are they formed? Our answer is an hypothesis. They are formed by chemical and mechanical aggregation from matters diffused throughout space by the mechanical energy of the sun; and by their fall they restore this energy. This would complete the round of nature, but the theory is not thereby demonstrated. Scientific demonstration is slow and painful, the work of time and patience. All that can now be presented are problems, but these are scientific problems. They are concerned with the details of an

---

* By Professor William Thomson.

elementary order, which science has a right to presume, and not with the abstract features of an external order, which science has no right to presume.

Following the publication of his "First Principles," there appeared a short essay by Mr. Spencer on "The Classification of the Sciences;" to which are added his "Reasons for dissenting from the Philosophy of M. Comte." We had a little hope that here at least Mr. Spencer's reputation for philosophical analysis, and for an extensive knowledge of the sciences, would stand proof, and be confirmed by a valuable result. Instead of this, we find nothing deserving attention from any one who does not find in his "First Principles" the germs of a great philosophy, except bad criticism, a perverted terminology, and fanciful discriminations.

Nearly all philosophers are agreed, we believe, in assigning logic and mathematics to a distinct division of the sciences, and these have with great propriety been denominated formal sciences, as distinguished from the real or material sciences. This propriety is quite independent of any metaphysical or critical theory which we may have about the origin or intrinsic character of mathematical and logical truth. Whether we regard the truths of formal science as really universal or not, their *presumed* universality is what determines their peculiar character and functions in science generally. But Mr. Spencer seems more solicitous to avoid an implication of a metaphysical doctrine, which these terms have, than to avail himself of their real scientific utility; and he uses, instead of them, the ambiguous and otherwise objectionable terms "abstract" and "concrete," and is obliged, consequently, to define and defend these in the sense in which he proposes to use them. Truths that have exemplification in nearly every class of facts of which we have precise knowledge, the axioms and postulates of which are implied, indeed, in all knowledge, may relatively to all other truths be properly regarded as *a priori* and formal or as the moulds into which these truths are cast. It may be, as Mr. Spencer thinks, that these truths are obtained by abstraction alone, from our experience of things; nevertheless, to make any reference in a classification to this circumstance is to sacrifice the proper objects of a classification to an extrinsic object, and is also open to the objection which seems to have prevailed with him, though he makes no explicit reference to it, against the more generally received terms "formal" and "material." "Formal" implies precisely what Mr. Spencer means by *wholly* abstract, and "material" what he means by *wholly* concrete; but he uses the unqualified terms "abstract" and "concrete" in these extreme senses. He gets confused about the distinction of "abstract" and "general," and thinks M. Comte and M. Littré have confounded them.

According to the most authentic usage, "abstract" and "general," though not the same, are not antithetical, as Mr. Spencer would have them to be. He says: "Abstractness means *detachment from* the incidents of particular cases. Generality means *manifestation in* numerous cases." *Total* detachment he means, for he uses "abstract" and "concrete" as exclusive contraries. In this use, however, Mr. Spencer is not alone; for the character of the process of abstraction, says Sir William Hamilton, has "been overlooked by philosophers, insomuch that they have opposed the terms *concrete* and *abstract* as exclusive contraries." But no philosopher before Mr. Spencer has attempted to establish any opposition between "abstract" and "general;" for though the "abstract" does not imply generality, yet generality is dependent on abstraction. "*Manifestation in* numerous cases" is the manifestation of what?—we would inquire of Mr. Spencer. Of anything but what must be obtained by abstraction? And yet he claims that his use of the words "abstract," "concrete," and "general" is the correct one. M. Littré's definition of abstractness as "subjective generality," does not appear to us a very happy one, but it is vastly superior to his critic's definitions.

In designating by the terms "abstract," "abstract-concrete," and "concrete" the divisions of the sciences which the words "formal," "mixed," and "material" have hitherto denoted, Mr. Spencer has only confused a subject already possessed of an adequately precise nomenclature. The *presumed* universality of mathematical and logical truth, the entirely empirical generality of merely descriptive sciences, and the union of these kinds of truth in general physics, are properly connoted by the terms already in use.

In Mr. Spencer's subdivisions of mathematics he has given a prominence to "Descriptive Geometry" which might be regarded as arising from the partiality of the civil engineer for a branch of his own art, were it not that he says:

"I was ignorant of the existence of this as a separate division of mathematics, until it was described to me by Mr. Hirst, whom I have also to thank for pointing out the omission of the subdivision 'Kinematics.' It was only when seeking to affiliate and define 'Descriptive Geometry' that I reached the conclusion that there is a negatively-quantitative mathematics, as well as a positively-quantitative mathematics. In explanation of the term negatively-quantitative, it will suffice to instance the proposition that certain three lines will meet in a point, as a negatively-quantitative proposition; since it asserts the absence of any quantity of space between their intersections. Similarly, the assertion that certain three points will always fall in a straight line is negatively-quantitative; since the conception of a straight line implies the negation of any lateral quantity or deviation."

The propositions selected by Mr. Spencer to illustrate what he calls "Descriptive Geometry" are by no means peculiar to or characteristic of the art to which mathematicians have given this name. In the most elaborate and extensive treatises no more is claimed for this art than that it is an account in a scientific order of certain methods of geometrical construction, useful in engineering and architecture, but inferior in scientific extension even to trigonometry, to which Mr. Spencer does not deign to descend. It is possible that Mr. Spencer has in mind certain propositions in the "Higher Geometry" concerning relations of position and direction in points and lines; but these cannot be made to stand alone or independently of dimensional properties, and if they could, they would be as appropriately named "qualitative" mathematics as "negatively-quantitative." In short, this is the most flagrant application of "the principle of contraries" in classification which has ever come to our notice. If Mr. Spencer proposes to select from mathematics all positively-quantitative problems and propositions for one branch, and all negatively-quantitative ones for the other, he must reconstruct, if he can, the whole science, and the question of terminology will then be a question between him and his brothers in his own craft.

Having treated first in order the second part of Mr. Spencer's "First Principles," which comprises his "Laws of the Knowable," we now turn to the consideration of his doctrine of "the Unknowable," and his position before the religious world.

This position has been greatly misunderstood, and Mr. Spencer himself has contributed much to the misunderstanding. He has appeared as a champion for what is sound in the older philosophy, and one of his avowed objects is to reconcile the truths of religion with those of science. He is anxious not to be thought a positivist, and he publishes as an appendix to his "First Principles" a response to his reviewer in the *Revue des Deux Mondes*, to show that he is not a positivist or a follower of M. Comte.

It requires only a little thoughtful attention to the speculations of Mr. Spencer and M. Comte to see that they are radically unlike, not only in the details of doctrine, but in their ostensible aims. The religious world, however, though perhaps a little too trusting and a little dull of thought, has very acute feelings, and a fine sagacity in apprehending the religious drift of a system of philosophy. It began to have suspicions, but it was, nevertheless, anxious to see the truths of science reconciled with those of religion, and so it has continued to listen to Mr. Spencer.

There can be no doubt of the earnestness and moral honesty of Mr. Spencer's writings. He is conscious of a generous purpose, and is actuated by the modern form of religious sentiment, —moral idealism, or a belief in the moral perfectibility of things in general. He only lacks a distinct consciousness of his exact position with reference to older forms of religious sentiment. He imagines that his philosophy can conciliate these also. This conciliation is effected, he thinks, by presenting the unknowable as a subject of contemplation,—the abstract unknowable, not an entity or a subject for propositions and beliefs. Beliefs about the unknowable are absurd, thinks Mr. Spencer. It is only in the existence of the unknowable as implied in the existence and limits of the knowable that we can believe, and this becomes more and more distinct as the knowable becomes more distinct in its conditions and limits.

"Thus the consciousness of an Inscrutable Power manifested to us through all phenomena has been growing ever clearer, and must eventually be freed from its imperfections. The certainty that on the one hand such a Power exists, while on the other hand its nature transcends intuition and is beyond imagination, is the certainty towards which intelligence has from the first been progressing. To this conclusion science inevitably arrives as it reaches its confines; while to this conclusion religion is irresistibly driven by criticism. And satisfying as it does the demands of the most rigorous logic at the same time that it gives the religious sentiment the widest possible sphere of action, it is the conclusion we are bound to accept without reserve or qualification.

"Some do indeed allege that though the Ultimate Cause of things cannot really be thought of by us as having specified attributes, it is yet incumbent upon us to assert these attributes. Though the forms of our consciousness are such that the Absolute cannot in any manner or degree be brought within them, we are nevertheless told that we must represent the Absolute to ourselves under these forms. As writes Mr. Mansel in the work from which I have already quoted largely, 'It is our duty then to think of God as personal; and it is our duty to believe that he is infinite.'

"That this is not the conclusion here adopted needs hardly be said. If there be any meaning in the foregoing arguments, duty requires us neither to affirm or deny personality. Our duty is to submit ourselves with all humility to the established limits of our intelligence, and not perversely to rebel against them. Let those who can believe that there is eternal war set between our intellectual faculties and our moral obligations. I for one admit no such radical vice in the constitution of things.

"This, which to most will seem an essentially irreligious position, is an essentially religious one,—nay, is *the* religious one to which, as already shown, all others are but approximations."

We are inclined to think, nevertheless, that the older forms of religious sentiment, instead of being satisfied with this, and accepting it in lack of a better reconciliation, will resort rather to formularies and the fine arts. Religious sentiments are essentially constructive. They must have propositions, or something to believe,—something to give entire, free, and hearty assent to. Strings of abstract incomprehensible terms, with the copulas all left out,—nothing to believe in except our own ignorance (however respectable this may be),—will never do. If thought cannot furnish the copulas, feeling can and will.

But, we must repeat that the philosophy of Sir William Hamilton went as far in the direction of empiricism as was possible without renouncing the interests to which philosophy has always been devoted.   Hamilton's doctrine aimed only at this,—to show that unbelief or negative dogmatism was unfounded, and to open the way for the authority of religious feeling.

Mr. Mansel, correctly apprehending the drift of Sir William Hamilton's doctrine, elaborated it still further, and supplied what was wanting to make it a religious philosophy, namely, the authority of religious feeling; but it was the authority of the religious feelings of his own sect, of course.   This movement, apparently in behalf of the Established Church, roused great opposition to the doctrines of Hamilton on the part of dissenting theologians.   They attacked what had been before called in question, the empirical doctrines to which, while admitting and defending them theoretically, Hamilton opposed what is peculiarly his own philosophy, as a practical defense of religion.   But any other sectarians were just as competent to supply the defects of Hamilton's philosophy as Mr. Mansel. They had only to advance the authority of *their* religious feelings into the vacant place.   Controversy would have gone on just as before.   Only the irreligious would have been excluded from the field.   But the vacant place was historically preoccupied by Mr. Mansel, and it was thought necessary by the others to carry the whole position.

Thus religious controversy blinded both the friends and the foes of religious philosophy in regard to the true scope and position of Sir William Hamilton's doctrine.   He has come to be regarded by both parties as the great modern champion of philosophical empiricism, whereas he only cited it against Cousin and the German rationalists, and proposed as his own contribution to philosophy that which is regarded by Mr. Spencer as a defect and an inconsistency in his philosophy.

"The Conditioned," says Hamilton, "is a mean between two extremes, two inconditionates, exclusive of each other, neither of which *can be conceived as possible*, but of which, on the principles of contradiction and excluded middle, one must be admitted as *necessary*.   On this opinion, therefore, reason is shown to be weak, but not deceitful.   The mind is not represented as conceiving two propositions subversive of each other as equally possible; but only as unable to understand as possible either of two extremes, one of which, however, on the ground of their mutual repugnance, it is compelled to recognize as true. We are thus taught the salutary lesson, that the capacity of thought is not to be constituted into the measure of existence; and are warned from recognizing the domain of our knowledge as necessarily co-extensive with the horizon of our faith. And by a wonderful revelation we are thus, in the very consciousness of our inability to conceive aught above the relative and finite, inspired with a belief in the existence of something unconditioned beyond the sphere of all comprehensible reality."

Of this passage, in which Sir William Hamilton first stated his own peculiar doctrine, though less clearly than in his subsequent writings, Mr. Spencer says:

"By the laws of thought, as Sir William Hamilton has interpreted them, he finds himself forced to the conclusion, that our consciousness of the absolute is a pure negation. He nevertheless finds that there does exist in consciousness an irresistible conviction of the real 'existence of something unconditioned.' And he gets over the inconsistency by speaking of this conviction as a 'wonderful revelation,' 'a belief' with which we are 'inspired'; thus apparently hinting that it is supernaturally at variance with the laws of thought. [!] Mr. Mansel is betrayed into a like inconsistency,"—

which Mr. Spencer proceeds to point out.

Strange inconsistency indeed, if it be true, between that which is mistaken by his critic as the essence of his philosophy, and that which, being the real essence, is regarded as an inconsistency. Supposing Sir William Hamilton and Mr. Mansel are really arguing in the interests of empiricism, he tries to help them out, and supply another proof of "the relativity of all knowledge;" yet he finds in some of the statements of his friends an implication of "a grave error." He thinks they deny by implication that we can "rationally affirm the positive existence of anything beyond phenomena;" whereas what they are all along trying to prove is, that we *can* rationally affirm what we cannot positively conceive or construe to thought. This includes what Mr. Spencer calls "the incomplete thoughts of an indefinite consciousness," and more. It even signifies that we can and do rationally affirm not only what is incompletely thought of, but that of which we can only think the meanings, or the relations of the terms by which it is expressed.

Mr. Spencer believes that we have an indefinite consciousness of the Absolute and of Cause, but not one which will warrant any other proposition than that which is implied in this consciousness, namely, that it is not distinct. That we can be distinctly ignorant is the highest religious truth he has to offer. In setting forth this his contribution to religious philosophy, he characterizes the argument of his predecessors thus :

"Truly to realize in thought any one of the propositions of which the argument consists, the unconditioned must be represented as positive, not negative. How then can it be a legitimate conclusion from the argument, that our consciousness of it is negative? An argument, the very construction of which assigns to a certain term a certain meaning, but which ends in showing that this term has no such meaning, is simply an elaborate suicide."

But really the argument of which Mr. Spencer has proved his total misapprehension is not an argument about meanings at all, but about the supposed objects of thought which the terms of the argument denote. To conceive the meaning of a proposition and to conceive the proposition itself, or to conceive the fact which the proposition expresses, are not the same; though in confounding them Mr. Spencer does not stand alone. The question is about the mind's ability, right, or duty to believe what, as stated in a proposition, is stated in terms which, while their meanings are clear, cannot be united in a judgment, either by proof from what is truly known, or by intuition. If two such propositions stand in mutual contradiction, says Sir William Hamilton, one of them must be true, or the laws of thought are false; and he offers the alternative of absolute or philosophical scepticism, a suspension of all judgments, or a belief in something inconceivable. He offers it of course only formally; for a decision in favor of scepticism is self-contradictory, a judgment that all judgments are false, which ends in that painful uncertainty exhibited in the sophism of the liar, to which we referred in treating of Mr. Spencer's Psychology. The choice between having judgments and having none is, of course, only a paradoxical mode of presenting the absurdity which cannot really be committed, but which is implied in certain confusions of thought. It was to remove these confusions by clear philosophical statements, and not to prove anything, that Hamilton's doctrine of the conditioned was propounded.

We have now completed our survey of the principal philosophical works of Mr. Spencer, a writer whose pretensions aim at a system of truth which shall formulate all legitimate human knowledge, but whose performance of the part he has undertaken gives little hope of success in what yet remains to do. The number of topics which we have been led to consider in this survey illustrates the versatility of our author, and the number in regard to which we have been compelled to deny his conclusions illustrates his incompetency for the further development of his encyclopedic abstractions.

LIMITS OF NATURAL SELECTION.*

Few scientific theories have met with such a cordial reception by the world of scientific investigators, or created in so short a time so complete a revolution in general philosophy, as the doctrine of the derivation of organic species by Natural Selection; perhaps in this respect no other can compare with it when we consider the incompleteness of the proofs on which it still relies, or the previous prejudice against the main thesis implied in it, the theory of the development or transmutation of species. The Newtonian theory of gravity, or Harvey's theory of the circulation of the blood, in spite of the complete and overwhelming proofs by which these were soon substantiated, were much longer in overcoming to the same degree the deeply-rooted prejudices and preconceptions opposed to them. In less than a decade the doctrine of Natural Selection had conquered the opposition of the great majority of the students of natural history, as well as of the students of general philosophy; and it seems likely that we shall witness the unparalleled spectacle of an all but universal reception by the scientific world of a revolutionary doctrine in the lifetime of its author; though by the rigorous tests of scientific induction it will yet hardly be entitled to more than the rank of a very probable hypothesis. How is this singular phenomenon to be explained? Doubtless in great part by the extraordinary skill which Mr. Darwin has brought to the proof and promulgation

* From the North American Review, October, 1870.

of his views. To this, Mr. Wallace thus testifies in the Preface to his book : *

"The present work will, I venture to think, prove that I both saw at the time the value and scope of the law which I had discovered, and have since been able to apply it to some purpose in a few original lines of investigation. But here my claims cease. I have felt all my life, and I still feel, the most sincere satisfaction that Mr. Darwin had been at work long before me, and that it was not left for me to attempt to write 'The Origin of Species.' I have long since measured my own strength, and know well that it would be quite unequal to that task. Far abler men than myself may confess that they have not that untiring patience in accumulating, and that wonderful skill in using large masses of facts of the most varied kinds,—that wide and accurate physiological knowledge,—that acuteness in devising, and skill in carrying out, experiments, and that admirable style of composition, at once clear, persuasive, and judicial,—qualities which, in their harmonious combination, mark out Mr. Darwin as the man, perhaps of all men now living, best fitted for the great work he has undertaken and accomplished."

But the skillful combination of inductive and deductive proofs with hypothesis, though a powerful engine of scientific discovery, must yet work upon the basis of a preceding and simpler induction. Pythagoras would never have demonstrated the "forty-seventh," if he had not had some ground of believing in it beforehand. The force and value of the preceding and simpler induction have been obscured in this case by subsequent investigations. And yet that more fundamental evidence accounts for the fact that two such skillful observers and reasoners as Mr. Wallace and Mr. Darwin arrived at the same convictions in regard to the derivation of species, in entire independence of each other, and were constrained to accept the much-abused and almost discarded "transmutation hypothesis." And both moreover reached, independently, the same explanation of the process of derivation. This was obviously from their similar experiences as naturalists ; from the force of the same obscure and puzzling facts which their studies of the geographical distributions of animals and plants had brought to their notice, though the Malthusian doctrine of

---

* Contributions to the Theory of Natural Selection. A Series of Essays. By Alfred Rupell Wallace, London, 1870.

population was, doubtless, the original source of their common theory. Mr. Darwin, in the Introduction to his later work on "The Variation of Animals and Plants under Domestication," attributes the beginnings of his speculations to the phenomena of the distributions of life over large continental areas, and in the islands of large archipelagoes, and especially refers to the curious phenomena of life in the Galapagos Islands in the Pacific Ocean. Mr. Wallace, in his first essay, originally published in 1855, four years earlier than "The Origin of Species," refers to the same class of facts, and the same special facts in regard to the Galapagos Islands, as facts which demand the transmutation hypothesis for their sufficient explanation.

While then much is to be credited to the sagacity and candor of these most accomplished travelers and observers in appreciating the force of obscure and previously little studied facts, yet their theoretical discussions of the hypothesis brought forward to explain them have been of still more importance in arousing an ever-increasing activity in the same field, and in creating a new and most stimulating interest in the external economy of life,—in the relations of living beings to the special conditions of their existence. And so the discussion is no longer closet work. It is no web woven from self-consuming brains, but a vast accumulation of related facts of observation, bound together by the bond of what must still be regarded as an hypothesis,—an hypothesis, however, which has no rival with any student of nature in whose mind reverence does not, in some measure, neutralize the aversion of the intellect to what is arbitrary.

In anticipating the general acceptance of the doctrine which Mr. Darwin and Mr. Wallace have done so much to illustrate, we ought to except those philosophers who, from a severe, ascetic, and self-restraining temper, or from preoccupation with other researches, are disposed to regard such speculations as beyond the proper province of scientific inquiry. But to stop short in a research of "secondary causes," so long as experience or reason can suggest any derivation of laws and relations in nature which must otherwise be accepted

as ultimate facts, is not agreeable to that Aristotelian type of
mind which scientific culture so powerfully tends to produce
Whatever the theological tendencies of such a mind, whether
ultimate facts are regarded by it as literally arbitrary, the de
crees of an absolute will, or are summarily explained by wha
Professor De Morgan calls "that exquisite atheism, 'the natur
of things,'" it still cannot look upon the intricate system of
adaptations, peculiar to the organic world (which illustrate
what Cuvier calls "the principle of *the conditions of existence*
vulgarly called the principle of *final causes*"),—it cannot look
upon this as an arbitrary system, or as composed of facts in
dependent of all ulterior facts (like the axioms of mechanics o
arithmetic or geometry), so long as any explanation, not tan
tamount to arbitrariness itself, has any probability in the order o
nature.   This scientific instinct stops far short of an irreveren
attitude of mind, though it does not permit things that clain
its reverence to impede its progress.   And so a class of facts
of which the organical sciences had previously made some us
as instruments of scientific discovery, but which was appropri
ated especially to the reasonings of Natural Theology, ha
fallen to the province of the discussions of Natural Selection
and has been wonderfully enlarged in consequence.   It canno
be denied that this change has weakened the force of the *ar
guments* of Natural Theology; but it is simply by way of sub
traction or by default, and not as offering any arguments op
posed to the main conclusions of theology.   "Natural Selec
tion is not inconsistent with Natural Theology," in the sens
of refuting the main conclusions of that science; it onl
reduces to the condition of an arbitrary assumption one im
portant point in the interpretation of special adaptations in or
ganic life, namely, the assumption that in such adaptation
foresight and special provision is shown, analogous to the de
signing, anticipatory imaginings and volitions in the menta
actions of the higher animals, and especially in the mind o
man.

Upon this point the doctrine of Natural Selection assume
only such general anticipation of the wants or advantages o

an animal or plant as is implied in the laws of inheritance. That is, an animal or plant is produced adapted to the *general* conditions of its existence, with only such anticipations of a change or of varieties in these conditions as is implied in its *general* tendency to vary from the inherited type. Particular uses have no special causal relations to the variations that occur and become of use. In other words, Natural Selection, as an hypothesis, does not assume, and, so far as it is based on observation, it affords no evidence, that any adaptation is specially anticipated in the order of nature. From this point of view, the wonderfully intricate system of special adaptations in the organic world is, at any epoch of its history, altogether retrospective. Only so far as the past affords a type of the future, both in the organism itself and in its external conditions, can the conditions of existence be said to determine the adaptations of life. As thus interpreted, the doctrine of Final Causes is deprived of the feature most obnoxious to its opponents, that abuse of the doctrine "which makes the cause to be engendered by the effect." But it is still competent to the devout mind to take a broader view of the organic world, to regard, not its single phases only, but the whole system from its first beginnings as presupposing all that it exhibits, or has exhibited, or could exhibit, of the contrivances and adaptations which may thus in one sense be said to be foreordained. In this view, however, the organical sciences lose their traditional and peculiar value to the arguments of Natural Theology, and become only a part of the universal order of nature, like the physical sciences generally, in the principles of which philosophers have professed to find no sign of a divinity. But may they not, while professing to exclude the *idea* of God from their systems, have really included him unwittingly, as immanent in the very thought that denies, in the very systems that ignore him?

So far as Natural Theology aims to prove that the principles of utility and adaptation are all-pervasive laws in the organic world, Natural Selection is not only not inconsistent, but is identical with it. But here Natural Selection pauses. It does not go on to what has been really the peculiar province of Natural

Theology, to discover, or trace the analogies of organic adaptations to proper designs, or to the anticipations of wants and advantages in the mental actions of man and the higher animals. In themselves these mental actions bear a striking resemblance to those aspects of organic life in general, which Natural Selection regards; and according to the views of the experiential psychologist, this resemblance is not a mere analogy. In themselves, and without reference to the external uses of these mental actions, they are the same generalized reproductions of a past experience as those which the organic world exhibits in its laws of inheritance, and are modified by the same tentative powers and processes of variation, but to a much greater degree. But here the resemblance ceases. The relations of such mental actions to the external life of an organism, in which they are truly prophetic and providential agencies, though founded themselves on the observation of a past order in experience, are entirely unique and unparalleled, so far as any assumption in the doctrine of Natural Selection, or any proofs which it adduces are concerned. Nevertheless a greater though vaguer analogy remains. *Some* of the wants and adaptations of men and animals are anticipated by their designing mental actions. Does not a like foreseeing power, ordaining and governing the whole of nature, anticipate and specially provide for *some* of its adaptations? This appears to be the distinctive position in which Natural Theology now stands.

We have dwelt somewhat at length on this aspect of our author's subject, with reference to its bearing on his philosophical views, set forth in his concluding essay on "The Limits of Natural Selection as applied to Man," in which his theological position appears to be that which we have just defined. We should like to quote many passages from the preceding essays, in illustration of the principle of utility and adaptation, in which Mr. Wallace appears at his best; but one example must suffice. "It is generally acknowledged that the best test of the truth and completeness of a theory is the power which it gives us of prevision"; and on this ground Mr. Wallace justly claims great weight for the following inquiry into the "use of the gaudy colors of many caterpillars," in the essay on Mimicry, etc., p. 117:

"Since this essay was first published, a very curious difficulty has been cleared up by the application of the general principle of protective coloring. Great numbers of caterpillars are so brilliantly marked and colored as to be very conspicuous even at a considerable distance, and it has been noticed that such caterpillars seldom hide themselves. Other species, however, are green or brown, closely resembling the colors of the substances on which they feed; while others again imitate sticks, and stretch themselves out motionless from a twig, so as to look like one of its branches. Now, as caterpillars form so large a part of the food of birds, it was not easy to understand why any of them should have such bright colors and markings as to make them specially visible. Mr. Darwin had put the case to me as a difficulty from another point of view, for he had arrived at the conclusion that brilliant coloration in the animal kingdom is mainly due to sexual selection, and this could not have acted in the case of sexless larvæ. Applying here the analogy of other insects, I reasoned, that since some caterpillars were evidently protected by their imitative coloring, and others by their spiny or hairy bodies, the bright colors of the rest must also be in some way useful to them. I further thought, that as some butterflies and moths were greedily eaten by birds while others were distasteful to them, and these latter were mostly of conspicuous colors, so probably these brilliantly colored caterpillars were distasteful and therefore never eaten by birds. Distastefulness alone would, however, be of little service to caterpillars, because their soft and juicy bodies are so delicate, that if seized and afterwards rejected by a bird they would almost certainly be killed. Some constant and easily perceived signal was therefore necessary to serve as a warning to birds never to touch these uneatable kinds, and a very gaudy and conspicuous coloring, with the habit of fully exposing themselves to view, becomes such a signal, being in strong contrast with the green and brown tints and retiring habits of the eatable kinds. The subject was brought by me before the Entomological Society (see Proceedings, March 4, 1867), in order that those members having opportunities for making observations might do so in the following summer," etc.

Extensive experiments with birds, insectivorous reptiles, and spiders, by two British naturalists, were published two years later, and fully confirmed Mr. Wallace's anticipations. His book is full of such curious matters.

In a controversial essay called "Creation by Law," an answer to various criticisms of the doctrine of Natural Selection, Mr. Wallace is equally happy and able; and in his essay on

"The Action of Natural Selection on Man," he shows a wonderful sagacity and skill in developing a new phase of his subject, while meeting, as in so many other cases, obstacles and objections to the theory. It appears, both by geological evidence and by deductive reasonings in this essay, that the human race is singularly exempt from variation and the action of Natural Selection, so far as its merely physical qualities are concerned. This follows from theoretical considerations, since the race has come to depend mainly on its mental qualities, and since it is on these, and not on its bodily powers, that Natural Selection must act. Hence the small amount of physical differences between the earliest men of whom the remains have been found and the men of the present day, as compared to differences in other and contemporary races of mammals. We may generalize from this and from Mr. Darwin's observation on the comparatively extreme variability of plants, that in the scale of life there is a gradual decline in physical variability, as the organism has gathered into itself resources for meeting the exigencies of changing external conditions; and that while in the mindless and motionless plant these resources are at a *minimum*, their *maximum* is reached in the mind of man, which, at length, rises to a level with the total order and powers of nature, and in its scientific comprehension of nature is a summary, an epitome of the world. But the scale of life determined by the number and variety of actual resources in an organism ought to be distinguished from the rank that depends on a high degree of specialty in particular parts and functions, since in such respects an organism tends to be highly variable.

But Mr. Wallace thinks, and argues in his concluding essay, that this marvelous being, the human mind, cannot be a product of Natural Selection; that some, at least, of the mental and moral qualities of man are beyond the jurisdiction and measure of utility; that Natural Selection has its limits, and that among the most conspicuous examples of its failure to explain the order of nature are the more prominent and characteristic distinctions of the human race. Some of these, according to Mr. Wallace, are physical; not only the physical instruments of man's mental nature, his voluminous brain, his cunning hand, the structure and power of his vocal organs, but also a characteristic which appears to have no relation to his mental nature,—his nakedness. Man is distinguished from all soft and delicate skinned terrestrial mammals in having no hairy covering to protect his body. In other mammals the hair is a protection against rain, as is proved by the manner in which it is disposed,—a kind of argument, by the way, especially prized by Cuvier, which has acquired great validity since Harvey's reasonings on the valves of the veins.* The backs of these animals are more especially protected in this way. But it is from the back more especially that the hairy covering is missed in the whole human race; and it is so effectually abolished as a character of the species, that it never occurs even by such reversions to ancestral types as are often exhibited in animal races. How could this covering have ever been

---

* It is remarkable that our author should be so willing to attribute such a slight and unimportant character as the hair of animals, and even the lay of it, to Natural Selection, and, at the same time, should regard the absence of it from the human back as beyond the resources of natural explanations. We credit him, nevertheless, with the clearest appreciation, through his studies and reflections, of the extent of the action of the law which he independently discovered; which comprises in its scope, not merely the stern necessities of mere existence, but the gentlest amenities of the most favored life. Sexual Selection, with all its obscure and subtle influences, is a type of this gentler action, which ranges all the way in its command of fitnesses from the hard necessities of utility and warfare to the apparently useless superfluities of beauty and affection. Nay, more, a defect which, without subtracting from the attractions or any other important external advantage in an animal, should simply be the source of private discomfort to it, is certain to come under the judgments of this all-searching principle.

It is a fair objection, however, sometimes made against the theory of Natural Selection, that it abounds in loopholes of ingenious escape from the puzzling problems of nature; and that, instead of giving real explanations of many phenomena, it simply refers them in general terms to obscure and little known, perhaps wholly inadequate causes, of which it holds *omne ignotum pro magnifico.* But this objection, though good, so far as it goes, against the theory, is not in favor of any rival hypothesis, least of all of that greatest of unknown causes, the supernatural, which is magnificent indeed in adequacy, if it be only real, but whose reality must rest forever on the negative evidence of the insufficiency, not only of the known, but of all possible natural explanations, and whose sufficiency even is, after all, only the counterpart or reflection of their apparent insufficiencies. Hence the objection is a fair one only against certain phases of this theory, and against the tendency to rest satisfied with its imperfect explanations, or to regard them lightly as trivial defects. But to such criticisms the progress of the theory itself, in the study of nature, is a sufficient answer in general, and is a triumphant vindication of the mode of inquiry, against which such criticisms are sometimes unjustly made.

injurious, or other than useful to men? Or, if at any time in the past history of the race it was for any unknown reason injurious, why should not the race, or at least some part of it, have recovered from the loss and acquired anew so important a protection? Mr. Wallace is not unmindful of Mr. Darwin's doctrine of Correlated Variation, and the explanation it affords of useless and even injurious characters in animals; but he limits his consideration of it to the supposition that the loss of hair by the race might have been a physiological consequence of correlation with some past unknown hurtful qualities. From such a loss, however, he argues, the race ought to have recovered. But he omits to consider the possible correlation of the absence of hair with qualities not necessarily injurious, but useful, which remain and equally distinguish the race. Many correlated variations are quite inexplicable. "Some are quite whimsical: thus cats, which are entirely white and have blue eyes, are generally deaf," and very few instances could be anticipated from known physiological laws, such as homological relations. There is, however, a case in point, cited by Mr. Darwin, the correlation of imperfect teeth with the nakedness of the hairless Turkish dog. If the intermediate varieties between men and the man-apes had been preserved, and a regular connection between the sizes of their brains, or developments of the nervous system, and the amount of hair on their backs were observed, this would be as good evidence of correlation between these two characters as that which exists in most cases of correlation. But how in the absence of any evidence to test this or any other hypothesis, can Mr. Wallace presume to say that the law of Natural Selection cannot explain such a peculiarity? It may be that no valid proof is possible of any such explanation, but how is he warranted in assuming on that account some exceptional and wholly occult cause for it? There is a kind of correlation between the presence of brains and the absence of hair which is not of so obscure a nature, and may serve to explain in part, at least, why Natural Selection has not restored the protection of a hairy coat, however it may have been lost. Mr. Wallace himself signalizes this correlation in the preceding essay. It is that through which art supplies to man in a thousand ways the deficiencies of nature, and supersedes the action of Natural Selection. Every savage protects his back by artificial coverings. Mr. Wallace cites this fact as a proof that the loss of hair is a defect which Natural Selection ought to remedy. But why should Natural Selection remedy what art has already cared for? In this essay Mr. Wallace seems to us to have laid aside his usual scientific caution and acuteness, and to have devoted his powers to the service of that superstitious reverence for human nature which, not content with prizing at their worth the actual qualities and acquisitions of humanity, desires to intrench them with a deep and metaphysical line of demarkation.

There are, doubtless, many and very important limitations to the action of Natural Selection, which the enthusiastic student of the science ought to bear in mind; but they belong to the application of the principle of utility to other cases as well as to that of the derivation of human nature. Mr. Wallace regards the vocal powers of the human larynx as beyond the generative action of Natural Selection, since the savage neither uses nor appreciates all its powers. But the same observation applies as well to birds, for certain species, as he says in his essay on "The Philosophy of Birds' Nests," "which have naturally little variety of song, are ready in confinement to learn from other species, and become much better songsters." It would not be difficult to prove that the musical capacities of the human voice involve no elementary qualities which are not involved in the cadences of speech, and in such other powers of expression as are useful at least, if not indispensable, in language. There are many consequences of the ultimate laws or uniformities of nature, through which the acquisition of one useful power will bring with it many resulting advantages, as well as limiting disadvantages, actual or possible, which the principle of utility may not have comprehended in its action. This principle necessarily presupposes a basis in an antecedent constitution of nature, in principles of fitness, and laws of cause and effect, in the origin of which it has had no agency.

The question of the origin of this constitution, if it be a proper question, belongs to metaphysical philosophy, or, at least, to its pretensions. Strictly speaking, Natural Selection is not a cause at all, but is the mode of operation of a certain quite limited class of causes.* Natural Selection never made it come to pass, as a habit of nature, that an unsupported stone should move downwards rather than upwards. It applies to no part of inorganic nature, and is very limited even in the phenomena of organic life.

In his obvious anxiety to establish for the worth of human nature the additional dignity of metaphysical isolation, Mr. Wallace maintains the extraordinary thesis that "the brain of

---

* Though very limited in extent, this class is marked out only by the single character, that the efficient causes (of whatever nature, whether the forces of simple growth and re-production, or the agency of the human will), are yet of such a nature as to act through the principles of utility and choice. It includes in its range, therefore, developments of the simplest adaptive organic characters on one hand, and the growths of language and other human customs on the other. It has been objected that Natural Selection does not apply to the origin of languages, because language is an invention, and the work of the human will; and it is clear, indeed, that Natural, as distinguished from Artificial, Selection is not properly the cause of language, or of the custom of speech. But to this it is sufficient to reply, that the contrast of Natural and Artificial Selections is not a contrast of principles, but only of illustrations, and that the common principle of "the survival of the fittest" is named by Synecdoche from the broader though more obscure illustration of it. If it can be shown that the choice of a word from among many words as the name of an object or idea, or the choice of a dialect from among many varieties of speech, as the language of literature, is a universal process in the developments of speech and is determined by real, though special grounds of fitness, then this choice is a proper illustration of the principle of Natural Selection; and is the more so, with reference to the name of the principle, in proportion as the process and the grounds of fitness in this choice differ from the common volitions and motives of men, or are obscured by the imperfections of the records of the past, or by the subtleties of the associations which have determined it in the minds of the inventors and adopters of language. It is important, however, to distinguish between the origins of languages or linguistic customs, which are questions of philology, and the psychological question of the origin of language in general, or the origin in human nature of the inventions and uses of speech. Whether Natural Selection will serve to solve the latter question remains to be seen. In connection, however, with the resemblance, here noted, between the primitive, but regularly determined inventions of the mind and Natural Selection in its narrower sense, it is interesting to observe a corresponding resemblance between the theories of Free-Will and Creation, which are opposed to them. The objection that the origin of languages does not belong to the inquiries of Natural Selection, because language is an invention, and the work of Free-Will, thus appears to be parallel to the objection to Natural Selection, that it attempts to explain the work of Creation; and both objections obviously beg the questions at issue. But both objections have force with reference to the real and proper limitations of Natural Selection, and to the antecedent conditions of its action.

the savage is larger than he needs it to be"; from which he would conclude that there is in the size of the savage's brain a special anticipation or prophecy of the civilized man, or even of the philosopher, though the inference would be far more natural, and entirely consistent with Natural Selection, that the savage has degenerated from a more advanced condition. The proofs of our author's position consist in showing that there is a very slight difference between the average size of the savage's brain and that of the European, and that even in prehistoric man the capacity of the skull approaches very near to that of the modern man, as compared to the largest capacity of anthropoid skulls. Again, the size of the brain is a measure of intellectual power, as proved by the small size of idiotic brains, and the more than average size of the brains of great men, or "those who combine acute perception with great reflective powers, strong passions, and general energy of character." By these considerations "the idea is suggested of a surplusage of power, of an instrument beyond the needs of its possessor." From a rather artificial and arbitrary measure of intellectual power, the scale of marks in university examinations, as compared to the range of sizes in brains, Mr. Wallace concludes it to be fairly inferred, "that the savage possesses a brain capable, if cultivated and developed, of performing work of a kind and degree far beyond what he ever requires it to do." But how far removed is this conclusion from the idea that the savage has more brains than he needs! Why may it not be that all that he can do with his brains beyond his needs is only incidental to the powers which are directly serviceable? Of what significance is it that his brain is twice as great as that of the man-ape, while the philosopher only surpasses him one sixth, so long as we have no real measure of the brain power implied in the one universal characteristic of humanity, the power of language,—that is, the power to invent and use arbitrary signs?

Mr. Wallace most unaccountably overlooks the significance of what has always been regarded as the most important distinction of the human race,—its rationality as shown in language. He even says that "the mental requirements of savages, and the faculties actually exercised by them, are very little above those of animals." We would not call in question the accuracy of Mr. Wallace's observations of savages; but we can hardly accord equal credit to his accuracy in estimating the mental rank of their faculties. No doubt the savage mind seems very dull as compared with the sagacity shown by many animals; but a psychological analysis of the faculty of language shows that even the smallest proficiency in it might require more brain power than the greatest in any other direction. For this faculty implies a complete inversion of the ordinary and natural orders of association in the mind, or such an inversion as in mere parroting would be implied by the repetition of the words of a sentence in an inverse order,—a most difficult feat even for a philosopher. "The power of abstract reasoning and ideal conception," which Mr. Wallace esteems as a very great advance on the savage's proficiency, is but another step in the same direction, and here, too, *ce n'est que le premier pas qui coûte.* It seems probable enough that brain power proper, or its spontaneous and internal determinations of the perceptive faculties, should afford directly that *use* or *command* of a *sign* which is implied in language, and essentially consists in the power of turning back the attention from a suggested fact or idea to the suggesting ones, with reference to their use, in place of the naturally passive following and subserviency of the mind to the orders of first impressions and associations. By inverting the proportions which the latter bear to the forces of internal impressions, or to the powers of imagination in animals, we should have a fundamentally new order of mental actions; which, with the requisite motives to them, such as the social nature of man would afford, might go far towards defining the relations, both mental and physical, of human races to the higher brute animals. Among these the most sagacious and social, though they may understand language, or follow its significations, and even by indirection acquire some of its uses, yet have no direct *power of using,* and no power of *inventing* it.

But as we do not know, and have no means of knowing, what is the quantity of intellectual power, as measured by brains, which even the simplest use of language requires, how shall we be able to measure on such a scale the difference between the savage and the philosopher; which consists, not so much in additional elementary faculties in the philosopher, as in a more active and persistent use of such faculties as are common to both; and depends on the external inheritances of civilization, rather than on the organic inheritances of the civilized man? It is the *kind* of mental acquisition of which a race may be capable, rather than the amount which a trained individual may acquire, that we should suppose to be more immediately measured by the size of the brain; and Mr. Wallace has not shown that this *kind* is not serviceable to the savage. Idiots have sometimes great powers of acquisition of a certain low order of facts and ideas. Evidence upon this point, from the relations of intellectual power to the growth of the brain in children, is complicated in the same way by the fact that powers of acquisitions are with difficulty distinguished from, and are not a proper measure of, the intellectual powers, which depend directly on organic conditions, and are independent of an external inheritance.

But Mr. Wallace follows, in his estimations of distinct mental faculties, the doctrines of a school of mental philosophy which multiplies the elementary faculties of the mind far beyond any necessity. Many faculties are regarded by this school as distinct, which are probably only simple combinations or easy extensions of other faculties. The philosopher's mental powers are not necessarily different in their elements from those which the savage has and needs in his struggle for existence, or to maintain his position in the scale of life and the resources on which he has come to depend. The philosopher's powers are not, it is true, the direct results of Natural Selection, or of utility; but may they not result by the elementary laws of mental natures and external circumstances, from faculties that *are* useful? If they imply faculties which are useless to the savage, we have still the natural alternative left us, which Mr. Wallace does not consider, that savages, or all the races of savages now living, are degenerate men, and not the proper representatives of the philosopher's ancestors. But this alternative, though the natural one, does not appear to us as necessary; for we are not convinced that "the power of conceiving eternity and infinity, and all those purely abstract notions of form, number, and harmony, which play so large a part in the life of civilized races," are really so "entirely outside of the world of thought of the savage" as our author thinks. [Are they not rather implied and virtually acquired in the powers that the savage has and needs,—his powers of inventing and using even the concrete terms of his simple language? The fact that it does not require Natural Selection, but only the education of the individual savage, to develop in him these results, is to us a proof, not that the savage is specially provided with faculties beyond his needs, nor even that he is degenerated, but that mind itself, or elementary mental natures, in the savage and throughout the whole sentient world, involve and imply such relations between actual and potential faculties; just as the elementary laws of physics involve many apparently, or at first sight distinct and independent applications and utilities.] Ought we to regard the principle of " suction," applied to the uses of life in so many and various animal organisms, as specially prophetic of the mechanical invention of the pump and of similar engines? Shall we say that in the power of "suction" an animal possesses faculties that he does not need? Natural Selection cannot, it is true, be credited with such relations in development. But neither can they be attributed to a special providence in any intelligible sense. They belong rather to that constitution of nature, or general providence, which Natural Selection presupposes.

The theories of associational psychology are so admirably adapted to the solution of problems, for which Mr. Wallace seems obliged to call in the aid of miracles, that we are surprised he was not led by his studies to a more careful consideration of them. Thus in regard to the nature of the moral sense, which Mr. Wallace defines in accordance with the intuitional theory as "a feeling,—a sense of right and wrong,—in our nature, antecedent to, and independent of, experiences of utility."—this sense is capable of an analysis which meets and answers very simply the difficulties he finds in it on the theory of Natural Selection. The existence of feelings of approval and disapproval, or of likings and aversions to certain classes of actions, and a sense of obligation, are eminently useful in the government of human society, even among savages. These feelings may be associated with the really useful and the really harmful classes of actions, or they may not be. Such associations are not determined simply by utility, any oftener than beliefs are by proper evidence. But utility tends to produce the proper associations; and in this, along with the increase of these feelings themselves, consists the moral progress of the race. Why should not a fine sense of honor and an uncompromising veracity be found, then, among savage tribes, as in certain instances cited by Mr. Wallace; since moral feelings, or the motives to the observance of rules of conduct, lie at the foundation of even the simplest human society, and rest directly on the utility of man's political nature; and since veracity and honor are not merely useful, but indispensable in many relations, even in savage lives? Besides, veracity being one of the earliest developed instincts of childhood, can hardly with propriety be regarded as an original moral instinct, since it matures much earlier than the sense of obligation, or any feeling of the sanctity of truth. It belongs rather to that social and intellectual part of human nature from which language itself arises. The desire of communication, and the desire of communicating the truth, are originally identical in the ingenuous social nature. Is not this the source of the "mystical sense of wrong," attached to untruthfulness, which is, after all, regarded by mankind at large as so venial a fault? It needs but little early moral discipline to convert into a strong moral sentiment so natural an instinct. Deceitfulness is rather the acquired quality, so far as utility acts directly on the development of the individual, and for his advantage; but the native instinct of veracity is founded on the more primitive utilities of society and human intercourse. Instead, then, of regarding veracity as an original moral instinct, "antecedent to, and independent of, experiences of utility," it appears to us more natural to regard it as originally an intellectual and social instinct, founded in the broadest and most fundamental utilities of human nature.

The extension of the moral nature beyond the bounds of the necessities and utilities of society does not require a miracle to account for it; since, according to the principles of the associational psychology, it follows necessarily from the elementary laws of the mind. The individual experiences of utility which attach the moral feelings to rules of conduct are more commonly those of rewards and punishments, than of the direct or natural consequences of the conduct itself; and associations thus formed come to supersede all conscious reference to rational ends, and act upon the will in the manner of an instinct. The uncalculating, uncompromising moral imperative is not, it is true, derived from the individual's direct experiences of its utility; but neither does the instinct of the bee, which sacrifices its life in stinging, bear any relation to its individual advantage. Are we warranted, then, in inferring that the sting is useless to the bee? Suppose that whole communities of bees should occasionally be sacrificed to their instinct of self-defense, would this prove their instinct to be independent of a past or present utility, or to be prophetic of some future development of the race? Yet such a conclusion would be exactly parallel to that which Mr. Wallace draws from the fact that savages some times deal honorably with their enemies to their own apparent disadvantage. It is a universal law of the organic world, and a necessary consequence of Natural Selection, that the individual comprises in its nature chiefly what is useful to the race, and only incidentally what is useful to itself; since it is the race, and not the individual, that endures or is preserved. This contrast is the more marked in proportion as a race exhibits a complicated polity or social form of life; and man, even in his savage state, "is more political than any bee or ant." The doctrine of Natural Selection awakens a new interest in the problems of psychology. Its inquiries are not limited to the origin of species. "In the distant future," says Mr. Darwin, "I see open fields for far more important researches. Psychology will be based on a new foundation,—that of the necessary acquirements of each mental power and capacity by gradation. Light will be thrown on the origin of man and his history." More light we are sure can be expected from such researches than has been discovered by Mr. Wallace, in the principles and analysis of a mystical and metaphysical psychology.

The "origin of consciousness," or of sensation and thought, is relegated similarly by Mr. Wallace to the immediate agency or interposition of a metaphysical cause, as being beyond the province of secondary causes, which could act to produce it under the principle of Natural Selection. And it is doubtless true, nay, unquestionable, that sensation as a simple nature, with the most elementary laws of its activity, does really belong to the primordial facts in that constitution of nature, which is presupposed by the principle of utility as the ground or condition of the fitnesses through which the principle acts. In like manner the elements of organization, or the capacities of living matter in general, must be posited as antecedent to the mode of action which has produced in it, and through its elementary laws, such marvelous results. But if we mean by "consciousness" what the word is often and more properly used to express,—that total and complex structure of sensibilities, thoughts, and emotions in an animal mind, which is so closely related to the animal's complex physical organization,—so far is this from being beyond the province of Natural Selection, that it affords one of the most promising fields for its future investigations.* Whatever the results of such investigations,

* In further illustration of the range of the explanations afforded by the principle of Natural Selection, to which we referred in our note, page 108, we may instance an application of it to the more special psychological problem of the development of the individual mind by its own experiences, which presupposes, of course, the innate powers and mental faculties derived (whether naturally or supernaturally) from the development of the race. Among these native faculties of the individual mind is the power of reproducing its own past experiences in memory and belief; and this is, at least, analogous, as we have said, to the reproductive powers of physical organisms, and like these is in itself an unlimited, expansive power of repetition. Human beliefs, like human desires, are naturally illimitable. The generalizing instinct is native to the mind. It is not the result of habitual experiences, as is commonly supposed, but acts as well on *single* experiences, which are capable of producing, when unchecked, the most unbounded beliefs and expectations of the future. The only checks to such unconditional natural beliefs are *other* and equally unconditional and natural beliefs, or the contradictions and limiting conditions of experience. Here, then, is a close analogy, at least, to those fundamental facts

we may rest assured that they will not solve; will never even propound the problem peculiar to metaphysics (if it can prop-

of the organic world on which the law of Natural Selection is based; the facts, namely, of the "rapid increase of organisms," limited only by "the conditions of existence," and by competition in that "struggle for existence" which results in the "survival of the fittest." As the tendency to an unlimited increase in existing organisms is held in check only by those conditions of their existence which are chiefly comprised in the like tendencies of other organisms to unlimited increase, and is thus maintained (so long as external conditions remain unchanged) in an unvarying balance of life; and as this balance adjusts itself to slowly changing external conditions, so, in the history of the individual mind, beliefs which spring spontaneously from simple and single experiences, and from a naturally unlimited tendency to generalization, are held mutually in check, and in their harmony represent the properly balanced experiences and knowledges of the mind, and by adaptive changes are kept in accordance with changing external conditions, or with the varying total results in the memory of special experiences. This mutual limitation of belief by belief, in which consists so large a part of their proper *evidence*, is so prominent a feature in the beliefs of the rational mind, that philosophers had failed to discover their true nature, as elementary facts, until this was pointed out by the greatest of living psychologists, Professor Alexander Bain. The mutual tests and checks of belief have, indeed, always appeared to a great majority of philosophers as their only proper evidence; and beliefs themselves have appeared as purely intellectual phases of the mind. But Bain has defined them, in respect to their ultimate natures, as phases of the will; or as the tendencies we have to *act* on mere experience, or to *act* on our simplest, most limited experiences. They are tendencies, however, which become so involved in intellectual developments, and in their mutual limitations, that their ultimate results in rational beliefs have very naturally appeared to most philosophers as purely intellectual facts; and their real genesis in experience has been generally discredited, with the exception of what are designated specially as "empirical beliefs."

It may be objected that the generative process we have here described bears only a remote and fanciful analogy, and not an essential resemblance, to Natural Selection in the organic world. But to this it is, perhaps, sufficient to reply (as in the case of the origin of language), that if "the survival of the fittest" is a true expression of the law,—it is to Mr. Herbert Spencer we owe this most precise definition, —then the development of the individual mind presents a true example of it; for our knowledges and rational beliefs result, *truly and literally*, from the survival of the fittest among our original and spontaneous beliefs. It is only by a figure of speech, it is true, that this "survival of the fittest" can be described as the result of a "struggle for existence" among our primitive beliefs; but this description is equally figurative as applied to Natural Selection in the organic world.

The application of the principle to mental development takes for granted, as we have said, the faculties with which the individual is born, and in the human mind these include that most efficient auxiliary, the faculty of using and inventing language. How Natural Selection could have originated this is not so easy to trace, and is an almost wholly speculative question; but if the faculty consists essentially, as we have supposed, in a preponderance of the active and spontaneous over the passive powers of the brain, effecting the turning-back or reflective action of the mind, while the latter simply result in the following-out or sagacious habit, we see at least that the contrast need not depend on the absolute size of the brain, but only on the *proportion* of the powers that depend on its quantity to those that depend on its quality. We should naturally suppose, therefore, that the earliest men were probably not very sagacious creatures, perhaps much less so than the present uncivilized races. But they were, most likely, very social; even more so, perhaps, than the sagacious savage; for there was needed a strong motive to call this complicated and difficult mental action into exercise; and it is even now to be observed that sagacity and

erly be called a problem), the origin of sensation or simple consciousness, the problem *par excellence* of pedantic garrulity or
philosophical childishness. Questions of the special physical
antecedents, concomitants, and consequents of special sensations will doubtless continue to be the legitimate objects of
empirical researches and of important generalizations; and
such researches may succeed in reducing all other facts of actual
experience, all our knowledge of nature, and all our thoughts
and emotions to intelligible modifications of these simple and
fundamental existences; but the attempt to reduce sensation
to anything but sensation is as gratuitous and as devoid of any
suggestion or guidance of experience, as the attempt to reduce
the axioms of the mathematical or mechanical sciences to
simpler orders of universal facts. In one sense material phenomena, or physical objective states, are causes or effects of
sensations, bearing as they do the invariable relations to them
of antecedents, or concomitants, or consequents. But these
are essentially empirical relations, explicable perhaps by more
and more generalized empirical laws, but approaching in this
way never one step nearer to an explanation of material conditions by mental laws, or of mental natures by the forces of
matter. Matter and mind co-exist. There are no scientific
principles by which either can be determined to be the cause

---

sociability are not commonly united in high degrees even among civilized men. Growths
both in the quantity and quality of the brain are, therefore, equally probable in the history of
human development, with always a preponderance of the advantages which depend upon
quantity. But the present superiority of the most civilized races, so far as it is independent
of any external inheritance of arts, knowledges, and institutions, would appear to depend
chiefly upon the *quality* of their brains, and upon characteristics belonging to their moral
and emotional natures rather than the intellectual, since the intellectual acquisitions of
civilization are more easily communicated by education to the savage than the refine-
ments of its moral and emotional characteristics. Though all records and traces of this
development are gone, and a wide gulf separates the lowest man from the highest brute
animal, yet elements exist by which we may trace the succession of utilities and advantages that have determined the transition. The most essential are those of the social nature of man, involving mutual assistance in the struggle for existence. Instrumental to
these are his mental powers, developed by his social nature, and by the reflective character of his brain's action into a general and common intelligence, instead of the specialized instincts and sagacities characteristic of other animals; and from these came language, and thence all the arts, knowledges, governments, traditions, all the external inheritances, which, reacting on his social nature, have induced the sentiments of morality,
worship, and refinement; at which gazing as in a mirror he sees his past, and thinks it
his future.

of the other. Still, so far as scientific evidence goes, mind exists in direct and peculiar relations to a certain form of matter,
the organic, which is not a different kind, though the properties of no other forms are in themselves capable, so far as scientific observation has yet determined, of giving rise to it.
The materials and the forces of organisms are both derived
from other forms of matter, as well as from the organic; but
the organic form itself appears to be limited to the productive
powers of matters and forces which already have this form.

The transcendental doctrine of development (which is not
wholly transcendental, since it is guided, at least vaguely, by the
scientific principles of cause and effect, or by the continuities
and uniformities of natural phenomena) assumes that in the
past course of nature the forms as well as the materials and
forces of organic matter had at one time a causal connection
with other forms of material existence. Mental natures, and
especially the simplest, or sensations, would have had, according to this assumption, a more universal relation of immediate
connection than we now know with properties of the sort that
we call material. Still, by the analogies of experience they
cannot be regarded as having been either causes or effects of
them. Our ignorances, or the as yet unexplored possibilities
of nature, seem far preferable to the vagueness of this theory,
which, in addition to the continuities and uniformities universally exhibited in nature, assumes transcendentally, as a universal first principle, the law of *progressive change*, or a law
which is *not* universally exemplified by the course of nature.
We say, and say truly, that a stone has no sensation, since it
exhibits none of the signs that indicate the existence of sensations. It is not only a purely objective existence, like everything else in nature, except our own individual self-consciousness,
but its properties indicate to us no other than this purely objective existence, unless it be the existence of God. To suppose
that its properties could possibly result in a sensitive nature, not
previously existing or co-existing with them, is to reason entirely
beyond the guidance and analogies of experience. It is a purely
gratuitous supposition, not only metaphysical or transcendental,
but also materialistic; that is, it is not only asking a foolish ques-

tion, but giving a still more foolish answer to it. In short, the metaphysical problem may be reduced to an attempt to break down the most fundamental antithesis of all experience, by demanding to know of its terms which of them is the other. To this sort of fatuity belongs, we think, the mystical doctrine which Mr. Wallace is inclined to adopt, "that FORCE is a product of MIND"; which means, so far as it is intelligible, that forces, or the physical antecedents and conditions of motion (apprehended, it is true, along with motion itself, through our sensations and volitions), yet bear to our mental natures the still closer relation of resemblance to the prime agency of the Will; or it means that "all force is probably will-force." Not only does this assumed mystical resemblance, expressed by the word "will-force," contradict the fundamental antithesis of subject and object phenomena (as the word "mind-matter" would), but it fails to receive any confirmation from the law of the correlation of the physical forces. All the motions of animals, both voluntary and involuntary, are traceable to the efficiency of equivalent material forces in the animal's physical organization. The cycles of equivalent physical forces are complete, even when their courses lie through the voluntary actions of animals, without the introduction of conscious or mental conditions. The sense of effort is not a form of force. The painful or pleasurable sensations that accompany the conversions of force in conscious volitions are not a consciousness of this force itself, nor even a proper measure of it. The Will is not a measurable quantity of energy, with its equivalents in terms of heat, or falling-force, or chemical affinity, or the energy of motion, unless we identify it with the vital energies of the organism, which are, however (unfortunately for this hypothesis), the causes of the involuntary movements of an animal, as well as of its proper volitions considered from their physical side.

But Mr. Wallace is inclined to the opinion that the Will is an incident force, regulating and controlling the action of the physical forces of the vital machine, but contributing, even in this capacity, some part at least to the actual moving forces of the living frame. He says:

"However delicately a machine may be constructed, with the most exquisitely contrived detents to release a weight or spring by the exertion of the smallest possible amount of force, *some* external force will always be required; so in the animal machine, however minute may be the changes required in the cells or fibres of the brain, to set in motion the nerve currents that loosen or excite the pent-up forces of certain muscles, *some force* must be required to effect those changes."

And this force he supposes to be the Will. This is the most intelligible materialism we have ever met with in the discussions of this subject. It is true that in a machine, not only the main efficient forces, but also the incident and regulating ones, are physical forces; and however small the latter may be, they are still of the same nature, and are comparable in amount with the main efficient forces. But is not this one of the most essential differences between a machine and a sensitive organism? Is it impossible, then, that nature has contrived an infinitely more perfect machine than human art can invent,— machinery which involves the powers of art itself, if it be proper to call that contrivance a machine, in which the regulating causes are of a wholly different nature from the efficient forces? May it not be that sensations and mental conditions, generally, are regulating causes which add nothing, like the force of the hand of the engineer to the powers which he controls in his machine, and subtract nothing, as an automatic apparatus does, from such powers in the further regulation of the machine? We may not be able to understand how such regulation is possible; how sensations and other mental conditions can restrain, excite, and combine the conversions of physical forces in the cycles into which they themselves do not enter; though there is a type of such regulation in the principles of theoretical mechanics, in the actions of forces which do not affect the quantities of the actual or potential energies of a system of moving bodies, but simply the form of the movement, as in the rod of the simple pendulum. Such regulation in the sensitive organism is more likely to be an ultimate inexplicable fact; but it is clear that even in a machine the amounts of the regulating forces bear no definite relations to the powers they control, and might, so far as these are directly concerned, be reduced to nothing as forces; and in many cases they are reduced to a *minimum* of the force of friction. They must, however, be *something* in amount in a machine, *because they are physical*, and, like all physical forces, must be derived in quantity from pre-existing forms of force. To infer from this that the Will must add something to the forces of the organism is, therefore, to assume for it a material nature. But Mr. Wallace escapes, or appears to think (as others think who hold this view) that he escapes, from complete materialism by the doctrine of the freedom of the Will. Though he makes the Will an efficient physical force, he does not allow it to be a physical effect. In other words, he regards the Will as an absolute source of physical energy, continually adding, though in small amounts, to the store of the forces of nature; a sort of molecular leakage of energy from an absolute source into the nervous system of animals, or, at least, of men. This, though in our opinion an unnecessary and very improbable hypothesis, is not inconceivable. It is improbable, inasmuch as it denies to the Will a character common to the physical forces with which the Will is otherwise assimilated by this theory,—the character, namely, of being an effect in measurable amount as well as a cause, or the character of belonging to cycles of changes related by invariable quantities; but as we do not regard the conservation of force as a *necessary* law of the universe, we are able to comprehend Mr. Wallace's position. It is the metaphysical method of distinguishing a machine from a sensitive organism. But we do not see why Mr. Wallace is not driven by it to the dilemma of assuming free-wills for all sentient organisms; or else of assuming, with Descartes, that all but men are machines. The latter alternative would, doubtless, redound most effectively to the metaphysical dignity of human nature. Mr. Wallace appears to think that unless we can attribute to the Will *some* efficiency or quantity of energy, its agency must be regarded as a nullity, and our apparent consciousness of its influence as an illusion; but this opinion appears to be based on the still broader assumption, which seems to us erroneous, that all causation is reducible to the conversions of equivalent physical energies. It may be true (at least we are not prepared to dispute the assumption) that every case of real causation involves such conversions or changes in forms of energy, or that every effect involves changes of position and motion. Nevertheless, every case of real causation may still involve also another mode of causation.

A much simpler conception than our author's theory, and one that seems to us far more probable is that the phenomena of conscious volition involve in themselves no proper efficiencies or forces coming under the law of the conservation of force, but are rather natural types of causes, purely and absolutely *regulative*, which add nothing to, and subtract nothing from, the quantities of natural forces. No doubt there is in the actions of the nervous system a much closer resemblance than this to a machine. No doubt it is automatically regulated, as well as moved, by physical forces; but this is probably just in proportion as its agency —as in our habits and instincts—is removed from our conscious control. All this machinery is below, beyond, external, or foreign to our consciousness. The profoundest, most attentive introspection gains not a glimpse of its activity, nor do we ever dream of its existence; but both by the laws of its operations, and by the means through which we become aware of its existence, it stands in the broadest, most fundamental contrast to our mental natures; and these, so far from furnishing a type of physical efficiency in our conscious volitions, seem to us rather, in accordance with their general contrast with material phenomena, to afford a type of purely regulative causes, or of an absolutely forceless and unresisted control and regulation of those forces of nature which are comprised in the powers of organic life. Perhaps a still higher type of such regulation is to be found in those "laws of nature," which, without adding to, or subtracting from, the real forces of nature, determine the order of their conversions by "*fixed*, *stated*, or *settled*" rules of succession; and these may govern also, and probably do govern, the successions of our mental or self-conscious states, both in themselves and in their relations to material conditions. Simple, absolute, invariable rules of succession in phenomena, both physical and mental, constitute the most abstract conception we can have of causal relations; but they appear under two chief classes, the physical laws which determine the possible relations of the forms of force, and those which are also concerned in the still further determination of its actual orders of succession, or which, by their combinations in the intricate web of uniformities in nature, both mental and physical, determine the events in particular that in relation to the laws of force are only determined in general. The proper laws of force, or of the conversions of energy, are concerned exclusively with relations in space. Relations in time are governed by the other class of laws. Thus, in the abstract theory of the pendulum, the phenomena of force involved are limited simply to the vertical rise and fall of the weight, upon which alone the amounts of its motions depend. The times of its vibrations are determined by the regulating length of the rod, which in theory adds nothing to, and subtracts nothing from, the efficient mutually convertible forces of motion and gravity. What is here assumed in theory to be true, we assume to be actually and absolutely true of mental agencies.

But it may be said, and it often is said, " that this theory of the Will's agency is directly contradicted in both its features by consciousness; that we are immediately conscious both of energy and freedom in willing."· There is much in our volitional consciousness to give countenance to this contradiction; but it is only such as dreams give to contradictions of rational experience. The words " force," " energy," " effort," " resistance," " conflict," all point to states of feeling in our volitional consciousness which seem to a superficial observation to be true intuitions of spontaneous self-originated causes; and it is only when these states of feeling are tested by the scientific definitions and the objective measure of forces, and by the orders of the conversions of force, that they are found to be only vague, subjective accompaniments, instead of distinct objective apprehensions or perceptions of what "force" signifies in science. Such tests prove them to be like the complementary or subjective colors of vision. In one sense they are intuitions of force, our only intuitions of it (as the aspects of nature are our only intuitions of the system of the world); but they are not true perceptions, since they do not afford, each feeling in itself, definite and invariable indications of force as an objective existence, or as affecting all minds alike. Even the sense of weight is no proper measure of weight as an element of force; and the muscular effort of lifting is only a vague and variable perception of this conversion of force, and does not afford even a hint of the great law of the conservation and convertibility of forces, but, on the contrary, seems to contradict it. The muscular feeling of resistance to motion or to a change of motion is an equally vague measure of *inertia*. Indeed, the feelings of weight and resistance, which are often regarded as intuitions of gravity and inertia, are insusceptible of precise measurement or numerical comparison; and though capable of being trained to some degree of precision in estimating what is properly measured by other means, they could never have revealed through their unaided indications the law of the fixed and universal proportionality of these two forces. The feeling of effort itself (more or less intense, and more or less painful, according to circumstances, which are quite irrelevant to its apparent effect) appears by the testimony of consciousness to be the immediate cause of the work which is done,—work really done by forces in the vital organism, which only the most recondite researches of science have disclosed. But if this much-vaunted authority of immediate consciousness so blunders in even the simplest cases, how can our author or any judicious thinker trust its unconfirmed, unsupported testimony in regard to the agency of the Will? Is it not like trusting the testimony of the senses as to the immobility of the earth?

With hardly a point, therefore, of Mr. Wallace's concluding essay are we able to agree; and this impresses us the more, since we find nothing in the rest of his book which appears to us to call for serious criticism, but many things, on the contrary, which command our most cordial admiration. We account for it by the supposition that his metaphysical views, carefully excluded from his scientific work, are the results of an earlier and less severe training than that which has secured to us his valuable positive contributions to the theory of Natural Selection. Mr. Wallace himself is fully aware of this contrast, and anticipates a scornful rejection of his theory by many who in other respects agree with him.

The doctrines of the special and prophetic providences and decrees of God, and of the metaphysical isolation of human nature, are based, after all, on barbaric conceptions of dignity, which are restricted in their application by every step forward in the progress of science. And the sense of security they give us of the most sacred things is more than replaced by the ever-growing sense of the universality of inviolable laws, — laws that underlie our sentiments and desires, as well as all that these can rationally regard in the outer world. It is unfortunate that the prepossessions of religious sentiment in favor of metaphysical theories should make the progress of science always seem like an indignity to religion, or a detraction from what is held as most sacred; yet the responsibility for this belongs neither to the progress of science nor to true religious sentiment, but to a false conservatism, an irrational respect for the ideas and motives of a philosophy which finds it more and more difficult with every advance of knowledge to reconcile its assumptions with facts of observation.

THE GENESIS OF SPECIES.*

It is now nearly twelve years since the discussion of that "mystery of mysteries," the origin of species, was re-opened by the publication of the first edition of Mr. Darwin's most remarkable work. Again and again in the history of scientific debate this question had been discussed, and, after exciting a short-lived interest, had been condemned by cautious and conservative thinkers to the limbo of insoluble problems or to the realm of religious mystery. They had, therefore, sufficient grounds, *a priori*, for anticipating that a similar fate would attend this new revival of the question, and that, in a few years, no more would be heard of the matter; that the same condemnation awaited this movement which had overwhelmed the venturesome speculations of Lamarck and of the author of the "Vestiges of Creation." This not unnatural anticipation has been, however, most signally disappointed. But what can we say has really been accomplished by this debate; and what reasons have we for believing that the judgment of conservative thinkers will not, in the main, be proved right after all, though present indications are against them? One permanent consequence, at least, will remain, in the great additions to our knowledge of natural history, and of general physiology, or theoretical biology, which the discussion has produced; though the greater part of this positive contribution to science is still to be credited directly to Mr. Darwin's works, and even to his original researches. But, besides this, an advantage has been gained which cannot be too highly estimated. Orthodoxy has been won over to the

---

* From the North American Review, July, 1871.

doctrine of evolution. In asserting this result, however, we are obliged to make what will appear to many persons important qualifications and explanations. We do not mean that the heads of leading religious bodies, even in the most enlightened communities, are yet willing to withdraw the dogma that the origin of species is a special religous mystery, or even to assent to the hypothesis of evolution as a legitimate question for scientific inquiry. We mean only, that many eminent students of science, who claim to be orthodox, and who are certainly actuated as much by a spirit of reverence as by scientific inquisitiveness, have found means of reconciling the general doctrine of evolution with the dogmas they regard as essential to religion. Even to those whose interest in the question is mainly scientific this result is a welcome one, as opening the way for a freer discussion of subordinate questions, less trammeled by the religious prejudices which have so often been serious obstacles to the progress of scientific researches.

But again, in congratulating ourselves on this result, we are obliged to limit it to the doctrine of evolution in its most general form, the theory common to Lamarck's zoölogical philosophy, to the views of the author of the "Vestiges of Creation," to the general conclusions of Mr. Darwin's and Mr. Wallace's theory of Natural Selection, to Mr. Spencer's general doctrine of evolution, and to a number of minor explanations of the processes by which races of animals and plants have been derived by descent from different ancestral forms. What is no longer regarded with suspicion as secretly hostile to religious beliefs by many truly religious thinkers is that which is denoted in common by the various names "transmutation," "development," "derivation," "evolution," and "descent with modification." These terms are synonymous in their primary and general signification, but refer secondarily to various hypotheses of the processes of derivation. But there is a choice among them on historical grounds, and with reference to associations, which are of some importance from a theological point of view. "Transmutation" and "development" are under ban. "Derivation" is, perhaps, the most innocent word; though "evolution" will probably prevail, since in spite of its etymological implication, it has lately become most acceptable, not only to the theological critics of the theory, but to its scientific advocates; although, from the neutral ground of experimental science, "descent with modification" is the most pertinent and least exceptionable name.

While the general doctrine of evolution has thus been successfully redeemed from theological condemnation, this is not yet true of the subordinate hypothesis of Natural Selection, to the partial success of which this change of opinion is, in great measure, due. It is, at first sight, a paradox that the views most peculiar to the eminent naturalist, whose work has been chiefly instrumental in effecting this change of opinion, should still be rejected or regarded with suspicion by those who have nevertheless been led by him to adopt the general hypothesis, —an hypothesis which his explanations have done so much to render credible. It would seem, at first sight, that Mr. Darwin has won a victory, not for himself, but for Lamarck. Transmutation, it would seem, has been accepted, but Natural Selection, its explanation, is still rejected by many converts to the general theory, both on religious and scientific grounds. But too much weight might easily be attributed to the deductive or explanatory part of the evidence, on which the doctrine of evolution has come to rest. In the half-century preceding the publication of the "Origin of Species," inductive evidence on the subject had accumulated, greatly outweighing all that was previously known; and the "Origin of Species" is not less remarkable as a compend and discussion of this evidence than for the ingenuity of its explanations. It is not, therefore, to what is now known as "Darwinism" that the prevalence of the doctrine of evolution is to be attributed, at least directly. Still, most of this effect is due to Mr. Darwin's work, and something undoubtedly to the indirect influence of reasonings that are regarded with distrust by those who accept their conclusions; for opinions are contagious, even where their reasons are resisted.

The most effective general criticism of the theory of Natural Selection which has yet appeared, and, at the same time, one which is likely to exert great influence in overcoming the re-

aining prejudice against the general doctrine of evolution, is
he work of Mr. St. George Mivart "On the Genesis of
pecies." Though the work falls short of what we might have
xpected from an author of Mr. Mivart's attainments as a
aturalist, yet his position before the religious world, and his
nquestionable familiarity with the theological bearings of his
ubject, will undoubtedly gain for him and for the doctrine of
volution a hearing and a credit, which might be denied to
he mere student of science. His work is mainly a critique of
Darwinism"; that is, of the theories peculiar to Mr. Darwin
nd the "Darwinians," as distinguished from the believers in
he general doctrine of evolution which our author accepts.
Ie also puts forward an hypothesis in opposition to Mr. Dar-
vin's doctrine of the predominant influence of Natural Selec-
ion in the generation of organic species, and their relation to
he conditions of their existence. On this hypothesis, called
Specific Genesis," an organism, though at any one time a
xed and determinate species, approximately adapted to sur-
ounding conditions of existence, is potentially, and by innate
ootential combinations of organs and faculties, adapted to
nany other conditions of existence. It passes, according to
he hypothesis, from one form to another of specific "mani-
estation," abruptly and discontinuously in conformity to the
mergencies of its outward life; but in any condition to which
t is tolerably adapted it retains a stable form, subject to varia-
ion only within determinate limits, like oscillations in a stable
quilibrium. For this conception our author is indebted to
Mr. Galton, who, in his work on "Hereditary Genius," "com-
ares the development of species with a many-faceted spheroid
umbling over from one facet or stable equilibrium to another.
The existence of internal conditions in animals," Mr. Mivart
dds (p. 111), "corresponding with such facets is denied by
oure Darwinians, but it is contended in this work that some-
hing may also be said for their existence."

There are many facts of variation, numerous cases of abrupt
hanges in individuals both of natural and domesticated species,
vhich, of course, no Darwinian or physiologist denies, and of
vhich Natural Selection professes to offer no direct explanation.

The causes of these phenomena, and their relations to external conditions of existence, are matters quite independent of the principle of Natural Selection, except so far as they may directly affect the animal's or plant's well-being, with the origin of which this principle is alone concerned. General physiology has classified some of these sudden variations under such names as "reversion" and "atavism," or returns more or less complete to ancestral forms. Others have been connected together under the law of "correlated or concomitant variations," changes that, when they take place, though not known to be physically dependent on each other, yet usually or often occur together. Some cases of this law have been referred to the higher, more fundamental laws of homological variations, or variations occurring together on account of the relationships of homology, or due to similarities and physical relations between parts of organisms, in tissues, organic connections, and modes of growth. Other variations are explained by the laws and causes that determine monstrous growths. Others again are quite inexplicable as yet, or cannot yet be referred to any general law or any known antecedents. These comprise, indeed, the most common cases. The almost universal prevalence of well-marked phenomena of variation in species, the absolutely universal fact that no two individual organisms are exactly alike, and that the description of a species is necessarily abstract and in many respects by means of averages,—these facts have received no particular explanations, and might indeed be taken as ultimate facts or highest laws in themselves, were it not that in biological speculations such an assumption would be likely to be misunderstood, as denying the existence of any real determining causes and more ultimate laws, as well as denying any known antecedents or regularities in such phenomena. No physical naturalist would for a moment be liable to such a misunderstanding, but would, on the contrary, be more likely to be off his guard against the possibility of it in minds otherwise trained and habituated to a different kind of studies. Mr. Darwin has undoubtedly erred in this respect. He has not in his works repeated with sufficient frequency his faith in the universality of the law of causation, in the phenomena of general physiology or theoretical biology, as well as in all the rest of physical nature. He has not said often enough, it would appear, that in referring any effect to "accident," he only means that its causes are like particular phases of the weather, or like innumerable phenomena in the concrete course of nature generally, which are quite beyond the power of finite minds to anticipate or to account for in detail, though none the less really determinate or due to regular causes. That he has committed this error appears from the fact that his critic, Mr. Mivart, has made the mistake, which nullifies nearly the whole of his criticism, of supposing that "the theory of Natural Selection may (though it need not) be taken in such a way as to lead men to regard the present organic world as formed, so to speak, *accidentally*, beautiful and wonderful as is confessedly the hap-hazard result" (p. 33). Mr. Mivart, like many another writer, seems to forget the age of the world in which he lives and for which he writes,—the age of "experimental philosophy," the very standpoint of which, its fundamental assumption, is the universality of physical causation. This is so familiar to minds bred in physical studies, that they rarely imagine that they may be mistaken for disciples of Democritus, or for believers in "the fortuitous concourse of atoms," in the sense, at least, which theology has attached to this phrase. If they assent to the truth that may have been meant by the phrase, they would not for a moment suppose that the atoms move fortuitously, but only that their conjunctions, constituting the actual concrete orders of events, could not be anticipated except by a knowledge of the natures and regular histories of each and all of them,—such knowledge as belongs only to omniscience. [The very hope of experimental philosophy, its expectation of constructing the sciences into a true philosophy of nature, is based on the induction, or, if you please, the *a priori* presumption, that physical causation is universal; that the constitution of nature is written in its actual manifestations, and needs only to be deciphered by experimental and inductive research; that it is not a latent invisible writing, to be brought out by the magic of mental anticipation or metaphysical meditation. Or, as

Bacon said, it is not by the "anticipations of the mind," but by the "interpretation of nature," that natural philosophy is to be constituted; and this is to presume that the order of nature is decipherable, or that causation is everywhere either manifest or hidden, but never absent.

Mr. Mivart does not wholly reject the process of Natural Selection, or disallow it as a real cause in nature, but he reduces it to "a subordinate rôle" in his view of the derivation of species. It serves to perfect the imperfect adaptations, and to meet within certain limits unfavorable changes in the conditions of existence. The "accidents" which Natural Selection acts upon are allowed to serve in a subordinate capacity and in subjection to a foreordained, particular, divine order, or to act like other agencies dependent on an evil principle, which are compelled to turn evil into good. Indeed, the only difference on purely scientific grounds, and irrespective of theological considerations, between Mr. Mivart's views and Mr. Darwin's is in regard to the *extent* to which the process of Natural Selection has been effective in the modifications of species. Mr. Darwin himself, from the very nature of the process, has never supposed for it, as a cause, any other than a co-ordinate place among other causes of change, though he attributes to it a superintendent, directive, and controlling agency among them. The student of the theory would gather quite a different impression of the theory from Mr. Mivart's account of it, which attributes to "Darwinians" the absurd conception of this cause as acting "alone" to produce the changes and stabilities of species; whereas, from the very nature of the process, other causes of change, whether of a known or as yet unknown nature, are presupposed by it. Even Mr. Galton's hypothetical "facets," or internal conditions of abrupt changes and successions of stable equilibriums, might be among these causes, if there were any good inductive grounds for supposing their existence. Reversional and correlated variations are, indeed, due to such internal conditions and to laws of inheritance, which have been ascertained inductively as at least laws of phenomena, but of which the causes, or the antecedent conditions in the organism, are unknown. Mr Darwin continually refers to variations as arising from unknown causes, but these are always such, so far as observation can determine their relations to the organism's conditions of existence, that they are far from accounting for, or bearing any relations to, the adaptive characters of the organism. It is solely upon and with reference to such adaptive characters that the process of Natural Selection has any agency, or could be supposed to be effective. If Mr. Mivart had cited anywhere in his book, as he has not, even a single instance of sudden variation in a whole race, either in a state of nature or under domestication, which is not referable by known physiological laws to the past history of the race on the theory of evolution, and had further shown that such a variation was an adaptive one, he might have weakened the arguments for the agency and extent of the process of Natural Selection. As it is, he has left them quite intact.

The only direct proofs which he adduces for his theory that adaptive as well as other combinations proceed from innate predeterminations wholly within the organism, are drawn from, or rather assumed in, a supposed analogy of the specific forms in organisms to those of crystals. As under different circumstances or in different media the same chemical substances or constituent substances assume different and distinct crystalline forms, so, he supposes, organisms are distinct manifestations of typical forms, one after another of which will appear under various external conditions. He quotes from Mr. J. J. Murphy's "Habit and Intelligence," that, "it needs no proof that in the case of spheres and crystals, the forms and structures are the effect and not the cause of the formative principle. Attraction, whether gravitative or capillary, produces the spherical form; the spherical form does not produce attraction. And crystalline polarities produce crystalline structure and form; crystalline structure and form do not produce polarities." And, by analogy, Mr. Murphy and our author infer that innate vital forces always produce specific vital forms, and that the vital forms themselves, or "accidental" variations of them, cannot modify the types of action in vital force. Now, although Mr. Murphy's propositions may need no proof, they will bear correction; and, clear as they appear to be, a better interpretation of the physical facts is needed for the purposes of tracing out analogy and avoiding paralogism. Strange as it may seem, Mr. Murphy's clear antitheses are not even partially true. No abstraction ever produced any other abstraction, much less a concrete thing. The abstract laws of attraction never produced any body, spherical or polyhedral. It was actual forces acting in definite ways that made the sphere or crystal; and the sizes, particular shapes, and positions of these bodies determined in part the action of these actual forces. It is the resultants of many actual attractions, dependent in turn on the actual products, that determine the spherical or crystalline forms. Moreover, in the case of crystals, neither these forces nor the abstract law of their action in producing definite angles reside in the finished bodies, but in the properties of the surrounding media, portions of whose constituents are changed into crystals, according to these properties and to other conditioning circumstances. So far as these bodies have any innate principle in them concerned in their own production, it is manifested in determining, not their general agreements, but their particular differences in sizes, shapes, and positions. The particular position of a crystal that grows from some fixed base or nucleus, and the particular directions of its faces, may, perhaps, be said to be *innate ;* that is, they were determined at the beginning of the particular crystal's growth.

Finding, therefore, what Mr. Murphy and Mr. Mivart suppose to be innate to be really in the outward conditions of the crystal's growth, and what they would suppose to be superinduced to be all that is innate in it, we have really found the contrast in place of an analogy between a crystal and an organism. For, in organisms, no doubt, and as we may be readily convinced without resort to analogy, there is a great deal that is really innate, or dependent on actions in the organism, which diversities of external conditions modify very little, or affect at least in a very indeterminate manner, so far as observation has yet ascertained. External conditions are, nevertheless, essential factors in development, as well as in mere increase or growth. No animal or plant is developed, nor do its developments acquire any growth without very special external conditions. These are quite as essential to the production of an organism as a crystalline nucleus and fluid material are to the growth and particular form of a crystal; and as the general resemblances of the crystals of any species, the agreements in their angles, are results of the physical properties of their food and other surrounding conditions of their growth, so the general resemblances of animals or plants of any species, their agreements in specific characters, are doubtless due, in the main, to the properties of what is innate in them, yet not to any abstraction. This is sufficiently conspicuous to "need no proof," and is denied by no Darwinian. The analogy is so close indeed between the internal determinations of growth in an organism and the external ones of crystals, that Mr. Darwin was led by it to invent his "provisional hypothesis of Pangenesis," or theory of gemmular reproduction. The gemmules in this theory being the perfect analogues of the hypothetical atoms of the chemical substances that are supposed to arrange themselves in crystalline forms, the theory rather gives probability to the chemical theory of atoms than borrows any from it. But we shall recur to this theory of Pangenesis further on.

General physiology, or physical and theoretical biology, are sciences in which, through the study of the laws of inheritance, and the direct and indirect effect of external conditions, we must arrive, if in any way, at a more and more definite knowledge of the causes of specific manifestations; and this is the end to which Mr. Darwin's labors have been directed, and have partially accomplished. Every step he has taken has been in strict conformity to the principles of method which the examples of inductive and experimental science have established. A stricter observance of these by Mr. Murphy and our author might have saved them from the mistake we have noticed, and from many others,—the "realism" of ascribing efficacy to an abstraction, making attraction and polarity produce structures and forms independently of the products and of the concrete matters and forces in them. A similar "realism" vitiates nearly all speculations in theoretical biology, which are not designedly, or even instinctively, as in Mr. Darwin's work, made to conform to the rigorous rules of experimental philosophy. These require us to assume no causes that are not true or phenomenally known, and known in some other way than in the effect to be explained; and to prove the sufficiency of those we do assume in some other way than by putting an abstract name or description of an effect for its cause, like using the words "attraction" and "polarity" to account for things the matters of which have *come together* in a *definite form*. It may seem strange to many readers to be told that Mr. Darwin, the most consummate speculative genius of our times, is no more a maker of hypotheses than Newton was, who, unable to discover the cause of the properties of gravitation, wrote the often-quoted but much misunderstood words, "*Hypotheses non fingo*." "For," he adds, "whatever is not deduced from the phenomena is to be called an hypothesis; and hypotheses, whether metaphysical or physical, whether of occult qualities or mechanical, have no place in experimental philosophy. In this philosophy particular propositions are inferred from the phenomena, and afterwards rendered general by induction. Thus it was that the impenetrability, the mobility, and the impulsive force of bodies, and the laws of motion and gravitation, were discovered. And to us it is enough that gravity does really exist and act according to the laws which we have explained, and abundantly serves to account for all the motions of the celestial bodies and of our sea." Thus, also, it is that the variability of organisms and the known laws of variation and inheritance, and of the influences of external conditions, and the law of Natural Selection, have been discovered. And though it is not enough that variability and selection do really exist and act according to laws which Mr. Darwin has explained (since the limits of their action and efficiency are still to be ascertained), yet it is enough for the present that Darwinians do not rest, like their opponents, contented with framing what Newton would have called, if he had lived after Kant, "*transcendental hypotheses*," which have no place in experimental philosophy. It may be said that Mr. Darwin has invented the hypothesis of Pangenesis, against the rules of this philosophy; but so also did Newton invent the corpuscular theory of light, with a similar purpose and utility.

In determining the limits of the action of Natural Selection, and its sufficiency within these limits, the same demonstrative adequacy should not, for obvious reasons, be demanded as conditions of assenting to its highly probable truth, that Newton proved for his speculation. For the facts for this investigation are hopelessly wanting. Astronomy presents the anomaly, among the physical sciences, of being the only science that deals in the concrete with a few naturally isolated causes, which are separated from all other lines of causation in a way that in other physical sciences can only be imitated in the carefully guarded experiments of physical and chemical laboratories. The study of animals and plants under domestication is, indeed, a similar mode of isolating with a view to ascertaining the physical laws of life by inductive investigations. But the theory of Natural Selection, in its actual application to the phenomena of life and the origin of species, should not be compared to the theory of gravitation in astronomy, nor to the principles of physical science as they appear in the natures that are shut in by the experimental resources of the laboratory, but rather to these principles as they are actually working, and have been working, in the concrete courses of outward nature, in meteorology and physical geology. Still better, perhaps, at least for the purposes of illustration, we may compare the principle of Natural Selection to the fundamental laws of political economy, demonstrated and actually at work in the production of the values and the prices in the market of the wealth which human needs and efforts demand and supply. Who can tell from these principles what the market will be next week, or account for its prices of last week, even by the most ingenious use of hypotheses to supply the missing evidence? The empirical economist and statistician imagines that he can discover some other principles at work, some predetermined regularity in the market, some "innate" principles in it, to which the general laws of political economy are subordinated; and speculating on them, might risk his own wealth in trade, as the speculative "vitalist" might, if anything could be staked on a transcendental hypothesis. In the same way the empirical weather-philosopher thinks he can discern regularities in the weather, which the known principles of mechanical and chemical physics will not account for, and to which they are subordinate. This arises chiefly from his want of imagination, of a clear mental grasp of these principles, and of an adequate knowledge of the resources of legitimate hypothesis to supply the place of the unknown incidental causes through which these principles act. Such are also the sources of most of the difficulties which Mr. Mivart has found in the application of the theory of Natural Selection.

His work is chiefly taken up with these difficulties. He does not so much insist on the probability of his own transcendental hypothesis, as endeavor to make way for it by discrediting the sufficiency of its rival; as if this could serve his purpose; as if experimental philosophy itself, without aid from "Darwinism," would not reject his metaphysical, occult, transcendental hypothesis of a specially predetermined and absolute fixity of species,—an hypothesis which multiplies species in an organism to meet emergencies,—the emergencies of theory,—much as the epicycles of Ptolemy had to be multiplied in the heavens. Ptolemy himself had the sagacity to believe that his was only a mathematical theory, a mode of representation, not a theory of causation; and to prize it only as representative of the facts of observation, or as "saving the appearances." Mr. Mivart's theory, on the other hand, is put forward as a theory of causation, not to save appearances, but to justify the hasty conclusion that they are real; the appearances, namely, of complete temporary fixity, alternating with abrupt changes, in the forms of life which are exhibited by the scanty records of geology and in present apparently unchanging natural species.

Before proceeding to a special consideration of Mr. Mivart's difficulties on the theory of Natural Selection, we will quote from Mr. Darwin's latest work, "The Descent of Man," his latest views of the extent of the action of this principle and its relations to the general theory of evolution. He says (Chapter IV):

"Thus a very large yet undefined extension may safely be given to the direct and indirect results of Natural Selection; but I now admit, after reading the essay by Nägeli on plants, and the remarks by various authors with respect to animals, more especially those recently made by Professor Broca, that in the earlier editions of my 'Origin of Species' I probably attributed too much to the action of Natural Selection, or the survival of the fittest. I have altered the fifth edition of the 'Origin' [the edition which Mr. Mivart reviews in his work] so as to confine my remarks to adaptive changes of structure. I had not formerly sufficiently considered the existence of many structures which appear to be, as far as we can judge, neither beneficial nor injurious; and this I believe to be one of the greatest oversights as yet detected in my work. I may be permitted to say, as some excuse, that I had two distinct objects in view: firstly, to show that species had not been separately created; and secondly, that Natural Selection had been the chief agent of change, though largely aided by the inherited effects of habit, and slightly by the direct action of the surrounding conditions. Nevertheless, I was not able to annul the influence of my former belief, then widely prevalent, that each species had been purposely created; and this led to my tacitly assuming that every detail of structure, excepting rudiments, was of some special, though unrecognized, service. Any one with this assumption in his mind would naturally extend the action of Natural Selection, either during past or present times, too far. Some of those who admit the principle of evolution, but reject Natural Selection, seem to forget, when criticising my work, that I had the above two objects in view; hence, if I have erred in giving to Natural Selection great power, which I am far from admitting, or in having exaggerated its power, which is in itself probable, I have at least, as I hope, done good service in aiding to overthrow the dogma of separate creations."

In one other respect Mr. Darwin has modified his views of the action of Natural Selection, in consequence of a valuable criticism in the North British Review of June, 1867; and Mr. Mivart regards this modification as very important, and says of it that "this admission seems almost to amount to a change of front in the face of the enemy." It is not, as we shall see, an important modification at all, and does not change in any essential particular the theory as propounded in the first edition of the "Origin of Species," but Mr. Mivart's opinion of it has helped us to discover what, without this confirmation, seemed almost incredible,—how completely he has misapprehended, not merely the use of the theory in special applications, which is easily excusable, but also the nature of its general operation and of the causes employed by it; thus furnishing an additional illustration of what he says in his Introduction, that "few things are more remarkable than the way in which it [this theory] has been misunderstood." One other consideration has also been of aid to us. In his concluding chapter on "Theology and Evolution," in which he very ably shows, and on the most venerable authority, that there is no necessary conflict between the strictest orthodoxy and the theory of evolution, he remarks (and quotes Dr. Newman) on the narrowing effect of single lines of study. Not only inabilities may be produced by a one-sided pursuit, but "a positive distaste may grow up, which, in the intellectual order, may amount to a spontaneous and unreasoning disbelief in that which appears to be in opposition to the more familiar concept, and this at all times." This is, of course, meant to apply to those who, from want of knowledge, lack interest in and even acquire a distaste for theological studies. But it also has other and equally important applications. Mr. Mivart, it would at first sight seem, being distinguished as a naturalist and also versed in theology, is not trammeled by any such narrowness as to disable him from giving just weight to both sides of the question he discusses. But what are the two sides? Are they the view of the theologian and the naturalist? Not at all. The debate is between the theologian and descriptive naturalist on one side, or the theologian and the student of natural history in its narrowest sense, that is, systematic biology; and on the other side the physical naturalist, physiologist, or theoretical biologist. Natural history and biology, or the general science of life, are very comprehensive terms, and comprise in their scope widely different lines of pursuit and a wide range of abilities. In fact, the sciences of biology contain contrasts in the objects, abilities, and interests of scientific pursuit almost as wide as that presented by the physical sciences generally, and the sciences of direct observation, description, and classification. The same contrast holds, indeed, even in a science so limited in its material objects as astronomy. The genius of the practical astronomer and observer is very different from that of the physical astronomer and mathematician; though success in this science generally requires nowadays that some degree of both should be combined. So the genius of the physiologist is different from that of the naturalist proper, though in the study of comparative anatomy the observer has to exercise some of the skill in analysis and in the use of hypotheses in which the student of the physical sciences displays his genius in the search for unknown causes. We may, perhaps, comprise all the forms of intellectual genius (excluding æsthetics) under three chief classes, namely, first, the genius that pursues successfully the researches for unknown causes by the skillful use of hypothesis and experiment; secondly, that which, avoiding the use of hypotheses or preconceptions altogether and the delusive influence of names, brings together in clear connections and contrasts in classification the objects of nature in their broadest and most real relations of resemblance; and thirdly, that genius which seeks with success for reasons and authorities in support of cherished convictions.

That Mr. Mivart may have the last two forms of genius, even in a notable degree, we readily admit; but that he has not the first to the degree needed for an inquiry, which is essentially a branch of physical science, we propose to show. We have already pointed out how his theological education, his schooling against Democritus, has misled him in regard to the meaning of "accidents" or accidental causes in physical science; as if to the physical philosopher these could possibly be an absolute and distinct class, not included under the law of causation, "that every event must have a cause or determinate antecedents," whether we can trace them out or not. The accidental causes of science are only "accidents" relatively to the intelligence of a man. Eclipses have the least of this character to the astronomer of all the phenomena of nature; yet to the savage they are the most terrible of monstrous accidents. The accidents of monstrous variation, or even of the small and limited variations normal in any race or species, are only accidents relatively to the intelligence of the naturalist, or to his knowledge of general physiology. An accident is what cannot be anticipated from what we know, or by any intelligence, perhaps, which is less than omniscient.

But this is not the most serious misconception of the accidental causes of science, which Mr. Mivart has fallen into. He utterly mistakes the particular class of accidents concerned in the process of Natural Selection. To make this clear, we will enumerate the classes of causes which are involved in this process. In the first place, there are the external conditions of an animal's or plant's life, comprising chiefly its relations to other organic beings, but partly its relations to inorganic nature, and determining its needs and some of the means of satisfying them. These conditions are consequences of the external courses of events or of the partial histories of organic and inorganic nature. In the second place, there are the general principles of the fitness of means to ends, or of supplies to needs. These comprise the best ascertained and most fundamental of all the principles of science, such as the laws of mechanical, optical, and acoustical science, by which we know how a leg, arm, or wing, a bony frame, a muscular or a vascular system, an eye or an ear, can be of *use*. In the third place, there are the causes introduced by Mr. Darwin to the attention of physiologists, as normal facts of organic nature, the little known phenomena of variation, and their relations to the laws of inheritance. There are several classes of these. The most important in the theory of Natural Selection are the diversities *always existing* in any race of animals or plants, called "individual differences," which *always* determine a better fitness of some individuals to the general conditions of the existence of a race than other less fortunate individuals possess. The more than specific agreements in characters, which the best fitted individuals of a race must thus exhibit, ought, if possible, according to Cuvier's principles of zoölogy, to be included in the description of a species (as a norm or type which only the *best* exhibit), instead of the rough averages to which the naturalist really resorts in defining species by marks or characters that are variable. But probably such averages in variable characters are really close approximations to the characters of the best general adaptation; for variation being, so far as known, irrespective of adaptation, is as likely to exist to the same extent on one side of the norm of utility as on the other, or by excess as generally as by defect. Though variation is irrespective of utility, its limits are not. Too great a departure from the norm of utility must put an end to life and its successions. Utility therefore, in conjunction with the laws of inheritance, determines not only the middle line or safest way of a race, but also the bounding limits of its path of life; and so long as the conditions and principles of utility embodied in a form of life remain unchanged, they will, together with the laws of inheritance, maintain a race unchanged in its average characters.

"Specific stability," therefore, for which theological and descriptive naturalists have speculated a transcendental cause, is even more readily and directly accounted for by the causes which the theory of Natural Selection regards than is specific change. But just as obviously it follows from these causes that a change in the conditions and resources of utility, not only may but must change the normal characters of a species, or else the race must perish. Again, a slow and gradual change in the conditions of existence must, on these principles, slowly change the middle line or safest way of life (the descriptive or graphic line); but always, of course, this change must be within the existing limits of variation, or the range of "individual differences." A change in these limits would then follow, or the range of "individual differences" would be extended, at least, so far as we know, in the direction of the change. That it is widened or extended to a greater range by rapid and important changes in conditions of existence, is a matter of observation in many races of animals and plants that have been long subject to domestication or to the capricious conditions imposed by human choice and care. This phenomenon is like what would happen if a roadway or path across a field were to become muddy or otherwise obstructed. The traveled way would swerve to one side, or be broadened, or abandoned, according to the nature and degree of the obstruction, and to the resources of travel that remained. This class of variations, that is, "individual differences," constant and normal in a race, but having different ranges in different races, or in the same race under different circumstances, may be regarded as in no proper sense accidentally related to the advantages that come from them; or in no other sense than a tendril, or a tentacle, or a hand searching in the dark, is accidentally related to the object it succeeds in finding. And yet we say properly that it was by "accident" that a certain tendril was put forth so as to fulfill its function, and clasp the particular object by which it supports the vine; or that it was an accidental movement of the tentacle or hand that brought the object it has secured within its grasp. The search was, and continues to be, normal and general; it is the particular success only that is accidental; and this only in the sense that lines of causation, stretching backwards infinitely, and unrelated except in a first cause, or in the total order of nature, come together and by their concurrence produce it. Yet over even this concurrence "law" still presides, to the effect that for every such concurrence the same consequences follow.

But Mr. Mivart, with his mind filled with horror of "blind chance," and of "the fortuitous concourse of atoms," has entirely overlooked the class of accidental variations, on which, even in the earlier editions of the "Origin of Species," the theory of Natural Selection is based, and has fixed his attention exclusively on another class, namely, abnormal or unusual variations, which Mr. Darwin at first supposed might also be of service in this process. The error of his critic might, perhaps, be regarded as due to Mr. Darwin's failure to distinguish sufficiently the two classes, as well as to his overlooking, until it was pointed out in the article in the "North British Review," before referred to, the fact that the latter class could be of no service; if it were not that Mr. Mivart's work is a review of the last edition of the "Origin of Species" and of the treatise on "Animals and Plants under Domestication," in both of which Mr. Darwin has emphatically distinguished the two classes, and admitted that it is upon the first class only that Natural Selection can normally depend; though the second class of unusual and monstrous variations may give rise, by highly improbable though possible accidents, to changes in the characters of whole races. Mr. Mivart characterizes this admission by the words we have quoted, that "it seems almost to amount to a change of front in the face of the enemy"; of which it might have been enough to say, that the strategy of science is not the same as that of rhetorical disputation, and aims at cornering facts, not antagonists But Mr. Mivart profits by it as a scholastic triumph over he esy, which he insists upon celebrating, rather than as a correction of his own misconceptions of the theory. He continues throughout his book to speak of the variations on which Natural Selection depends as if they were all of rare occurrence, like abrupt and monstrous variations, instead of being always present in a race; and also as having the additional disadvantage of being "individually slight," "minute," "insensible," "infinitesimal," "fortuitous," and "indefinite." These epithets are variously combined in different passages, but his favorite compendious formula is, "minute, fortuitous, and indefinite variations." When, however, he comes to consider the enormous time which such a process must have taken to produce the present forms of life, he brings to bear all his forces, and says (p. 154): "It is not easy to believe that less than two thousand million years would be required for the totality of animal development by no other means than minute, fortuitous, occasional, and intermitting variations in all conceivable directions." This exceeds very much—by some two hundred-fold—the length of time Sir William Thomson allows for the continuance of life on the earth. It is difficult to see how, with such uncertain "fortuitous, occasional, and intermitting" elements, our author could have succeeded in making any calculations at all. On the probability of the correctness of Sir William Thomson's physical arguments "the author of this book cannot presume to advance an opinion; but," he adds (p. 150), "the fact that they have not been refuted pleads strongly in their favor when we consider how much they tell against the theory of Mr. Darwin." He can, it appears, judge of them on his own side.

For the descriptive epithets which Mr. Mivart applies to the variations on which he supposes Natural Selection to depend he has the following authority. He says (p. 35): "Now it is distinctly enunciated by Mr. Darwin that the spontaneous variations upon which his theory depends are individually slight, minute, and insensible. He says *(Animals and Plants under Domestication*, Vol. II, p. 192): 'Slight individual differences, however, suffice for the work, and are probably the sole differ-

ences which are effective in the production of new species.'"
After what we have said as to the real nature of the differences
from which nature selects, it might be, perhaps, unnecessary
to explain what ought at least to have been known to a naturalist, that by "individual differences" is meant the differences
between the individuals of a race of animals or plants; that
the slightness of them is only relative to the differences between
the characters of species, and that they may be very considerable in themselves, or their effects, or even to the *eye* of the
naturalist.   How the expression "slight individual differences"
could have got translated in the writer's mind into "individually slight, minute, and insensible" ones, has no natural explanation.   But this is not the only instance of such an unfathomable translation in Mr. Mivart's treatment of the theory of
Natural Selection.   Two others occur on page 133.   In the
first he says : " Mr. Darwin abundantly demonstrates the variability of dogs, horses, fowls, and pigeons, but he none the less
shows the *very small* extent to which the goose, the peacock,
and the guinea-fowl have varied.   Mr. Darwin attempts to
explain this fact as regards the goose by the animal being
valued only for food and feathers, and from no pleasure having
been felt in it on other accounts.   He adds, however, at the
end, the striking remark, which concedes the whole position,
'but the goose seems to have *a singularly inflexible organization.*'"   The translation is begun in the author's italics, and
completed a few pages further on (p. 141), where, recurring
to this subject, he says : "We have seen that Mr. Darwin himself implicitly admits the principle of specific stability in asserting the singular inflexibility of the organization of the goose."
This is what is called in scholastic logic, *Fallacia a dicto
secundum quid ad dictum simpliciter.*   The obvious meaning,
both from the contexts and the evidence, of the expression,
"singularly inflexible," is that the goose has been much less
changed by domestication than other domestic birds.   But this
relative inflexibility is understood by Mr. Mivart as an admission
of an *absolute* one, in spite of the evidence that geese have varied from the wild type, and have individual differences, and
even differences of breeds, which are sufficiently conspicuous,

even to the eye of a goose. The next instance of Mr. Mivart's translations (p. 133) is still more remarkable. He continues: "This is not the only place in which such expressions are used. He [Mr. Darwin] elsewhere makes use of phrases which quite harmonize with the conception of a normal specific constancy, but varying greatly and suddenly at intervals. Thus he speaks of a *whole organism seeming to have become plastic and tending to depart from the parental type* ('Origin of Species,' 5th edit., 1869, p. 13)." The italics are Mr. Mivart's. The passage from which these words are quoted (though they are not put in quotation-marks) is this: "It is well worth while carefully to study the several treatises on some of our old cultivated plants, as on the hyacinth, potato, even the dahlia, etc.; and it is really surprising to note the endless points in structure and constitution in which the varieties and sub-varieties differ slightly from each other. The whole organization seems to have become plastic, and tends to depart *in a slight degree* from that of the parental type." The words that we have italicized in this quotation are omitted by Mr. Mivart, though essential to the point on which he cites Mr. Darwin's authority, namely, as to the organism "varying greatly and suddenly at intervals." Logic has no adequate name for this fallacy; but there is another in Mr. Mivart's understanding of the passage which is very familiar,—the fallacy of ambiguous terms. Mr. Darwin obviously uses the word "plastic" in its secondary signification as the name of that which is "capable of being moulded, modeled, or fashioned to the purpose, as clay." His critic quite as obviously understands it in its primary signification as the name of anything "having the power to give form." But this is a natural enough misunderstanding, since in scholastic philosophy the primary signification of "plastic" is the prevailing one.

Such being Mr. Mivart's misconceptions of the principle of Natural Selection, and such their source, it would be useless to follow him in his tests of it by hypothetical illustrations from the history of animals; but we are bound to make good our assertion that his difficulties have arisen, not only from his want of a clear mental grasp of principles, but also from an inadequate knowledge of the resources of legitimate hypothesis to supply the unknown incidental causes through which the principle has acted. These deficiencies of knowledge and imagination, though more excusable, are not less conspicuous in his criticisms than the defects we have noticed. He says (p. 59): "It may be objected, perhaps, that these difficulties are difficulties of *ignorance ;* that we cannot explain them, because we do not know *enough* of the animals." It is not surprising that he adds: "But it is here contended that this is not the case; it is not that we merely fail to see how Natural Selection acted, but that there is a positive incompatibility between the cause assigned and the results." And no wonder that he remarks at the close of the chapter (Chapter II): "That minute, fortuitous, and indefinite variations could have brought about such special forms and modifications as have been enumerated in this chapter seems to contradict, not imagination, but reason."

In this chapter on "Incipient Structures," two facts are quite overlooked,—the one, which is so conspicuous in the principles of comparative anatomy, how few the fundamental structures are, which have been turned to such numerous uses; that is, how meagre have been the resources of Natural Selection, so far as it has depended on the occurrence of structures which were of no previous use, or were not already partially useful in directions in which they have been modified by the selection and inheritance of "individual differences"; the other, how important to Natural Selection have been the principles of indirect utility and "correlated acquisition," dependent as they are on ultimate physical laws. The human hand is still useful in swimming, and the fishes' fins could even be used for holding or clasping, if there were occasion for it. We might well attribute the paucity of indifferent types of structure to the agency of the rarest accidents of nature, though not in a theological sense. Animals and plants are no longer dependent for improvement on their occurrence, and, perhaps, never were after their competition and struggle for existence had fully begun. It is so much easier for them to turn to better account powers that they already possess in small degrees. Previously to such a competition and struggle, when the whole field of the inorganic conditions of life was open to simple organisms, they were doubtless much more variable than afterwards. But variability would then have been, as it is now, in no absolute sense accidental. On the contrary, variation, instead of comparative stability in species, would have been the most prominent normal feature of life. The tentative powers of life, trying all things, but not holding fast to that which is good, or not so firmly as afterwards, instead of its hereditary features, would have been its most characteristic manifestation. Our author's general difficulty in this chapter is as to how variations too small to have been of use could have been preserved, and he is correct in thinking that it could not be by Natural Selection, or the survival of the fittest, but wrong in thinking that variations are generally so rare or so insignificant, even in present forms of life as to require a power other than those of life in general to bring them forth when needed, or to produce them in useful amounts.

The first example of the working of Natural Selection is the well-known case of the neck of the giraffe. This, it has been imagined, though not by Mr. Darwin, was produced by its supposed use in aiding this animal to feed on the foliage of trees, and by the occasional advantage of length of neck to the highest reaching individuals, when in drought and scarcity the ground vegetation and lower foliage were consumed enabling them to survive the others and in continuing the species, to transmit this advantage to their offspring. Without denying that this is an excellent hypothetical illustration of the process of Natural Selection, Mr. Mivart attacks its probability as a matter of fact. In reply to it he says: "But against this it may be said, in the first place, that the argument proves too much; for, on this supposition, many species must have tended to undergo a similar modification and we ought to have at least several forms similar to the giraffe developed from different *Ungulata*," or hoofed beasts. We would even go further than Mr. Mivart, and hold that, on the hypothesis in question, not only several forms, but the whole order of *Ungulata*, or large portions of it, should have been similarly modified; at least those inhabiting regions subject to droughts and presenting the alternative of grazing on the ground and browsing on the foliage of high trees. But as these alternatives do not universally exist in regions inhabited by such animals, very long necks would not, perhaps, if this hypothesis were true, characterize the whole order; as the habit of herding does, for example. We may observe, however, that this illustration from the giraffe's neck is not an *argument* at all, and proves nothing, though the hypothesis employed by it is very well called in question by Mr. Mivart's criticism. But can Mr. Mivart suppose that, having fairly called in question the importance of the high-feeding use of the giraffe's neck, he has thereby destroyed the utility of the neck altogether, not only to the theory of Natural Selection, but also to the animal itself? Is there, then, no important use in the giraffe's neck? Is it really the monstrosity it appears to be, when seen out of relation to the normal conditions of the animal's life? But if there be any utility left in the neck, as a teleologist or a believer in Final Causes would assume without question, and in spite of this criticism, then this other utility might serve the purposes of Natural Selection even better perhaps than that of the mistaken hypothesis. If Mr. Mivart had approached this subject in the proper spirit, his criticism would probably have led him to an important observation, which his desire to discredit a much more important discovery has hidden from his view. He would have inquired what are the conditions of existence of the Ungulates generally and of the giraffe in particular, which are so close pressing and so emphatically attest the grounds of their severest struggle for life, as to be likely to cause in them the highest degree of specialty and adaptation. The question of food is obviously not concerned in such a struggle, for this order of animals lives generally upon food which is the most abundant and most easily obtained. Mr. Mivart compares his objection to one that has been made against Mr. Wallace's views as to the uses of color in animals, that "color being dangerous, should not exist in nature,' or

that "a dull color being needful, all animals should be so colored." He quotes Mr. Wallace's reply, but does not take the
clue to the solution of his difficulty respecting the giraffe's neck,
which it almost forces on him. This reply was, that many animals can afford brilliant colors, and their various direct uses
or values, when the animals are otherwise provided with sufficient protection, and that brilliant colors are even sometimes
indirectly protective. The quills of the porcupine, the shells of
tortoises and mussels, the very hard coats of certain beetles, the
stings of certain other insects, the nauseous taste of brilliantly
colored caterpillars, and other instances, are given as examples
of protection with color. Now, what bearing has this on the
long neck of the giraffe? According to Mr. Mivart, who is
himself at this point on the defensive, it is as follows. He says:
"But because many different kinds of animals can elude the
observation or defy the attack of enemies in a great variety of
ways, it by no means follows that there are any similar number
and variety of ways for attaining vegetable food in a country
where all such food other than the lofty branches of trees
has been destroyed. In such a country we have a number
of vegetable-feeding Ungulates, all of which present minute
variations as to the length of the neck." Mr. Mivart is apparently not aware that he is here arguing, not against the theory
of Natural Selection, but against a subordinate and false hypothesis under it. But if he thinks thus to undermine the
theory, it must be because he is not aware of, or has not
present to his imagination, the numberless ingenuities of nature, and the resources of support the theory has to rest upon.

There can be no doubt that the neck of the giraffe, whatever
other uses it can be put to, and it is put to several, is pre-eminently useful as a *watch-tower*. Its eyes, large and lustrous,
"which beam with a peculiarly mild but fearless expression,
are so placed as to take in a wider range of the horizon than is
subject to the vision of any other quadruped. While browsing
on its favorite acacia, the giraffe, by means of its laterally pro-
jecting orbits, can direct its sight so as to anticipate a threat-
ened attack in the rear from the stealthy lion or any other foe
of the desert." When attacked, the giraffe can defend itself

by powerful blows with its well-armed hoofs, and even its short horns can inflict fatal blows by the sidelong swing of its neck. But these are not its only protections against danger. Its nostrils can be voluntarily closed, like the camel's, against the sandy, suffocating clouds of the desert. "The tail of the giraffe looks like an artificially constructed fly-flapper; and it seems at first incredible," says Mr. Darwin, "that this could have been adapted for its present purpose by successive slight modifications, each better and better fitted, for so trifling an object as to drive away flies; yet we should pause before being too positive, even in this case, for we know that the distribution and existence of cattle and other animals in South America absolutely depend on their power of resisting the attacks of insects; so that individuals which could, by any means, defend themselves from these small enemies, would be able to range into new pastures, and thus gain a great advantage. It is not that the larger quadrupeds are actually destroyed (except in rare cases) by flies, but they are incessantly harrassed and their strength reduced, so that they are more subject to disease, or not so well enabled in a coming dearth to search for food, or to escape from beasts of prey."

This passage recalls our main problem, which does not concern the giraffe alone, but all the Ungulates; and its solution will show that this order of animals exhibits, almost as well as Mr. Wallace's examples, the resources that nature has for the protection of animals that have the disadvantage, not, indeed, generally of brilliant colors, but of exposure by living exclusively on bulky and comparatively innutritious food. Nearly all the resources of defensive warfare are exhausted in their specialties of protection. The giraffe alone is provided with a natural watch-tower, but the others are not left without defense. All, or nearly all, live in armies or herds, and some post sentinels around their herds. The numerous species of the antelope resort to natural fortifications or fastnesses. "They are the natives for the most part of the wildest and least accessible places in the warmer latitudes of the globe, frequenting the cliffs and ledges of mountain rocks or the verdure-clad banks of tropical streams, or the oases of the desert." Other tribes depend on their fleetness, and on hiding in woods like the deer. Others, again, on great powers of endurance in flight and long marches, like the camels with their commissaries of provision. Others, again, with powerful frames, like the rhinoceros and the bisons, resort to defensive attack. The ruminant habits and organs of large numbers are adapted to rapid and dangerous foraging, and to digestion under protection from beasts of prey and insects.

But Mr. Mivart, with little fertility of defense for the theory of Natural Selection, is still not without some ingenuity in attack. He objects, in the second place, that the longest necked giraffes, being by so much the larger animals, would not be strong in proportion, but would need more food to sustain them, a disadvantage which would, perhaps, more than outbalance the neck in times of drought; and he cites Mr. Spencer's ingenious speculations on the relations of size, food, and strength, in confirmation of this objection. But he forgets or overlooks the important physiological law of the compensation or economy of growth which prevails in variations. A longer neck does not necessarily entail a greater bulk or weight on the animal as a whole. The neck may have grown at the expense of the hind parts in the ancestors of the giraffe. If we met with an individual man with a longer neck than usual, we should not expect to find him heavier, or relatively weaker, or requiring more food on that account.

But let us pass to the next illustration of the insufficiency of Natural Selection. This is the difficulty Mr. Mivart finds in attributing to this cause various cases of mimicry or protective resemblances of animals to other animals, or to other natural objects. In some insects this is carried to a wonderful extent. Thus, some which imitate leaves when at rest, in the sizes, shapes, colors, and markings of their wings, "extend the imitation even to the very injuries on those leaves made by the attacks of insects or fungi." Thus Mr. Wallace says of the walking-stick insects: "One of these creatures, obtained by myself in Borneo, was covered over with foliaceous excrescences of a clear olive-green color so as exactly to resemble a stick grown over by creeping moss or jungermannia. The Dyak who brought it me assured me it was grown over with moss, although alive, and it was only after a most minute examination that I could convince myself it was not so." And in speaking of the leaf-butterfly, he says: "We come to a still more extraordinary part of the imitation, for we find representations of leaves in every stage of decay, variously blotched and mildewed, and pierced with holes, and in many cases irregularly covered with powdery black dots, gathered into patches and spots, so closely resembling the various kinds of minute fungi that grow on dead leaves that it is impossible to avoid thinking, at first sight, that the butterflies themselves have been attacked by real fungi." Upon these passages Mr. Mivart remarks: "Here imitation has attained a development which seems utterly beyond the power of the mere 'survival of the fittest' to produce. How this double mimicry can importantly aid in the struggle for life seems puzzling indeed, but much more so how the first beginnings of the imitation of such injuries in the leaf can be developed in the animal into such a complete representation of them; *a fortiori*, how simultaneous and similar first beginnings of imitations of such injuries could ever have been developed in several individuals, out of utterly indifferent and indeterminate infinitesimal variations in all conceivable directions."

What ought to have been first suggested to a naturalist by this wonderful mimicry is, what clever entomologists some insectivorous birds must have become to be able to press the conditions of existence and the struggle for life in these insects to such a degree of specialty. But this, after all, is not so very wonderful, when we consider what microscopic sight these birds must have acquired and what practice and exclusive interest in the pursuit! We may feel pretty confident, however, that neither Natural Selection nor any occult or transcendental cause has ever carried protective mimicry beyond eyesight, though it may well be a better eyesight than that even of a skillful naturalist. There is no necessity to suppose, with our author, that the variations on which this selection depended were either simultaneous, or infinitesimal, or indifferent, for "individual differences" are always considerable and generally greatest in directions in which variations have already most recently occurred, as in characters in which closely allied races differ most from each other; but, doubtless, a very long time was required for these very remarkable cases of mimicry to come to pass. The difficulties they present resemble those of the development of sight itself, on which Mr. Mivart comments elsewhere; but in these particular cases the conditions of "hide and seek" in the sport of nature offer correlated difficulties, which, like acid and alkali, serve to neutralize each other. In these cases, four distinct forms of life of widely diverse origins, or very remotely connected near the beginnings of life itself, like four main branches of a tree, have come together into closest relations, as parts of the foliage of the four main branches might do. These are certain insectivorous birds, certain higher vegetable forms, the imitated sticks or leaves, certain vegetable parasites on them, and the mimicking insects. But the main phenomenon was and is the neck-and-neck race of variation and the selection between the powers of hiding in the insect and the powers of finding in the bird. Mr. Mivart overlooks the fact that variations in the bird are quite as essential to the process as those of the insect, and has chosen to consider elsewhere the difficulties which the developments of the eye present, and to consider them in equal independence of its obvious uses. The fact that these, as well as other extraordinary cases of mimicry, are found only in tropical climates, or climates equable not only in respect to short periodic but also secular changes, accords well with the probable length of time in which this competition has been kept up; and the extraordinary, that is, rare character of the phenomenon agrees well with the probable supposition that it has always begun in what we call in science "an accident." If its beginnings were common, their natural consequences would also be common, and would not be wonderful; and if it arose from a destructive, unintelligent, evil principle,—from Ahriman,—it has, at least, shown how the course of nature has been able to avoid destruction, to the astonishment of human intelligence, and how Oromasdes has been able to defeat his antagonist by turning evil into good.

Let us take next Mr. Mivart's treatment of a supposed origin of the mammary, or milk glands:

" Is it conceivable," he asks (p. 60), "that the young of any animal was ever saved from destruction by accidentally sucking a drop of scarcely nutritious fluid from an accidentally hypertrophied cutaneous gland of its mother? And even if one was so, what chance was there of the perpetuation of such a variation? On the hypothesis of 'Natural Selection' itself we must assume that, up to that time, the race had been well adapted to the surrounding conditions; the temporary and accidental trial and change of conditions, which caused the so-sucking young one to be the 'fittest to survive' under the supposed circumstances, would soon cease to act, and then the progeny of the mother, with the accidentally hypertrophied sebaceous glands, would have no tendency to survive the far-outnumbering descendants of the normal ancestral form."

Here, as before, Mr. Mivart stakes the fate of the theory on the correctness of his own conceptions of the conditions of its action. He forgets, first of all, that the use of a milk gland in its least specialized form requires at least a sucking mouth, and that sucking mouths and probosces have very extensive uses in the animal kingdom. They are good for drinking water and nectar, and are used for drawing blood as well as milk; and, without reference to alimentation, are still serviceable for *support* to parasitical animals. Might not the young, which before birth are, in a high degree, parasitical in all animals, find it highly advantageous to continue the habit after birth, even without reference to food, but for the generally quite as important use of protection against enemies, by clinging by a sucking mouth to the body of its dam? If this should cause sebaceous glands to become hypertrophied and ultimately a valuable or even an exclusive source of nutrition, it would, perhaps, be proper to describe the phenomenon as an unintended or accidental, but not as a rare or improbable one. Moreover, though on the theory of Natural Selection (or, indeed, on any theory of the continuance of a race by modifications of structures and habits), the race must, while it lives, be fitted to live, yet it need be no more fitted to do so than to survive in its offspring. No race is so well fitted to its general conditions of existence, but that some individuals are better fitted than others, and have, on the average, an advantage. And new resources do not imply abandonment of the old, but only additions to them, giving superiorities that are almost never superfluous. How, indeed, but by accidents of the rarest occurrence, could variation (much less selection) give superfluous advantages, on the whole, or except temporarily and so far as normal variations anticipate in general, regular, or usual changes in the conditions of existence? We have, to be sure, on the hypothesis we have proposed, still to account for the original of the sucking mouth, though its numerous uses are obvious enough, on the really uniform and unvarying types of natural law, the laws of inorganic physics, the principles of suction. But we are not ambitious to rival nature in ingenuity, only to contrast its resources with those of our naturalist.

His next example is a criticism of the theory of Sexual Selection. Speaking of apes, he says: "When we consider what is known of the emotional nature of these animals and the periodicity of its intensification, it is hardly credible that a female would often risk life or limb through her admiration of a trifling shade of color or an infinitesimally greater, though irresistibly fascinating degree of wartiness." Is it credible that Mr. Mivart can suppose that the higher or spiritual emotions, like affection, taste, conscience, ever act *directly* to modify or compete with the more energetic lower impulses, and not rather by forestalling and indirectly regulating them, as by avoiding temptation in the case of conscience; or by establishing social arrangements, companionships, friendships, and more or less permanent marriages in the case of sexual preferences? All such arrangements, all grounds for the action of taste or admiration, or any but the most monstrous friendships, are prevented or removed in the lives of caged beasts. His example and his inference from it are as much as if an explorer should discover a half-famished tribe of savages sustaining life upon bitter and nauseous food, and should conclude that not only these but all savages, the most provident, or even all men, are without any choice in food, and that in providing for future wants they are influenced by no other considerations than the grossest cravings of appetite.

But to return to Natural Selection. The next example is

that of the rattling and expanding powers of poisonous snakes. The author says that "in poisonous serpents, also, we have structures which, at all events, at first sight, seem positively hurtful to these reptiles. Such are the rattle of the rattlesnake and the expanding neck of the cobra, the former serving to warn the ear of the intended victim as the latter warns the eye." This "first sight" is all the use our author discovers in these organs; but why should these warnings be intended or used to drive away intended *victims* rather than *enemies?* Or is it among the intentions of nature to defeat those of the serpent? If the effects of such "warnings" really were to deprive these snakes of their proper food, would not experience itself and intelligence be sufficient in the wily serpent to correct such perverse instincts? It is, indeed, at first sight, curious that certain snakes, though these are the sluggish kinds, and cannot so easily escape their enemies by flight as others can, should be provided, not only with poisonous fangs, but with these means of warning either victims or dangerous enemies. But Mr. Wallace has furnished a clew to their correlation by his example of the relations between conspicuous colors and nauseous tastes in many caterpillars, the color serving as a sign of the taste and warning birds not to touch these kinds. The poisonous fang and its use are expensive and risky means of defense; the warnings associated with them are cheap and safe. But if, as is very likely, these "warnings" are also used against intended victims, they can only be used either to paralyze them with terror or allure them from curiosity, or to produce in them that curious and paralyzing mixture of the two emotions, alarm and something like curiosity, which is all that is probably true of the supposed powers of fascination* in serpents. Perhaps, also, the rattle serves to inspire the sluggish snake itself with courage; and in this case the rattle will serve

---

* This is a real condition of mind in the subject of it; a condition in which interest or emotion gives to an idea such fixity and power that it takes possession at a fatal moment of the will and acts itself out; as in the fascination of the precipice. It is not, however, to be regarded as a natural contrivance in the mental acquisitions of the victims for the benefit of the serpent any more than the serpent's warnings are for their benefit; but as a consequence of ultimate mental laws in general, of which the serpent s faculties and habits take advantage.

all the purposes that drums, trumpets, and gongs do in human warfare. The swaying body and vibrating tongue of most snakes, and the expanding neck and the hood of the cobras, may serve for banners. But the rattle has also been supposed to serve as a sexual call, very much as the inspirations of warfare are turned into the allurements of the tournament, or as gongs also serve to call travelers to dinner. What poverty of resources in regard to the relations of *use* in the lives of animals thus distinguishes our naturalist from the natural order of things! What wealth and capital are left for the employments and industries of Natural Selection!

In the next chapter Mr. Mivart charges the theory of Natural Selection with inability to account for independent similarities of structure; "that it does not harmonize with the co-existence of closely similar structures of diverse origin," like the dental structures in the dog and in the carnivorous marsupial, the Thylacine, closely similar structures and of exactly the same utilities, though belonging to races so diverse that their common ancestors could not have been like them in respect to this resemblance. But these structures really differ in points not essential to their utilities; in characters which, though inconspicuous, are marks of the two great divisions of mammalia, to which these animals belong. Mr. Mivart here attacks the theory in its very citadel, and has incautiously left a hostile force in his rear. He has claimed in the preceding chapter for Natural Selection that it ought to have produced several independent races of long-necked Ungulates, as well as the giraffe; so that, instead of pursuing his illustrations any further, we may properly demand his surrender. Of course Natural Selection requires for similar products similar means and conditions; but these are of such a general sort that they belong to wide ranges of life; and as it does not act by "blind chance," or theological accidents, but by the invariable laws of nature and the tentative powers of life, it is not surprising that it often repeats its patterns independently of descent, or of the copying powers of inheritance.

That the highest products of nature are not the results of the mere forces of inheritance, and do not come from the birth of latent powers and structures, seems to be the lesson of the obscure discourse in which Jesus endeavored to instruct Nicodemus the Pharisee. How is it that a man can be born again, acquire powers and characters that are not developments of what is already innate in him? How is it possible when he is old to acquire new innate principles, or to enter a second time into his mother's womb and be born? The reply does not suggest our author's hypothesis of a life turning over upon a new "facet," or a new set of latent inherited powers. Only the symbols, water and the Spirit, which Christians have ever since worshiped, are given in reply; but the remarkable illustration of the accidentality of nature is added, which has been almost equally though independently admired. "Marvel not that I said unto thee, Ye must be born again. The wind bloweth where it listeth, and thou hearest the sound thereof, but canst not tell whence it cometh and whither it goeth; so is every one that is born of the Spirit." The highest products of nature are the outcome of its total and apparently accidental orders; or are born of water and the Spirit, which symbolize creative power. To this the Pharisee replied: "How can these things be?" And the answer is still more significant: "Art thou a master of Israel and knowest not these things?" We bring natural evidences, "and ye receive not our witness. If I have told you earthly (natural) things, and ye believe not, how shall ye believe if I tell you heavenly (supernatural) things?" The bearing of our subject upon the doctrine of Final Causes in natural history has been much discussed and is of considerable importance to our author's theory and criticism. But we propose, not only to distinguish between this branch of theology and the theories of inductive science on one hand, but still more emphatically, on the other hand, between it and the Christian faith in divine superintendency, which is very liable to be confounded with it. The Christian faith is that even the fall of a sparrow is included in this agency, and that as men are of more value than many sparrows, so much more is their security. So far from weakening this faith by showing the connection between value and security, science and the theory of Natural Selection have confirmed it. The very agencies that give values to life secure them by planting them most broadly in the immutable grounds of utility. But Natural Theology has sought by Platonic, not Christian, imaginations to discover, not the relations of security to value, but something *worthy* to be the source of the value considered as *absolute*, some particular worthy source of each valued end. This is the motive of that speculation of Final Causes which Bacon condemned as sterile and corrupting to philosophy, interfering, as it does, with the study of the facts of nature, or of what *is*, by preconceptions, necessarily imperfect as to what *ought to be;* and by deductions from assumed *ends*, thought worthy to be the purposes of nature. The naturalists who "take care not to ascribe to God any intention," sin rather against the spirit of Platonism than that of Christianity, while obeying the precepts of experimental philosophy. Though, as our author says, in speaking of the moral sense and the impossibility, as he thinks, that the accumulations of small repugnances could give rise to the strength of its abhorrence and reprobation; though, as he says, " no stream can rise higher than its source "; while fully admitting the truth of this, we would still ask, Where is its source ? Surely not in the little fountains that Platonic explorers go in search of, *a priori*, which would soon run dry but for the rains of heaven, the water and the vapor of the distilling atmosphere. Out of this come also the almost weightless snow-flakes, which, combined in masses of great gravity, fall in the avalanche. The results of moralizing Platonism should not be confounded with the simple Christian faith in Divine superintendence. The often-quoted belief of Professor Gray, "that variation has been led along certain beneficial lines, like a stream along definite lines of irrigation," might be interpreted to agree with either view. The lines on which variations are generally useful are lines of search, and their particular successes, dependent, it is true, on no theological or absolute accidents, may be regarded as being lines of beneficial variations, seeing that they have resulted through laws of nature and principles of utility in higher living forms, or even in continuing definite forms of life on the earth. But thousands of movements of variation, or efforts of search, have not succeeded to one that has.   These are not continued along evil lines, since thousands of forms have perished in consequence of them for every one that has survived.

The growth of a tree is a good illustration of this process, and more closely resembles the action of selection in nature generally than might at first sight appear; for its branches are selected growths, a few out of many thousands that have begun in buds; and this rigorous selection has been effected by the accidents that have determined in surviving growths superior relations to their supplies of nutriment in the trunk and in exposure to light and air.   This exposure (as great as is consistent with secure connection with the sources of sap) seems actually to be sought, and the form of the tree to be the result of some foresight in it.   But the real seeking process is budding, and the geometrical regularity of the production of buds in twigs has little or nothing to do with the ultimate selected results, the distributions of the branches, which are different for each individual tree.   Even if the determinate variations really existed,—the "facets" of stable equilibrium in life, which Mr. Mivart supposes,—and were arranged with geometrical regularity on their spheroid of potential forms, as leaves and buds are in the twig, they would probably have as little to do with determining the ultimate diversities of life under the action of the selection which our author admits, as phyllotaxy has to do with the branching of trees.   But phyllotaxy, also, has its utility.   Its orders are the best for packing the incipient leaves in the bud, and the best for the exposure to light and air of the developed leaves of the stem.   But here its utility ends, except so far as its arrangements also present the greatest diversity of finite elements, within the smallest limits, for the subsequent choice of successful growths; being *the nearest approaches that finite regularity could make* to "indefinite variations in all conceivable directions."   The general resemblance of trees of a given kind depends on no formative principle other than physical and physiological properties in the woody tissue, and is related chiefly to the tenacity, flexibility, and vascularity of this tissue, the degrees of which might almost be inferred from the general form of the tree.   It cannot be doubted, in the case of the tree, that this tentative though regular budding has been of service to the production of the tree's growth, and that the particular growths which have survived and become the bases of future growths were determined by a beneficial though accidental order of events under the total orders of the powers concerned in the tree's development. But if a rigorous selection had not continued in this growth, no proper branching would have resulted. The tree would have grown like a cabbage. Hence it is to selection, and not to variation,—or rather to the *causes* of selection, and not to those of variation,—that species, or well-marked and widely separated forms of life, are due. If we could study the past and present forms of life, not only in different continents, which we may compare to different individual trees of the same kind, or better, perhaps, to different main branches from the same trunk and roots, but could also study the past and present forms of life in different planets, then diversities in the general outlines would probably be seen similar to those which distinguish different kinds of trees, as the oak, the elm, and the pine; dependent, as in these trees, on differences in the physical and physiological properties of living matters in the different planets,—supposing the planets, of course, to be capable of sustaining life, like the earth, or, at least, to have been so at some period in the history of the solar system. We might find that these general outlines of life in other planets resemble elms or oaks, and are not pyramidal in form like the pine, with a "crowning" animal like man to lead their growths. For man, for aught we know or could guess, but for the highly probable accidents of nature, which blight the topmost terminal bud and give ascendency to some lateral one, except for these accidents, man *may* have always been the crown of earthly creation, or always "man," if you choose so to name and define the creature who, though once an ascidian (when the ascidian was the highest form of life), *may* have been the *best* of the ascidians. This would, perhaps, add nothing to the present value of the race, but it might satisfy the Platonic demand that the race, though not derived from a source quite worthy of it, yet should come from the *best* in nature.

We are thus led to the final problem, at present an apparently insoluble mystery, of the origin of the first forms of life on the earth. On this Mr. Darwin uses the figurative language of religious mystery, and speaks "of life with its several powers being originally breathed by the Creator into a few forms or into one." For this expression Mr. Mivart takes him to task, though really it could mean no more than if the gravitative properties of bodies were referred directly to the agency of a First Cause, in which the philosopher professed to believe; at the same time expressing his unwillingness to make hypotheses, that is, transcendental hypotheses, concerning occult modes of action. But life is, indeed, divine, and there is grandeur in the view, as Mr. Darwin says, which derives from so simple yet mysterious an origin, and "from the war of nature, from famine and death, the most exalted object which we are capable of conceiving, namely, the production of the higher animals." Mr. Mivart, however, is much more "advanced" than Mr. Darwin on the question of the origin of life or archigenesis, and the possibility of it as a continuous and present operation of nature. He admits what is commonly called "spontaneous generation," believing it, however, to be not what in theology is understood by "spontaneous," but only a sudden production of life by chemical synthesis out of inorganic elements. The absence of decisive evidence on this point does not deter him, but the fact that the doctrine can be reconciled to the strictest orthodoxy, and accords well with our author's theory of sudden changes in species, appears to satisfy him of its truth. The theory of Pangenesis, on the other hand, invented by Mr. Darwin for a different purpose, though not inconsistent with the very slow generation of vital forces out of chemical actions,—slow, that is, and insignificant compared to the normal actions and productions of chemical forces,—is hardly compatible with the sudden and conspicuous appearance of new life under the microscope of the observer. This theory was invented like other provisional theories,—like Newton's corpuscular theory of light, like the undulatory theory of light (though this is no longer provisional), and like the chemical theory of atoms,—for the purpose of giving a material or visual basis to the phenomena and empirical laws of life in general, by embodying in such supposed properties the phenomena of development, the laws of inheritance, and the various modes of reproduction, just as the chemical theory of atoms embodies in visual and tangible properties the laws of definite and multiple proportions, and the relations of gaseous volumes in chemical unions, together with the principle of isomerism and the relations of equivalent weights to specific heats. The theory of Pangenesis presents life and vital forces in their ultimate and essential elements as perfectly continuous, and in great measure isolated from other and coarser orders of forces, like the chemical and mechanical, except so far as these are the necessary theatres of their actions. Gemmules, or vital molecules, the smallest bodies which have separable parts under the action of vital forces, and of the same order as the scope of action in these forces,—these minute bodies, though probably as much smaller than chemical molecules as these are smaller than rocks or pebbles, may yet exist in unorganized materials as well as in the germs of eggs, seeds, and spores, just as crystalline structures or chemical aggregations may be present in bodies whose form and aggregation are mainly due to mechanical forces. And, as in mechanical aggregations (like sedimentary rocks), chemical actions and aggregations slowly supervene and give in the metamorphosis of these rocks an irregular crystalline structure, so it is supposable that finer orders of forces lying at the heart of fluid matter may slowly produce imperfect and irregular vital aggregations. But *definite* vital aggregations and *definite* actions of vital forces exist, for the most part, in a world by themselves, as distinct from that of chemical forces, actions, and aggregations as these are from the mechanical ones of dynamic surface-geology, which produce and are embodied in visible and tangible masses through forces the most directly apparent and best understood; or as distinct as these are from the internal forces of geology and the masses of continents and mountain formations with which they deal; or as distinct again as these are from the actions of gravity and the masses in the solar system; or, again, as these are from the unknown forces and conditions that regulate sidereal aggregations and movements. And as to the size of the gemmules, the various orders of molecular sizes are limited in our powers of conception only by the needs of hypothesis in the representation of actual phenomena, under visual forms and properties. Sir William Thomson has lately determined the probable sizes of chemical molecules from the phenomena of light, and experiments relating to the law of the "conservation of force." According to these results, these sizes are such that if a drop of water were to be magnified to the size of the earth, its molecules, or parts dependent on the forces of chemical physics, would be seen to range from the size of a pea to that of a billiard-ball. But there is no reason to doubt that in every such molecule there are still subordinate parts and structures; or that, even in these parts, a still finer order of parts and structures exists, at least to the extent of assimilated growth and *simple* division. Mr. Darwin supposes such growths and divisions in the vital gemmules; but our author objects (p. 230) that, " to admit the power of spontaneous division and multiplication in such rudimentary structures seems a complete contradiction. The gemmules, by the hypothesis of Pangenesis, are the ultimate organized components of the body, the absolute organic atoms of which each body is composed; how then *can* they be divisible? Any part of a gemmule would be an impossible (because *less* than possible) quantity. If it is divisible into still smaller organic wholes, as a germ-cell is, it must be made up, as the germ-cell is, of subordinate component atoms, which are then the *true* gemmules." But this is to suppose what is not implied in the theory (nor properly even in the chemical theory of atoms), that the sizes of these bodies are any more constant or determinate than those of visible bodies of any order. It is the order only that is determinate; but within it there may be wide ranges of sizes. A billiard-ball may be divided into parts as small as a pea, or peas may be aggregated into masses as large as a billiard-ball, without going beyond the order of forces that produce both sizes. Our author himself says afterwards and in another connection (p. 290), " It is possible that, in some minds, the notion may lurk that such powers are simpler and easier to understand, because the bodies they affect are so minute! This absurdity hardly bears stating. We can easily conceive a being so small that a gemmule would be to it as large as St. Paul's would be to us." This argument, however, is intended to discredit the theory on the ground that it does not tend to simplify matters, and that we must rest somewhere in " what the scholastics called 'substantial forms.'" But this criticism, to be just, ought to insist, not only that vital phenomena are due to "a special nature, a peculiar innate power and activity," but that chemical atoms only complicate the mysteries of science unnecessarily; that corpuscles and undulations only hide difficulties; and that we ought to explain very simply that crystalline bodies are produced by " polarity," and that the phenomena of light and vision are the effects of "luminosity." This kind of simplicity is not, however, the purpose which modern science has in view; and, consequently, our real knowledges, as well as our hypotheses, are much more complicated than were those of the schoolmen. It is not impossible that vital phenomena themselves include orders of forces as distinct as the lowest vital are from chemical phenomena. May not the contrast of merely vital or vegetative phenomena with those of *sensibility* be of such orders? But, in arriving at *sensibility*, we have reached the very elements out of which the conceptions of size and movement are constructed,—the elements of the tactual and visual constructions that are employed by such hypotheses. Can sensibility and the movements governed by it be derived directly by chemical synthesis from the forces of inorganic elements? It is probable, both from analogy and direct observation, that they cannot (though some of the believers in " spontaneous generation" think otherwise); or that they cannot, except by that great alchemic experiment which, employing all the influences of nature and all the ages of the world, has actually brought forth most if not all of the definite forms of life in the last and greatest work of creative power.

EVOLUTION BY NATURAL SELECTION.*

The physical problem, proposed independently and almost simultaneously near the beginning of this century by three eminent men of genius, Goethe, Geoffroy St. Hilaire, and the elder Darwin, *how* animals and plants came to have the structures and habits that characterize them as distinct species, this question which was proposed in place of the teleological inquiry, *why* they were so produced, has now fairly become a simple question for scientific investigation. There is no longer any doubt that this effect was by some natural process, and was not by a formless creative fiat. Moreover, there scarcely remains any doubt that this natural process connects the living forms of the present with very different forms in the past; and that this connection is properly described in general terms as "descent with modification." The question has thus become narrowed down to the inquiry, What is the nature of this modification, or what are the causes and the modes of action by which such modifications have been effected?

This is a great step in scientific progress. So long as a doubt remained about the fact that such modifications have been effected, and that present living forms are the results of them, the inquiry, how they were effected, belonged to the region of profitless speculation,—profitless except for this, that speculative minds, boldly laying aside doubts which perplex and impede others, and anticipating their solution, have often in the history of science, by preparing a way for further progress, greatly facilitated their actual solution. Difficulties and questions lying beyond such doubts—walls to scale after outworks

* From the North American Review, July, 1872.

and ditches are passed—do not inspire the cautious with courage. And so the scientific world waited, though prepared with ample force of evidence, and hesitated to take the step which would bring it face to face with the questions of the present and the future. Darwin's "Origin of Species," by marshaling and largely reinforcing the evidences of evolution, and by candidly estimating the opposing evidence, and still more by pointing out a way to the solution of the greatest difficulty, gave the signal and the word of encouragement which effected a movement that had long been impending.

The "that," the fact of evolution, may be regarded as established. The "how," the theory or explanation of it, is the problem immediately before us. Its solution will require many years of patient investigation, and much discussion may be anticipated, which will doubtless sometimes degenerate into acrimonious disputes, more especially in the immediate future, while what may be called the dialectics of the subject are being developed, and while the bearings and the limits of views and questions are being determined, and conceptions and definitions and kinds of arguments appropriate to the discussion, are the subjects on which it is necessary to come to a common understanding. It is highly desirable that this discussion should be as free as possible from mere personalities, and there is strong hope that it may be kept so through the manners and methods of procedure established by means of the experience which the history of modern science affords. That it is impossible, however, to avoid errors of this sort altogether, is evident from the provocations experienced and keenly felt by some of the noblest of modern students of science in the establishment of theories in modern astronomy, and of theories in geology, to which may now be added the theory of evolution. That the further discussion of rival hypotheses on the causes and modes of evolution will profit by these older examples may be hoped, since there have grown up general methods of investigation and discussion, which prescribe limits and precautions for hypothesis and inference, and establish rules for the conduct of debate on scientific subjects, that have been of the greatest value to the progress of science, and will, if faithfully observed, doubtless direct the present discussion to a successful issue.

These methods are analogous in their purposes to the general rules in courts of law, and constitute the principles of method in experimental philosophy, or in philosophy founded on the sciences of observation. They serve to protect an investigation, by demanding that it shall be allowed on certain pretty strict conditions (in the conduct of experiments and observations, and in the formation and verification of hypotheses) to proceed without hindrance from prejudice for any existing doctrine or opinion. An investigation may thus start from the simplest basis of experience, and, for this purpose, may waive, yet without denying, any presumption or conclusion held in existing theories or doctrines. Again, these rules protect an investigation from a one-sided criticism or *ex parte* judgment, since they demand of the criticism or judgment the same judicial attitude that is demanded of the investigation. Advocacy, and especially the sort that is of essential value in courts of law, where two advocates are set against each other, each with the duty of presenting only what can be said for his own side, and where the same judge and jury are bound to hear both, is singularly out of place in a scientific discussion, unless in oral debate before the tribunal of a scientific society. Moreover, there are no burdens of proof in science. Such advocacy in a published work claiming scientific consideration is almost an offense against the proprieties of such discussions. To collect together in one place all that can be said for an hypothesis, and in another all that can be said against it, is at best a clumsy and inconvenient method of discussion, the natural results of which may best be seen in the present condition of theological and religious doctrines. These practical considerations are of the utmost importance for the attainment of the end of scientific pursuit; which is not to arrive at decisions or judgments that are probably true, but is the discovery of the real truths of nature, for which science can afford to wait, and for which suspended judgments are the soundest substitutes.

No work of science, ancient or modern, dealing with prob-

lematic views and doctrines, has more completely conformed
to these principles, or more fully justified them by its success,
than the "Origin of Species." For its real or principal success
has been in convincing nearly all naturalists, a majority of
whom, at least, were still unconvinced, of the truth of the
theory of evolution; and this has resulted from its obvious
fairness and spirit of caution almost as much as from the preponderance of the evidences for the theory when thus presented. And the very same qualities of spirit and method
governed the leading and more strictly original design of the
work, which cannot, however, yet be said to be a complete
success, namely, the *explanation* of evolution by natural selection. That Mr. Darwin himself is fully convinced of the truth
of this explanation is sufficiently evident. He holds that natural selection is the principal or leading cause in determining the
changes and diversities of species, though not the only cause of
the development of their characters. Conspicuously at the close
of the Introduction in the first edition of the work, and in all
subsequent editions, occur these words : "I am convinced that
Natural Selection has been the most important, but not the exclusive, means of modification." That the work is not a merely
dialectical performance is clear; and it is equally clear that
in proportion to the strength of the author's conviction is his
solicitude to give full and just weight to all valid objections to
it. In this respect the work stands in marked contrast to much
that has been written on the subject and in reply to it.

Once to leave the vantage-ground of scientific method and
adopt the advocate's *ex parte* mode of discussion almost necessitates a continuance of the discussion under this most inconvenient form. Mr. Mivart's "Genesis of Species," which we
examined in this Review last July, though a conspicuous example of such a one-sided treatment of a proper scientific question,
was by a writer so distinguished for his attainments in science
that his criticism could not well be passed by without notice;
and, having also the character of a popular treatise, it came
within a wider province of criticism that that of strictly scientific reviews. Our notice of his work was chiefly devoted to sup-
plying something of what could be and had been said in favor

of the theory thus criticised, both by way of defining and defending it. We also followed the author to some extent into the consideration of a subject, namely, the general philosophical and theological bearings of this theory, which does not, we endeavored to show, belong properly to the discussion, and ought to be kept in abeyance, so long, at least, as the laws of experimental philosophy are observed in the conduct of the inquiry. One of the first questions asked in past times in regard to physical hypotheses, which have now become established theories or doctrines of science, was, if they were orthodox, or at least theistic; and the negative decision of this question by what was deemed competent authority determined temporarily and in a measure the fate of the hypothesis and the standing of those who held to it. It was to be hoped that, in the light of such a history, this discussion could be spared the question, at least till the hypothesis could be fairly tried, when, if it should be found wanting in scientific validity, its banishment to the limbo of exploded errors might, without much harm, be changed to a severer sentence; and, if it should withstand the tests of purely scientific criticism, the same means of reconciling it to orthodoxy would doubtless be found as in the case of older physical hypotheses. Mr. Mivart himself claimed and argued a similar exemption for the general theory of evolution, or rather attempted the later office of reconciliation, or the affording of proofs of its conformity to the most venerable and authoritative decisions of orthodoxy. But he appeared unwilling to allow either such an exemption, or the possibility of an accordance with orthodoxy, to the theory of natural selection, for he more than once quoted and applied to the discussion of this theory the saying and supposed opinions of an heretical heathen philosopher, Democritus.

In his reply to our criticisms,[*] he wonders who could have so misled us as to make us suppose that his was a "theological education" and a "schooling against Democritus"; the fact being just the reverse of this, his education being in that phi-

---

[*] See the number of the North American Review for April, 1872. Mr. Mivart has reprinted his reply, without notice of the present essay, in his volume entitled, "Lessons from Nature," London, 1876.

losophy of "nescience," out of the evils and fallacies of which he had at length struggled. Clearly we were misled by the author himself. Our error, slight except as a biographical one, would have been amended if we had referred the character of his criticism to his theological *studies*. This would have left the period in his life in which he acquired his mode of thought and discussion as undetermined, as it was unimportant to the point of our criticism; since, through the influence of these studies, or similar dialectical pursuits, his unquestionable abilities appeared to us to have been developed, and, as we believe, misapplied. It was the bringing in of "the fortuitous concourse of atoms," and "blind chance," "accidents," and "hap-hazard results," in a discussion with which they had no more to do, and no less, than they have to do with geology, meteorology, politics, philosophical history, or political economy. It was this irrelevancy in his criticism which we regarded as oblivious of the age in which we live and for which he wrote,—the age of experimental philosophy. Mr. Mivart thinks he is clear of all blame for speaking of the theory of natural selection as liable "to lead men to regard the present organic world as formed, so to speak, *accidentally*, beautiful and wonderful as is confessedly the hap-hazard result," since he qualified the word "accidentally" by the phrase "so to speak." The real fault was in speaking so at all.

Accidents in the ordinary every-day sense are causes in every concrete course of events,—in the weather, in history, in politics, in the market,—and no theory of these events can leave them out. Explanation of the events consists in showing how they will result, or have resulted, through certain fixed principles or laws of action from the occasions or opportunities, which such accidents present. Given the state of the atmosphere over a large district in respect to temperature, moisture, pressure, and motion,—none of which could have been anticipated without similar data for a short time before, all in fact being accidents,—and the physical principles of meteorology might enable us to explain the weather that immediately follows. So with the events of history, etc. In no other sense are accidents supposed as causes in the theory of natural selection. Accidental variations and surrounding conditions of existence, and the previous condition of the organic world, (none of which could have been anticipated from anything we actually know, all in fact being "accidents")—these are the causes which present the occasions or opportunities through which principles of utility and advantage are brought to bear in changing structures and habits, and improving their adaptations. If this is like the philosophy of Democritus, or any other excommunicated philosopher of antiquity, and is, therefore, to be condemned for the heresy, then all the sciences with which we have compared it, and many others, the conquests of human intelligence, must share the condemnation.

We dwelt in our review, perhaps unnecessarily, on the fact that accidents in this sense, and in the theory of natural selection, as well as elsewhere, are relative to our knowledge of causes; that the same event, like an eclipse of the sun, might be an accident to one mind, and an anticipated event to another. We did so because we could not understand otherwise why our author should single out the theory of natural selection from analogous theories and sciences for a special criticism of this sort; or except on the idea that the accidents in natural selection were supposed by him to be exceptional, and of the type which Democritus is reputed to have put in the place of intelligent design, or on the throne of Nous. We did not, as Mr. Mivart imagines, think him "ignorant that the various phenomena which we observe in nature have their respective phenomenal antecedents," nor suppose that he "held the opinion that phenomena of variation, etc., are not determined by definite, invariable, physical antecedents." We only thought that, knowing better,—knowing that "natural selection," like every other physical theory, dealt with physical causes and their laws,—he was unjust and inconsistent in condemning the employment of it, as a leading or prominent cause, in explanation of the phenomena of the organic world, in the manner in which he did; except on the hypothesis, which we repudiated in behalf of experimental philosophy but without positively attributing it to him,—the hypothesis of absolute accidents. It was inconsistency and irrelevancy which we meant to attribute to him.

That he supposed absolute accidents to be meant in the ancient atheistical philosophy appeared from a passage in his chapter on Theology and Evolution (p. 276), in which he speaks of the kind of action we might expect in physical nature from a theistic point of view, as an action "which is orderly, which *disaccords* with the action of blind chance and with the 'fortuitous concourse of atoms' of Democritus." But in his reply to us he repudiates the idea that this old philosophy held events to be accidental in the strict sense; and he further says of us that we "know very well that Democritus and Empedocles and their school no more held phenomena to be undetermined or unpreceded by other phenomena than do their successors at the present day." We are far from being so well informed, or willing to accept this as a statement of our views. For, in the first place, the terms "undetermined" and "unpreceded" are not synonymous. Moreover, so far as phenomena are determined, they are "orderly," "harmonize with man's reason" (p. 275), though in their complexity they may be quite beyond the power of any man's imagination to represent or disentangle; and, as our author has said, they are what we might expect "from a theistic point of view."

Whether Democritus believed in absolute accidents or not we do not know. Little is really known of his opinions in this respect. The question has been disputed, but not decided. All his works are lost, except a few quoted sentences and maxims. He is in a peculiarly exposed condition for an attack from any one disposed to be his opponent. The words ascribed to him are unprotected by contexts, or by the scruples an opponent might feel about their meaning were he assigning to him his place in the history of speculation. It is very likely that he did not hold to absolute accidents as occurring in the course of nature; though it is very doubtful whether he was so thoroughly convinced as his "successors of the present day" are of the universality of the "law of causation," or that *every* event must have determinant antecedents. The conception of cause, as based by experimental science on the elementary invariable orders of phenomenal successions, is, even at the present day, altogether too precise and abstract for the apprehension of a mind untrained by scientific studies. How much more so must it have been when among the old Ionian philosophers the first crude conceptions of science were being fashioned by attempts at discovering the physical bond of union and the inchoate form of nature, regarded as a universe. It is an anachronism to speak of these philosophers as materialists and atheists, since the distinctions and questions which could make such a classification intelligible had not yet been proposed. And it is equally an anachronism to attribute even to later thinkers, like Democritus, such a conception of physical causation as only the latest and maturest products of scientific thought have rendered definite.

There can be no antithesis in the problem of the beginning of the world between accident and law, that is, between accident and the orderly movements which imply determinant antecedents. The real antithesis is between accident and miracle, that is, between accident and the extraordinary action of pre-existent designing intelligence; and in this relation Accident can only have an absolute meaning, equivalent in fact to Destiny or Fate, when unintelligible. Unintelligible Destiny or "blind chance" is directly opposed to the intelligible Destiny which is the principle of "law" in nature; though these have often been confounded as equally fatalistic and atheistical. Mr. Mivart, however, does not confound them; for he has said that the latter is what we might expect from a theistic point of view. It is altogether likely, however, that the Democritus to whom the former meaning could be attributed as a characteristic one is not the real thinker, but is a myth; or is rather the orthodox lay-figure of atheism of the theological studio.

The reputation for atheism which the real Democritus doubtless had may have come from a cause which has often produced it in the history of physical science. He invented a theory of atoms with which he attempted physical explanations quite in advance of previous speculations. And the invention of physical hypotheses has often been regarded as an invasion of the province and jurisdiction of divine power and a first cause. For men rarely allow the explanation of any important effect in nature to remain an open question. If observed or inferred physical causes do not suffice, invisible or even spiritual ones are invented; and thus the ground is preoccupied, and closed against the inquiries of the physical philosopher. It is probably the general direction or tendency of these inquiries, rather than any positive positions or results at which they may arrive, which puts the physical philosopher in an apparently irreligious attitude. For in following out the consequences of physical hypotheses into the details of natural phenomena, reasoning from supposed causes to their effects, his interests and his modes of thought are the reverse of those of mankind in general, and of the religious mind. He appears to turn his back on divinity, and though seeking to approach nearer the first cause, or the total order of nature, his aspect of looking downward from a proximate principle through a natural order appears to the popular view to be darkened by a sombre shadow. The theory of universal gravitation was condemned on this account for impiety by even so liberal and enlightened a thinker as Leibnitz. This seems very strange to us now, since the law of gravitation is almost as familiar as fire, or even gravity itself. When in ancient times any one had burned his fingers, or been bruised by a fall, one did not, except perhaps in early childhood, attribute the harm to a person, a spirit, or a god, but to the qualities of fire or gravity; yet the sounds of the thunder were still referred directly to Zeus. We all remember how in the "Clouds" of Aristophanes the comic poet puts impiety in the mouth of Socrates, or the doctrine that Zeus does not exist, and that it is ethereal Vortex, reigning in his stead, which drives the clouds and makes them rain and thunder. Such a view of physical inquiries is not confined to comic poets or their audiences. The meteorological sophists of that day were in very much the same position as the Darwinian evolutionists of the present time.

However important it may be to bear these considerations in mind, there is, as we have said, no more occasion to do so with reference to the theory of natural selection than with reference to many other analogous theories, not only in physical science, like those of meteorology and geology (including the theory of evolution), but also in sociological science, like theories of political economy, and those theories of history which explain the growth of institutions, governments, and national characteristics. The comparison of the continuous order in time of the organic world and its total aspect at any period, to the progressive changes and the particular aspect at any time of the weather, will, doubtless, strike many minds as inapt, since the latter phenomena are the type to us of indetermination and chance, while the former present to us the most conspicuous evidences of orderly determination and design. This contrast, though conspicuous, is, nevertheless, not essential to the contrasted orders themselves. The movements in one are almost infinitely slower than in the other. We see a single phase and certain orderly details in one. We see only confused and rapid combinations and successions in the other. One is seen in fine, the other in gross form. But looked at from the same point of view, regarding each as an *ensemble* of details in time and space, they are equally without definite order or intelligible plan; "beautiful and wonderful as is," according to Mr. Mivart, "the hap-hazard result." It is in the intimate and comparatively minute parts of the organic world in individual structures or organisms that the beautiful and wonderful order is seen. When we look at great groups, like the floras and faunas of various regions, or at past geological groupings,—the shifting clouds, as it were, of organic life,—this order disappears or is hidden for the most part. There remains enough of apparent order to indicate continuity in time and space, but hardly anything more. Perfectly as the individual organism may exhibit adaptations or the applications of principles of utility, there is no definite clew in it to the cause of the particular combination of uses which it embodies, or to its existence in a particular region, or at a particular period in the history of the world, or to its co-existence with many other quite independent particular forms. But in precise analogy with what is conspicuously regular and indicative of simple laws in the organic world, correspond the intimate elementary changes of the atmosphere, some of which, like the fall and even the formation of rain and snow, the development and disappearance of clouds, are almost as simple exhibitions of natural laws as experiments in the laboratory. What, even in the laboratory, can exceed the beauty, simplicity, and completeness of that exemplification of definite physical laws which the fall of dew on clear, calm nights demonstrates? Moreover, there are in the successions of changes in the weather sufficient traces of order to indicate a continuity in space and time corresponding to the geographical distributions and geological successions of the organic world. The elementary orders, which exhibit ultimate physical laws in simple isolation, are, in their aggregate and complex combination, the causes of the successions of changes in the weather and the source of whatever traces of order appear in them, and are thus analogous to what the theory of natural selection supposes in the organic world, namely, that the adaptations, or the exhibitions of simple principles of utility in structures, are in their aggregate and complex combinations the causes of successive and continuous changes in forms of life.

Far more important, however, than such analogies in the doctrine of evolution is the clear understanding of what the theory of natural selection undertakes to explain, and what is the precise and essential nature of its supposed action. There appears to be much confusion on this subject, arising probably from the influence of preconceived opinions concerning the nature both of the matters explained and the mode of explanation, or, in other words, concerning the nature of the changes which take place in species and the relations of them to this cause. These would seem, at first sight, very simple matters for conception, and difficult only in the evidences and the adequacy of the explanation. Such appeared, and still appears, to be the opinion of Mr. Mivart.

Perhaps the best way to make a difficult theory plain is the negative one of correcting the misconceptions of it as they arise. This is what we attempted in our former review with reference to the character of the variations from which nature normally and for the most part selects. But new difficulties have emerged in Mr. Mivart's later writings which deserve consideration. In his answer to Professor Huxley, in the January number of the "Contemporary Review" (p. 170), he says of the theory of natural selection, "That the benefit of the individual in the struggle for life was announced as the one determining agent, fixing slight beneficial variations into enduring characters," for which he thinks it quite incompetent. And again, in reply to us (p. 453), he speaks of " *The* origin, not, of course, of slight variations, but of the fixing of these in definite lines and grooves"; and this origin, he believes, cannot be natural selection. And we believe that his conclusions are right! That is, if the more obvious meaning of these expressions are their real ones. They appear to mean that natural selection will not account for the unvarying continuance in succeeding generations of *simple* changes made accidentally in individual structures (whether the change be large or small), or will not account for the direct conversion of a *simple* change in a parent into a permanent alteration of its offspring. Such is the apparent meaning of these expressions, but they might possibly be taken as loose expressions of the opinion that this cause will not account for permanent changes in the *average* characters, or mid-points, about which variations oscillate; and, in this case, we believe that he is wrong. This permanency must not be understood, however, as meaning that changes cease, but only that they are not reversed. The same cause, natural selection, prevents such reversion, on the whole, and except in individual cases which it exterminates.

The first and obviously intended meaning of these expressions has let in light upon the author's own theory and his general difficulty about the theory of natural selection, which we did not have before. They show how fundamentally the matter has been misconceived, either by him or by us. That we did not more fully perceive this fundamental difference doubtless arose from a tacit assumption of the principle of "specific stability" in his earlier criticisms, which was explicitly treated of in a later chapter and as a subordinate topic. This, as we shall find, is the source of the most serious misunderstanding. We were not aware that any one supposed that particular variations ever became *fixed* and heritable changes in the characters of organisms by the direct agency of natural selection, or, indeed, by any other known cause. The proper effect of this cause is not to fix variations, though it must *determine their averages and limit their range*, and must act directly to increase the useful ones and diminish the injurious; or rather to permit the one and forbid the other, and when these are directly opposed to each other, it must act to shift the average or normal character, instead of fixing it. Variation as a constant and normal phenomenon of organization, exhibited chiefly in the ranges of individual differences, is, as it were, the agitation or irregular oscillation that keeps the characters of species from getting too closely *fixed* in "definite lines and grooves," through the too rigid inheritance of ancestral traits; or it is a principle of alertness that keeps them ever ready for movement and change in conformity to changing conditions of existence. What fixes species (when they are fixed) is the continuance of the same advantages in their structures and habits, or the same conditions for the action of selection, together with the force of long-continued inheritance.

This, though almost trite from frequent repetition, appears a very difficult conception for many minds, probably on account of their retaining the old stand-point of philosophy. It would appear that Mr. Mivart is really speaking of the *fixed* species of the old and still prevalent philosophy, or about *real* species, as they are commonly called. Natural selection cannot, of course, account for these figments. Their true explanation is in the fact that naturalists formerly assumed, without proper evidence, that a change too slow for them to perceive directly could not exist, and that characters widely prevalent and so far advanced as to become permanently adapted to very general and unchanging conditions of existence, like vertebral and articulate structures, the numbers and positions of the organs of locomotion in various animals, the whorl and the spiral arrangement of leaves in plants, and similar homological resemblances, could never have been vacillating and uncertain ones. It was not many years ago that a distinguished writer in criticising the views of Lamarck affirmed that "the majority of naturalists agree with Linnæus in supposing that all the individuals propagated from one stock have certain distinguishing characters in common, which never vary, and which have remained the same since the creation of each species." The influence of this opinion still remains, even with naturalists who would hesitate to assert categorically the opinion itself. This comes, doubtless, from the fact that long-prevalent doctrines often get stamped into the very meanings of words, and thus acquire the character of axioms. The word "species" became synonymous with *real* or *fixed* species, or these adjectives became pleonastic. And this was from the mere force of repetition, and without valid foundation in fact, or confirmation from proper inductive evidence.

Natural selection does not, of course, account for a fixity that does not exist, but only for the adaptations and the diversities in species, which may or may not be changing at any time. They are fixed only as the "fixed" stars are fixed, of which very many are now known to be slowly moving. Their fixity, when they are fixed, is temporary and through the accident of unchanging external conditions. Such is at least the assumption of the theory of natural selection. Mr. Mivart's theory seems to assume, on the other hand, that unless a species or a character is tied to something it will run away; that there is a necessity for some internal bond to hold it, at least temporarily, or so long as it remains the *same* species. He is entitled, it is true, to challenge the theory of natural selection for proofs of its assumption, that "fixity" is not an essential feature of natural species; for, in fact, so far as direct evidence is concerned, this is an open question. Its decision must depend chiefly on the preponderance of indirect and probable evidences in the interpretation of the "geological record," a subject to which much space is devoted, in accordance with its importance, in the "Origin of Species." Technical questions in the classification and description of species afford other evidences, and it is asserted by naturalists that a very large number of specimens, say ten thousand, is sufficient, in some departments of natural history, to break down any definition or discrimination even of living species. Other evidences are afforded by the phenomena of variation under domestication. Mr. Mivart had the right, and may still have it, to resist all this evidence, as not conclusive; but he is not entitled to call upon the theory of natural selection for an explanation of a feature in organic structures which the theory denies in its very elements, the *fixity* of species. This is what he has done,—implicitly, as it now appears, in his book, and explicitly in his later writings.

The question of zoölogical philosophy, "Whether species have a real existence in nature," in the decision of which naturalists have so generally agreed with Linnæus, refers directly and explicitly to this question or the fixity of essential characters, and to the assumption that species must remain unaltered in these respects so long as they continue to exist, or until they give birth to new species; or, as was formerly believed, give place in perishing to new independent creations. The distinction involved in this question in the word *real* should not be confounded, as it might easily be, with the distinction in Logic of "real kinds" from other class-names. Logic recognizes a principal division in class-names, according as these are the names of objects which agree with each other and differ from other objects in a very large and indefinite number of particulars or attributes, or are the names of objects which agree only in a few and a definite number of attributes. The former are the names of "real kinds," and include the names of natural species, as man, horse, etc., and of natural genera, as whale, oak, etc. These classes are "real kinds," not because the innumerable particulars in which the individual members of them agree with each other and differ from the members of other classes, are themselves fixed or invariable in time, but because this sort of agreement and difference is fixed or continues to appear. An individual hipparion resembled its immediate parents and the other offspring of them as closely as, or, at least, in the same intimate manner in which one horse resembles another, namely, in innumerable details. But this is not opposed to the conception that the horse is descended from the hipparion by insensible steps of gradation or continuously. For examples of names that are not the names of "real kinds," we may instance such as denominate objects that are an inch in length, or in breadth, or are colored black, or are square, or (combining these particulars) that are as black square inches. These objects may be made of paper, or wood, or ivory, or differ in all other respects except the enumerated and definite particulars. They are not "real" or natural "kinds," but factitious ones.

The confusion which, as we have said, might arise between the "real kinds" of Logic, and the *real* species of biological speculation, would depend on a vagueness in the significance of the word "real," which in common usage combines in uncertain proportions two elementary and more precise ideas, that of fixedness and that of breadth of relationship. Both these marks of reality are applied habitually as tests of it. Thus if an object attests its existence to several of my senses, is seen, heard, touched, and is varied in its relations to these senses, and moreover is similarly related to the senses of another person, as evinced by his testimony, then I know that the object is real, and not a mere hallucination or invention of my fantasy; though it may disappear immediately afterwards in an unexplained manner, or be removed by some unknown but supposable agency. Here the judgment of reality depends on breadth of relationship to my experience and sources of knowledge. Or again I may only *see* the object, and consult no other eyes than my own; but seeing it often, day after day, in the same place, I shall judge it to be a real object, provided its existence is conformable to the general possibilities of experience, or to the test of "breadth." Here the test of reality is "fixity" or continuance in time. That natural species are real in one of these senses, that individuals of a species are alike in an indefinite number of particulars, and resemble each other intimately, is unquestionable as a fact, and is not an invention of the understanding or classifying faculty, and is moreover the direct natural consequence of the principles of inheritance. In this sense species are equivalent to large natural stocks or races existing for a limited but indeterminate number of generations. That they are real in the other sense, or fixed in time absolutely in respect to any of the particulars of their resemblance, whether these are essential (that is, useful for discrimination and classification) or are not, is far from being the axiom it has seemed to be. It is, on the contrary, highly improbable that they are so, though this is tacitly assumed, as we have seen, in criticisms of the theory of natural selection, and in the significance often attached to the word "species" in which the notions of fixedness and distinctiveness have coalesced. It is true that without this significance in the word "species" the names and descriptions of organic forms could not be permanently applicable. No system of classification, however natural or real, could be final. Classification would, indeed, be wholly inadequate as a representation of the organic world on the whole, or as a sketch of the "plan of creation," and would be falsely conceived as revealing the categories and thoughts of creative intelligence,—a consequence by no means welcome to the devout naturalist, since it seems to degrade the value of his work. But this may be because he has misconceived its true value, and dedicated to the science of divinity what is really the rightful inheritance of natural or physical science.

If instead of implicitly assuming the principle of specific stability in the earlier chapters of his book, and deferring the explicit consideration of it to a later chapter and as a special topic, Mr. Mivart had undertaken the establishment of it as the essential basis of his theory (as indeed it really is), he would have attacked the theory of natural selection in a most vital point; and if he had succeeded, all further criticism of the theory would have been superfluous. But without success in establishing this essential basis, he leaves his own theory, and his general difficulties concerning the theory of natural selection, without adequate foundation. The importance of natural selection in the evolution of organic species (its predominent influence) depends entirely on the truth of the opposite assumption, the *instability* of species. The evidences for and against this position are various, and are not adequately considered in the author's chapter on this subject. Moreover, some of the evidences may be expected to be greatly affected by what will doubtless be the discoveries of the immediate future. Already the difficulties of discrimination and classification in dealing with large collections have become very great in some departments of natural history, and even in paleontology the gradations of fossil forms are becoming finer and finer with almost every new discovery; and this in spite of the fact that nothing at all approaching to evidence of continuity can rationally be expected from the fragmentary geological record.   To this evidence must be added the phenomena of variation under domestication.   The apparent limits of the changes which can be effected by artificial selection are not, as they have been thought, proofs of the doctrine of "specific stability," or of the opinion of Linnæus, but only indications of the dependence of variation on physiological causes, and on laws of inheritance; and also of the fact that the laws of variation and the action of natural selection are not suspended by domestication, but may oppose the aims and efforts of artificial selection.   The real point of the proof afforded by these phenomena is that permanent changes may be effected in species by insensible degrees.   They are permanent, however, only in the sense that no tendency to reversion will restore the original form, except by the action of similar causes.

Against the conclusions of such inductive evidences the vague analogies of the organic to the inorganic world would avail little or nothing, even if they were true.   They avail little or nothing, consequently, in confirmation of them in being proved false; as we showed one analogy to be in the illustration given by our author, namely, the supposed analogy of specific characters in crystals to those of organisms; and his inference of abrupt changes in organic species, corresponding by this analogy to changes in the mode or species of crystallization, which the same substance undergoes in some cases with a change of surrounding conditions, such as certain other substances may introduce by their presence.   A complete illustration of the chemical phenomenon is afforded by the crystals of sulphur.   Crystals produced in the wet way, or from solution in the bisulphide of carbon, are of a species entirely distinct from those formed in the dry way, or from the fused mineral; and there are many other cases of these phenomena of *dimorphism* and *polymorphism*, as they are called.   We recur to this topic, not on account of its importance to the discussion, but because Mr. Mivart accuses us of changing a quotation from Mr. J. J. Murphy, so that he "is unlucky enough to be blamed for what he never said, or apparently thought of saying." We have looked with true solicitude for the evidences of the truth of this charge, and find them to be as follows: We transcribed from Mr. Mivart's book these sentences, as quoted by him (p. 185), from Mr. Murphy: "It needs no proof that in the case of spheres and crystals, the forms and *the* structures are the effect, and not the cause, of the formative principle*s*. Attraction, whether gravitative or capillary, produces the spherical form; the spherical form does not produce attraction. And crystalline polarities produce crystalline structure and form; crystalline structure and form do not produce *crystalline* polarities." The superfluous letter and words, which we have put in italics, were omitted in the printing, we do not know how, but it looks like an unwarrantable attempt in a final revision of proofs to improve the English of the quotation. Certainly the changes were of no advantage to our criticism, especially as they only have the effect to render the antithesis, which was the object of the criticism, slightly weaker. It is impossible to see how these changes have exposed Mr. Murphy to undeserved censure. We blamed him and Mr. Mivart, not for the use of abstractions as causes,—a use, which, as Mr. Mivart says, we ourselves make whenever it is convenient, but for asserting the antithesis of cause and effect between abstractions both of which are descriptive of effects, namely, the character of the attractions, gravitative and capillary, which produce spherical forms *vs.* the spherical form itself; and the polar character of the forces that produce crystals *vs.* the crystalline form and structure. Each of these effects (both in the case of the sphere and of the crystal) is doubtless a concause or condition that goes to the determination of the other. The spherical form arranges and determines the resultants of the elementary forces, and thus indirectly determines itself, or determines that action of the elementary forces thus combined, which results in the maintenance or stable equilibrium of the spherical form. Again, in crystallization the already formed bodies, with the particular directions of their faces and axes, determine in part how the resultants of elementary polar forces will act in the further growth of the crystal, or in the repair of a broken one; and the elementary forces, thus determined and combined, result in the crystalline form and structure. Thus both of the effects which are put in the antithesis of cause and effect in the above quotation are also partial agents. They act and react on each other in the production of actual crystals.

But this point was of importance to the discussion only as exhibiting a kind of "realism" by which scientific discussion is very liable to be confused. In this case, the wordy profundity was not quite so bald and conspicuous as the ordinary putting of a single-worded abstract description of an effect for its cause, since it consisted in putting one of two such abstractions as the cause of the other. More important, as affecting the truth of the supposed analogy of *species* in crystals to those of organisms, was our statement which Mr. Mivart confesses is utterly beyond him, and which, as he certainly has misinterpreted it, we may be pardoned for repeating and explaining. We said, "Moreover, in the case of crystals, neither these forces [the elementary] nor the abstract law of their action in producing definite *angles* reside in the finished bodies, but in the properties of the surrounding media, portions of whose constituents are changed into crystals, according to these properties and other conditioning circumstances." Our author has made us say "crystals" where we said "angles," though the unintelligible character of the sentence ought to have made him the more cautious in copying it. We said "angles" because these are prominent marks of the *species* of the crystal; and this species we referred to the nature of the fluid material out of which the crystal is formed, and to the modifying influences of the presence of other substances, when the crystallization takes place from solutions, or in the wet way. The fact that the determination of the *species* of a crystal is not in any germ or nucleus or anything belonging in a special way to the particular crystal itself, but is in the molecular forces of the fluid solution, makes the analogy of species in crystals to those of organisms not only vague but false. What is really effected by the introduction of a foreign substance, acid or alkali, in the solution, is a change, not in such accidents as the surrounding conditions are to an organism, but is a change of the essential forces, which *ought* to change the character or species of the crystal suddenly, discretely, or discontinuously; and it has not, therefore, the remotest likeness to such suppositions as that a duck might be hatched from a goose's egg, or a goose from a duck's; or that a horse might have been the foal of an hipparion.

Notwithstanding that our statement was "utterly beyond" our author, he has ventured the following confident comments (p. 460): "If this is so," he says, "then when a broken crystal completes itself, the determining forces reside exclusively in the media, and not at all in the crystal with its broken surface! The first atoms of a crystal deposited arrange themselves entirely according to the forces of the surrounding media, and their own properties are utterly without influence or effect in the result!" The marks of exclamation appended to these statements ought to have been ours, since nothing in the statements themselves has the remotest dependence on anything we said; but on the contrary these statements are directly opposed to the objections we made to Mr. Murphy's antitheses. They might be deducible, perhaps, from our proposition, in the form to which it was altered through the substitution of the word "crystals" for "angles," by supposing the concrete actual crystals to be referred to, instead of their *species*, of which these angles are prominent marks. But we had insisted that neither the resulting form, nor the resultants of elementary forces, are exclusively effects, or exclusively causes in the formation or in the mending of actual crystals; yet the *species* of the crystal is fully determined by what is outside of it, or by causes that may be abruptly changed by a change in the medium. Hence the phenomena of *dimorphism* and *polymorphism*, and similar chemical phenomena, have nothing in common with the hypothesis of "specific genesis."

Several similar misunderstandings of more special criticisms in our review tempt us (chiefly from personal considerations) to undertake their rectification; but our object in this article is only to further the discussion, so far as it can be done under the inconvenient form of polemical discussion, by removing confusions and misunderstandings in essential matters. Hence we shall not dwell upon the discussion of what may be called hypotheses of the second degree, or hypothetical illustrations of the action of natural selection. It was a part of Mr. Mivart's plan, in attacking the hypothesis of the predominant agency of natural selection in the origination of species, to discredit a number of subordinate hypotheses, as well as to challenge the theory to offer any adequate ones for the explanation of certain extraordinary structures. We considered in detail several objections of this sort, though we might have been content with simply pointing out a sufficient answer in the logical weakness of such a mode of attack. The illustrations of the theory which have been proposed have not in general at all the force of arguments; they have it only where the utility of a structure is simple and obvious and can be shown by direct evidence to be effective in developing the structure out of accidental beginnings, and even in perfecting it, as in cases of the mimicry of certain insects, for the sake of a protection, which is thus really acquired. In general, the illustrations serve only to show the mode of action supposed in the theory, without pretending to reconstruct the past history of an animal, even by the roughest sketch; or to determine all the uses of any structure, or their relative importance.

To discredit these particular secondary hypotheses has no more weight as an argument against the theory than the hypotheses themselves have in confirmation of it. To be convinced on general grounds that such a structure as that of the giraffe's neck was developed by insensible steps from a more common form of the neck in Ungulates, through the oscillations of individual differences, and by the special utilities of the variations which have made the neck longer in some individuals than in others, or through the utilities of these to the animals under the special conditions of their past existence, is very different from believing that this or that particular use in the structure was *the* utility (to adopt our author's favorite form of definiteness) which governed the selection or deter-

mined the survival of the fittest. *The* use which may be presumed in general to govern selection is a combination, with various degrees of importance, of all the actual uses in a structure. There can be no more propriety in demanding of the theory of natural selection that it should assign a special use, or trace out the history hypothetically of any particular structure in its relations to past conditions of existence, than there would be in demanding of political economy that it should justify the correctness of its general principles by success in explaining the record of past prices in detail, or accounting in particular for a given financial anomaly. In either case, the proper evidence is wanting. Any instance, however, of a structure which could be conclusively shown (a very difficult kind of proof) to exist, or to be developed in any way, without reference in the process of development to any utility whatever, past or present, or to any past forms of the structure, would, indeed, go far towards qualifying the evidence, otherwise mostly affirmative, of the predominant agency of natural selection.

We may remark by the way that Mr. Mivart's definite thesis, "that natural selection is not *the* origin of species," is really not *the* question. No more was ever claimed for it than that it is the most influential of the agencies through which species have been modified. Lamarck's principle of the direct effect of habit, or actual use and disuse, has never been abandoned by later evolutionists; and Mr. Darwin has given much more attention to its proof and illustration in his work on "Variation under Domestication" than any other writer. Moreover, the physiological causes which produce reversions and correlations of growth, and which, so far as they are known, are quite independent of natural selection, are also recognized as causes of change. But all these are subordinated in the theory to the advantage and consequent survival of the fittest in the struggle for life, or to natural selection. Upon this point we must refer our readers to the "Additions and Corrections" in the lately published sixth edition of the "Origin of Species"; in which also all the objections brought forward by Mr. Mivart, which had not previously been examined in the work, are fully considered; and, we need hardly add, far more thoroughly and adequately than could be possible for us, or in the pages of this Review.

We will, nevertheless, give, in sheer self-defense, the correction of one perversion of our criticism. Mr. Mivart had argued in his book that the use of the giraffe's long neck for browsing on the foliage of trees, and the advantage of it in times of drought, could not be the cause of its gradual increase by selection; since this advantage, if a real one, would be equally an advantage to all Ungulates inhabiting the country of the giraffe, or similar regions; and that the other Ungulates, at least in such regions, ought to have been similarly modified. We allowed that there was force in the objection, but we were mistaken. The very conditions of the selection must have been a competition which would have soon put a large majority of the competitors out of the lists, and have narrowed the contest to a few races, and finally to the individuals of a single race. All the rest must have early given up the struggle for life in this direction; since a slight increase in the length of the neck could have been of no advantage if the reach of it still fell far short of the unconsumed foliage. The success of the survivors among them must have been won in some other direction, like the power of rapid and wide ranging, or organs better adapted to close grazing. For a fuller development and illustration of this reply we must refer to Chapter VII. in the new edition of the "Origin of Species," in which most of Mr. Mivart's objections are considered. We attempted a reply to this objection in a direction in which his own remarks led us. Granting that the advantage of a long neck would have been equally an advantage to all Ungulates in South Africa; that there was no alternative or substitute for it; and that the use of the neck for high reaching in times of drought could not *therefore* have been *the* efficient cause of its preservation and increase through selection; still there were other and very important uses in such a neck, to which these objections do not apply, and through which there would be advantages in the struggle for life, that would determine competition only among the individuals of a single race; while those of other races would compete with each other on other grounds. Mr. Mivart

admitted that there might be several lines of advantage in means of *protection* or *defense;* and cited instances from Mr. Wallace, showing, for example, that a dull color, useful for concealing an animal, would not be an advantage to those animals which are otherwise sufficiently protected, and do not need concealment. The use of the giraffe's neck, then, as a means of defense and offense, for which there was ample evidence, its use as a watch-tower and as a weapon of offense, would be raised by Mr. Mivart's objection to greater prominence, and might be the principal ground of advantage and competition between giraffe and giraffe, or one herd of them and another, with reference to protection from the larger beasts of prey; an advantage which would be incessant instead of occasional, like the high-reaching advantage in times of drought. *The* use, as we have said, means, with reference to the advantage in the struggle for life, the combination of all the uses that are of importance to the preservation of life. Accordingly we demanded whether Mr. Mivart, having made a special objection to the *importance* of *one* use, as affording advantages and grounds for selection (an objection which we allowed, though unwarrantably), we demanded whether he could possibly suppose that this exhausted the matter, or that the supposed small importance of this use precluded the existence of uses more important which *would* afford grounds of advantage and competition in the struggle for life.

As would be the case with one having the true "philosophical habit of mind," to be distinguished from the "scientific," Mr. Mivart's notice was attracted to the *form* in which we made this inquiry, rather than to the material import of it, and "as we might *a priori* expect to be the case," he showed "that breadth of view, freedom of handling, and flexibility of mind" which he believes to characterize the true philosopher, as contrasted with the mere physicist; but in a manner which appears to us to characterize rather the mere dialectician. With great fertility of invention he attempts the interpretation of our inquiry (which we grant was not sufficiently explicit for the "philosophical habit of mind"). The first interpretation is playful, and too delicate a jest to be transplanted to our pages. The next is, on the other hand, altogether too serious. He asks in return (p. 463), whether we can suppose "that he ever dreamed that the structures of animals are not useful to them. or that his position is an altogether anti-teleological one." No, we certainly do not. We only suppose that his position is not sufficiently teleological to interest him in the inquiry, and that he has overlooked many uses in the structures of animals, to which his special objections do not apply, and has vainly imagined, that by making those he felt called upon to examine as few and as faint as possible (except for the purpose of inspiring the agreeable emotion of admiration), he has reduced them to mere luxuries, having little or no value as grounds of advantage in the actual, incessant, and severe struggle to which all life is subject. "Nothing is easier than to admit in words the truth of the universal struggle for life, or more difficult"—even Mr. Darwin finds it so—"than constantly to bear this conclusion in mind. Yet unless it be thoroughly engrained in the mind, the whole economy of nature, with every fact in distribution, rarity, abundance, extinction, and variation, will be dimly seen or quite misunderstood."

Supposing us possessed by some such idea as that his "position is an altogether anti-teleological one," Mr. Mivart observes that we proceed "to exhibit the giraffe's neck in the character of a 'watch-tower.' But," he adds, "this leaves the question just where it was before. Of course I concede most readily and fully that it *is* a most admirable watch-tower, as it also *is* a most admirable high-reaching organ, but this tells us nothing of its *origin*. In both cases the long neck is most useful *when you have got it;* but the question is how it *arose*, and in this species *alone*. And similar and as convincing arguments could be brought against the watch-tower theory of origin as against the high-reaching theory, and not only this, but also against every other theory which could possibly be adduced." It appears that Mr. Mivart is prepared, *a priori*, to meet any number of foes of this sort that may present themselves singly. But *the* use, that is, all the essential uses of a structure, do not thus present themselves to our consideration and criticism. To deal adequately with the problem, we need the power to con-

eive how closely the uses lie to the actual necessities of life; ow, while we may be admiring in imagination the almost superfluous bounties of nature, this admirable watch-tower and igh-reaching organ may just be failing to save the poor animal, so highly endowed, from a miserable death. A lion, hose stealthy approach it would have detected, if a few inches more in the length of its neck, or in those of its companions, ad enabled it, or them, to see a few rods further, or over some intervening obstacle, has meantime sprung upon the wretched east, and is drawing its life-blood. This, if we were aware of t, would be the proper occasion to turn our admiration upon the fine endowments of the lion. Or, continuing our contemplation of the giraffe, it may be that its admirable high-reaching organ has just failed to reach the few remaining leaves near the tops of trees, which might have served to keep up its trength against the attacks of its enemies, or enabled it to eal more effective blows with its short horns, so admirably placed as weapons of offense; or might have served to sustain t through the famine and drought, till the returning rains would have given it more cause for gratitude (and us more occasion for admiration), for a few additional inches of its neck than for all the rest. Meantime, for the lack of these inches, our giraffe may have sickened and perished miserably, ailing in the competition and struggle for life. This need not tagger the optimist. The bounty of nature is not exhausted in giraffes. We can still admire the providential structure of the tree, which by its high-reaching branches has preserved some of its foliage from destruction by these beasts, and perhaps thereby saved not only its own life, but that of its kind. The occasions of destruction, even in the best guarded, most highly endowed lives, are all of the nature of accidents, and are generally as slight as the individual advantages are, for which so much influence is claimed in the theory of natural selection. Even death from old age is not a termination preordained in the original powers of any life, but is the effect of accumulated causes of this sort. Much of the destruction to which life is subject* is *strictly fortuitous so far as* either the

---

* The fortuity or chance is here, as in all other cases, a relative fact. The *strictest* use of the word applies to events which could not be anticipated except by omnis-

general powers or individual advantages in structures and habits are concerned; and is, therefore, quite independent of the effects of these advantages. Hence these effects are not thereby limited; for though a form of life presses, and is pressed upon, in all directions, yet it presses forward no less in the directions of its advantages.

The "philosophical habit of mind," which Mr. Mivart admires for its "breadth of view, freedom of handling, and flexibility of mind," is sometimes optimistic, sometimes pessimistic in its views of providence in nature, according as this flexible mind has its attention bent by a genial or morose disposition to a bright or dark aspect in things. But, whichever it is, it is generally extreme or absolute in its judgments. The "scientific" mind, which Mr. Mivart contrasts with it, and believes to be characterized by "a certain rigidity and narrowness," is held *rigidly* to the truth of things, whether good or bad, agreeable or disagreeable, admirable or despicable, and is *narrowed* to the closest, most uncompromising study of facts, and to a training which enables it to render in imagination the truest account of nature as it actually exists. The "scientific" imagination is fashioned by physical studies after the patterns of nature itself. The "philosophical habit of mind," trained in the school of human life, is the habit of viewing and interpreting nature according to its own dispositions, and defending its interpretations and attacking others with the skill and weapons of forensic and dialectical discussions. The earlier physical philosophers, the "physicists" of the ancient school, were "philosophers" in our author's sense of the term. They had not the "scientific" mind, since to them nature was a chaos

---

cience. To speak, therefore, of an event as *strictly accidental* is not equivalent to regarding it as undetermined, but only as determined in a manner which cannot be anticipated by a finite intelligence (see Mr. Mivart's Reply, p. 458). There are degrees in the intelligibility of things, according to human means and standards. Events like eclipses, which are the most normal and predictable of all events to the astronomer, are to the savage pure accidents; and with still lower forms of intelligence events are unforeseen which are familiar anticipations in the intelligence of the savage. To believe events to be *designed* or not, according as they are or are not predictable by us, is to assume for ourselves a complete and absolute knowledge of nature which we do not possess. Hence faith in a *designing* intelligence, supreme in nature, is not the result of any capacity in our own intelligence to comprehend the design, and is quite independent of any distinctions we may make, relative to our own powers of prediction, between orderly and accidental events.

hardly less confused than human affairs, and was studied with the same "breadth of view, freedom of handling, and flexibility of mind" which are fitted for and disciplined by such affairs. They were wise rather than well informed. Their observation was guided by tact and subtilty, or fine powers of discrimination, instead of by that machinery of knowledge and the arts which now fashions and guides the "scientific" mind. Thus the theory of atoms of Democritus has little resemblance to the chemical theory of atoms, since "the modern theory is the law of definite proportions; the ancient theory is merely the affirmation of indefinite combinations." Indefinite, or at least inexplicable, combinations meet the modern student of science, both physical and social, at every step of his researches, and in all the sciences with which we have compared the theory of natural selection. He does not stop to lay hold upon these *a priori*, with the loose though flexible grasp of the "philosophical habit of mind," but studies the intimate and elementary orders in them, and presumes them to be made up of such orders, though woven in infinite and inexplicable complexity of pattern.

The division which Mr. Mivart makes in kinds of intellectual ability, the "philosophical" and "scientific," and regards as a more real distinction than the threefold division we proposed,* is really determined by a broad distinction in the object-matter of thought and study, and is not in any way inconsistent with what we still regard as an equally real but more elementary one, which is equivalent in fact to the logical division of "hypothesis," "simple induction," and "deduction." These are not, indeed, co-ordinate as logical elements, since induction and deduction exhaust the simple elements of understanding when unaided by trained powers of perception and imagination. But practically, as habits of thought and disciplined skill in the study of nature and human affairs, they are distinct and divergent modes of investigation, partly determined by the character of the problem,—whether it be to explain a fact, or to properly name and classify it, or to prove it from assumed or admitted premises. Skill in the formation and verification of hypothesis,

* See ante p. 141

dependent on a power of imagination, which physical studies discipline peculiarly, belongs peculiarly to the student of physical science; and though, perhaps, "a poor monster," as Mr. Mivart says, when without an adequate basis in more strictly inductive studies, yet in that division of labors and abilities, on which the economy and efficiency of scientific investigation so largely depends, there is no propriety in thus regarding him, so long as co-operation in the pursuit of truth produces a symmetrical whole; not, indeed, complete in a single mind, except so far as it is erudite or instructed beyond the range of its special abilities, but in that solid general progress of science which such co-operation promotes.

EVOLUTION OF SELF-CONSCIOUSNESS.

It has come to be understood, and very generally allowed, that the conception of the origin of man as an animal race, as well as the origin of individual men within it, in accordance with the continuity of organic development maintained in the theory of evolution, does not involve any very serious difficulties, or difficulties so great as are presented by any other hypothesis of this origin, not excepting that of "special creation"; —if that can be properly called a hypothesis, which is, in fact, a resumption of all the difficulties of natural explanation, assuming them to be insuperable and summarizing them under a single positive name. Yet in this evolution, the birth of self-consciousness is still thought by many to be a step not following from antecedent conditions in "nature," except in an incidental manner, or in so far only as "natural" antecedents have prepared the way for the "supernatural" advent of the self-conscious soul.

Independently of the form of expression, and of the false sentiment which is the motive of the antithesis in this familiar conception, or independently of its mystical interest, which has given to the words "natural" and "supernatural" their commonly accepted meanings, there is a foundation of scientific truth in the conception. For the word "evolution" conveys a false impression to the imagination, not really intended in the scientific use of it. It misleads by suggesting a continuity in the *kinds* of powers and functions in living beings, that is, by suggesting transition by insensible steps from one *kind* to another, as well as in the *degrees* of their importance and exercise at different stages of development. The truth is, on the contrary, that according to the theory of evolution, new uses of old

---

* From the North American Review, April, 1873.

powers arise discontinuously both in the bodily and mental natures of the animal, and in its individual developments, as well as in the development of its race, although, at their rise, these uses are small and of the smallest importance to life. They seem merged in the powers to which they are incident, and seem also merged in the special purposes or functions in which, however, they really have no part, and which are no parts of them. Their services or functions in life, though realized only incidentally at first, and in the feeblest degree, are just as distinct as they afterwards come to appear in their fullest development. The new uses are related to older powers only as *accidents*, so far as the special services of the older powers are concerned, although, from the more general point of view of natural law, their relations to older uses have not the character of accidents, since these relations are, for the most part, determined by universal properties and laws, which are not specially related to the needs and conditions of living beings. Thus the uses of limbs for swimming, crawling, walking, leaping, climbing, and flying are distinct uses, and are related to each other only through the general mechanical principles of locomotion, through which some one use, in its first exercise, may be incident to some other, though, in its full exercise and perfection of special service, it is independent of the other, or has only a common dependence with the other or more general conditions.

Many mental as well as bodily powers thus have mixed natures, or independent uses; as, for example, the powers of the voice to call and allure, to warn and repel, and its uses in music and language; or the numerous uses of the human hand in services of strength and dexterity. And, on the contrary, the same uses are, in some cases, realized by independent organs as, for example, respiration in water and in the air by gills and lungs, or flight by means of fins, feathers, and webs. The appearance of a really new power in *nature* (using this word in the wide meaning attached to it in science), the power of flight in the first birds, for example, is only involved potentially in previous phenomena. In the same way, no act of self-consciousness, however elementary, may have been realized before man's first self-conscious act in the animal world; yet the act may have been involved potentially in pre-existing powers or causes. The derivation of this power, supposing it to have been observed by a finite angelic (not animal) intelligence, could not have been foreseen to be involved in the mental causes, on the conjunction of which it might, nevertheless, have been seen to depend. The angelic observation would have been a purely empirical one. The possibility of a subsequent analysis of these causes by the self-conscious animal himself, which would afford an explanation of their agency, by referring it to a rational combination of simpler elements in them, would not alter the case to the angelic intelligence, just as a rational explanation of flight could not be reached by such an intelligence as a consequence of known mechanical laws; since these laws are also animal conditions, or rather are more general and material ones, of which our angelic, spherical * intelligence is not supposed to have had any experience. Its observation of the conditions of animal flight would thus also be empirical; for an unembodied spirit cannot be supposed to analyze out of its general experiences the mechanical conditions of movement in animal bodies, nor, on the other hand, to be any more able than the mystic appears to be to analyze the conditions of its own intelligence out of its experiences of animal minds.

The forces and laws of molecular physics are similarly related to actual human intelligence. Sub-sensible properties and powers can only be empirically known, though they are "visualized" in the *hypotheses* of molecular movements and forces. Experimental science, as in chemistry, is full of examples of the discovery of new properties or new powers, which, so far as the conditions of their appearance were previously known, did not follow from antecedent conditions, except in an incidental manner,—that is, in a manner *not then foreseen* to be involved in them; and these effects became afterwards predictable from what had become known to be their antecedent conditions only by the empirical laws or rules which inductive experimentation had established. Neverthe-

---

* For an intellect complete without appendages of sense or locomotion, see Plato's Timæus, 33, 34.

less, the phenomena of the physical or chemical laboratory, however new or unprecedented, are very far from having the character of miracles, in the sense of supernatural events. They are still *natural* events; for, to the scientific imagination, *nature* means more than the continuance or actual repetition of the properties and productions involved in the course of ordinary events, or more than the *inheritance* and reappearance of that which appears in consequence of powers which have made it appear before. It means, in general, those kinds of effects which, though they may have appeared but once in the whole history of the world, yet appear dependent on conjunctions of causes which *would always* be followed by them. One experiment is sometimes, in some branches of science, (as a wide induction has found it to be in chemistry, for example,) sufficient to determine such a dependence, though the particular law so determined is a wholly empirical one; and the history of science has examples of such single experiments, or short series of experiments, made on general principles of experimentation, for the purpose of ascertaining empirical facts or laws, qualities, or relations, which are, nevertheless, generalized as universal ones. Certain "physical constants," so called, were so determined, and are applied in scientific inference with the same unhesitating confidence as that inspired by the familiarly exemplified and more elementary "laws of nature," or even by axioms. Scientific research implies the *potential* existence of the natures, classes, or kinds of effects which experiment brings to light through instances, and for which it also determines, in accordance with inductive methods, the previously unknown conditions of their appearance. This research implies the *latent* kinds or natures which mystical research contemplates (erroneously, in some, at least, of its meditations) under the name of "the supernatural."

To make any event or power supernatural in the mystic's regard requires, however, not merely that it shall be isolated and unparalleled in nature, but that it shall have more than an ordinary, or merely scientific, interest to the mystic's or to the *human* mind. The distinctively human or self-conscious interest, or sentiment, of self-consciousness gives an emphasis to the contrast named "natural and supernatural," through which mysticism is led to its speculations or assumptions of correspondingly emphatic contrasts in real existences. For mysticism is a speculation interpreting as matters of fact, or real existences outside of consciousness, impressions which are only determined within it by emphasis of attention or feeling. It is for the purpose of deepening still more, or to the utmost that its interest suggests, the really profound distinction between human and animal consciousness, or for the purpose of making the distinction *absolute*, of deepening this gulf into an unfathomable and impassable one, that mysticism appears to be moved to its speculations, and has imbued most philosophy and polite learning with its conceptions. Mental philosophy, or metaphysics, has, consequently, come down to us from ancient times least affected by the speculative interests and methods of modern science. Mysticism still reigns over the science of the mind, though its theory in general, or what is common to all theories called mystical, is very vague, and obscure even in the exclusively religious applications of the term. This vagueness has given rise to the more extended use and understanding of the term as it is here employed, which indicates little else than the generally apprehended *motive* of its speculations, or the feelings allied to all its forms of conception. These centre in the feeling of absolute worthiness in self-consciousness, as the source, and at the same time the perfection of existence and power. The naturalist's observations on the minds of men and animals are impertinences of the least possible interest to this sense of worth, very much as the geologist's observations are generally to the speculator who seeks in the earth for hidden mineral treasures.

Mysticism in mental philosophy has apparently gained, so far as it has been materially affected by such observations, a relative external strength, dependent on the real feebleness of the opposition it has generally met with from lovers of animals and from empirical observers and thinkers, in whom a generous sympathy with the manifestations of mind in animals and a disposition to do justice to them have been more conspicuous than the qualities of clearness or consistency. For, in the comparisons which they have attempted they have generally sought to break down the really well-founded distinctions of human and animal intelligence, and have sought to discredit the theory of them in this way, rather than by substituting for it a rational, scientific account of what is real in them. The ultimate metaphysical mystery which denies all comparison, and pronounces man a paragon in the kinds, as well the degrees, of his mental faculties, is, as a solution, certainly *simpler*, whatever other scientific excellence it may lack, than any solution that the difficulties of a true scientific comparison are likely to receive.

It is not in a strictly empirical way that this comparison can be clearly and effectively made, but rather by a critical re-examination of the phenomena of self-consciousness in themselves, with reference to their possible evolution from powers obviously common to all animal intelligences, or with reference to their potential, though not less natural, existence in mental causes, which could not have been known to involve them before their actual manifestation, but may, nevertheless, be found to do so by an analysis of these causes into the more general conditions of mental phenomena. Mystical metaphysics should be met by scientific inquiries on its own ground, that is, dogmatically, or by theory, since it despises the facts of empirical observation, or attributes them to shallowness, misinterpretation, or errors of observation, and contents itself with its strength as a system, and its impregnable self-consistency. Only an explanation of the phenomena of human consciousness, equally clear and self-consistent with its own, and one which, though not so simple, is yet more in accordance with the facts of a wider induction, could equal it in strength. But this might still be expected as the result of an examination of mental phenomena from the point of view of true science; since many modern sciences afford examples of similar triumphs over equally ancient, simple, and apparently impregnable doctrines. The history of science is full, indeed, of illustrations of the impotence, on one hand, of exceptional and isolated facts against established theory, and of the power, on the other hand, of their organization in new theories to revolutionize beliefs. The physical doctrine of a *plenum*, the doctrine of epicycles and vortices in astronomy, the corpuscular theory of optics, that of cataclysms in geology, and that of special creations in biology, each gave way, not absolutely through its intrinsic weakness, but through the greater success of a rival theory which superseded it. A sketch only is attempted in this essay of some of the results of such an examination into the psychological conditions, or antecedents, of the phenomena of self-consciousness; an examination which does not aim at diminishing, on the one hand, the real contrasts of mental powers in men and animals, nor at avoiding difficulties, on the other, by magnifying them beyond the reach of comparison.

The terms "science" and "scientific" have come, in modern times, to have so wide a range of application, and so vague a meaning, that (like many other terms, not only in common speech, but also in philosophy and in various branches of learning, which have come down to us through varying usages) they would oppose great difficulties to any attempts at defining them by *genus* and difference, or otherwise than by enumerating the branches of knowledge and the facts, or relations of the facts, to which usage has affixed them as names. Precision in proper definition being then impossible, it is yet possible to give to these terms so general a meaning as to cover all the knowledge to which they are usually applied, and still to exclude much besides. As the terms thus defined coincide with what I propose to show as the character of the knowledge peculiar to men, or which distinguishes the minds of men from those of other animals, I will begin with this definition. In science and in scientific facts there is implied a conscious purpose of including particular facts under general facts, and the less general under the more general ones. Science, in the modern use of the term, consists, essentially, of a knowledge of things and events either as effects of general causes, or as instances of general classes, rules, or laws; or even as isolated facts of which the class, law, rule, or cause is sought. The conscious purpose of arriving at general facts and at an adequate statement of them in language, or of bringing particular facts under explicit general ones, determines for any knowledge a scientific character.

Many of our knowledges and judgments from experience in practical matters are not so reduced, or sought to be reduced, to explicit principles, or have not a theoretical form, since the major premises, or general principles, of our judgments are not consciously generalized by us in forms of speech. Even matters not strictly practical, or which would be merely theoretical in their bearing on conduct, if reduced to a scientific form, like many of the judgments of common-sense, for example, are not consciously referred by us to explicit principles, though derived, like science, from experience, and even from special kinds of experience, like that of a man of business, or that of a professional adept. We are often led by being conscious of a sign of anything to believe in the existence of the thing itself, either past, present, or prospective, without having any distinct and general apprehension of the connection of the sign and thing, or any recognition of the sign under the general character of a sign. Not only are the judgments of common-sense in men, both the inherited and acquired ones, devoid of heads, or major premises (such as "All men are mortal"), in deductive inference, and devoid also of distinctly remembered details of experience in the inferences of induction, but it is highly probable that this is all but exclusively the character of the knowledges and judgments of the lower animals. Language, strictly so called, which some of these animals also have, or signs *purposely used* for communication, is not only required for scientific knowledge, but a second step of generalization is needed, and is made through reflection, by which this use of a sign is itself made an object of attention, and the sign is recognized in its general relations to what it signifies, and to what it has signified in the past, and will signify in the future. It is highly improbable that such a knowledge of knowledge, or such a *re*-cognition, belongs in any considerable, or effective, degree to even the most intelligent of the lower animals, or even to the lowest of the human race. This is what is properly meant by being "rational," or being a "rational animal." It is what I have preferred to call "scientific" knowledge; since the growing vagueness and breadth of application common to all ill-comprehended words (like "Positivism" in recent times) have given to "scientific" the meaning probably attached at first to "rational." This knowledge comes from reflecting on what we know in the common-sense, or semi-instinctive form, or making what we know a field of renewed research, observation, and analysis in the generalization of major premises. The line of distinction between such results of reflection, or between scientific knowledge and the common-sense form of knowledge, is not simply the dividing line between the minds of men and those of other animals; but is that which divides the knowledge produced by outward attention from that which is further produced by reflective attention. The former, throughout a considerable range of the higher intelligent animals, involves veritable judgments of a complex sort. It involves combinations of minor premises leading to conclusions through implicit major premises in the enthymematic reasonings, commonly employed in inferences from signs and likelihoods, as in prognostications of the weather, or in orientations with many animals. This knowledge belongs both to men and to the animals next to men in intelligence, though in unequal degrees.

So far as logicians are correct in regarding an enthymeme as a reasoning, independently of its statement in words; or in regarding as a rational process the passing from such a sign as the human nature of Socrates to the inference that he will die, through the data of experience concerning the mortality of other men,—data which are neither distinctly remembered in detail nor generalized explicitly in the formula, "all men are mortal," but are effective only in making mortality a more or less clearly understood part of the human nature, that is, in making it one of the attributes *suggested* by the name "man," yet not separated from the essential attributes by the contrasts of subject and attributes in real predication,—so far, I say, as this can be regarded as a reasoning, or a rational process, so far observation shows that the more intelligent dumb animals reason, or are rational. But this involves great vagueness or want of that precision in the use of signs which the antitheses of essential and accidental attributes and that of proper predication secure. There is little, or no, evidence to show that the animals which learn, to some extent, to comprehend human speech have an analytical comprehension of real general propositions, or of propositions in which both subject and predicate are general terms and differ in meaning. A merely verbal general proposition, declaring only the equivalence of two general names, might be comprehended by such minds, if it could be made of sufficient interest to attract their attention. But this is extremely doubtful, and it would not be as a *proposition*, with its contrasts of essential and added elements of conception that it would be comprehended. It would be, in effect, only repeating in succession two general names of the same class of objects. Such minds could, doubtless, comprehend a single class of objects, or an indefinite number of resembling things by several names; that is, several signs of such a class would recall it to their thoughts, or revive a representative image of it; and they would thus be aware of the equivalence of these signs; but they would not attach precision of meaning and different degrees of generality to them, or regard one name as the name or sign of another name; as when we define a triangle to be a rectilinear figure, and a figure of three sides.

Only one degree of generality is, however, essential to inference from signs, or in enthymematic reasoning. Moreover, language in its relation to thought does not consist exclusively of spoken, or written, or imagined words, but of signs in general, and, essentially, of internal images or successions of images, which are the representative imaginations of objects and their relations; imaginations which severally stand for each and all of the particular objects or relations of a *kind*. Such are the visual imaginations called up by spoken or written concrete general names of visible objects, as "dog" or "tree"; which are vague and feeble as images, but effective as notative, directive, or guiding elements in thought. These are the internal signs of things and events, and are instruments of thought in judgment and reasoning, not only with dumb animals but also with men, in whom they are supplemented, rather than supplanted, by names. But being of feeble intensity, and little under the influence of distinct attention or control of the will, compared to actual perceptions and to the voluntary movements of utterance and gesture, their nature has been but dimly understood even by metaphysicians, who are still divided into two schools in logic,—the conceptualists and the nominalists. The "concepts" of the former are really composed of these vague and feeble notative images, or groups of images, to which clearness and distinctness of attention are given by their associations with outward (usually vocal) signs. Hence a second degree of observation and generalization upon these images, as objects in reflective thought, cannot be readily realized independently of what would be the results of such observations, namely, their associations with outward signs. Even in the most intelligent dumb animal they are probably so feeble that they cannot be associated with outward signs in such a manner as to make these distinctly appear as substitutes, or signs equivalent to them.

So far as images act in governing trains of thought and reasoning, they act as signs; but, with reference to the more vivid outward signs, they are, in the animal mind, merged in the things signified, like stars in the light of the sun. Hence, language, in its narrower sense, as the instrument of reflective thought, appears to depend directly on the intensity of significant, or representative, images; since the power to attend to these and intensify them still further, at the same time that an equivalent outward sign is an object of attention, would appear to depend solely on the relative intensities of the two states, or on the relations of intensity in perception and imagination, or in original and revived impressions. The direct power of attention to intensify a revived impression in imagination does not appear to be different in kind from the power of attention in perception, or in outward impressions generally. But this direct power would be obviously aided by the indirect action of attention when fixed by an outward sign, provided attention could be directed to both at the same time; as a single glance may comprehend in one field of view the moon or the brighter planets and the sun, since the moon or planet is not hidden like the stars, by the glare of day.

As soon, then, as the progress of animal intelligence through an extension of the range in its powers of memory, or in revived impressions, together with a corresponding increase in the vividness of these impressions, has reached a certain point (a progress in itself useful, and therefore likely to be secured in some part of nature, as one among its numerous grounds of selection, or lines of advantage), it becomes possible for such an intelligence to fix its attention on a vivid outward sign, without losing sight of, or dropping out of 'distinct attention, an image or revived impression; which latter would only serve, in case of its spontaneous revival in imagination, as a sign of the same thing, or the same event. Whether the vivid outward sign be a real object or event, of which the revived image is the counterpart, or whether it be a sign in a stricter meaning of the term,—that is, some action, figure, or utterance, associated either naturally or artificially with all similar objects or events, and, consequently, with the revived and representative image of them,—whatever the character of this outward sign may be, provided the representative image, or inward sign, still retains, in distinct consciousness, its power as such, then the outward sign may be consciously recognized as a substitute for the inward one, and a consciousness of simultaneous internal and external suggestion, or significance, might be realized; and the contrast of thoughts and things, at least in their power of suggesting that of which they may be coincident signs, could, for the first time, be perceptible. This would plant the germ of the distinctively human form of self-consciousness.

Previously to such a simultaneous consciousness of movements in imagination and movements in the same direction arising from perception, realized through the comparative vividness of the former, all separate and distinct consciousness of the inward sign would be eclipsed, and attention would pass on to the thought suggested by the outward sign. A similar phenomenon is frequently observed with us in successions of inward suggestions, or trains of thought. The attention often skips intermediate steps in a train, or appears to do so. At least, the memory of steps, which appear essential to its rational coherency, has ceased when we revive the train or repeat it voluntarily. This happens even when only a few moments have elapsed between the train and its repetition. Some writers assert that the omitted steps are immediately forgotten in such cases, on account of their feebleness,—as we forget immediately the details of a view which we have just seen, and remember only its salient points; while others maintain that the missing steps are absent from consciousness, even in the original and spontaneous movements of the train; or are present only through an unconscious agency, both in the train and its revival. This being a question of memory, reference cannot be made to memory itself for the decision of it. To decide whether a thing is completely forgotten, or has never been experienced, we have no other resource than rational analogy, which, in the present case, appears to favor the theory of oblivion, rather than that of latent mental ties and actions; since oblivion is a *vera causa* sufficient to account for the difference between such revived trains and those in which no steps are missed, or could be rationally supposed to have been present. The theory of "latent mental agency" appears to confound the original spontaneous movement of the train with what appears as its representative in its voluntary revival. This revival, in some cases, really involves new conditions, and is not, therefore, to be rationally interpreted as a precisely true recollection. If repeated often, it will establish direct and strong associations of contiguity between salient steps in the train which were connected at first by feebler though still conscious steps. The complete obliteration of these is analogous, as I have said, to the loss, in primary forms of memory, of details which are present to consciousness in actual first perceptions.

If, as more frequently happens, the whole train, with all its steps of suggestion, is recalled in the voluntary revival of it (without any sense of missing steps), the feebler intermediate links, that in other cases are obliterated, would correspond to the feebler, though (in the more advanced animal intelligences) comparatively vivid, mental signs which have in them the germ, as I have said, of the human form of self-consciousness. The growth of this consciousness, its development from this germ, is a more direct process than the production of the germ itself, which is only incidental to previous utilities in the power of memory. Thought, henceforward, may be an object to thought in its distinct contrast, as an inward sign, with the outward and more vivid sign of that which they both suggest, or revive from memory. This contrast is heightened if the outward one is more strictly a sign; that is, is not the perception of an object or event, of which the inward and representative image is a counterpart, but is of a different nature, for instance some movement or gesture or vocal utterance, or some graphic sign, associated by contiguity with the object or event, or, more properly, with its representative image. The "concept" so formed is not a thing complete in itself, but is essentially a cause, or step, in mental trains. The outward sign, the image, or inward sign, and the suggested thought, or image, form a train, like a train which might be wholly within the imagination. This train is present, in all its three constituents, to the first, or immediate, consciousness, in all degrees of intelligence; but in the revival of it, in the inferior degrees of intelligence, the middle term is obliterated, as in the trains of thought above considered. The animal has in mind only an image of the sign, previously present in perception, followed now immediately by an image of what was suggested through the obliterated mental image. But the latter, in the higher degrees of intelligence, is distinctly recalled as a middle term. In the revival of past trains, which were first produced through outward signs, the dumb animal has no consciousness of there having been present more than one of the two successive signs, which, together with the suggested image, formed the actual train in its first occurrence. The remembered outward sign is now a thought, or image, immediately suggesting or recalling that which was originally suggested by a feebler intermediate step.

In pure imaginations, not arising by actual connections through memory, the two terms are just the same with animals as in real memory; except that they are not felt to be the representatives of a former real connection. The contrast of the real and true with the imaginary and false is, then, the only general one of which such a mind could be aware in the phenomena of thought. The contrast of thought itself with perception, or with the actual outward sign and suggestion of the thought, is realized only by the revival in memory of the feeble connecting link. This effects a contrast not only between what is real and what is merely imaginary, but also between what is out of the mind and what is within it. The minute difference in the force of memory, on which this link in the chain of attention at first depended, was one of immense consequence to man. This feeble link is the dividing region, interval, or cleft between the two more vivid images; one being more vivid as a direct recollection of an actual outward impression, and the other being more vivid, or salient, from the interest or the motives which gave it the prominence of a thought demanding attention ; either as a memory of a past object or event of interest, or the image of something in the immediate future. The disappearance altogether of this feeble link would, as I have said, take from the images connected by it all contrast with any pair of steps in a train, except a consciousness of reality in the connection of these images in a previous experience.*

---

* It appears, at first sight, a rash hypothesis to imagine so extensive an action of illusion as I have supposed in the revivals of memory,—a self-vouching faculty of which, in general, the testimony cannot be questioned,—since each recall asserts for itself an identity with what is recalled by it, either in past outward experiences or in previous revivals of them. But the hypothesis of uniform, or frequent, illusions in individual judgments of memory is not made in contradiction of experiences in general, including those remembered, when reduced to rational consistency. The familiar fact that no memory, even of an immediately past experience, is an adequate reproduction of everything that must have been present in it in actual consciousness, and must have received more or less attention, is familiarly verified by repeating the remembered experiences. Memory itself thus testifies to its own fallibility. But this is not all. Illusion in an opposite direction, the more than adequate revival of some experiences, so far as vividness and apparently remembered details are concerned, affects our memories of dreams, demonstrably in some, presumably in many. What is commonly called a dream is not what is present to the imagination in sleep, but what is believed, often illusively, to have been present; and is, doubtless, in general, more vivid in memory and furnished with more numerous details, owing to the livelier action of imagination in waking moments. The liveliness of an actual dream is rather in its dominant feeling or interest than in its images.

The order of internal events, or the order of suggestion in actual dreams, is often reversed in the waking memories of them. A dream very long and full of details, as it appears in memory, and taking many words to relate, is sometimes recalled from the

To exemplify this somewhat abstruse analysis, let us examine what, according to it, would be the mental movements in a

suggestions and trains of thought in sleep which are comprised in the impressions of a few moments. Such a dream usually ends in some startling or interesting event, which was a misinterpretation in sleep of some real outward impression, as a loud or unusual noise, or some inward sensation, like one of hunger, thirst, heat, cold, or numbness, which really stood in sleep at the beginning of the misremembered train of thought, instead of constituting its *dénouement* in a remembered series of real incidents. The remembered dream *seems* to have been an isolated series of such incidents, succeeding each other in the natural order of experience; but this appearance may well arise from the absence of any remembered indications of a contrary order; or from the absence, on one hand, of a consciousness in sleep of anything more vivid than the actual dream, and the real feebleness, on the other hand, of the dream itself in respect to everything in it except the salient incident, or the dominant interest, which caused it to be remembered along with the feeble sketch of suggested incidents. Surprise at incongruities in parts of trains often constitutes this interest.

If the waking imagination really fills out this sketch, and avouches the whole without check from anything really remembered, the phenomenon would be perfectly accordant with what is known of the dealings of imagination with real experiences, and with what is to be presumed of the comparative feebleness of its powers in sleep. A remembered dream would thus be, in some cases, a twofold illusion,—an illusion in sleep arising from misinterpreted sensations, and an illusion in memory concerning what was actually the train of thoughts excited by the mistake, the train being in fact often inverted in such an apparent recollection. Savages and the insane believe their dreams to be real experiences. The civilized and sane man believes them to be true memories of illusions in sleep. A step farther in the application of the general tests of true experience would reduce some dreams to illusive memories of the illusions of sleep.

There does not appear on analysis, made in conformity to the reality of experiences in general, that there is any intrinsic difference between a memory and an imagination, the reality of the former being dependent on extrinsic relations, and the outward checks of other memories. Memory, as a whole, vouches for itself, and for all its mutually consistent details, and banishes mere imaginations from its province, not as foreigners, but on account of their lawlessness, or incoherence with the rest of its subjects, and it does so through the exercise of what is called the judgments of experience, which are in fact mnemonic summaries of experiences (including instinctive tendencies). The imaginations of the insane are in insurrection against this authority of memory in general experience, or against what is familiarly called "reason." When sufficiently vivid, or powerful, and numerous, they usurp the powers of state, or the authority of memory and free intelligent volition. "Reason" is then said to be "dethroned."

The unreality of some dreams would thus appear to be more complete than they are in general discovered to be by mature, sane, and reflective thought, and by indirect observations upon their conditions and phenomena. The supposition of a similar illusion in the phenomena of reflection on the immediately past, or passing, impressions of the mind affords an explanation of a curious phenomenon, not uncommon in waking moments, which is referred to by many writers on psychology, namely, the phenomenon of experiencing in minute detail what appears also to be recalled as a past experience. Some writers have attempted to explain this as a veritable revival, by a passing experience, of a really past and very remote one, either in our progenitors, as some evolutionists suppose; or in a previous life, or in some state of individual existence, otherwise unremembered, as the mystic prefers to believe; a revival affected by an actual coincidence, in many minute particulars, of a present real experience with a really past one. But if a passing real experience could be supposed to be divided, so to speak, or to make a double impression in memory,—one the ordinary impression of what is imme-

man,—let him be a sportsman,—and a domestic animal,—let
it be his dog,—on hearing a name,—let it be the name of
some game, as " fox." The general character of the phenomena in both would be the same on the actual first hearing of
this word. The word would suggest a mental image of the
fox, then its movements of escape from its hunters, and the
thought would pass on and dwell, through the absorbing in
terest of it, on the hunter's movements of pursuit, or pass on
even to the capture and destruction of the game. This would,
doubtless, recall to the minds of the hunter and his hound one
or more real and distinctly remembered incidents of the sort.
Now if we suppose this train of thought to be revived (as undoubtedly it is capable of being, both in the man and the dog),
it will be the same in the man's mind as on its first production ;
except that the name "fox" will be thought of as an auditory,
or else a vocal image, instead of being heard ; and the visual
image of the fox will be recalled by it with all the succeeding
parts of the repeated train. ✓ But in the dog, either the auditory image of the name will not be recalled, since the vocal
image does not exist in his mind to aid the recall (his voluntary vocal powers not being capable of forming it even in the
first instance) ; or if such an auditory image arises, the representative visual or olfactory * one will not appear in distinct
consciousness. His attention will pass at once from either of
these signs, but from one only to the more intense and interesting parts of the train,—to the pursuit and capture of the
game, or to actually remembered incidents of the kind. Either the first or the immediate sign will remain in oblivion.

Hence the dog's dreams, or trains of thought, when they are
revivals of previous trains, or when they rise into prominent
consciousness in consequence of having been passed through

diately past, and the other a dream-like impression filled out on its immediate revival in
reflection with the same details,—the supposition would be in accordance with what is
really known of some dreams, and would, therefore, be more probable than the above
explanations. It is possible to trust individual memories too far, even in respect to what
is immediately past, as it is to trust too far a single sense in respect to what is immediately present. Rational consistency, in all experiences, or in experience on the whole,
✓is the ultimate test of reality or truth in our judgments, whether these are "intuitive,"
or consciously derived.

* Images in dogs are supposed to depend largely on the sense of smell.

before, omit or skip over the steps which at first served only as suggesting and connecting signs, following now only the associations of contiguity, established in the first occurrence of the train between its more prominent parts. The suggested thought eclipses by its glare the suggesting one. The interest of an image, or its power to attract attention and increased force, depends in the dog only on its vividness as a memory, or as a future purpose or event, and very little, if at all, on its relations and agency as a *sign*. Images, as well as outward signs, serve, as I have said, in the dumb animals as well as in man in this capacity; but this is not *recognized* by the animal, since those parts of a train which serve only as signs are too feeble to be revived in the repeated train; and new associations of mere contiguity in the prominent parts of it take their places. All that would be recognized in the animal mind by reflection on thought as thought, or independently of its reality as a memory, an anticipation, or a purpose, would be its unreality, or merely imaginary character.

If, on the contrary, a greater intensity, arising from a greater power of simple memory, should revive the feebler parts in repeated trains of thought, to the degree of attracting attention to them, and thus bringing them into a more distinct and vivid consciousness, there might arise an interest as to what they are, as to what are their relations, and where they belong, which would be able to inspire and guide an act of distinct reflection. A thought might thus be determined as a representative mental image; and such acts of reflection, inspired also by other motives more powerful than mere inquisitiveness, would by observation, analysis, and generalization (the counterparts of such outward processes in the merely animal mind) bring all such representative images, together with real memories and anticipations, into a single group, or subjective connection. The recognition of them in this connection is the knowledge of them as *my* thoughts, or *our* thoughts, or as phenomena of the mind.

When a thought, or an outward expression, acts in an animal's mind or in a man's, in the capacity of a sign, it carries forward the movements of a train, and directs attention away from itself to what it signifies 'or suggests; and consciousness is concentrated on the latter. But being sufficiently vivid in itself to engage distinct attention, it determines a new kind of action, and a new faculty of observation, of which the cerebral hemispheres appear to be the organs. From the action of these, in their more essential powers in memory and imagination, the objects or materials of reflection are also derived. Reflection would thus be, not what most metaphysicians appear to regard it, a fundamentally new faculty in man, as elementary and primordial as memory itself, or the power of abstractive attention, or the function of signs and representative images in generalization; but it would be determined in its contrasts with other mental faculties by the nature of its objects. On its subjective side it would be composed of the same mental faculties—namely, memory, attention, abstraction —as those which are employed in the primary use of the senses. It would be engaged upon what these senses have furnished to memory; but would act as independently of any orders of grouping and succession presented by them, as the several senses themselves do of one another. To this extent, reflection is a distinct faculty, and though, perhaps, not peculiar to man, is in him so prominent and marked in its effects on the development of the individual mind, that it may be regarded as his most essential and elementary mental distinction in kind. For differences of degrees in causes may make differences of kinds in effects.

Motives more powerful than mere inquisitiveness about the feebler steps or *mere* thoughts of a revived train, and more efficient in concentrating attention upon them, and upon their functions as signs, or suggesting images, would spring from the social nature of the animal, from the uses of mental communication between the members of a community, and from the *desire* to communicate, which these uses would create. And just as an outward sign associated with a mental image aids by its intensity in fixing attention upon the latter, so the *uses* of such outward signs and the motives connected with their employment would add *extensive* force, or interest, to the energy of attention in the cognition of this inward sign;

and hence would aid in the reference of it and its sort to the subject *ego*,—a being already known, or distinguished from other beings, as that which wills, desires, and feels. That which wills, desires, and feels is, in the more intelligent domestic animal, known by the proper name, which the animal recognizes and answers to by its actions, and is a consciousness of its individuality. It is not known or recognized by that most generic name " I "; since phenomena common to this individual and to others, or capable of being made common through the communications of language, are not distinctly referred to the individual self by that degree of abstractive attention and precision which an habitual exercise of the faculty of reflection is required to produce. But, in the same manner, the word "world," which includes the conscious subject in its meaning, would fail to suggest anything more to such an intelligence than more concrete terms do,—such as what is around, within, near, or distant from consciousness; or it would fail to suggest the *whole* of that which philosophers divide into *ego* and *non-ego*, the outward and inward worlds. A contrast of this whole to its parts, however divided in predication, or the antithesis of subject and attributes, in a divisible unity and its component particulars, would not be suggested to an animal mind by the word "world." The "categories," or forms and conditions of human understanding, though doubtless innate in the naturalist's sense of the term, that is inherited, are only the ways and facilities of the higher exercise of the faculty of reflection. They are, doubtless, ways and facilities that are founded on the ultimate nature of mind; yet, on this very account, are universal, though only potential in the animal mind generally; just as the forms and conditions of *locomotion* are generally in the bodies of plants; forms and conditions founded on the ultimate natures or laws of motion, which would be exemplified in plants, if they also had the power of changing their positions, and are indeed exemplified in those forms of vegetable life that are transported, such as seeds, or can move and plant themselves, like certain spores.

The world of self-conscious intellectual activity,—the world of mind,—has, doubtless, its ultimate unconditional laws, everywhere exemplified in the actual phenomena of abstractive and reflective thought, and capable of being generalized in the reflective observations of the philosopher, and applied by him to the explanation of the phenomena of thought wherever manifested in outward expressions, whether in his fellow-men, or in the more intelligent dumb animals. Memory, in the effects of its more powerful and vivid revivals in the more intelligent animals, and especially in the case of large-brained man, presents this new world, in which the same faculties of observation, analysis, and generalization as those employed by intelligent beings in general, ascertain the marks and classes of phenomena strictly mental, and divide them, as a whole class, or *summum genus*, from those of the outward world. The distinction of subject and object becomes thus a classification through observation and analysis, instead of the intuitive distinction it is supposed to be by most metaphysicians. Intuitive to some extent, in one sense of the word, it doubtless is; that is, facilities and predispositions to associations, which are as effective as repeated experiences and observations would be, and which are inherited in the form of instincts, doubtless have much to do in bringing to pass this cognition, as well as many others, which appear to be innate, not only in the lower animals but also in man.

The very different aim of the evolutionist from that of his opponents—the latter seeking to account for the *resemblances* of mental actions in beings supposed to be radically different in their mental constitutions, while the former seeks to account for the *differences* of manifestation in fundamentally similar mental constitutions—gives, in the theory of evolution, a philosophical *rôle* to the word "instinct," and to its contrast with intelligence, much inferior to that which this contrast has had in the discussions of the mental faculties of animals. For the distinction of instinct and intelligence, though not less real and important in the classification of actions in psycho-zoölogy, and as important even as that of animal and vegetable is in general zoölogy, or the distinctions of organic and inorganic, living and dead, in the general science of life, is yet, like these, in its applications a vague and ill-defined distinction, and is most profitably studied in the subordinate classes of actions, and in the special contrasts which are summarized by it. Under the naturalist's point of view, the contrasts of dead and living matters, inorganic and organic products, vegetable and animal forms and functions, automatic and sentient movements, instinctive and intelligent motives and actions, are severally rough divisions of *series*, which are clearly enough contrasted in their extremities, but ill defined at their points of division. Thus, we have the long series beginning with the processes of growth, nutrition, and waste, and in movements independent of nervous connections, and continued in processes in which sensations are involved, first vaguely, as in the processes of digestion, circulation, and the general stimulative action of the nervous system; then distinctly, as in the stimulative sensations of respiration, winking, swallowing, coughing, and sneezing, more or less under general control or the action of the will. This series is continued, again, into those sensations, impulses, and consequent actions which are wholly controllable, though spontaneously arising; and thence into the motives to action which are wholly dependent on, or involved in, the immediate controlling powers of the will,—a series in which the several marks of distinction are clearly enough designated in the abstract, as the colors of the spectrum are by their names, but are not clearly separated in the concrete applications of them.

Again, we have the series of voluntary actions, beginning at the connections between perceptions, emotions, and consequent actions, which are strictly instinctive. These, though inherited, are independent of the effects of higher, and more properly voluntary, actions in the individual's progenitors, as well as in himself. When they are not simple ultimate and universal laws of mental natures, or elementary mental connections, they are combinations produced through their serviceableness to life, or by natural selection and exercise, that is in the same general manner in which bodily organs, powers, and functions are produced or altered. Such connections between perceptions, emotions, and consequent actions, derived through natural selection, or even those that are ultimate laws, and determine, in a manner not peculiar to any species, the conditions and uses of serviceable actions,—are *instinctive* connections, or powers of *instinct*, in a restricted but perfectly definite use of the word. But following immediately in the series of voluntary actions are, first, the inherited effects of habits, and next, habits properly so called, or effects produced by higher voluntary actions in the individual. *Habits* properly so called, and *dispositions*, which are the inherited effects of habits, are not different in their practical character or modes of action from true instincts; but differ only in their origin and capacity of alteration through the higher forms of volition. The latter, or proper, volitions are connections between the occasions, or external means and conditions of an action, and the production of the action itself through the *motive of the end*, and not through emotions or by any other ties instinctively uniting them. They are joined by the foreseen ulterior effect of the action, or else through a union produced by its influence. The desirableness of what is effected by an action connects its occasions, or present means and conditions, with the action itself, and causes its production through the end felt in imagination. The influence of the end, or ulterior motive in volition, may not be a consciously recognized part of the action, or a distinctly separated step in it, and will actually cease to be the real tie when a series of repeated volitions has established a habit, or a fixed association between them and their occasions, or external conditions. This connection in habits is, as we have said, closely similar to strictly instinctive connections, and is indistinguishable from them independently of questions of origin and means of alterations.

Independently of these questions, the series of voluntary actions starting from the strictly instinctive joins to them natural dispositions, or the inherited effects of habit, and passes on to habits properly so called, thence into those in which the ulterior motives of true volitions are still operative, though not as separate parts of consciousness, and thence on to mere faculties of action, or to those actions in which such a motive is still the sole effective link, though quite faded out of distinct attention, or attended to with a feeble and intermittent consciousness. Thence it comes finally to the distinct recognition in reflective thought of an ulterior motive to an action. The ulterior motive, the end or good to be effected by an action, anticipated in imagination, joins the action to its present means and conditions in actual volitions, or else joins it in imagination with some future occurrence of them in an *intention*, or a predetermination of the will. These ulterior motives, ends, or determinations of an action through foreseen consequences of it, may be *within* the will, in the common and proper meaning of the word, when it is spoken of as free, or unconstrained by an outward force, or necessity; or they may be *without* it, like instinctive tendencies to which the will is said to *consent* or *yield*, as well as in other cases to be *opposed*. The motives within the will, either distinctly or vaguely operative, or completely superseded by forces of habit, constitute the individual's character.

To summarize all the steps and contrasts of these series under the general heads of intelligence and instinct would be, from the evolutionist's and naturalist's point of view, only a rough classification, like that of living beings into animals and plants; and any attempts at investigating the distinctions and classes of mental natures by framing elaborate definitions of this summary contrast would be like concentrating all the energies of scientific pursuit in biography, and staking its success on the question whether the sponge be an animal or a plant. This is, in fact, the scholastic method, from which modern science is comparatively, and fortunately, set free; being contented with finding out more and more about beings that are unmistakably animals or plants, and willing to study the nature of the sponge by itself, and defer the classification of it to the end. The more ambitious scholastic method is followed in the science of psycho-zoölogy by those who seek, in an ultimate definition of this sort, to establish an impassable barrier between the minds of men and those of the lower animals,—being actuated apparently by the naïve, though generous, motive of rendering the former more respectable, or else of defending a worth in them supposed to be dependent on such a barrier. This aim would be confusing at least, if not a false one, in a strictly scientific inquiry.

Although the definition of the subject world through the distinction in memory of the phenomena of signification from those of outward perception, would be a classification spontaneously arising through inherited facilities and predispositions to associations, which are as effective as repeated experiences would be, it must still be largely aided by the voluntary character of outward signs,—vocal, gestural, and graphic,—by which all signs are brought under the control of the will, or of that most central, active personality, which is thus connected externally and actively, as well as through the memory, with the inward signs or the representative mental images. These images are brought by this association under stronger and steadier attention; their character, as representative images or signs, is more distinctly seen in reflection, and they are not any longer merely guides in thought, blindly followed. They form, by this association, a little representative world arising to thought at will. Command of language is an important condition of the effective cognition of a sign as such. It is highly probable that the dog not only cannot utter the sound "fox," but cannot revive the sound as heard by him. The word cannot, therefore, be of aid to him in fixing his attention in reflection on the mental image of the fox as seen or smelt by him. But the latter, spontaneously arising, would be sufficient to produce a lively train of thoughts, or a vivid dream. • It by no means follows from his deficiencies of vocal and auditory imagination that the dog has not, in some directions, aid from outward signs, and some small degree of reflective power, though this, probably, falls far short of the clear division of the two worlds realized in the cognition of "*cogito*." Thus, he has at command the outward sign of the chase, incipient movements of his limbs, such as he makes in his dreams; and this may make the mental image of the chase, with its common obstacles and incidents, distinct in his imagination, in spite of the greater interest which carries the thoughts of his dream forward to the end of the pursuit, the capture of the game. He may even make use of this sign, as he in fact does when he indicates to his master by his movements his eagerness for a walk or for the chase.

Command of signs, and, indeed, all the volitional or active powers of an animal, including attention in perception, place it in relation to outward things in marked contrast with its passive relations of sensation and inattentive or passive perception. The distinctness, or prominence, in consciousness given by an animal's attention to its perceptions, and the greater energy given by its intentions or purposes to its outward movements, cannot fail to afford a ground of discrimination between these as causes, both of inward and outward events, and those outward causes which are not directly under such control, but form an independent system, or several distinct systems, of causes. This would give rise to a form of self-consciousness more immediate and simple than the intellectual one, and is apparently realized in dumb animals. They, probably, do not have, or have only in an indistinct and ineffective form, the intellectual cognitions of *cogito* and *sum;* but having reached the cognition of a contrast in subject and object as *causes* both in inward and outward events, they have already acquired a form of subjective consciousness, or a knowledge of the *ego.* That they do not, and cannot, name it, at least by a general name, or understand it by the general name of " I " or *ego*, comes from the absence of the attributes of *ego* which constitute the intellectual self-consciousness. A dog can, nevertheless, understand the application of his own proper name to himself, both in the direct and the indirect reference of our language to his conduct or his wants; and can also understand the application to himself of the general name,—" dog." He cannot say, " I am a dog," and probably has but the faintest, if any, understanding of what the proposition would mean if he could utter it; though he probably has as much understanding, at least, as the parrot has in saying, " I am Poll." For there are, in these propositions, two words expressing the abstractest ideas that the human mind can reach. One of them, " I," is the name of one of the two *summa genera*, *ego* and *non-ego*, into which human consciousness is divisible. " I am a dog," and "Camp is a dog," would mean much the same to Camp; just as " I am a child," and " John is a child " are not clearly distinguished by John even after he has acquired considerable command of language. The other word, "am," is a form of the substantive verb expressing existence in general, but further determined to express the *present* existence of the *speaker* or *subject.* These further determinations, in tense, number, and persons, are, however, the most important parts of meaning in the various forms of the substantive verb to the common and barbarous minds, from which we and the philosophical grammarian have received them. The substantive verb is, accordingly, irregular in most languages under the form of a grammatical paradigm. In this form the philosophical grammarian subordinates to the infinitive meaning of a word those determinations which, in the invention of words, were apparently regarded as leading ideas in many other cases as well as in the substantive verb, and were expressed by words with distinct etymologies.

Not only the dog and other intelligent dumb animals, but some of the least advanced among human beings, also, are unable to arrive at a distinct abstraction of what is expressed by "to be," or "to exist." Being is concreted, or determined, to such minds down, at least, to the conception of living or acting; to a conception scarcely above what is implied in the actions of the more intelligent animals, namely, their apprehension of themselves as agents or patients with wills and feelings distinct from those of other animals, and from the forces and interests of outward nature generally. "Your dog is here, or is coming, and at your service," is a familiar expression in the actions of dogs not remarkable for intelligence. A higher degree of abstraction and generalization than the simple steps, which are sufficient, as we have seen, for inference in enthymematic reasonings to particular conclusions, would be required in reflection; and a more extensive and persistent exercise of the faculty of reflection, aided by voluntary signs or by language, than any dumb animal attains to, would be needed to arrive at the cognition of *cogito* and *sum.* This is a late acquisition with children; and it would, indeed, be surprising if the mind of a dumb animal should attain to it. But there is little ground in this for believing, with most metaphysicians, that the cognition is absolutely *sui generis,* or an ultimate and underived form of knowledge; or that it is not approached gradually, as well as realized with different degrees of clearness and precision, as the faculty of reflection becomes more and more exercised.

That a dumb animal should not know itself to be a thinking being, is hardly more surprising than that it should not be aware of the circulation of its blood and other physiological functions; or that it should not know the anatomy of its frame or that of its nervous system, or the seat of its mental faculties, or the fact that the brain is much smaller in it, in proportion to the size of its body, than in man. Its reflective observation may be as limited in respect to the phenomena of thought as the outward observation of most men is in respect to these results of scientific research. And, on the other hand, the boasted intellectual self-consciousness of man is a knowledge of a subject, not through all its attributes and phenomena, but only through enough of them in general to determine and distinguish it from outward objects, and make it serve as the subject of further attributions or predications, as reflective observation makes them known. The abstract forms of this knowledge, the laws of logic and grammar, and the categories of the understanding, which are forms of all scientific knowledge, are all referable to the action of a *purpose* to know, and to fix knowledge by precise generalization; just as the mechanical conditions of flight are referable to the purpose to fly and to secure the requisite means. Generalization already exists, however, with particular acts of inquisitiveness in the animal mind; and there is required only the proper degree of attention to signs in order to make it act in accordance with laws which, *if they are universal and necessary laws of the mind*, are equally laws of the animal intelligence, though not actually exemplified in it; just as the laws of locomotion are not actually exemplified in the bodies of plants, but are still potential in them.

The inferior and savage races of men, whose languages do not include any abstract terms like truth, goodness, and sweetness, but only concrete ones, like true, good, and sweet, would hardly be able to form a conception, even a vague and obscure one, of the mystic's research of omniscience in the profundities of self-consciousness. They ought on this account, perhaps, to be regarded as races distinct from that of these philosophers, at least mentally, and to be classed, in spite of their powers of speech and limited vocabularies, with the dumb, but still intelligent, animals. If, however, the theory above propounded be true, this greatest of human qualities, intelligent self-consciousness, understood in its actual and proper limits, would follow as a consequence of a greater brain, a greater, or more powerful and vivid, memory and imagination, bringing to light, as it were, and into distinct consciousness, phenomena of thought which reflective observation refers to the subject, already known in the dumb animal, or distinguished as an active cause from the forces of outward nature, and from the wills of other animals. The degrees of abstraction and the successively higher and higher steps of generalization, the process which, in scientific knowledge, brings not only the particulars of experience under general designations, but, with a conscious purpose, brings the less general under the more general, or gives common names not only to each and all resembling objects and relations, but also more general common names to what is denoted by these names, thus grouping them under higher categories,—this process brings together the several forms of self-consciousness. Willing, desiring, feeling, and lastly thinking, also, are seen in thought to belong together, or to the same subject; and by thinking they are brought under a common view and receive a common name, or several common names, to wit, "my mind," "me," "I," "my mental states."

By still further observation, comparison, and analysis on the part of philosophers, this step is seen to be the highest degree of abstraction, since nothing appears to be common to all my mental states, except their belonging together and acting on one another, along with their common independence of other existences in this mutual action. The word "I" is discovered by philosophers to be a word without meaning or determination, or to be as meaningless as the words "thing," "being," "existence," which are subjects stripped of all attributes. "I" is the bare subject of mental phenomena. The word points them out, but does not declare anything of their nature by its meaning, essence, or implied attribution, which is, in fact, no meaning at all. Hence philosophers have placed this term, or name, over against that which is not, or in contrast with all other existences. Common language has no name for the latter, and so philosophers were compelled to call it the *non-ego*, in order to contrast these two highest categories, or *summa genera*, into which they divide all of which we are, or may be, conscious. Grammatical science, however, furnished convenient substitutes for these words. *Ego* and *non-ego* were named "subject" and "object." Yet these terms so applied do not retain any meanings. "Subject" is applicable to denote the *ego*, rather than the *non-ego*, only because it is the positive or more prominent term of the antithesis in its grammatical application, like "active and passive." Sir William Hamilton undertakes, however, to assign them meanings in psychology by representing the *object* as that which *is thought about*, and the *subject* as that which *thinks*, or *acts*, or that in which the thought or action inheres. But this definition is given from the active subject's point of view, and not from the whole scope of the subject-attributes. We act, indeed, in volition and attentive perception on the outer world or *non-ego ;* but in sensation and passive perception we are the objects influenced, governed, or acted on by this outer world. Moreover, from the point of view of the effects of thinking, both the *object* and *subject* are the subjects of attribution. We attribute qualities to external objects, and, at the same time, to their mental images, which, in their capacity as representative images, or internal signs of objects and relations, are called up and separately attended to in the human consciousness, and are, in turn, referred or attributed to the conscious subject, or to its memory and understanding.

These images, in their *individual* capacity, are not to be distinguished, even in human consciousness, from the object of perception. . It is in their specific, or notative, function as signs, and as referring back to memories of like experiences, which they summarize, that they are separately and subjectively cognized. *Individually* they are divisible only into real and unreal, or into remembered and imagined combinations of particular impressions. As inward and mine they are "concepts," or thoughts directing the processes of thought, and are specially related to my will and its motives. The classification of events as inward and outward does not necessarily imply that the scientific process depends on each man's experiences of their connections alone; for the forms of language, and what is indirectly taught in learning a language, guide observation in this matter largely; and so, also, very probably, do inherited aptitudes, ties, or tendencies to combination, which have the same effect in associating the particulars of the individual's experiences as the frequent repetitions of them in himself would have, and are, indeed, by the theory of evolution, the consequences of such repeated experiences in the individual's progenitors. Such a reference of the distinction of subject and object to instinctive tendencies in our minds is not equivalent to the metaphysical doctrine that this distinction is intuitive. For this implies more than is meant by the word "instinctive" from the naturalist's point of view. It implies that the cognition is absolute; independent not only of the individual's experiences, but of all possible previous experience, and has a certainty, reality, and cogency that no amount of experience could give to an empirical classification.

The metaphysical dogmas, for which this formula is given, deserve but a passing scientific consideration. Truths independent of all experience are not known to exist, unless we exclude from what we mean by "experience" that experience which we have in learning the meanings of words and in agreeing to definitions and the conventions of language, on the ground that they depend solely, or may be considered as depending solely, on a lexical authority, from which a kind of necessity proceeds, independent of reality in the relations and connections of the facts denoted by the words. It is possible that laws exist absolutely universal, binding fate and infinite power as well as speech and the intelligible use of words; but it is not possible that the analytical processes of any finite intellect should discover what particular laws these are. Such

an intellect may legislate with absolute freedom in the realm
of definition and word-making, provided it limits itself to its
autonomy, and does not demand of other intellects that they
shall be governed by such laws as if they were of universal
application in the world of common experience. It is also
possible that beliefs, or convictions, exist, supposed by the
mystic to be independent of all ordinary forms of particular
experience, "which no amount of experience could produce";
but it is not true that there are any universal or scientific beliefs
of this kind.   The effects of inherited aptitudes, and of early,
long-continued, and constantly repeated experiences in the individual, together with the implications of language itself, in
fixing and in giving force and certainty to an idea or a belief,
have, probably, not been sufficiently considered by those metaphysicians who claim a preternatural and absolute origin for
certain of our cognitions; and also, perhaps, the more dogmatic
among these thinkers over-estimate the force and certainty of
the beliefs, or mistake the *kind* of necessity they have. The
essential importance, the necessity and universality in language,
of pronominal words or signs, should not be mistaken for a real
a priori necessity in the relations expressed by them.   Metaphysicians should consider that *ego* and *non-ego*, as real existences, are not individual phenomena, but groups with
demonstrative names the least possible determined in meaning,
or are the most abstract subjects of the phenomena of experience, though determined, doubtless, in their applications partly
by spontaneous, instinctive, or natural and inherited tendencies
to their formation.

This view of the origin of the cognition of *cogito* is equally
opposed to the schemes of "idealism" and "natural realism,"
which divide modern schools of philosophy.   According to the
"idealists," the conscious subject is immediately known, at least
in its phenomena, and the phenomena are intuitively known to
belong to it; while the existence of anything external to the
mind is an inference from the phenomena of self, or a reference
of some of them to external causes.   Objects are only known
mediately "by their effects on *us*."   Against this view the
"natural realist" appeals effectively to the common-sense, or

natural judgment of unsophisticated minds, and is warranted by this judgment in declaring that the object of consciousness is *just as immediately* known as the subject is. But natural realism goes beyond this judgment and holds that both the subject and object are absolutely, immediately, and equally known through their essential attributes in perception. This is more than an unlearned jury are competent to say. For if by immediacy we mean the relation which a particular *unattributed* phenomenon has to consciousness in general, we are warranted in saying that immediately, or without the step of attribution, subject and object are undistinguished in consciousness. Thus, the sensations of sound and color and taste and pleasure and pain, and the emotions of hope and fear and love and hate, *if not yet referred to their causes, or even classified as sensations and emotions,* belong to neither world exclusively. But so far as any man can remember, no such unattributed or unclassified states of consciousness are experienced. He cannot say, however, that they cannot exist, or (what is worse for the theory) that a state of consciousness cannot be wrongly attributed or classified. All states of consciousness are, it is true, referred to one or the other, or partly to each of the two worlds; and this attribution is, in part at least, instinctive, yet not independent of all experience, since it comes either from the direct observation of our progenitors, or, possibly, through the natural selection of them; that is, possibly through the survival of those who rightly divided the worlds, and did not often mistake a real danger for a dream or for an imagined peril, nor often mistake a dream of security for real safety. If, however, we mean by immediacy such an instinctive attribution, independent of repeated connections of attributes in their subject through the individual's own experiences, then "natural realism" is most in accordance with our view, with such exceptions as the mistakes and corrections of dreams and hallucinations imply, and excepting the ontological or metaphysical positions that are assumed in it.

If the natural realist is not also an evolutionist (and usually he is not), then his meaning of intuitions must be that they are absolute and underived universal facts of connection in phenomena. He must suppose that distinct phenomena have stamped upon them indelible marks of their ultimate highest class, equivalents for " I " and "not-I," as the individuals of a herd of cattle are branded with the mark of their owner. Such an immutable mark would, however, render the mistakes of insanity, hallucinations, and dreams impossible, or else would refer them (as has actually been supposed *) to the mystery of the existence of evil,—a convenient disposition of philosophical puzzles. In the doctrine of evolution the meaning of the word "intuition" does not imply immutability in the connections of instinctively combined phenomena, except where such connection is an ultimate law of nature, or is the simplest causal connection, like the laws of motion, or the laws of logic, regarding logic as a science and not merely as an art. The intuition of space in the blind might be, from this point of view, a different combination of sensibilities from that in other men ; and the interpretation of sensations of hearing or sight in hallucinations as being caused by outward objects, when, in reality, they arise from disturbances or abnormal conditions of the nervous system, would not be an interpretation involving violations of ultimate laws, or suspensions in rebellious Nature of relations between cause and effect. Variations in intuitions and instinctive judgments would be as natural and explicable as errors of judgment are in the experiences of the individual man. But the doctrine of natural realism, independently of that of evolution and the implied mutability of instincts, has insurmountable difficulties.

Idealism, on the other hand, appears to contradict not the abnormal, so much as the common, phenomena of consciousness. It seems to be related to the modern sciences of physics and physiology very nearly as natural realism is to scholastic logic and ontology. Dating from the time of Descartes, it appears, in all its forms, to depend on a more exact knowledge of the bodily apparatus and outward physical causes of perception than the ancients possessed. This knowledge made it evident that perception, and even sensation, are fully determined or realized in the brain only through other parts of the

---

* Dr. McCosh, On the Intuitions of the Mind, etc.

bodily apparatus, and through outward forces and movements like those of pressure and vibration. That the perception, or sensation, is experienced, or is seated, in the brain, was a natural and proper conclusion. That the apparent object of perception is not only distant from what thus appeared to be the seat of the perception, but that a long series of usually unknown, or unnoticed, movements intervenes between it and this apparent seat,—these facts gave great plausibility to a confused interpretation of the phenomena, namely, that the perception is first realized as a state of the conscious *ego*, and, afterwards, is referred to the outward world through the associations of general experience, as an effect produced upon us by an otherwise unknown outward cause. On similar grounds a similar misinterpretation was made of the phenomena of volition, namely, that a movement in ourselves, originally and intuitively known to be *ours*, produces an effect in the outward world at a distance from us, through the intervention of a series of usually unknown (or only indirectly known) agencies. Remote effects of the outer world on us, and our actions in producing remote effects on it, appeared to be the first or intuitive elements in our knowledge of these phenomena, all the rest being derived or inferential. This was to confound the seat of sensation or perception in the brain with its proper subjectivity, or the reference of it to the subject.

The position in the brain where the last physical condition for the production of a sensation is situated is, no doubt, properly called the place or seat of the sensation, especially as it is through the movements of the brain with other special nervous tracts, and independently of any movements out of the nervous system, that like sensations are, or can be, revived, though these revived ones are generally feebler than those that are set in movement by outward forces. Nevertheless, this physiological seat of a sensation is no part of our direct knowledge of it. *A priori* we cannot assign it any place, nor decide that it has, or has not, a place. The place which we do assign it, in case it is outward, is the place determined by a great variety of sensations and active forms of consciousness experienced in the

localization of the object to which it is referred.   It is only by
the association (either spontaneous and instinctive, or acquired)
of this sensation with those sensations and actions that are
involved in the localization of the object, that we arrive at
any notion of its locality.   If we do not form any such associations of it with otherwise determined localities, and if it
and its kind remain after much experience unlocalized, or only
vaguely localized in our bodies, it is then, *but not till then*, referred to the conscious self as a subjective phenomenon.   There
remains the alternative, of course, in the theory of evolution,
that the negative experiences, which would thus determine the
subjective character of a phenomenon, may be the experiences
of our progenitors, and that our judgment of this character
may be, in many cases, an instinctive one, arising from the inherited effects of these former experiences.   Otherwise this
judgment in the individual mind, and from its own experiences,
would appear to be posterior, in point of time, to its acquaintance with the object world, since this judgment would be determined by the *absence* of any uniform connection in the phenomenon with the phenomena of locality.   Instead of being,
as the theories of idealism hold, first known as a phenomenon
of the subject *ego*, or as an effect upon us of an hypothetical
outward world, its first unattributed condition would be, by
our view, one of neutrality between the two worlds.

In dissenting, therefore, from both extremes,—the theory
of idealism and that of natural realism, or assenting to the latter only as qualified by the theory of evolution,—I have supposed both theories to be dealing with the two worlds only as
worlds of phenomena, without considering the metaphysical
bearings and varieties of them with respect to the question of
the cognition of non-phenomenal existences, on the grounds of
belief in an inconceivable and metaphysical matter or spirit;
for, according to the view proposed as a substitute for these
extremes, subject and object are only names of the highest
classes, and are not the names of inconceivable substrata of
phenomena.   Ontology or metaphysics would not be likely to
throw much original light on the scientific evolution of self-
consciousness; but it becomes itself an interesting object of

study as a phase of this evolution seen in the light of science. When one comes to examine in detail the supposed cognitions of super-sensible existences, and the faculty of necessary truth which is called "the reason," or else is described in its supposed results as the source of necessary beliefs or convictions, or of natural and valid hypotheses of inconceivable realities, great difficulty is experienced, on account of the abstract character of the beliefs, in distinguishing what is likely to be strictly inherited from what is early and uniformly acquired in the development of the faculty of reflection, and especially from what is imbibed through language, the principal philosophical instrument of this faculty.   The languages employed by philosophers are themselves lessons in ontology, and have, in their grammatical structures, implied conceptions and beliefs common to the philosopher and to the barbarian inventors of language, as well as other implications which the former takes pains to avoid.   How much besides he ought to avoid, in the correction of conceptions erroneously derived from the forms of language, is a question always important to be considered in metaphysical inquiries.

The conception of *substance*, as a nature not fully involved in the contrast of essential and accidental attributes, and the connection, or co-existence, of them in our experiences; or the conception of substance as also implying the real, though latent, co-existence of all attributes in an existence unknown to us, or known only in a non-phenomenal and inconceivable way,—this conception needs to be tested by an examination of the possible causes of it as an effect of the forms of language and other familiar associations, which, however natural, may still be misleading.   To the minds of the barbarian inventors of language, words had not precise meanings, for definition is not a barbarian accomplishment.   Hence, to such minds, definite and precise attributions, as of sweetness to honey and sugar, or light to the day, to the heavenly bodies, or to fire, are strongly in contrast with the vagueness which appears to them inherent in substantive names,—inherent not as vagueness, however, but as *something else*.   Such names did not clearly distinguish persons and things, for the day and the heavenly bodies were personal, and fire apparently was an animal or a spirit. Removing as much as possible of mere crudeness from such conceptions, predication would yet appear to be a reference of something distinctly known to something essentially unknown, or known only by one or a few attributes needed to distinguish it by a name, as proper names distinguish persons. The meaning of this name, and the conception of it as meaning much more, and as actually referring to unapparent powers of bringing to light attributes previously unknown,—powers manifested in an actual effect when a new attribute is added in predication,—this vague, ill-defined, and essentially hidden meaning is assimilated in grammar, and thence in philosophy, to an agent putting forth a new manifestation of itself in a real self-assertion.

The contrast of "active and passive" in the forms of verbs illustrates how the barbaric mind mounted into the higher regions of abstraction in language through concrete imaginations. The subject of a proposition, instead of being thought of as that vaguely determined group of phenomena with which the predicate is found to be connected, was thought either to perform an action on an object as expressed through the transitive verb, or to be acted on by the object as expressed through the passive fôrm, or to put forth an action absolute, expressed by the neuter verb, or to assert its past, present, or future existence absolutely, and its possession of certain properties as expressed by the substantive verb, and by the copula and predicate. This personification of the subject of a proposition, which is still manifested in the forms and terminology of grammar, is an assimilation of things to an active, or at least demonstrative, self-consciousness or personality. It had hardly reached the degree of abstraction needed for the clear intellectual self-consciousness of *cogito*. It rather implied that things also think. The invention of substantive names for attributes, that is, abstract names, like goodness or truth,—an invention fraught with most important consequences to human knowledge,—brought at first more prominently forward the realistic tendencies which philosophers have inherited from the barbarian inventors of language. Abstract names do not seem to have been meant at first to be the direct names of attributes, or collections of attributes, as " goodness " and " humanity," but to be the names of powers (such as make things good, or make men what they are), names which appear to be results of the earliest conscious or scientific analysis in the progress of the human mind, but which are strongly tainted still by the barbaric conception of words as the names of active beings. Abstract words were not, however, as active or demonstrative as their savage progenitors, the concrete general substantives. They appear rather as artificers, or the agents which build up things, or make them what they are. But, by means of them, concrete general names were deprived of their powers and reduced to subjection. To have direct general names, and to have general powers, seem to be synonymous to savage and semi-barbarous mind.

I have spoken as if all this were a matter of past history, instead of being an actually present state of philosophical thought, and a present condition of some words in the minds of many modern thinkers. The misleading metaphors are, it is true, now recognized as metaphors; but their misleading character is not clearly seen to its full extent. The subjects of propositions are still made to do the work, to bear the impositions, to make known the properties and accidents expressed by their predicates, or to assert their own existence and autonomy, just so far as they are supposed to be the names of anything but the assemblages of known essential qualities or phenomena actually co-existent in our experiences, that is of the qualities which their definitions involve, and to which other attributes are added (but from which they are not evolved) in real predication; or just so far as they are supposed to be the names of unknown and imperceptible entities. Names are directly the designations of things, not of hidden powers, or wills, in things. But it is not necessary to regard them as precisely definable, or as connoting definite groups of qualities or the essential attributes of things, in order that they may fulfill the true functions of words; for they are still only the names of things, not of wills in things, on the one hand, nor of "concepts" or thoughts in us, on the other hand. They are synonyms of "concepts," if we please to extend synonymy so as to include the whole range of the *signs* of things; but both the "concept" and its verbal synonym may be, and generally are, *vague*. For just as in the major premises of syllogisms the subject is, in general, a co-designation of two undivided parts of a class of objects, one known directly to have, or lack, the attributes affirmed or denied in this premise, and the other part, judged by induction to be also possessed, or not possessed of them,—a co-designation in which the conclusion of the syllogism is virtually contained, so as to make the syllogism appear to be a *petitio principii* (as it would be but for this implied induction*),— so in the simple naming of objects the names may be properly regarded as the names of groups of qualities, in which groups the qualities are partly known and partly unknown, predication in real (not verbal) propositions being the conversion of the latter into the former. But in this view of the functions of words, it is necessary, at least, to suppose enough of the known attributes of objects to be involved in the meanings of their names to make the applications of the names distinct and definite. Names, with the capacity they would thus acquire, or have actually had, in spite of metaphysics, of having their meanings modified or changed, are best adapted to the functions of words in promoting the progress of knowledge. From this use of words their essences, both the apparent and the inscrutable, have disappeared altogether, except so far as the actual existence and co-existence of the known attributes of objects are implied by names, or so far as the co-existence of these with previously unknown ones is also implied by the use of names as the subjects of propositions. No inscrutable powers in words or things, nor any immutable connections among the attributes called essential, are thus imposed upon the use of words in science.

Metaphysicians, on the other hand, in nearly all that is left to the peculiar domain of their inquiries, possess their problems and solutions in certain words, such as "substance," "cause," "matter," "mind," which still retain, at least in metaphysical usage, the barbaric characters we have examined. Matter and mind, for example, still remain, not only with meta-

---

* See Mill's Logic, Book II., chapter iii.

physicians, but also with the vulgar, designations of unknown inscrutable powers in the outward and inward worlds, or powers which, according to some, are known only to a higher form of intuition through the faculty of "Reason"; or, being really inscrutable and inconceivable by any human faculty, as others hold, are, nevertheless, regarded as certainly existent, and attested by irresistible natural beliefs. That beliefs in beings, unknown and unknowable, are real beliefs, and are natural (though more so to some minds than to others), seems *a priori* probable on the theory of evolution, without resorting to the effects of early training and the influence of associations in language itself, by which the existence of such beliefs is accounted for by some scientific philosophers. But the authority which the theory of evolution would assign to these beliefs is that of the conceptions which barbarous and vulgar minds have formed of the functions of words, and of the natures which they designate. Inheritance of these conceptions, that is, of aptitudes or tendencies to their formation, and the continued action of the causes so admirably analyzed by Mr. Mill,* through which he proposes to account for these beliefs directly, and which have retained, especially in the metaphysical conception of "matter," the barbarian's feelings and notions about real existence as a power to produce phenomena, are sufficient to account for the existence of these beliefs and their cogency, without assigning them any force as authorities.

That some minds have inherited these beliefs, or the tendency to form them, more completely than others, accords with a distinction in the mental characters of philosophers which Professor Masson makes in his work on Recent British Philosophy, and illustrates by the philosophies of Mr. Carlyle, Sir W. Hamilton, and Mr. Mill, namely, the differences arising from the degrees in which the several thinkers were actuated by an "ontological faith," or an "ontological feeling or passion," which, according to Professor Masson, has in the history of the world amounted to "a rage of ontology," and has been the motive of wars and martyrdoms. This passion would appear,

---

* See Mill's Examination of Hamilton, chapter xi.

according to the theory of evolution, to be a survival of the barbarian's feelings and notions of phenomena as the outward show of hidden powers in things, analogous to his own expressions in language and gesture of his will or interior activity. As he assigned his own name, or else the name "I," to this active inward personality, and not to the group of external characters by which he was known to his fellow-barbarians ; and as he also named and addressed them as indwelling spirits, so he seemed to apply his general designations of things. The traces of this way of regarding names and things, surviving in the grammatical inventions and forms of speech, which the barbarian has transmitted to us, include even the sexes of things. The metaphysical meanings of the terms "substance," "matter," "mind," "spirit," and "cause" are other traces. The metaphysical realism of abstract terms appears, in like manner, to be a trace of an original analysis of motives in the powers of things to produce their phenomena, analogous to the barbarian's analysis of motives in his own will or those of his fellows.

According to Professor Masson, Sir W. Hamilton was strongly actuated by "the ontological passion." This would mean, according to our interpretation of it, that he had inherited, or had partly, perhaps, imbibed from his philosophical studies, the barbarian's mode of thought. And it appeared in the metaphysical extension which he gave to the doctrine of natural realism, which, with him, was not merely the doctrine of the equal immediacy and the instinctive attribution of subjective and objective phenomena, but included also natural beliefs in the equal and independent, though hidden, existences of the metaphysical substrata of matter and mind. He was, nevertheless, so far influenced by modern scientific modes of thought that he did not claim for these natural beliefs at all the character of cognitions, nor did he claim determinate conception of these existences except as to their mutual independence. He rejected the metaphysician's invention of a faculty of "reason," cognizant of supersensible realities ; and really contradicted himself in claiming, with most modern thinkers, that knowledge of phenomena is the only possible knowledge, while he held that belief in what could not thus be known had the certainty of knowledge, and was in effect knowledge, though he did not call it knowledge.*

Another point in Sir W. Hamilton's philosophy illustrates our theory on a different side. While contending for the equal immediacy of our knowledge of subject and object, he, nevertheless, held that the phenomena of the subject had a superior certainty to those of the object, on the ground that the latter could be doubted (as they were by certain idealists) without logical contradiction, while the former could not be, since to doubt the existence of the subject would be to doubt the doubt, and thus neutralize it. To say nothing of other objections to this as a criterion of subjective certainty, it is obvious that it has no cogency as applied to the metaphysical, or non-phenomenal, existence of the subject. To doubt that a doubt inheres in a non-phenomenal subject, is not to doubt the existence of the doubt itself as a phenomenon, or even as a phenomenon referable to the subject group of phenomena. In regard to the impossibility of doubting the existence of this subject group, which, as including the doubt itself, would thus neutralize it, we ought to distinguish between a doubt of a doubt as a mere phenomenon of consciousness generally, that is as unattributed either to subject or object, and the doubt of the validity of the attribution of it to the subject. There can be logical contradiction only in respect to attribution, either explicit or implicit, and so far as the doubt is merely a phenomenon of which nothing is judged or known but its actual existence in consciousness, a doubt of it, though impossible, is yet not so on grounds of logical contradiction. Its actual presence would be the only proof of its presence, its actual absence the only proof of its absence. But this is equally true of all phenomena in consciousness, generally. If in reflection we examine whether a color of any sort is present, we have inquired, not merely about the bare existence of a phenomenon of which the phenomenon itself could alone assure us, but about its classes, whether it is a color or not, and what sort of a color; and we should attribute it, if present, to the object world, or the object group of

---

* See Mill's Examination of Hamilton, chapter v.

phenomena, by the very same sort, if not with the same degree, of necessity which determines the attribution of a doubt to the subject-consciousness. If now, having attributed the color or the doubt to its proper world, we should call in question the existence of this world, we should contradict ourselves; and this would be the case equally whether the attribution was made to the outward world, as of the color, or to the inward world, as of the doubt.

There may be different kinds of reflective doubt about either phenomenon. We should not ordinarily be able to question seriously whether the doubt belonged to the class "doubts," its resemblance to others of the class being a relation of phenomena universal and too clear to be dismissed from attention; and the color would call up its class with equal cogency, as well as the class of surfaces or spaces in which it appears always inherent. But we might doubt, nevertheless, seriously and rationally, whether a doubt had arisen from rational considerations in our minds, or from a disease of the nervous system, from hypochondriasis, or low spirits. So also in regard to the color and the forms in which it appears embodied, we may reasonably question whether the appearence has arisen from causes really external, or from disease, as in hallucinations.

There remains one other source of misunderstanding about the comparative certainty of "I think," and of that which I think about. The attributions contained in the latter may be particular, empirical, and unfamiliar, or based on a very limited experience and on *this account* may be uncertain; while the very general and highest attribution of the thought to myself will be most certain. The superior certainty of the clause "I think" over that which I think about disappears, however, as soon as the latter is made an attribution of equal simplicity, generality, and breadth in my experience; as when I say, "I think that there is an outer world," or, "I think that beings beside me exist." "To think that I think," is not more properly the formula of consciousness in general than "To think that a being not-I is thought about." It is not even the complete formula of *self*-consciousness, which, as we have seen, has several forms not necessarily coeval. To think that I will, that I desire, that I feel, is, as we have seen, to refer these several forms of consciousness to the thinking subject; or, more properly, to refer willing, desiring, feeling, and thinking all to the same subject "I"; which is related to the latter attribute more especially, merely because the name "I" is given only in and through the recognition of this attribute in the cognition of *cogito*. To infer the existence of the subject from the single attribute of thinking would be to unfold only in part its existence and nature; though it would note that attribute of the subject through the recognition of which in reflection its name was determined and connected with its other attributes.

The latter, namely, our volitions, desires, and feelings, are in general so obscure in respect to the particular causes which precede them and are anterior to their immediate determination or production, that introspective observation in reflection can penetrate only a little way, and is commonly quite unable to trace them back to remote causes in our characters, organizations, and circumstances. Hence, the conception of the causes of our own inward volitions, or our desires and intentions, as being of an inscrutable, non-phenomenal nature, would naturally arise. But this conception would probably be made much more prominent in the unreflective barbarian's mind, by his association of it with the obscurity to him of the inward, or personal, causes of outward actions and expressions in others. Darkness is seen where light is looked for and does not appear. Causes are missed where research is made without success. We are conscious of minds in other men and in other animals only through their outward expressions. The inward causes are not apparent or directly known to us as phenomena; and though the inference of their existence is not in all cases, even with men, made through analogy, or from an observation of their connections with similar outward actions and expressions in ourselves, but is grounded, doubtless, in many cases on an instinctive connection between these expressions in others and *feelings*, at least, in ourselves, yet we do not think of them as really inscrutable in their natures, but only as imperceptible to our outward senses. They have their representatives in the phenomena of our imaginations. These would be but vaguely conceived, however, in many cases. Even reverence in the barbarian's mind might prevent him, as an obedient subject, from attempting to fathom or reproduce in his own imagination the thoughts and intentions of his majesty the king. Reverence is not, however, in any case, an unreflective or thoughtless feeling. It would not be like the feelings of the sheep, which, not being able to comprehend through its own experience the savage feelings of the wolf, would only interpret his threatening movements as something fearful, or would connect in an instinctive judgment these outward movements only with anticipated painful consequences. Reverence in the loyal barbarian subject would not go so far as to make his king appear a mere automaton, as the wolf might seem to the sheep. The commands of his king, or of his deity, would be to him rather the voice of a wisdom and authority inscrutable, the outward manifestation of mysterious *power*, the type of metaphysical causation. Accordingly, we find that a capacity for strong, unappropriated feelings of loyalty and reverence, demanding an object for their satisfaction, have also descended to those thinkers who have inherited " the ontological passion." It would, therefore, appear most probable, that the metaphysician's invincible belief in the conception of the will as a mysterious power behind the inward phenomena of volition, and as incapable of analysis into the determinations of character, organization, and circumstances, arises also from inherited feelings about the wills of other men rather than from attentive observation of the phenomena of his own.

Science and scientific studies have led a portion of the human race a long way aside from the guidance of these inherited intellectual instincts, and have also appeared able to conquer them in many minds to which in youth they seemed invincible. Positivists, unlike poets, become—are not born—such thinkers. The conception of the causes of phenomena, with which these studies render them familiar, had small beginnings in the least noble occupations and necessities of life, and in the need of knowing the future and judging of it from present signs. From this grew up gradually a knowledge of natural phenomena, and phenomena of mind also, both in their outward and combined orders or laws and in their intimate and elementary successions, or the "laws of nature." The latter are involved in the relation of effects to their "physical" causes, so called because metaphysicians have discovered that they are not the same sort of powers as those which the invincible instincts look for as ultimate and absolute in nature. But this is not a new or modern meaning of the word "cause." It was always its practical, common-sense, every-day meaning;—in the relations of means to ends; in rational explanations and anticipations of natural events; in the familiar processes and observations of common human life ; in short, in the relations of phenomena to phenomena, as apparent causes and effects. This meaning was not well defined, it is true; nor is it now easily made clear, save by examples; yet it is by examples, rather than by a distinct abstraction of what is common to them, that the use of many other words, capable of clear definition, is determined in common language. The relations of invariable succession in phenomena do not, except in ultimate laws where the phenomena are simple or elementary, define the relation of phenomenal cause and effect; for, as it has been observed, night follows day, and day follows night invariably, yet neither is the cause of the other. These relations belong to the *genus* of natural successions. The relation of cause and effect is a *species* of this *genus*. It means an *unconditional*, invariable succession; *independence* of other orders of succession, or of all orders not involved in it.

The day illuminates objects; the night obscures them; the sun and fires warm them; the clouds shed rain upon them; the savage animal attacks and hurts others : these facts involve natural orders, in which relations of cause and effect are apparent, and are indicated in the antitheses of their terms as the subjects and objects of transitive propositions. But these relations are only indicated; they are not explicitly set forth. Metaphysics undertakes their explication by referring the illumination, obscurity, warmth, rain and hurt to *powers* in the day, the sun and fires, the clouds, and the animal. Modern metaphysics would not go so far as to maintain, in the light of science, that the powers in these examples are inscrutable, or incapable of further analysis. Nevertheless, when the analysis is made, and the vision of objects, for example, is understood to arise from the incidence of the light of the sun on the air and on objects, and thence from reflections on all surfaces of objects, and thence again from diffused reflections falling partly on our eyes, and so on to the full realization of vision in the brain, all according to determinate laws of succession,—an analysis which sets forth those *elementary* invariable orders, or *ultimate* and independent laws of succession in phenomena, to which, in their independent combinations, science refers the relations of cause and effect;—when this analysis has been made, then metaphysics interposes, and, from its ancient habits of thought, ascribes to the elementary antecedent a *power* to produce the elementary consequent. Or when the effect, as in vision, follows from the ultimate properties and elementary laws of great numbers of beings and arrangements,—the sun, the medium of light, the air, the illuminated objects, the eye, its nerves and the brain,—and follows through a long series of steps, however rapid, from the earliest to the latest essential antecedent, metaphysics still regards the whole process, with the elementary powers involved, as explicated only in its *outward* features. There is still the mystery inherent in the being of each elementary antecedent, of its power to produce its elementary consequent; and these mysterious powers, combined and referred to the most conspicuous essential conditions of the effect (like the existence of the sun and the eye), make in the whole a mystery as great as if science had never inquired into the process.

Metaphysics demands, in the interest of mystery, *why* an elementary antecedent is followed by its elementary consequent. But this question does not arise from that inquisitiveness which inspires scientific research. It is asked to show that it cannot be answered, and hence that all science rests on mystery. It is asked from the feelings that in the barbarian or the child forbid or check inquiry. But, being a question, it is open to answer; or it makes legitimate, at least, the counter-question, When can a question be properly asked? or, What is the purpose of asking a question? Is it not to discover the causes, classes, laws, or rules that determine the existence, properties, or production of a thing or event? And when these are discovered, is there any further occasion for inquiry, except in the interest of feelings which would have checked inquiry at the outset? The feelings of loyalty and reverence, instinctive in our natures, and of the utmost value in the history of our race, as the mediums of co-operation, discipline, and instruction, are instincts more powerful in some minds than in others, and, like all instincts, demand their proper satisfaction. From the will, or our active powers, they demand devotion; from the intellect, submission to authority and mystery. But, like all instincts, they may demand too much; too much for their proper satisfaction, and even for their most energetic and useful service to the race, or to the individual man. Whether it is possible for any one to have too much loyalty, reverence, love, or devotion, is, therefore, a question which the metaphysical spirit and mode of thought suggest. For in the mystic's mind these feelings have set themselves up as absolute excellencies, as money sets itself up in the mind of the miser. And it is clear that, under these absolute forms, it is difficult to deny the demand. It is only in respect to *what is* reverenced, loved, or worshiped, or *what* claims our allegiance, that questions of how much of them is due can be rationally asked.

To demand the submission of the intellect to the mystery of the simplest and most elementary relations of cause and effect in phenomena, or the restraint of its inquisitiveness on reaching an ultimate law of nature, is asking too much, in that it is a superfluous demand. The intellect in itself has no disposition to go any further, and, on the other hand, no impulse to kneel before its completed triumph. The highest generality, or universality, in the elements or connections of elements in phenomena, is the utmost reach both in the power and the desire of the scientific intellect. Explanation cannot go, and does not rationally seek to go, beyond such facts. The invention of *noumena* to account for ultimate and universal properties and relations in phenomena arises from no other necessity than the action of a desire urged beyond the normal prompt-ings of its power. To demand of the scientific intellect that it shall pause in the interest of mystery at the movements of a falling body or at the laws of these movements, is a misappro-priation of the quality of mystery. For mystery still has its uses; and, in its useful action, is an ally of inquisitiveness, in-citing and guiding it, giving it steadiness and seriousness, op-posing only its waywardness and idleness. It fixes attention, even inquisitive attention, on its objects, and in its active form of wonder "is a highly philosophical affection." So also de-votion, independently of its intrinsic worth in the mystic's re-gard, has its uses; and these determine its rational measure, or how much of it is due to any object. In its active forms of usefulness and duty, it is an ally of freedom in action, op-posing this freedom only in respect to what would limit it still more, or injuriously and on the whole.

The metaphysical modes of thought and feeling foster, on the other hand, the sentiments of mystery and devotion in their passive forms, and as attitudes of the intellect and will, rather than as their inciting and guiding motives. These attitudes, which are symbolized in the forms of religious worship, were no doubt needed to fix the attention of the barbarian, as they are still required to fix the attention of the child upon serious contemplations and purposes. Obedience and absolute sub-mission are, at one stage of intellectual and moral development, both in a race and in the individual, required as the conditions of discipline for effecting the more directly serviceable and freer action of the mind and character under the guidance of rational loyalty and reverence. The metaphysical modes of thought and feeling retain these early habits in relations in which they have ceased to be serviceable to the race, or to the useful development of the individual, especially when in the mystic's regard obedience has acquired an intrinsic worth, and submission has become a beatitude. The scientific habit of thought, though emancipated from any such outward supports and constraints, is yet not wanting in earnestness of purpose and serious interests, and is not without the motives of devotion and mystery, or their active guidance in the directions of usefulness and duty, and in the investigations of truth. It does not stand in awe before the unknown, as if life itself depended on a mysterious and capricious will in that unknown; for awe is habitual only with the barbarian, and is a useful motive only in that severe instruction which is exacted by the wants, insecurities, and necessities of his life, while among the partially civilized it often constrains the thoughtless by a present fear to avoid or resist evils really greater than what is feared, though less obvious to the imagination.

Nevertheless, the whole nature of the modern civilized man includes both these opposing tendencies in speculation, the metaphysical and scientific; the disposition to regard the phenomena of nature as they appeared naturally and serviceably in the primitive use of language and reflection, and the disposition of the Positivist to a wholly different interpretation of them. A conflict between them arises, however, only where either disposition invades the proper province of the other; where both strive for supremacy in the 'search for a clearer knowledge of these phenomena, or where both aim to satisfy the more primitive and instinctive tendencies of the mind. In the forms of ontological and phenomenological, or metaphysical and positive philosophies, this conflict is unavoidable and endless. Deathless warriors, irreconcilable and alternately victorious, according to the nature of the ground, or to advantages of position, continually renew their struggles along the line of development in each individual mind and character. A contrast of tendencies analogous to this, which involves, however, no necessary conflict, is shown in the opposition of science and poetry; the one contemplating in understanding and in fixed positive beliefs the phenomena which the other contemplates through firmly established and instinctive tendencies, and through interests, which for want of a better name to note their motive power, or influence in the will, are also sometimes called beliefs. Disputes about the nature of what is called "belief," as to what it is, as well as to what are the true grounds òr causes of it, would, if the meanings of the word were better discriminated in common usage, be settled by the lexicographer; for it is really an ambiguous term. Convictions of half-truths, or intimations of truth, coupled with deep feeling, and impressed by the rhythms and alliterations of words, are obviously different from those connections which logic and evidence are calculated to establish in the mind.

The poet inherits in his mental and moral nature, or organic memory, and in his dispositions of feeling and imagination, the instinctive thoughts and feelings which we have supposed habitual and useful in the outward life of the barbarian. In the melody of his verses he revives the habits which were acquired, it is believed, in the development of his race, long before any words were spoken, or were needed to express its imaginations, and when its emotions found utterance in the music of inarticulate tones. The poet's productions are thus, in part, reproductions, refined or combined in the attractive forms of art, of what was felt and thought before language and science existed; or they are restorations of language to a primeval use, and to periods in the history of his race in which his progenitors uttered their feelings, as of gallantry, defiance, joy, grief, exultation, sorrow, fear, anger, or love, and gave expression to their light, serious, or violent moods, in modulated tones, harsh or musical; or later, in unconscious figures of speech, expressed without reflection or intention of communicating truth. For, as it has been said, it is essential to eloquence to be heard, but poetry is expression to be only overheard. In supposing this noble savage ancestry for the poet, and for those who overhear in him, with a strange delight and interest, a charm of naturalness and of novelty combined by the magic of his art, it is not necessary to conclude that all savage natures are noble, or have in them the germs of the poet's inspiration. It is more probable that most of the races which have remained in a savage state have retained a more primitive condition, in many respects, than that of civilized men, because they lacked some qualities possessed by the *noble* savage which have advanced him to the civilized state, and because they have been isolated from the effects of such qualities either to improve or exterminate them. The noble savage is not, at any rate, now to be found. Weeding out the more stupid and brutal varieties has, doubtless, been the effective method of nature in the culture of the nobler qualities of men, at least in that state of nature which was one of warfare.

It is a common misconception of the theory of evolution to suppose that any one of contemporary races, or species derived from a common origin, fully represents the characters of its progenitors, or that they are not all more or less divergent forms of an original race; the ape, for example, as well as the man, from a more remote stock, or the present savage man, as well as the civilized one, from a more recent common origin. Original differences within a race are, indeed, the conditions of such divergences, or separations of a race into several; and original superiorities, though slight at first and accidental, were thus the conditions of the survival of those who possessed them, and of the extinction of others from their struggles in warfare, in gallantry, and for subsistence. The secondary distinctions of sex, or contrasts in the personal attractions, in the forms, movements, aspects, voices, and even in some mental dispositions of men and women, are, on the whole, greatest in the races which have accomplished most, not merely in science and the useful arts, but more especially in the arts of sculpture, painting, music, and poetry. And this in the theory of evolution is not an accidental conjunction, but a connection through a common origin. Love is still the theme of poets, and his words are measured by laws of rhythm, which in a primeval race served in vocal music, with other charms, to allure in the contests of gallantry. There would, doubtless, have arisen from these rivalries a sort of self-attention,* or an outward self-consciousness, which, together with the consciousness of themselves as causes distinct from the wills or agencies of other beings, and as having feelings, or passive powers, and desires, or latent volitions, not shared by others, served in the case of the primitive men as bases of reference in their first attention to the phenomena of thought in their minds, when these became sufficiently vivid to engage attention in the revival of trains of images through acts of reflection. The consummate self-consciousness, expressed by "I think," needed for its gen-

---

* See Darwin's Expression of the Emotions in Men and Animals. Theory of Blushing, chapter xiii.

esis only the power of attending to the phenomena of thought as signs of other thoughts, or of images revived from memory, with a reference of them to a subject; that is, to a something possessing other attributes, or to a group of co-existent phenomena. The most distinct attention to this being, or subject, of volitions, desires, feelings, outward expressions, and thoughts required a name for the subject, as other names were required for the most distinct attention to the several phenomena themselves.

This view of the origin of self-consciousness is by no means necessarily involved in the much more certain and clearly apparent agency of natural selection in the process of development. For natural selection is not essentially concerned in the *first* production of any form, structure, power, or habit, but only in perpetuating and improving those which have arisen from any cause whatever. Its agency is the same in preserving and increasing a serviceable and heritable feature in any form of life, whether this service be incidental to some other already existing and useful power which is turned to account in some new direction, or be the unique and isolated service of some newly and arbitrarily implanted nature. Whether the powers of memory and abstractive attention, already existing and useful in outward perceptions common to men and others of the more intelligent animals, were capable in their higher degrees and under favorable circumstances (such as the gestural and vocal powers of primeval man afforded them) of being turned to a new service in the power of reflection, aided by language, or were supplemented by a really new, unique, and inexplicable power, in either case, the agency of natural selection would have been the same in preserving, and also in improving, the new faculty, provided this faculty was capable of improvement by degrees, and was not perfect from the first. The origin of that which through service to life has been preserved, is to this process arbitrary, indifferent, accidental (in the logical sense of this word), or non-essential. This origin has no part in the process, and is of importance with reference to it only in determining how much it has to do to complete the work of creation. For if a faculty has small beginnings, and rises to great importance in the development of a race through natural selection, then the process becomes an essential one. But if men were put in possession of the faculties which so pre-eminently distinguish them by a sudden, discontinuous, arbitrary cause or action, or without reference to what they were before, except so far as their former faculties were adapted to the service of the new ones, then selection might only act to preserve or maintain at their highest level faculties so implanted. Even the effects of constant, direct use, habit, or long-continued exercise might be sufficient to account for all improvements in a faculty. The latter means of improvement must, indeed, on either hypothesis, have been very influential in increasing the range of the old powers of memory, attention, and vocal utterance through their new use.

The outward physical aids of reflective thought, in the articulating powers of the voice, do not appear to have been firmly implanted, with the new faculty of self-consciousness, among the instincts of human nature; and this, at first sight, might seem to afford an argument against the acquisition by a natural process of any form of instinct, since vocal language has probably existed as long as any useful or effective exercise of reflection in men. That the faculty which uses the voice in language should be inherited, while its chief instrument is still the result of external training in an art, or that language should be "half instinct and half art," would, indeed, on second thought, be a paradox on any other hypothesis but that of natural selection. But this is an economical process, and effects no more than what is needed. If the instinctive part in language is sufficient to prompt the invention and the exercise of the art,* then the inheritance of instinctive powers of articulation would be superfluous, and would not be effected by selection; but would only come in the form of inherited effects of habit,—the form in which the different degrees of aptitude for the education of the voice appear to exist in different races of men. Natural selection would not effect anything, indeed,

* In the origin of the languages of civilized peoples, the distinction between powers of tradition, or *external inheritance*, and proper invention in art becomes a very important one, as will be shown farther on.

for men which art and intelligence could, and really do, effect,
—such as clothing their backs in cold climates with hair or fur,
—since this would be quite superfluous under the furs of other
animals with which art has already clothed them. The more
instinctive language of gestures appears also to have only indirect relations to real serviceableness, or to the grounds of
natural selection, and to depend on the inherited effects of
habit, and on universal principles of mental and physiological
action.*

The language of gestures may, however, have been sufficient
for the realization of the faculty of self-consciousness in all that
the metaphysician regards as essential to it. The primitive
man might, by pointing to himself in a meditative attitude,
have expressed in effect to himself and others the "I think,"
which was to be, in the regard of many of his remote descendants,
the distinguishing mark, the outward emblem, of his essential
separation from his nearest kindred and progenitors, of his metaphysical distinction from all other animals. This consciousness and expression would more naturally have been a source
of proud satisfaction to the primitive men themselves, just as
children among us glory most in their first imperfect command
of their unfolding powers, or even in accomplishments of a
unique and individual character when first acquired. To the
civilized man of the present time, there is more to be proud
of in the immeasurable consequences of this faculty, and in
what was evolved through the continued subsequent exercise
of it, especially through its outward artificial instruments in
language,—consequences not involved in the bare faculty itself. As being the pre-requisite condition of these uses and inventions, it would, if of an ultimate and underived nature, be
worthy the distinction, which, in case it is referable to latent
natures in pre-existing faculties, must be accorded to them in
their higher degrees. And if these faculties are common to all
the more intelligent animals, and are, by superior degrees
only, made capable of higher functions, or effects of a new and
different kind (as longer fins enable a fish to fly), then the main
qualitative distinction of the human race is to be sought for in

---

* See Darwin's Expression of the Emotions in Man and Animals.

these effects, and chiefly in the invention and use of artificial language.

This invention was, doubtless, at first made by men from social motives, for the purpose of making known to one another, by means of arbitrarily associated and voluntary signs, the wishes, thoughts, or intentions clearly determined upon in their imaginations. Even now, children invent words, or, rather, attribute meanings to the sounds they can command, when they are unable to enunciate the words of the mother tongue which they desire for the purposes of communication. It is, perhaps, improper to speak of this stage of language as determined by conscious invention through a recognized motive, and for a *purpose* in the subjective sense of this word. It is enough for a purpose (in its objective sense) to be served, or for a service to be done, by such arbitrary associations between internal and external language, or thought and speech, however these ties may, in the first instance, be brought about. The intention and the invention become, however, conscious acts in reflection when the secondary motives to the use of language begin to exert influence, and perhaps before the latter have begun to be reflectively known, or recognized, and while they are still acting as they would in a merely animal mind. These motives are the needs and desires (or, rather, the use and importance), of making our thoughts clearer to ourselves, and not merely of communicating them to others. Uncertainty, or perplexity from failures of memory or understanding, render the mnemonic uses of vivid external and voluntary signs the agents of important services to reflective thought, when these signs are already possessed, to some extent, for the purposes of communication. These two uses of language,—the social, and the meditative or mnemonic,—carried to only a slight development, would afford the means of recognizing their own values, as well as the character of the inventions of which languages would be seen to consist. Invention in its true sense, as a reflective process, would then act with more energy in extending the range of language.

Command of language is a much more efficient command of thought in reflective processes than that which is implied in the simplest form of self-consciousness. It involves a command of memory to a certain degree. Already a mental power, usually accounted a simple one, and certainly not involved in "I think," or only in its outward consequences, has been developed in the power of the will over thought. Voluntary memory, or reminiscence, is especially aided by command of language. This is a tentative process, essentially similar to that of a search for a lost or missing external object. Trials are made in it to revive a missing mental image, or train of images, by means of words; and, on the other hand, to revive a missing name by means of mental images, or even by other words. It is not certain that this power is an exclusively human one, as is generally believed, except in respect to the high degree of proficiency attained by men in its use. It does not appear impossible that an intelligent dog may be aided by its attention, purposely directed to spontaneous memories, in recalling a missing fact, such as the locality of a buried bone.

In the earlier developments of language, and while it is still most subject to the caprices and facilities of individual wills (as in the nursery), the character of it as an invention, or system of inventions, is, doubtless, more clearly apparent than it afterwards becomes, when a third function of language rises into prominence. Traditions, by means of language, and customs, fixed by its conservative power, tend, in turn, to give fixity to the conventions of speech; and the customs and associations of language itself begin to prescribe rules for its inventions, or to set limits to their arbitrary adoption. Individual wills lose their power to decree changes in language; and, indeed, at no time are individual wills unlimited agents in this process. Consent given on grounds not always consciously determining it, but common to the many minds which adopt proposals or obey decrees in the inventions of words, is always essential to the establishment or alteration of a language. But as soon as a language has become too extensive to be the possible invention of any single mind, and is mainly a tradition, it must appear to the barbarian's imagination to have a will of its own; or, rather, sounds and meanings must appear naturally bound together, and to be the fixed names and expressions of wills in things. And later, when complex grammatical forms and abstract substantive names have found their way into languages, they must appear like the very laws and properties of nature itself, which nothing but magical powers could alter; though magic, with its power over the will, might still be equal to the miracle.   Without this power not even a sovereign's will could oppose the authority of language in its own domain.   Even magic had failed when an emperor could not alter the gender of a noun.   Education had become the imperial power, and schoolmasters were its prime ministers.

From this point in the development of language, its separations into the *varieties* of dialects, the divergences of these into *species*, or distinct languages, and the affinities of them as grouped by the glossologist into *genera* of languages, present precise parallels to the developments and relations in the organic world which the theory of natural selection supposes. It has been objected* to the completeness of these parallels that the process of development in languages is still under the control of men's wills.   Though an individual will may have but little influence on it, yet the general consent to a proposed change is still a voluntary action, or is composed of voluntary actions on the part of the many, and hence is essentially different from the choice in natural selection, when acting within its proper province.   To this objection it may be replied, that a general consent to a change, or even an assent to the reasons for it, does not really constitute a voluntary act in respect to the whole language itself; since it does not involve in itself any intention on the part of the many to change the language. Moreover, the conscious intention of effecting a change on the part of the individual author, or speaker, is not the agent by which the change is effected; or is only an incidental cause, no more essential to the process than the causes which produce variations are to the process of natural selection in species. Let the causes of variation be what they may,—miracles even,— yet all the conditions of selection are fulfilled, provided the va-

---

* See article on Schleicher and the Physical Theory of Language, in Professor W. D. Whitney's Oriental and Linguistic Studies.

riations can be developed by selection, or will more readily occur in the selected successors of the forms in which they first appear in useful degrees. These conditions do not include the prime causes of variations, but only the causes which facilitate their action through inheritance, and ultimately make it normal or regular.

So, also, the reasons or motives which in general are not consciously perceived, recognized, or assented to, but none the less determine the consent of the many to changes in language, are the real causes of the selection, or the choice of usages in words. Let the cause of a *proposed* change in language be what it may—an act of free will, a caprice, or inspiration even —provided there is something in the proposition calculated to gain the consent of the many,—such as ease of enunciation, the authority of an influential speaker or writer, distinctness from other words already appropriated to other meanings, the influence of vague analogies in relations of sound and sense (accidental at first, but tending to establish fixed roots in etymology, or even to create instinctive connections of sound and sense),—such motives or reasons, common to the many, and not their consenting wills, are the causes of choice and change in the usages of speech. Moreover, these motives are not usually recognized by the many, but act instinctively. Hence, there is no intention in the many, either individually or collectively, to change even a single usage,—much less a whole language. The laws or constitution of the language, as it exists, appear, even to the reflecting few, to be unchanged; and the proposed change appears to be justified by these laws, as corrections or extensions of previous usages.

The case is parallel to the developments of legal usages, or principles of judicial decisions. The judge cannot rightfully change the laws that govern his judgments; and the just judge does not consciously do so. Nevertheless, legal usages change from age to age. Laws, in their practical effects, are ameliorated by courts as well as by legislatures. No new principles are consciously introduced; but interpretations of old ones, and combinations, under more precise and qualified statements, are made, which disregard old decisions, seemingly by new and better definitions of that which in its nature is unalterable, but really, in their practical effects, by alterations, at least in the proximate grounds of decision; so that nothing is really unalterable in law, except the intention to do justice under universally applicable principles of decision, and the instinctive judgments of so-called natural law.

In like manner, there is nothing unalterable in the traditions of a language, except the instinctive motives to its acquisition and use, and some instinctive connections of sense and sound. *Intention*—so far as it is operative in the many who determine what a language is, or what is proper to any language—is chiefly concerned in *not* changing it; that is, in conforming to what is regarded by them as established usage. That usages come in under the form of good and established ones, while in fact they are new though good inventions, is not due to the intention of the speakers who adopt them. The intention of those who consciously adopt new forms or meanings in words is to conform to what appears legitimate; or it is to fill out or improve usages in accordance with existing analogies, and not to alter the essential features in a language. But unconsciously they are also governed by tendencies in themselves and others, —vague feelings of fitness and other grounds of choice which are outside of the actual traditions of speech; and, though a choice may be made in their minds between an old and a really new usage, it is commonly meant as a truly conservative choice, and from the intention of not altering the language in its essence, or not following what is regarded as a deviation from correct usage. The actual and continuous changes, completely transforming languages, which their history shows, are not, then, due to the intentions of those who speak, or have spoken, them, and cannot, in any sense, be attributed to the agency of their wills, if, as is commonly the case, their intentions are just the reverse. For the same wills cannot act from contradictory intentions, both to conserve and to change a language on the whole.

It becomes an interesting question, therefore, when in general anything can be properly said to be effected by the will of man. Man is an agent in producing many effects, both in nature and in himself, which appear to have no different general character from that of effects produced by other animals, even the lowest in the animal series, or by plants, or even by inorganic forces. Man, by transporting and depositing materials, in making, for example, the shell-mounds of the stone age, or the works of modern architecture and engineering, or in commerce and agriculture, is a geological agent; like the polyps which build the coral reefs, and lay the foundations of islands, or make extensions to mainlands; or like the vegetation from which the coal-beds were deposited; or like winds, rains, rivers, and the currents of the ocean; and his agency is not in any way different in its general character, and with reference to its geological effects from that of unconscious beings. In relation to these effects his agency is, in fact, unconscious, or at least *unintended*. Moreover, in regard to internal effects, the modification of his own mind and character by influences external to himself, under which he comes accidentally, and without intention; many effects upon his emotions and sentiments from impressive incidents, or the general surroundings of the life with which he has become associated through his own agency,—these, as unintended effects, are the same in general character, as if his own agency had not been concerned in them,—as if he had been without choice in his pursuits and surroundings.

Mingled with these unintended effects upon himself, there are, of course, others, either actually or virtually intended, and, therefore, his own effects. If, for example, in conformity with surrounding fashions of dress, he should choose to clothe himself, and should select some one from the existing varieties in these fashions, or should even add, *consciously*, a new feature to them from his individual taste in dress, in each case he would be acting from intention, and the choice would be his own. But so far as he has thus affected the proportions among these varieties, or tends further to affect them by his example, the action is not his own volition, unless we include *within* the will's agency what is properly said to act either *through* or *upon* the will; namely, that which, by an undistinguished influence, guides taste and choice in himself and the others who follow unconsciously his example. Those influences of example and instinctive, or even educated, tastes, which are not raised by distinct attention into conscious motives, would not be allowed by the metaphysician to be parts in the will's action. It would not be *within* but *through* its action that these influences would produce their unintended effects. According to the less definite and precise *physical* theory of the will's action, these effects might be regarded as voluntary; but then the choice would not be different in its character from that effected through other kinds of physical agency. On neither theory, therefore, can unintended effects, or the effects of unrecognized causes acting through the will, be regarded as different in their character from the general results of selection in nature. On the physical theory of the will, man's agency is merged in that of nature generally; but according to the metaphysician's more definite understanding of voluntary actions, which is also that of common usage, *intention* would appear to be the mark by which to determine whether anything is the effect of the will of man, except in an accidental or non-essential manner.

An apparently serious objection to this test arises, however, in reference to another mark of voluntary action, and of the efficacy of the will. The mark of *responsibility* (the subject of moral or legal discipline, the liability to blame or punishment) is justly regarded as the mark of free human agency. But the limits set by this mark are beyond what is actually *intended* in our actions. We are often held responsible, and properly, for more than we intend, or for what we *ought* to have intended. The absence of intention (namely, of the intention of doing differently) renders us liable to blame, when it is involved in the absence of the more general intention of doing right, or of doing what the discipline of responsibility has commanded or implied in its commands. Carelessness, or want of forethought, cannot be said to involve intention in any case, but in many cases it is blameworthy or punishable; since in such cases moral discipline presupposes or presumes intention, or else seeks, as in the case of children, by punishment to turn attention upon moral principles, and upon what is implied in them, whether set forth in instincts, examples, precepts, or commandments. But this extension of the sphere of personal agency and accountability to relations in which effects upon will and character are sought to be produced by moral and legal discipline, its extension beyond what the will itself produces in its direct action, has nothing to do with strictly scientific or theoretical inquiries concerning effects, in which neither the foreseeing nor the obedient will can be an agent or factor, but of which the intellect is rather the recorder, or mere accountant.

If the question concerning the origin of languages were, Who are responsible for their existence and progressive changes, or ought to be credited for improvements, or blamed for deficiences in them? or if the question were, How men might or should be made better inventors, or apter followers of the best inventions,—there would then be some pertinency in insisting on the agency of man in their developments,—an agency which, in fact, like his agency in geology, is incidental to his real volitions, and is neither involved in what he intends nor in what he could be made to intend by discipline. So far as human intentions have had anything to do with changes in the traditions of language, they have, as we have said, been exerted in resisting them. Hence the traditions of language, with all the knowledge, histories, arts, and sciences involved and embodied in them, are developments incidental, it is true, to the existence and exercise of self-consciousness, and of free or intelligent wills, yet are developments around and outside of them, so to speak, and were added to them rather than evolved from them. These developments were added through their exercise and serviceableness as powers which stand to the more primitive ones of self-conscious thought and volition in relations similar to those we have seen to exist between the latter and the still more primitive powers of mind in memory and attention.

These relations come, first, from turning an old power to a new account; or making a new use of it, when the power, developed for other uses, acquires the requisite energy (as when the fins of a fish become fitted for flying); or when the revivals of memory become vivid enough to make connecting thoughts in a train distinct and apparent as mere signs to a reflective attention. Secondly, the new use increases the old power by its exercise and serviceableness (as flying and its value to life make the fins of the fish still longer), or as the exercise and importance to life of reflective thought make the revivals of memory still more vivid, and enlarge its organ, the brain. Traditions of language, or established artifices of expression, are related to new uses in a power, now in turn become sufficiently energetic, which at first was only the power of associating the sounds of words with thoughts, and thence with their objects, and which was incidental to the distinct recognition of thoughts as signs, or suggestions, of other thoughts. Developed by exercise and its serviceableness to life to the point, not only of making readily and employing temporarily such arbitrary associations, but also of fixing them and transmitting them as a more or less permanent language, or system of signs, this power acquired, or was turned to, a use involving immeasurable consequences and values.

To choose arbitrarily for preservation and transmission one out of many arbitrary associations of sounds with a meaning could not have been a rational or intelligent act of free will, but ought rather to be attributed to chance, lot, or fate; or to *will*, in the narrower sense of the word in which one man is said to have more than another, or to be more willful, that is, persistent in his caprices. To make by decree any action permanent and regular which in itself is transient or accidental requires *will*, it is true, in one sense, or *sticking to a point, merely because it has been assumed ;* as some children do in imposing their inventions upon their associates. This degree of arbitrariness appears necessary to the step in the use of signs which made them traditions of language, permanent enough to be the roots of a continued growth in it,—a growth which must, however, have determined more and more the selections of new words, and new uses in old ones, through motives common to the many speakers of a language; such as common fancies, instinctive tendencies, facilities, allegiance to authority, and associations in general—the vague as well as distinct ones—which were common to many speakers. These causes would act instinctively, or unconsciously, as well as by design. Tyranny in the growth of language, or the agency of arbitrary wills, persisting in their caprices, must have disappeared at an early date, or must have become insignificant in its effects upon the whole of any established language. Intentional choice would henceforward have the *design* generally of conserving or restoring a supposed good usage; though along with unintended preferences, instinctively followed, it would, doubtless, have the effect of slowly changing the usages of language on the whole. A happy suggestion of change would be adopted, if adopted consciously, with reference to its supposed conformity to the *genius* of the language, or to its will, rather than to the will of an individual dictator; and the influence of a speaker would depend on the supposition that he knew best how to use the language correctly, or was intimate with its genius. But suggestions of change would be more likely to be adopted unconsciously.

History can trace languages back only, of course, to the earliest times of their representations in phonetic writings or inscriptions; as palæontology can trace organic species back only to the earliest preservation of them as fossils in the rocks. In neither case do we probably go back to periods in which forms were subject to sudden or capricious variations. Natural selection would, therefore, define the most prominent action of the causes of change in both of them. But just as governments in all their forms depend on the fixedness and force of traditions, and as traditions gained this force through the wills of those in the past who established them by arbitrary decrees, and induced in others those habits of respect and obedience which now preserve them, so in language there was, doubtless, a time when *will* was the chief agent in its formation and preservation. But it was Will in its narrower sense, which does not include all that is commonly meant by volitional action. The latter involves, it is true, persistence in some elements,— a persistence in memory and thought of consciously recognized motives, principles, purposes, or intentions. Volition is an action through memory, and not merely from a present stimulus, and is accompanied, when free or rational, by the recognition in thought of the motive, the proximate cause of the action, the reasons for it, or the immediate and present tendency to it, which is referred back in turn, but is not analyzed, nor usually capable of being analyzed introspectively into still more remote antecedents in our histories, inherited disposition, characters, and present circumstances. Those causes which are even too feeble to be introspectively recognized are not, of course, the source whence the force or energy of will is derived; but independently of their *directive* agency, this force is indistinguishable from that of pure spontaneity or vital energy. In like manner, the force of water in a system of river-courses is not determined by its beds and banks, but is none the less guided by them. This water-force in the first instance, and from time to time, alters its courses, but normally flows within predetermined courses; as the energy of will flows normally within the directive, but alterable, courses of character and circumstances. The really recognized motives in ordinary volition generally include more than the impulse or satisfaction of adhering to an assumed position, or to a purpose, for the will's sake, as in mere will, or willfulness which is an overflow, so to speak, of energy, directed only by its own inertia, though often useful in altering character, or the courses of volition, both in the will itself and the wills of others. The habit of conscious persistence, involved in will, but most conspicuous in self-will, was, together with its correlatives, respect and obedience, doubtless serviceable to the rulers of primeval men, the authors of human government; and was, doubtless, developed through this serviceableness before it was turned to new uses in the institution of arbitrary customs and traditions. It thus illustrates anew the general principle shown in the several previous steps of this progress, namely, the turning of an old power to a new account, or making a new use of it, when the power has acquired the requisite energy; and the subsequent further increase of the power through serviceableness and exercise in its new function.

This power in the wills of the political, military, and religious leaders of men must soon, after producing the apotheosis of the more influential among them, have been converted into the sacred force of tradition; that is, into the *fas* or commands of languages themselves; and of other arbitrary customs. Henceforth and throughout all the periods included in the researches of comparative philology in which written remains of languages are to be found, it is probable that no man has consciously committed, or had the power to commit, the sin of intentionally altering their traditions, except for reasons common to many speakers and afforded by the traditions themselves.

THE CONFLICT OF STUDIES.*

Among the most advanced nations, in this age of sceptical inquiry,—an age sceptical in the old and good sense of the word (noting that close examination of a subject which orthodox philosophers and divines have for so many centuries stamped with a black mark),—in this age nothing seems likely to escape a radical re-examination by discussion and experiment. Those matters for which a genuine loyalty might still be counted on to conserve past usages, the means, influences, and appliances to which scholars and men of culture acknowledge their deepest indebtedness, have not proved exceptions.

That there should, if possible, be a science of education, founded on something more than the traditions of the art or the success of past usages, appears to be the present demand of reformers. The wide-spread and growing conviction, that universities have not advanced their knowledge of their duties to mankind or to their several nations at the same pace as other useful institutions, and that legislative interference ought to undertake what the incumbents of university places have neglected, has given so great alarm to the latter, that they have turned a most energetic and earnest attention to the subject. The discussion, so far, has developed little more than the many-sidedness and extreme difficulties in practice of the problems of education. This, together with the zeal exhibited by the best university men, to bring all the light they possess or can command to bear on the discussion, will doubtless serve the purpose about which they seem most solicitous,—the

* From the North American Review, July, 1875.

purpose of avoiding, if possible, revolutionary measures, and the "danger that *any* reform should be adopted because *some* reform is required." *

The problems of the higher general education of the universities,—what it should be, whether a simple *curriculum* or a variety of courses; what constitutes nowadays, a liberal education; what are its ends; what are their relative degrees of importance in a general education, or in one preparatory in a general way, as the lower school training is, to more specific studies or pursuits,—these problems have rather been exhibited in their difficulties than advanced towards a solution by recent discussions. It is well observed by Mr. Pattison, Rector of Lincoln College, Oxford, that the difficulties in which elementary education is implicated, great as they are, are difficulties of action:—"How to carry through what we know ought to be done." "The university question is quite otherwise." "There would be little difficulty in getting anything done, if we could see our way clearly to what we do want." To make the reformers outside of the universities feel this, and feel that the problem can only be solved by men practically acquainted with the business of education, seems to be one of the aims of university writers. Yet, we imagine that those who demand reform, in the name of the nation, look upon these writers as they would upon men pursuing other kinds of business, who, in the practice of means honored by long usage, and especially in devising the secondary and subsidiary means, are apt to have but dim perceptions of the ends to which the machinery or appliances of the art are as a whole, or should be, adapted. The means of the higher education, like all other means in practices of which the ends are manifold, conflicting, and only vaguely conceived, are naturally enough sought for by these writers in that kind of experience which is embodied in customs and institutions, rather than in philosophy or in a scientific analysis of the experience.

Next to the claim which their acquaintance with the details of practice gives to university writers on education, they rely

* Suggestions on Academical Organization, with especial Reference to Oxford. By Mark Pattison, B. D. 1868.

on this slowly developed *experiment* (as they would like to have it regarded) which the past usages of universities offer to observation; although without definite purposes or guiding questions, not implicated in an experience, its evidence can hardly with propriety be regarded as *experimental.* It is quite true, and a just complaint of conservative thinkers, that the projects of reformers, the proposed changes in subjects, text-books, and methods of the higher education, have no better title to be regarded as experiments philosophically devised. Most criticisms on what universities have done heretofore are expressions of little more than dissatisfaction with the choice of text-books, or even of subjects, or with methods of teaching and examination in subjects, in which the critics either have failed, or have reached only a slight proficiency; and advice is most freely proffered by those who are least acquainted with the matters in which they demand reform.

Upon a recent discussion in a scientific periodical con-cerning what modern elementary treatise is best adapted to take the place of Euclid (now considered antiquated by the reformers, though still supported by Cambridge and used in the best English schools), Mr. Todhunter * observes that, "what appeared singular to persons accustomed to inquiries about education, was the readiness of persons to offer advice with most imperfect knowledge of the circumstances." We may add, that what strikes the latter sort of persons as equally singular, is the firm reliance of conservative thinkers like Mr. Todhunter, on his acquaintance with these circumstances, not merely as affording evidence that existing practices are good, or can be made very good without revolution, but that they are practically the best. Mr. Todhunter is doubtless right in claiming that no text-book in elementary geometry has yet been proved superior to Euclid; but he does not appear to us quite justly aware of the disadvantages to which all novelties in the trials and experiences (we will not say experiments) in education are unavoidably exposed. The very complete and elaborate machinery of examinations in the classics and

---

* The Conflict of Studies, and other Essays on Subjects connected with Education. By I. Todhunter, M. A., F. R. S. London, 1873.

mathematics, to which Cambridge and the best English schools have given so much studious attention, would be wanting to all modern studies, and would need to be devised with equal care before the old and new experiences could be fairly compared.

The main question at issue needs to be cleared of many false charges and false arguments, which are as good or as bad on one side as the other, before any substantial progress can be made. Mr. Todhunter's essays will, no doubt, do service in this way. No one could be found in any seat of learning better qualified as an expert witness (the capacity in which he appears to prefer to engage in the discussion, rather than as an advocate). A long residence at Cambridge, and much experience in lecturing, and in examinations on mathematical subjects are his main qualifications. Intimate acquaintance with the working of the machinery of examinations, and with the adaptation of mathematical studies to different minds, makes his testimony of great value, however little regard may be had for his opinions expressed as an advocate. It is interesting to find such testimony as the following: That the majority of the younger students of a university, not distinguished in their school-days for mathematical taste and power, have been "either persons of ability whose attention was fully occupied with studies different from mathematics, or persons of scanty attainments and feeble power, who could do little more than pass the ordinary examination. I can distinctly affirm that the cases of hopeless failures in Euclid were very few; and the advantages derived from the study, even by men of feeble ability, were most decided. In comparing the performance in Euclid with that in arithmetic and algebra, there could be no doubt that the Euclid had made the deepest and most beneficial impression; in fact, it might be asserted that this constituted by far the most valuable part of the whole training to which such persons were subjected."

So far as this is testimony to the practicability of mathematical studies for all minds, it is valuable. The testimony to the value of such studies to those whose abilities are of a decidedly different bent from the mathematical may still be questioned.   Throughout his essays Mr. Todhunter's sole standard of value in a university study is that quality in it by which the machinery of lectures, text-books, and "pass" and competitive examinations, with emoluments and honors, can be made of direct assistance to the student.   On this standard he has a decided preference for the studies of the old *curriculum.* For these, and for advanced modern studies in applied mathematics, adequate tests of examination, and rewards of assistance, and honor for success in them are means which are within a university's power to devise or command.   To lay out courses and afford material aids in studies are all that remain of what a university can do for a student, unless it is so fortunate at times as to secure the services of men of genius (not to be reckoned among its ordinary resources), who have the rare faculty of stimulating the student to hard work by the interest they impart to their teachings.   On this ground Mr. Todhunter seems to us to be strong.   It may be justly demanded of a university not to think too highly of its resources, and to set its machinery aside on occasions in favor of greatly endowed teachers.

It is unfortunately too true, however, that such teachers have not always had the genius or sense to know that the exception is only properly made in favor of such as themselves. They have very frequently shown determined hostility to any use of methods which differ from the action of their own spontaneous powers of discipline, and which are really all the poor means that a seat of learning can constantly and systematically provide.   This hostility could be just only if the man of genius were endowed with untiring and immortal vigor, or could educate by his inspiration a like genius in one or more of his pupils, who might then take his place.   A natural genius for teaching any subject—by which we mean for making the pupil an accurate and hard worker in it, like his master—is as powerless to reproduce itself in a pupil as university examinations are.   We cannot by examinations, Mr. Todhunter observes, "*create* learning or genius; it is uncertain whether we can infallibly discover them; what we detect is simply the examination-passing-power of the candidate."   Sir Humphrey Davy said "that his greatest discovery in science was Michael Faraday." Genius does not make a genius, but discovers him. Nothing more, not so much even, could fairly be expected of the best-devised system of examinations.

"The adaptability of subjects to the exigencies of examinations" is almost the sole test which our author applies to the question of what shall be the course or courses proper to a higher general education, although he professes not to lay too great stress on this consideration, seeing that it is quite inapplicable to courses arranged for self-training. In regard to the value of the natural and experimental sciences this test appears to be with him quite decisive, though he thinks, if candidates were few and time ample, effective examinations in these subjects might be devised. It appears to us that this work falls within the province of a university's duties and is made feasible, so far as the number of students seeking honors through competitive examinations is concerned, if the university also makes it one of its duties, as our own Harvard has done, to lay out various courses, adapted to special classes of intellectual tastes. But even if the "examination-values" of modern subjects should never be made equal to that of the subjects of the old *curriculum*, this does not justify the university in not making such provision and affording such aids as it can for the action of a more genuine motive to study than its ordinary machinery seeks to bring into service. It is true that, without rigid and just competitive examinations, these ulterior motives of emolument and honor could not be fairly applied to studies in which they might be of very great service; but modern subjects might in themselves, and not unfrequently do, inspire the pupil and exact from him labors in a degree comparable to the influence of the most eminent teachers. Moreover, proficiency in them is capable of tests by teachers who closely follow the student's work, and by such original work in written theses as the study may inspire. One way in which the more immediate and genuine motive, the love of a study, could be made the more efficacious, is not to tempt the student away from it by too great rewards for proficiency in those studies which have a greater adaptability to examinations.

It is quite natural that the importance of a study as a means of general education should be constantly confounded, by one with Mr. Todhunter's experience, with what the university can do directly in aid of it, or with its "examination-value." Although it is true that no other studies compare with the mathematical in the exercise they require, when properly taught, of the active powers of intellect, or the inventive and imaginative faculties of the mind, yet it is not true that the mind need always be in a merely receptive attitude toward such studies as history or the natural sciences. Mr. Todhunter admits that, in the study of a new language, it is not altogether the receptive attention that is exercised. His chief objection to other studies compared to the mathematical are, however, that they afford no problems in their earlier stages; and, as he adds, "it is scarcely conceivable that examination papers in history or the natural sciences can offer any tolerable equivalent in merit and importance to the problems of mathematics." But it may be said, on the other hand, that mathematics offers nothing but the most uninviting entertainment to a receptive attention. Its truths, independently of the problems they suggest, have a weariness even for the adept; while languages, history, and the natural sciences, though not exercising the mind with problems in the earliest stages of the study, could and should be made to do so as soon as the active powers of intellect are mature enough. The student may be made to *seek* for more authentic or intelligible evidence both in history and the natural sciences than what his text-books afford; or he may be led to investigate these subjects by comparing various authorities, or by original research; though how he could be effectively led in this search by the requisitions of a formal competitive examination is not so easily determined. To many thinkers on the subject of education this last consideration would only tell against the rigidity of the type of competitive examinations, which has been developed in Cambridge from the studies of the old *curriculum* and in modern mathematics.

It is quite true that the great qualities required and developed in philosophers by original research in experimental sciences are not produced, or even approached, by the repetition of their experiments. These, from being the devices of the most vigorous activity of genius, become, in the experimental lecture-room, or even in the student's own hands in the laboratory, comparatively unimproving amusements. It is one of the weaknesses of genius to recommend enthusiastically (what is generally quite impracticable) the course by which it has manifested itself and reached conspicuous eminence. Nevertheless we attribute much more value to a first-hand acquaintance with experimental processes than our author appears to do. What he considers as a defect for which "some considerable drawback should be made from the educational value of experiments, so called," is their failure. This would certainly mingle unavoidable accidents confusedly with the merits of the student's performance in a set examination; and would, doubtless, disconcert the examining board or teacher, as it often has the most skillful lecturers. But these very failures have in them an important general lesson, especially useful in correcting impressions and mental habits formed by too exclusive attention to abstract studies, and have also special lessons in their respective sciences. From the general lesson is derived an adequate appreciation of the difference between abstract or conditional theorems in science, and their exhibition in concrete phenomena. The difficulty of isolating universal and simple principles from modifying and disturbing causes in actual experiments gives an impression of the nature of physical laws very unlike what the principles of geometry might give, when not corrected by such lessons from the failure of experiments. The actual circles and straight lines of geometry are easily made to embody very closely the theorems of the science. But this is not their real use. Geometrical diagrams are not specimens or examples of the universal truths of the science, but are rather a language—an ideographic language—by which these truths are expressed and inferred.

It is a curious illustration of the need geometrical studies of the Euclidean or ancient type have of guidance from a logic especially treating of its methods and limits, that a recent English work on Logic, in use in one of our principal universities (Jevons's "Elementary Lessons in Logic"), should have represented geometrical reasoning as a kind of induction,—a reasoning from a particular specimen to all other specimens. As well might we say that the repetition of the meaning of a proposition expressed in words, by expressing it in other words, or in the same words, first printed, then spoken, is an inductive process. It is true, and may explain this confusion, that the axioms and postulates of geometry are inductions from elementary constructions, real or imagined, which are subsequently used ideographically to express them and their combinations in the deductions of the science. Mr. Todhunter, in his essay on Elementary Geometry, avows himself opposed to the study of logic in conjunction with geometry, as of too small advantage compared to the addition that would be made to the labors of schoolmasters. The mere fact that Euclid expands his reasonings into full syllogistic completeness is not reason enough, we admit, for requiring additional work by the teacher and student in the study of syllogisms, or in the analysis and classification of arguments. This amplification of arguments was really made by Euclid to simplify, not to add to, the labors of students and teachers. But logic in a wider sense—that is, some account of what are the self-imposed restrictions of resource and method which characterize the ancient geometry —would, we believe, be of great service to intelligent students. It is to the struggle against these restrictions that the superior value of ancient geometry, as a mental discipline, is mainly attributed by the best writers. They are like the conditions and restrictions imposed on artists and poets in the conventions of the fine arts, or on youths as laws of games and athletic sports, to which the intellect, the conscience, and honor of youth are keenly alive. Such restrictions are in the very spirit of that spontaneous ambition for self-formation which characterizes the period of discipline; that is, the period from late childhood to or beyond middle youth.

In respect to the special value of experimental practice to the comprehension of a science, Mr. Todhunter makes a most singular remark, perhaps intended as a humorous one. After observing that boys would doubtless delight in such practice, as they would in any other physical pursuits, like foot-ball, as compared to mental exertion, he adds concerning the value there might be to the boy of seeing with his own eyes the facts of science illustrated, that it may be said the youth is thus made to *believe* the fact more confidently; and he then remarks: "I say that this ought not to be the case. If he does not believe the statement of his tutor,—probably a clergyman of mature knowledge, recognized ability, and blameless character,—his suspicions are irrational, and manifest a want of the power of appreciating evidence, a want fatal to his success in that branch of science which he is supposed to be cultivating." The power of appreciating the evidence of *testimony* would doubtless be shown to be deficient in the case supposed, or if the boy's *belief* was what the illustrations of experiment were useful in affecting. But the more direct effect of illustration is generally supposed to be to aid the *understanding* and *imagination*. A general statement about matters of which no illustrative or analogous instances have ever come under the student's notice is necessarily vague or even unintelligible, and is rather a subject of simple memory (or, so far as belief is concerned, of simple faith) than of rational comprehension. The latter consists in the ability to pass from the general to the particular, or from the abstract to the concrete, and to return again. This is the ladder of the intellect. Any number of formulæ, without a training of judgment and imagination by facts, any number of facts, without a training of the understanding by assured generalizations actually followed, if not originally made by the student, will fail to educate or discipline the faculty which is, *par excellence*, the mind. We do not set so high an estimate as many do on the value for discipline of experimental practice. Only enough of discipline in the actual practice of experiments to enable the student to study his textbook intelligently seems to us desirable for the purposes of a general education, and independently of an ambition or design of extending the boundaries of an experimental science. This might be· accomplished as our author suggests, and as Dr. Whewell believed, not by making the study of the facts in natural and experimental science a part of the business of a school, but rather a part of its recreations.

Mr. Todhunter apparently believes that "the amusing" has generally very little educational value; and much of what others would dignify by the name of "interesting" he seems disposed to place in this category. We should discriminate here between merely spontaneous and idle amusements and those pursuits which, because they happen to be interesting in themselves or at the outset, may not on this account be the less improving, or employ less energy or concentration of faculties than those which are hard or austere. Our author doubtless had in mind, however, a class of diversions lying in wait for unwary students, and forming inseparable parts of certain studies. His type of studies, the mathematical, are certainly not amusing. Even their interest to the adept is of a profoundly serious character. But most studies, besides the mathematical, have tempting by-paths leading from them; and geometry, even, is not without a danger of this sort. Mr. Todhunter says: "In my experience with pupils, I learned to look with apprehension on any exhibition of artistic skill among students of mathematics; for I am sure that it is not a fancy, but an actual fact, that such a power was in many cases an obstacle to success." This observation is given in illustration of the independence of each other of different kinds of observing powers. The chemist is not (as a chemist, we should add) better qualified than another man to be a botanical observer, and the like is true in other dissimilar studies. But there is a more instructive application of the author's observation on the relations of artistic taste to geometry. The facility for drawing appears to be the sole one incident to the study of geometry which tempts the student fatally into an attractive by-path from the difficult, unattractive road of the science. The comparative freedom from diverting attractions is one great advantage of mathematical studies, and we think that our author's esteem of them on this ground is just; though he appears to us not to distinguish clearly enough between the value of difficulty and the quality of irksomeness, which is not of the essence of difficulty. In the period of youth and discipline difficulties are courted and welcomed, and do not necessarily repel. On the contrary, the true end of disciplinary studies appears to be through habit to secure attractiveness, or the character of play for useful, though perhaps at first irksome exercises.

Athletic sports, to which the name "asceticism" was earliest applied in its secondary sense of improving exercises in self-formation, were not disagreeable exercises to the old Greeks; and although Mr. Todhunter looks upon their present prevalence in English universities with disfavor, he might have drawn from them lessons in the science and art of mental education. Even the training of the lower animals is not without instruction in this regard. Mathematical power, though attainable with more or less effort by nearly every one, as our author has testified, is so difficult of attainment, and so irksome to some minds, that it may well be doubted whether general training or a liberal education ought not to be sought in many cases in a different direction. Care should be taken, of course, that the tastes opposed to mathematical pursuits should not have as their chief the taste for merely amusing or diverting pursuits, as they very likely do in most cases. Mathematical abilities seem to us strikingly similar in their relations to education to the faculty of "retrieving" in hunting-dogs; notwithstanding that metaphysicians have attempted to distinguish with characteristic profundity between the mental powers of the lower animals and those of men by calling the capacity of the one for improvement in mental power susceptibility to *training*, and that of the other a capacity for *education*. It is a familiar fact to sportsmen, that unless the young dog shows a fondness for "fetching and carrying" it is almost useless to attempt to teach the accomplishment. For though fetching and carrying can always, with sufficient pains, be taught, yet the means of doing this also teach a vice which makes the faculty almost useless. The dog becomes "hard-mouthed" with his game. If an attempt to remedy this fault is resorted to by training him to carry anything which it is disagreeable to hold hard in the mouth, the animal will generally give up retrieving rather than the vice.

It is natural to suppose that the severe training needed to develop in some minds even a tolerable degree of proficiency ın mathematics will have some such effect; a narrowing effect similar to what excessive devotion to mathematical pursuits produces in minds of greater mathematical ability. "While engaged in these pursuits a student is really occupied with a symbolical language which is exquisitely adapted for a class of conceptions which it has to represent, but which is so far removed from the language of common life, that unless care be taken to guard against the evil the mathematician is in danger of finding his command over the vernacular diminished in proportion as he becomes familiar with the dialect of abstract science." To this testimony of our author on the disadvantage of mathematical training, we may add, that the supposed value of mathematics for training habits of accuracy is delusive. The accuracy belongs to the science objectively. There is no such thing as ambiguity or vagueness in it, or the possibility of misleading the student by these defects, except by gross carelessness on his part. He either understands fully and accurately a proposition, or a step in reasoning, or he does not understand it at all. There is in the study no discipline in detecting and avoiding the faults inherent in common language and in the expressions and reasonings of other classes of conceptions. As well might an athlete seek to become an acrobat by exercises on a wide, even, and guarded path.

Again our author says, "I do not suppose that the candidates who attain to the highest places in the Mathematical Tripos are deficient in knowledge and interest in other subjects; but I fear that omitting these more distinguished men, the remainder frequently betray a rude ignorance in much that is essential to a liberal education." But this disadvantage is not peculiar to mathematical studies. The concentration of a dull mind on any single but extensive study or class of conceptions (like the legal, for example) is apt to leave it in "rude ignorance" of many subjects, some knowledge of which, retained in the memory, is the sign, rather than the essence, of an effective liberal training. What constitutes a liberal education is, as we have said, an unsettled question, or is arbitrarily determined by conventional standards, which are less regarded now than formerly. But it obviously has, at least, these two general features; namely, an acquaintance with a wide variety of subjects, adequate and correct as far as it goes, but necessarily superficial, or at second hand; and, secondly, such a mastery of some one or two subjects in their methods and details, as will afford an adequate measure of the knowledge, or rather of the ignorance, of the mind, in respect to subjects of which it has only a smattering.

Another disadvantage in mathematical studies, admitted by our author, is the deficiency, as a means of discipline, of the modern and higher mathematics; a defect which is incident to their very perfections. When the perfect symbolism of the higher geometry is "cultivated for examination purposes, there is the great danger that the symbols may be used as substitutes for thought rather than as aids to thought." By this we suppose is meant that the abridged processes and notations of modern geometry make it possible for the candidate to carry the theorems and their proofs in mere memory for the most part, and without understanding, or without that rational memory, to which such symbolism is a true art; so that the examination will fail of its end. Yet in abstract subjects all thought is by means of symbols; whether these are the words of common language, the comparatively numerous and awkward steps in the expression and inference of theorems by the diagrams of the old geometry, or the refined, abridged, and effective notations of modern mathematics. The latter are substitutes for thought to the mathematician who has mastered them, in the same sense that a single philosophical term is a substitute for a paraphrase or definition. They save *useless* thought, or repetitions of thought when used as instruments of investigation, either in pure or applied mathematics; and though the thought that is thus avoided may be useful in mere discipline, yet it is mainly useful, we should suppose, by serving as a check, through an easy transition to intuition, for the guidance of reasoned processes, in which the mind still feels insecure.

The true value of these notations is objective; or is in that which most essentially distinguishes the modern from ancient geometry, its direct applicability to other sciences. The ancient geometry is no longer to the physical philosopher the misleading type it once was, of pure principles, or of rational comprehension. It is nevertheless, in one respect, as good a discipline as ever in the education of the mind, and is so on account of its very defects as an instrument of investigation. Its self-imposed restrictions of method adapt it pre-eminently to the spirit and uses of discipline. The modern mathematics are really as distinct from it in essential characteristics as from logic or grammar. Compared to ancient geometry, the objective ulterior value, the usefulness, independently of discipline, of the modern mathematics is immense. The various branches of exact physical science are closed studies to those who have not gained possession of this instrument of all exact inquiry. These can only view the outside of the temple. "Admission to its sanctuary, and to the privileges and feelings of a votary, is only to be gained," as Sir John Herschel says of astronomy, "by one means,—sound and sufficient knowledge of mathematics." The relative claims of this immediate use of a study and of its disciplinary use or "examination-value" are chiefly considered by writers on education in relation to the limits of time they propose for disciplinary studies in general. Mr. Todhunter objects to "the continuance of examinations far into the years of manhood," and also "regrets to see this discipline commenced at too early an age." In the former usage of his university, "when mathematical studies were regarded mainly as a discipline they were frequently entirely dropped or indefinitely postponed when the period of undergraduate discipline was completed." The most eminent scholars were thus sent forth from the universities, having made only a tantalizing approach to any direct use of mathematical skill, and deficient in a knowledge which many of them must afterwards have felt to be an essential part of a liberal education.

What we call the objective value of a science is what should be meant by calling it "useful knowledge." For if the specific utility of any knowledge is not indicated by calling it useful, this term can only mean that the value of the knowledge is not especially in itself, as distinguished from ignorance, error, or stupidity; or is not the kind of value which a well-ascertained but isolated, unrelated fact may yet have as a mere fact; such as the number of leaves on a given bush. In the acquisition and memory of such facts idiots not unfrequently emulate philosophers. The philosopher's advantage is that he has the power to select the related or the useful facts and to forget the rest. This selection is the prime function of intellect. The usefulness of knowledge is in its relatedness or ulterior value, whether as leading to other and wider ranges of knowledge, or as a discipline of the mind, or even as leading to "bread and butter." This last utility is what the unqualified term "useful" generally refers to in common language. Hence the objection to its employment. The popular teaching of natural and experimental sciences by lectures has in recent times been practiced apparently on the ground that they are useful in this sense. It is doubtless true that astronomy, chemistry, and physics are deserving of honor from the unlearned, as well as from scholars, on account of the great incidental services (not generally designed or anticipated in their pursuit) which they have rendered to the arts of life; or on account of their utility in the narrowest, most destitute sense of the word. Wealth and leisure are indispensable requisites to the philosopher's and scholar's pursuits; and it may be said that the means by which these are secured for their pursuits, in any community, ought to be prominent objects of their study and care. Yet, if such had been the motives of physical philosophers in their pursuits of such a subject as electrics, or magnetism and galvanism, if wider, vaguer, less-defined utilities, or relations of knowledge, had not been the almost exclusive motives of this pursuit, it is almost certain that the many useful applications of electrics in the arts would never have been reached. The same is true of other branches of physical and natural science and of applied mathematics. The utility of non-utilitarian motives (in the narrowest sense of the terms) justifies the motives even from the lowest grounds. Where it is demonstrable, as we might suppose it to be of comparative philology and the science of language, that the pursuit can never lead to any such results,* and is even deficient in applicability to university examination purposes, yet even here the spirit of the pursuit is the same as in natural and experimental science, and it is to this spirit, rather than to its occasional and incidental services, in unforeseen ways, that honor for the service is due.

Not only the knowledge which has thus been popularly honored, but all "useful knowledge," in this wide sense, should be fostered by the universities. That which, however, needs especially the care of the universities, is the knowledge which is not, and does not promise to be, useful in an economical sense; the pursuit of which is not stimulated by the prospects of rewards, in fees or wages, or in any ways proportionately to the exertion made. "If," says Mill, "we were asked for what end, above all others, endowed universities exist, or ought to exist, we should answer, 'To keep alive philosophy.'" It is, of course, in the devising and working of its machinery that the time and energies of the officers of a university are chiefly employed; by which young men are helped, encouraged, and tested in their pursuits of culture, and are then sent out into the world bettered in ability and character by the discipline they have received. "How," it may be asked, "can this be a service to philosophy, and to the knowledge which is useful only in a higher sense?" "Our obligations are to the nation, not to philosophy," the university officers might answer. "We are bound to see that the young men who come to us become thorough and accurate students of whatever studies they pursue, and become prepared for their duties in life by the discipline most conducive to accuracy and scholarship. The studies best adapted as means to these ends are the studies we must foster. We must be able to unmask ignorance in our 'pass' examinations; to reveal knowledge in our competitive ones; to compare competitors justly and to reward the most successful. If the studies chosen for these ends are not sufficiently philosophical, then we must sacrifice philosophy to our duty to the nation."

We believe we have not overstated in the above the views,

---

* The recognized political value to English rule in India of studies in these sciences by European scholars preclude, however, the supposition of even such an exception.

and the point of view, of the university men who think at all about the subject. Perhaps more attention to the claims of philosophy, or of a knowledge for the sake of a higher knowledge, would have avoided or remedied the defects which Mr. Todhunter finds in the Cambridge system of examinations. He is disposed apparently to go back to past usages, though he sees little to encourage the hope of a return. "In the study of mathematics formerly, as a discipline, a general knowledge of the principles was all that was required; now," he adds, " we insist on a minute investigation of every incidental part of a subject. Exceptions and isolated difficulties seem to receive undue attention on account of their utility for the examiner's purpose." Again he says, "As a general principle it may be said that the older practice in education was to aim at the discipline of the mind, and that the modern seeks to store it with information." And again, "It may be, I think, justly charged upon our examinations that the memory is over-cultivated and rewarded. As I have already said, examinations in some subjects, as in languages, for example, must necessarily be almost exclusively tests of the memory; but what we may regret to see is that in examinations in subjects with which the reasoning power is supposed to be mainly concerned, the memory should be severely taxed."

On the other hand he repels the charge against the examination system that it encourages *cramming*. This term as applied to various practices seems to him to lack any fixed definite meaning, other than an implied censure of rigorous examinations in general. He conjectures that one definite meaning in the word may relate to the tendency in examinations to over-cultivation and over-appreciation of the memory. But he denies that this is a fault or an avoidable one in such subjects as *language*, in which "it would seem, from the nature of the case, that the memory must be the principal faculty that is tested." Special and exclusive devotion to a single study in completing a school-boy's preparation for an examination does not appear to him to be properly called *cramming*, or at any rate to deserve the reprobation meant to be conveyed by "this absurd and unmeaning word." Mr. Todhunter's reprobation of this word, and of the criticism on examinations in general conveyed by its use, is a key to his whole theory of education; or at least defines the position from which his observations were made, and by which the bearings and value of his testimony should be estimated. There is, it seems to us, a slight inconsistency in objecting, as he does, to the value of natural and experimental sciences, as a discipline, on account of the time and pains needed for examinations in them, which he thinks would be excessive; at the same time admitting in regard to the studies he approves of, that undue attention to exceptions and isolated difficulties in them is given on account of the utility of these to the examiner's purpose. That is, he contrasts two kinds of studies in respect to defects, which it appears both would have, but which are really due to a system that does not admit, on account of these defects, of application to both kinds at once.

The examiner's purposes, the secondary or subsidiary means of discipline, are likely in his pursuit, as means are in all other pursuits, to receive undue attention, and the proximate means to the true ends to become ends in themselves; especially, as we have said, when custom or long usage has sanctioned them and affords the easiest escape from difficult questions. How to make the studies previously found useful in discipline still more useful; how to avoid defects in the examinations, to prevent the memory from doing the proper work of the reason in these tests of proficiency; how to prevent the evils, whatever they may be, of *cramming*, are the highest problems in education to which university men generally give their attention. To them it is a sufficient objection to modern studies as means of discipline that they are not fixed or finished sciences, but are constantly undergoing changes and improvements at the hands of special adepts, which are more fundamental than the changes, improvements, and expansions made in older subjects solely with reference to their use in education. In short, the officers of universities are as innocent of philosophy as most other men in business generally are. "The fashionable subjects of the day" disconcert the examiner. If these are capable of inspiring a patient and laborious attention in the student by their own inherent interest, it is well. This is the way in which they may be useful, but the professor and the examiner with his rewards of assistance and honor have no concern in it; or their duties are done by putting the new subjects into the highest examination papers.

The corporate spirit, the conscious union of aims and the purposes common to all in such a university, is not a very high one. Conservatism, reverence for the traditions of the university, attachment to it as a family of scholars, pride in it for the importance of its services to the nation and to mankind, are the sum of its conscious virtues, the limits of its aspirations. If so be philosophy seeks or can find entertainment in this family, she is welcome; but is still a guest, not an inmate. If it were not for the wealth or the appropriations of it which serve to consolidate these as well as other families, it might be otherwise. Philosophers were so named because they refused the pittances of schoolmasters; but it is difficult to see how they could have lived without them, or what was equivalent to them (though called by a different name), if they happened to be poor, as they generally were. But it is not perhaps by a disposal of means essentially different from what now prevails in universities, that a remedy for their defects is to be sought. It is rather by a different *spirit* of disposal. *In order that the distribution of assistance and honors might be perfectly just, a system has been devised which inevitably places inferior motives to study in the first rank of incitements.* A definite though factitious direction thus given to the efforts of teachers is the best excuse that can be clearly urged for this promotion of inferior incitements to study. Comparatively few candidates continue throughout their academic course to be stimulated by them, the majority being soon distanced; yet these few are those who least need or are really profited by such discipline; while the majority have their studies chosen for them on such irrelevant grounds as would be disregarded in a choice of courses arranged for self-training, namely, "the adaptability of subjects to the exigencies of examinations."

We admit the difficulties of reform, while insisting on its importance. It is at least one step towards it to recognize this importance, and to know, however painful the consciousness may be, that our loyalty and pride are not fixed upon the highest objects; that a justice which cannot go by favor is yet not the greatest justice. It is not the justice of natural families, nor of families of philosophers. These may not reach practically a very high type; they seek, however, for justice through other means than regulations; they love to receive it at the hands of honest and intelligent generosity, rather than win it from the hands of inflexible law. One would suppose that in a university, if anywhere among men, this dangerous, impracticable higher justice might find a seat; but an English university would be the last place where one would wisely seek for it. Such is the influence of competitive examinations, that the justice of them is more hostile to this rival than to any form of injustice. This may be because the rival is, in a university, a really formidable and dangerous one; so that it becomes the chief business of the reigning power to maintain its throne. At any rate Mr. Todhunter thinks it highly important that the justice of competitive examinations should be additionally guarded, by excluding teachers rigidly from the examinations of their own pupils in competition with others. This is indeed a confession of an inherent, rather than an incidental weakness in the system.

That the ends of a liberal education are manifold, and are vaguely conceived in their just proportions; that the means to the various ends, which may be consciously sought, are often conflicting; and that the attention of those who make education their business is definitely directed by a traditional *curriculum* to the subsidiary means of perfecting its use,—are perhaps sufficient explanations of the feeble attention given by scholars to the higher or ultimate ends of training. That our author, with all his study and experience in this subject, should have failed to discover any definite meaning in the word *cramming* beyond its implied censure of rigorous examinations is, therefore, not surprising. If we may venture to say in a sentence what the word commonly means, when used intelligently, we may say that a given amount of studious attention, either rational or merely mnemonic, given to a subject exclusively and for a short time, gives to the mind a different and a less persistent or valuable hold on the subject than the same amount and kind of attention spread over a longer time and interrupted by other pursuits. This mode of study and its defects are what we conceive the word *cram* is meant to express, and at the same time to censure.

All modes of study involve, of course, *repetitions* of such degrees of attention to a fact or conception or inference as the student's power can command. By these repetitions the memory is made firm and persistent. But there are two very different modes of repetition: first, by repeated acts of *direct* attention; secondly, by repeated recalls or recollections. The latter has two varieties, namely, being repeatedly reminded by associated thoughts or objects of the things remembered, and performing repeated acts of voluntary recollection or research in reminiscence. The last is the only *active* exercise of memory, and is, of course, most strengthening to a *command* of memory. But both these varieties, and especially the latter, require, for disciplinary exercise and trial, interposed intervals and diversions of attention; and the longer the intervals are, if not too long, the more the essential or rational, and the far-reaching or constructive associations of thought come into play, or the more the "reason" is cultivated, according to the common expression of this practically well-known fact. The reason is a slow growth, and cannot be forced in any study, though in some it may readily be blighted.

There is a popular opinion, shared by some philosophers, that great memory and sound judgment are incompatible, and the words *Beati memoria expectantes judicium* express this supposed incompatibility. And there is a basis, doubtless, for this belief. The more essential or rational and the far-reaching or constructive associations of thought are by far the most durable, and constitute the inner life, or sub-conscious action of thought; though the associations which are temporarily stronger are most readily commanded, or are parts of the present volitional power of the mind. In other words, the retentiveness of memory as distinguished from recollection, or from the power of ready recall, depends on the thoroughness of understanding, or on the number of links of mental habitude binding together and leading to the things remembered. The apparent contradiction, which Sir W. Hamilton regards as a real one, between the great learning of the philosophic scholar, Joseph Scaliger, and his statement that he had not a good memory but a good reminiscence, that proper names did not easily recur to him, but when thinking on them he could find them out, is a good illustration of the distinction between the readiness of a sensuous or first-hand memory by rote, and the more durable memory of a reflective and subtle understanding, which involves a greater real command with sufficient pains, though not so ready a command of remembered objects. There was no real inconsistency between Scaliger's confession and his great learning, or even the readiness of his memory on occasions. His own testimony is worth much more about his own memory than any contemporary's judgment from his talks, such as Sir W. Hamilton quotes in his Metaphysics (Lecture XXX). Reminiscence appears to have been used by him in the sense of a power of attention to recover what did not readily recur to him, and ought in this sense to be distinguished both from mere retentiveness and from readiness of recollection ; the latter being the sense in which he used the word *memory*. But so far are sound judgment and memory, in a wider sense than this, from being incompatible, that judgment is in fact a form of memory,—the most subtle and serviceable, though least readily commanded. It is the memory or the retentiveness of understanding, or of the generalizing faculty ; just as what is commonly called memory is the retentiveness of imagination, or of the faculty of individual and concrete representations. The soundness or excellence of both forms depends, of course, on the powers of attention and primary perception.

"That the memory is over cultivated and rewarded" by the incitements and exactions of examinations in Cambridge is what Mr. Todhunter admits. That this is due to the mode of study they encourage is what he has failed to see. The abuse to which examinations are liable of testing memory when the faculty of reason is the one under examination is a fault which Mr. Todhunter, as an examiner in mathematics, has seen, and against which he believes the examinations can and should be guarded; and it is not, therefore, he thinks, one which ought to condemn the system. And so far we go along with him, but the real defect of the system is subtler than this.

Examinations may be guarded against mistaking a simple memory of the lowest order, or mere memory, for a rational comprehension of a subject; but the faculties trained by mental discipline are not so simply classified as writers on education appear to think when they enumerate them as memory, reason, and invention or imagination. There are various kinds and orders of memory, and *the highest of these, together with the highest order of invention, involves the faculty called reason.* The faculties which ought to be tested by examination are properly *memory* and *invention* in their various orders, and in the kinds in which various studies have disciplined them. Examinations in languages and history are mainly tests of memory, Mr. Todhunter thinks; but how different are the orders of memory involved even in these! How different is the child's memory of stories from that of a student of comparative mythology! A quick, retentive child's memory will note every variation in repeated recitals of a tale, and will correct the story-teller on points which seem to the adult mind quite trivial, but are in fact to the child essential enough to make a different story. When the comparative mythologist, on the other hand, finds identity amidst the varieties of legendary tales of various races and nations, his memory of them is of a different order from the child's. History or language may be remembered in these different ways, and no *system* of competitive examinations would be able to detect the difference. A difficult construction in an author writing in an ancient or a foreign language might be satisfactorily construed by the candidate either because he retained in simple memory, as an isolated fact, the explanation of it given by his tutor (which might be more rational than the student could gather from a literal translation), or because he had, like his tutor, met and noted parallel or analogous constructions in the same or in other authors; thus exercising his reason in a still better way. How vastly superior, indeed, the latter form of memory is, in persistency, in utility for professional employments, and in the satisfaction of thought itself as a mental exercise! If this cannot be distinguished by formal examinations from lower orders of memory, the fact ought to tell against the system rather than against those studies which are ill-adapted to it, and which include almost all except mathematical studies; or even include these when the system is not elaborated to the perfection it now has in Cambridge.

A broad distinction in the kinds of mental association, dominant in different orders of memory, is familiar to psychologists, though apparently not to most writers on education. The associations of mere contiguity or consecutiveness are characteristic of the child's mind and of imaginative poetical persons. A low order of invention goes along with them, namely, the order of poetical or artistic invention, which is intellectually inferior, and is not cultivated systematically by universities, although valuable to the artist or poet, and highly influential in works of genius. If the memory dependent on this kind of association is naturally strong, and continues after childhood with but little systematic practice or effort, it may be regarded as a positive advantage to the mind, as a form of native strength; though the exercises and mental habits required for the cultivation of it are directly opposed to those needed for the cultivation of the higher or rational memory and invention. Committing pages of rhythmical verses or simple elegant prose to memory, though not exclusively dependent on associations of the lowest order, yet depends very largely on them, and interferes as a habit with the habits which bring into play the other kind of associations which psychologists have distinguished, namely, the associations of similarity. This kind of associations brings together resembling, analogous, or identical parts in different trains of contiguous or consecutive impressions, or drops from these trains into oblivion all the parts that have not with the rest ties of this sort, or else the contrasted ones of *dis*similarity. The associations of similarity are those of rational comprehension in memory and invention. They dissolve the ties of the other sort, which are relatively so strong in children, in natural·arithmeticians, and often in the undeveloped minds of idiots. The two sorts rarely exist together in great perfection, or except in men of eminent genius, whose native powers of attention are equal to those of two ordinary minds.

Hence for minds which schools and universities undertake to train, the needed discipline is not the training of two distinct and unrelated faculties (the memory and reason), by studies specifically chosen to test their proficiency; but it is the supplementing of a lower and original, or early developed form of memory and invention by a higher one, even at the expense of supplanting the lower in great measure. In the most rational of studies, the mathematical, the constituents which depend on mere memory, or the lowest kind of association, are the fewest, and the play of invention, in the constructive action of rational imagination, is the greatest. Perhaps the latter is too great for a symmetrical training of the mind; since, in a genuine pursuit of mathematics, the lower form of memory is apt with ordinary minds to be enfeebled by it. The lower form of memory is still a very valuable one; though the cheapness of books and writing-materials dispenses with many of its services. Even *cramming*, or the getting up of a subject in the shortest time, which depends largely on powers of retention of this sort, and but little on the fixed habits formed by studies more prolonged, might on this ground be commended; though *cramming* mathematics for examination would obviously not be the best course; since other studies, pursued properly, would more directly and profitably exercise these powers, by the concentration of attention.

The *ability* to "cram," which such work in the universities must, of course, cultivate, has been thought to be an element of success in various pursuits of life, as with the statesman, the general, the lawyer, and with men of business; but we are inclined to believe that the use in these pursuits of the lower form of memory is secured to successful men by their ability to stimulate its action on occasions by throwing into it their superior energies of purpose, emotion, or will, rather than by university practice of this sort. Light is thrown on this subject by the well-known facts in psychology, that the lower memory depends on two distinct causes, on the *repetition* and on the *intensity* of impressions; and that impressions which are at all relevant to states of strong emotion are more deeply and persistently impressed than under ordinary circumstances. Even trivial, irrelevant circumstances attending or coming under our notice in states of strong emotion are long retained in the memory. If this be the true explanation of the great service which the lower memory sometimes renders to eminent minds, it would follow that it is not by the direct cultivation of the memory, but rather by cultivating this cause of it that discipline can be useful; that is, by exercises which stimulate to energetic action the emotions and the will. Athletic training and exercises are of this sort, and though they do not employ the memory, may yet, by the sustained mental effort required in them, educate the character to a better command of memory on fitter occasions. No faculty is in general more susceptible of training than that of attention *in the directions in which it is spontaneous;* and, on the other hand, no faculty is more dependent on the native aptitudes and powers which direct it. The antithesis is due to the extreme generality of the term "attention," which includes in its meaning both the original or spontaneous powers of the mind, and those which discipline is capable of perfecting or improving with reference to any standard. Much of the superiority of eminent minds is, doubtless, in a native or early acquired degree and kind of power of attention, which none of the motives of direct discipline can create. This is true also of the lower animals; superior native or spontaneously acquired powers of attention being regarded by their trainers as indispensable to success in training them. Of this contrast between genius or native character and ordinary mental ability, genius itself is not in general made aware by comparison with ordinary standards, but usually attributes its success to a prolonged and patient concentration of an ordinary attention, which is merely voluntary; thus converting into a merit, or a moral superiority, what are really gifts of nature. But in this explanation of itself neither genius nor character takes account of the motives or the pleasures of action and effort which make patient labor and sacrifice easier for it than for inferior orders of minds, for whom moral incitements and rewards are, therefore, more needed ; and genius is apt to take no account of the finer quality of its powers of attention, which it attributes to the objects or the occasions to which its efforts are "accidentally directed." The pre-eminence of genius and of native character is really manifested in the equality of abilities to exceptionally difficult works; though it is made indubitably evident and a subject for fame and history only in performance which admits of comparison with the results of ordinary abilities.

Command of the lower memory is doubtless improved by the mastery of some one or two subjects; the more special and narrow they are, the better, perhaps, for saving time, and even if they do not belong to what is commonly accounted essential to a liberal education. It should, however, be such a mastery as is conducive to the formation of mental habits, and not such as can be compassed by *cramming*, or the exclusive study of any subject for a special purpose and in a limited time. A young officer of the Union army in our late struggle, in a letter written on the evening before the battle in which his life was sacrificed, attributed his previous successes, and rapid promotion to responsible duties, to a six months' study of *turtles* at the Zoölogical Museum of Harvard University, which was undertaken merely from the youthful instinct of mastery, or appreciation of the value of discipline, and was interrupted by the breaking out of the war and the young man's enlistment in the service. Perhaps, however, the independence of character which determined this choice of means for discipline was the real source of the success which the youth too modestly attributed to the discipline itself.

It is all-important in considering the problems of education to have clearly before our minds what are its true ends and its most direct proximate means. This is far more important, in a philosophical consideration of the subject, than any amount of evidence on the working of a system of subsidiary means supposed to be adapted to ends very ill understood. It is a far more important question than that to which answer is made in the testimony of experienced teachers and examiners as to the value of any system of examinations for testing a youth's "examination-passing-power." This testimony may be good evidence that a university is really doing, and doing faithfully, what it professes to do; but it is not a proof that its system is the best, or that its ideas of a liberal education are soundly based either in experience or philosophy. It is not a proof that philosophy is kept alive in such a university, even to the degree of inspiring a hope for attainment beyond the immediately practicable, or of creating any desire for a wider range of influence, or for a more comprehensive knowledge of its duties.

THE USES AND ORIGIN OF THE ARRANGE-
MENTS OF LEAVES IN PLANTS.*

In proposing to treat in this paper of the *origin* of some ot
the more common arrangements of leaves and leaf-like organs
in the higher orders of plants, I do not intend to make this
question the principal object of discussion, but propose only to
consider it so far as it affords useful hypotheses for the interpretation of some of the obscurer features in the main object
of this inquiry; namely, questions of the *uses* of these arrangements, or of their adaptations to the outward economy of the
plant's life, and to the conditions of its existence. If by such
a discussion hypothesis can be made to throw light on physiological questions, while seeking more directly to connect in a
continuous series the simpler and more general with the more
specific and complicated forms in vegetable life, it will gain for
itself a much greater interest and value than it would otherwise possess. It is, indeed, in this value of the principle of
Natural Selection, its value and use as a working hypothesis,
that its principal claim to respect consists. If any subsidiary
hypothesis under the theory serve only as a principle of connection, a thread on which we may arrange and more clearly
regard relationships that are the objects of a more promising
scientific inquiry, it will at least serve a useful purpose, and
even, perhaps, give greater plausibility to the theory in general
of the origin of organic forms through the agency ot their
utilities, or through the advantages these have given to surviving forms of life.

There is hardly any animal or plant, especially of the higher

---

*From the Memoirs of the American Academy of Arts and Sciences. Communicated
October 10, 1871.

orders, that has not in many of the characteristics of its structure very conspicuous adaptations to the outward conditions of its life,—to "the part it has to play in the world," or at least to the many values or advantages it has to secure. This fact has led many naturalists, whose opinion, until lately, and for a long time, has prevailed, to regard a living structure as principally, if not entirely, made up of subordinate parts or organs which exist for specific purposes, or are essentially concerned with special services to the general life of the organism, or even to life external to it, the general life of the world, or ultimately even to the highest and best life of the world. This doctrine deprived of its grander features, as the doctrine of Final Causes in natural history, and limited simply to the conception of the parts and characters of organic structures as all, or nearly all, related essentially to the preservation and continuance of the life itself which they embody, or to the principle of self-conservation, is the ground of the importance claimed for the principle of Natural Selection in the generation of organic species. But another school of naturalists, whose influence has been steadily gaining ground, has always strenuously opposed this view, and questioned the validity of the induction on which it rests. Though it is true that the higher animals and plants exhibit a great many special adaptations to the conditions of their existence, yet, it is objected, in a far greater number of characteristics they, in common with the rest of the organic world, exhibit no such adaptations. In those most important features of organic structures, which are now called genetic characters, and were formerly called affinities, few or no specific uses can in general be discovered; and it is considered unphilosophical to base an induction on the comparatively few cases of this class of characters which have obvious utilities It is thought unphilosophical to presume on such meagre grounds that all these characters are either now, or have been, of service to the life of the organism; thus confounding these genetic characters with those that are properly called adaptive. By positing this distinction of genetic and adaptive characters as a fundamental and absolute one, the theory of organic types opposes itself to the conception of utility as a property of organic structures in general, and conceives, on the other hand, that an organism consists essentially of certain constituent parts and characters which are of no service to its general life, and are ends, so far as we can know, in themselves; though other and subordinate ones may stand incidentally in this menial relation.

This contrast being a merely speculative difference of opinion, a reference to it, in a scientific inquiry, would be out of place were it not that scientific inquiries are almost never free from such biases. These almost always exert an unperceived influence, unless specially guarded against; and in calling attention here to this question in biological philosophy, it is only for the purpose of characterizing it as a strictly open question. As is so often the case in such debates, both sides are right and both wrong; right, so far as each refuses credence to the other's main and exclusive position, and wrong, so far as each claims it for its own. In other words, they are not properly inductive theories, awaiting and subject to verification, but arrogant dogmas, demanding unconditional assent. The bearing of this debate on the proper questions of science relates only to *method*, or to what are the directions in which scientific pursuit and hypothesis are legitimate. It is oftener by diverting or misdirecting scientific pursuit than in any other way that such speculative opinions are of serious importance; and in this way they are purely mischievous. The theory of types is undoubtedly right in refusing assent to the doctrine, as an established induction, that every part, arrangement, or function of an organism is of some special, though it may be unrecognized, service to its life; but it is wrong in assuming, on the other hand, that all attempts at discovering uses which are not present or obvious must be futile; or, in assuming that there are characteristic features in all organisms, which are not only at present of no use, but never could have been grounds of advantage. Again, the theory of the essential reference of every feature of an organism to the conditions of its existence is undoubtedly right in refusing assent to this assumption of essentially useless forms, and in affirming the legitimacy of inquiries concerning the utility of any feature whatever to the life of an organism, however far removed in appearance from any relations to its present conditions of existence. It is wrong, on the other hand, in confounding the legitimacy of this pursuit with the dogma in which, as a theory, it essentially consists, or in assuming as an established induction what is only a legitimate question or line of inquiry.

It is obvious, however, that a proper scientific judgment of these theories cannot be absolutely impartial, since one of them is opposed to scientific pursuit, and the other invites it. The theory of types, assuming that utility is only a superficial or incidental character, and not a property of organic forms and functions generally, occupies a negative and forbidding attitude towards what are really legitimate questions of science; and, from this point of view, judgment must be made in favor of the rival dogma. We ought to be on our guard, moreover, against this theory, since there is a strong natural, but erroneous and mischievous, tendency in the mind to fall back upon it from the difficulties of a baffled pursuit; and to regard as really ultimate those facts of which the causes and dependences elude our researches. This resort can never be justified so long as there remain any suggestions of explanation not altogether frivolous, or incapable of some degree of verification. We may safely maintain that this tendency to rest from the difficulties of scientific pursuit is the chief cause of the prevalence at the present time of the doctrine, which, when first propounded, was regarded as heterodox and dangerous, especially as it then seemed opposed to the doctrine of Final Causes. This apparent opposition has since, however, been made to disappear by a modification of the latter doctrine, which has incorporated in it this theory of types, by representing a type of structure as an ultimate feature in the general plan of creation, or as an end for which the successive manifestations and the adaptations of life exist, or to which they tend. According to this doctrine, it is not for the sake of the maintenance and continuance of the mere life, such as it is, or such as it can be, under the conditions of its existence, that adaptations exist in organisms; but it is for the sake of realizing in it certain predetermined special types of structure, which are ends in themselves, and to which the adaptive characters of the structure are subservient. Thus an elaborate and formidable philosophical theory has grown up, which stands in direct and forbidding opposition to such inquiries as the one proposed in this discussion.

If the theory were true, it would, indeed, be idle to ask what are the uses, and how could these have determined the origin of those special leaf arrangements in the higher plants, which have been observed by botanists, and discussed by mathematicians in the theory of Phyllotaxy. There is a sufficiently obvious utility in the general character of these arrangements with reference to the general external economy of vegetable life and the functions of leaf-like bodies; but this does not at first sight appear to regard the particular details, or the special laws of arrangement, with which the theory of Phyllotaxy is concerned. In these we have apparently reached ultimate features of structure, the origin or value of which in the plant's life it would, on the theory of types, be idle to seek. These are such excellent examples of what the theory of types supposes to be finalities in biological science, that botanists and mathematicians, with hardly an exception, have consented to regard them in this light. There is a difference of opinion, it is true, as to whether the several angular intervals between successive leaves around the stem, or the several angles of divergence between successive leaves in the spiral arrangements, ought to be regarded as modifications of a single typical angle to which they approximate in value, or as several distinct types. There is no difference of opinion, however, in regard to another distinction of types in leaf arrangements, which, to all appearance, are separated by entirely distinct characters; namely, the so-called spiral arrangements and those of the verticil or whorl. It is with the former chiefly that the mathematical theory of Phyllotaxy is concerned. The latter, or the verticil arrangements, though presenting a great variety of forms, are so obviously all of the same general and simple type, that they present no difficulties or problems for the exercise of mathematical skill. Their varieties consist simply in the number of leaves in the whorl. From two leaves placed oppositely, these whorls vary through all numbers to very large ones, and in all these varieties the simple law holds that the leaves of successive whorls, being of the same number and placed in each whorl at equal distances around the stem, like the spokes of a wheel, are so disposed that the leaves of the upper whorl stand directly over the angular spaces between those of the lower one. These features of arrangement are so obviously the same adaptations as those we shall find in the more complicated spiral arrangements, that I will consider them both together. They appear to be two solutions of the same problem in the economy of the higher vegetable life; though it is probable that the whorl arrangement is the inferior one. It approaches in simplicity most nearly to the alternate system among the spiral forms, though it is perfectly distinct from this. An opposition of leaves in the whorl is an accident or trivial circumstance dependent on the fact that the number of leaves in the whorl is in many cases an even one; while in the alternate arrangement this opposition is an essential character. This would not be strictly the case, indeed, if the theory were true that the alternate as well as the other spiral arrangements are only modifications of a single typical one. But an examination of the evidence will show very slight grounds for this opinion. No doubt, in the doctrine of development, all these arrangements must be considered as modifications of some single ancient form, though this, it is quite likely, was very different from the typical arrangement, or the perfect form, in the theory of Phyllotaxy. The important point, however, to be considered here, is, that on the theory of development there is properly no genetic connection between the opposition of leaves in whorls and those of the alternate arrangement. And, indeed, in the three-leaved systems of the two types the contrast is very marked; for the three leaves of such a whorl stand over the angular spaces between the three of the whorl below it, as in other arrangements of this type; while the three leaves of the spiral system or cycle stand severally directly over the three below them. The genetic relationships of the two great types will be specially considered when we come to the problem of the origin of both from simpler vegetable forms.

The names "system" and "cycle" are not so properly applicable to groups of leaves in the spiral arrangements as to those of whorls, and refer rather to abstract numbers, counted from any point we please, than to actually definite groups. The actual system, cycle, or group in these arrangements is of indefinite extent, or comprises the whole stem, so far as it is developed, and even extends into the undeveloped leaves of the terminal bud. In speaking of a cycle of leaves in these arrangements no definitely situated group is meant, but only a definite number counted from any one we may choose for an origin. In almost all arrangements of this type we find that, after thus counting some definite number of leaves from some one assumed as the first, we arrive next at a leaf which stands directly over the first. Such a group, so determined, makes what is called a cycle; or, as we may sometimes prefer to call it, a system. Within it leaves succeed each other at successively greater and greater heights, and are so placed around the stem that the same angular interval or angle of divergence is contained between any two successive ones. This angle of divergence is commensurate with the circumference, but is not always an aliquot part of it, as in the angular interval of the leaves of whorls. It is in many plants some multiple of an aliquot part, and in counting the leaves successively through the cycle, we have to turn several times around the stem. This number of revolutions, divided by the number of leaves in the cycle, is the ratio of the angle of divergence to the whole circumference; and the fraction expressing this ratio is used to denote the particular arrangement of such a system. Thus the fraction $\frac{1}{2}$ denotes the alternate arrangement, in which there are two leaves in one turn, the third leaf falling over the first. $\frac{1}{3}$ is the name of the three-leaved system, in which there are three leaves in one turn, the fourth falling over the first. $\frac{2}{5}$ is the name of the system in which five leaves occur in two turns and the sixth falls over the first. In order that such definite numerical systems, or cycles, should exist in the leaves of any plant, it is only necessary that the ratio of the angle of divergence to the circumference should be some proper fraction, and this fraction would be in the same way the name of the system. But any proper fraction whatever would have the property I have pointed out; namely, that after the number of leaves denoted by its denominator, and the number of turns denoted by its numerator, the next succeeding leaf would fall over the first. Whatever may be the purpose or advantage of the spiral arrangement, and of this feature in it, it is obvious that some other purpose is sought, or some other advantage gained, by the actual arrangements of this sort in nature; or else it would appear on the theory of types, that the typical properties of them are not fully determined by what we have yet observed respecting them. For, although there is a great variety of such arrangements, these do not include all the possible ones, nor even all the simplest. There must still be another principle of choice besides what determines the rational fraction and the spiral arrangement. What this is, is the problem of the mathematical theory of Phyllotaxy. The result of this investigation was a classification of all the fractions that occur in natural arrangements under the general form of the continued fraction

$$\cfrac{1}{a + \cfrac{1}{1 + \cfrac{1}{1 + \&c.,}}}$$

in which a may have the values, 1, 2, 3, or 4. The successive approximations of these four continued fractions give four series of proper fractions, which include all the arrangements that occur in nature. These series are for

$a = 1$ . . . . $\frac{1}{2}, \frac{2}{3}, \frac{3}{5}, \frac{5}{8}, \frac{8}{13},$ &c.

$a = 2$ . . . . $\frac{1}{2}, \frac{1}{3}, \frac{2}{5}, \frac{3}{8}, \frac{5}{13},$ &c.

$a = 3$ . . . . $\frac{1}{3}, \frac{1}{4}, \frac{2}{7}, \frac{3}{11}, \frac{5}{18},$ &c.

$a = 4$ . . . . $\frac{1}{4}, \frac{1}{5}, \frac{2}{9}, \frac{3}{14}, \frac{5}{23},$ &c.

The first series is not usually given, since they are the complements of the fractions of the second series, and express the same arrangements, but in an opposite direction around the circumference; or by supposing that the spiral line connecting the leaves is drawn from leaf to leaf the longer way round. Omitting then the first series, we shall still have in the others, as they stand, developed to five terms, many more fractions than have actually been observed, or could be observed in actual plants.

I propose in what follows to subject the mathematical induction expressed by these series to careful critical examination, to distinguish what is matter of actual observation from what is deduced from theory, and to ascertain with precision the amount of inductive evidence on which the theory of the typical angle rests. Pursuing the subject afterwards by a strictly inductive investigation, I shall estimate what there is of truth in the theory. This will lead, I think, to the rejection of the theory as it stands, or under the form of the typical angle, but will not render the observation on which it depends wholly nugatory. On the contrary, it will show that this observation really leads to the true explanation of the occurrence of only certain fractions in the spiral arrangements, and the more frequent occurrence of some of them than of others. It is a well-known property of the fractions of these series, that after the first two in each, the others can be deduced from the preceding ones, and continued indefinitely, by a very simple process. The numerator of each after the first two is equal to the sum of the numerators of the two preceding, and its denominator to the sum of their denominators. This law, as a matter of observation, was actually discovered only in the first four fractions of the first or second series, which are by far the commonest of actually observed arrangements in nature. Other less frequently occurring fractions were arranged on the same principle, and extended so as to give the last two series. The four series, or the three lower ones, contain, therefore, more than all the fractions that are known to belong to natural arrangements. This will be sufficiently evident when we observe that the fractions $\frac{5}{8}$ and $\frac{8}{13}$ in the first series, or their complements, $\frac{3}{8}$ and $\frac{5}{13}$, in the second series, would be indistinguishable in actual measurement; since they differ from each other by $\frac{1}{104}$, or by less than a hundredth, which is much less than can be observed, or than stems are often twisted by irregular growth. For the same reason we must reject all but the first three terms of the third and fourth series as being distinguishable only in theory. We are thus left with a very slight basis of facts on which to erect the superstructure of theory. We shall see further on a still more cogent reason for calling in question the validity of this induction; namely, that limiting the evidence as we are thus obliged to do, we have still left so large a number of actually observed arrangements, that they include almost all that are possible among equally simple and distinguishable fractions within the observed limits of natural arrangements; all, in fact, but two; namely, the fractions $\frac{4}{9}$ and $\frac{3}{7}$. The range is not a narrow one, but extends from $\frac{1}{6}$ to $\frac{4}{5}$, or from $\frac{1}{6}$ to $\frac{1}{2}$, since the fractions above $\frac{1}{2}$ are complements of those below, and express the same arrangements, but in an opposite direction around the circumference. The problem of Phyllotaxy, therefore, seems at first sight to be reduced to this; not why the other fractions do occur in nature, but why these two do not? But to answer the latter question is really also to answer the former, though it will go but very little way towards justifying the theory of the typical or unique angle. It will go much further if we exclude from this list of fractions those which are of very infrequent occurrence, namely, those peculiar to the third and fourth series; or, in other words, take account of the relative frequency in nature of the several arrangements. This, indeed, entirely changes the aspects of the question, for we find that, instead of two, there are six fractions of the simpler denominations (or within the limits of distinguishable values), which either do not occur in nature at all, or occur very rarely; while those that are common are four in number, or less than half of all. But we shall find that those of the six which occur rarely differ from the two really unique ones among them, and agree with the common ones in respect to the law on which the answer to our question really depends. This answer will be found to depend on the law which was observed in the first four fractions of the first or second series, and was extended in the continuation of these and the formation of the others. This law, or the dependence of these fractions on each other, was seen to be a simple case of the relations of dependence in the successive approximations of continued fractions, and thus led to the induction of these fractions; namely, the continued fraction

$$\cfrac{1}{1 + \cfrac{1}{1 + \cfrac{1}{1 + \&c.}}}$$ for the first series, or

$$\cfrac{1}{2 + \cfrac{1}{1 + \cfrac{1}{1 + \&c.}}}$$

for the second. The ultimate values of these continued fractions extended infinitely are complements of each other, as their successive approximations are, and are in effect the same fraction; namely, the irrational or incommensurate interval which is supposed to be the perfect form of the spiral arrangement. This does, in fact, possess in a higher degree than any rational fraction the property common to those which have been observed in nature; though practically, or so far as observation can go, this higher degree is a mere refinement of theory. For, as we shall find, the typical irrational interval differs from that of the fraction $\frac{3}{8}$ (and its complement differs from $\frac{5}{8}$) by almost exactly $\frac{7}{1000}$, a quantity much less than can be observed in the actual angles of leaf-arrangements. The conception of such a typical angle as an actual value in nature, and as a point of departure for more specialized ones, existing either among the normal patterns, or formative principles of vegetable life, as the theory of types supposes, or in some unknown law of development or physiological necessity,—such a conception is a very attractive one. And as exhibiting in the abstract and in its most perfect form a property peculiar, as we shall see, to natural arrangements, but belonging to them in inferior and in various degrees,—as exhibiting this separated from the property which such arrangements also have, by which they are divisible into limited systems or cycles,—from this point of view the conception acquires a valid scientific utility. But we should be on our guard against a misconstruction of it. There is no evidence whatever, and there *could* be none from observation, that any such separation of properties actually occurs in nature, or that one is superposed on the other in successive stages of development in the bud, or that this typical arrangement is first produced and subsequently modified into the more special ones,—into the limited systems or cycles represented by simple rational fractions. To suppose this is to confound abstractions with concrete existences, and would be an instance of the so-called "realism" in science, against which it is always so necessary to be on our guard. There is no reason to suppose that one rather than the other of these properties appears first in the incipient parts of the bud, or that either exists in any degree of perfection before the development of these parts has made considerable advance.

[The memoir proceeds to show by "a strictly inductive investigation," and to exemplify graphically by a large diagram, "what this property is which the typical or unique angle has in the abstract and in perfection, and to show what its utility is in the economy of vegetable life." The details are too technical and the investigation too mathematical to be reproduced here. It explains how this spiral arrangement]

would effect the most thorough and rapid distribution of the leaves around the stem, each new or higher leaf falling over the angular space between the two older ones which are nearest in direction so as to subdivide it in the same ratio, k, in which the first two, or any two successive ones, divide the circumference. But according to such an arrangement there could be no limited systems or cycles, or no leaf would ever fall exactly over any other; and, as I have said, we have no evidence, and could have none, that this arrangement actually exists in nature. To realize simply and purely the property of the most thorough distribution, the most complete exposure of the leaves to light and air around the stem, and the most ample elbow-room or space for expansion in the bud, is to realize a property that exists separately only in abstraction, like a line without breadth. Nevertheless practically, and so far as observation can go, we find that the last two fractions, $\frac{5}{8}$ and $\frac{8}{13}$, and all further ones of the first series, like $\frac{13}{21}$, etc., which are all indistinguishable as measured values in the plant, do actually realize this property with all needful accuracy. Thus $\frac{5}{8}=0.625$; $\frac{8}{13}=0.615$; and $\frac{13}{21}=0.619$; and differ from k by 0.007, 0.001, 0.003, respectively; or they all differ by inappreciable values from the quantity which might therefore be made to stand for all of them. But in putting k for all the values of the first series after the first three, it should be with the understanding that it is not so employed in its capacity as the grand type, or the source of the distributive character which they have; in its capacity as an irrational fraction,—but simply as being indistinguishable practically from these rational ones, and as being entirely consistent practically with the property that rational proper fractions also have of forming limited systems or cycles. Much mystification has come from the irrational character of this fraction; scepticism on the part of non-mathematical botanists, and mysticism on the part of mathematicians. The simpler or the first three fractions of this series have also in a less degree the same distributive quality, and so in a still less degree have the fractions of the two lower series. But all the fractions left among possible ones, within the limits considered, that are sufficiently simple to be readily identified, are the fractions $\frac{4}{7}$ and $\frac{5}{8}$, or their complements $\frac{3}{7}$ and $\frac{4}{9}$; and these exceptions, as I have said, are all the grounds of fact which at first sight give any plausibility to the theory of Phyllotaxy, or make its laws anything other apparently than the necessary consequences of purely numerical properties in the simpler fractions. Yet beside the fact that these two have not the distributive character of the others, the fact should be taken account of, that by confining ourselves to the limits $\frac{1}{2}$ to $\frac{4}{5}$ we have neglected several other simple fractions, that are even worse adapted for the purpose which the great majority appear to serve. These fractions are $\frac{5}{8}$, $\frac{6}{7}$, $\frac{7}{8}$, and $\frac{8}{9}$, or their complements. Moreover, we should consider that as the fractions peculiar to the two lower series are much less fitted for this purpose than those of the first series, so they are much less frequently found in nature.

Taking account of all these facts, we find the hypothesis that nature has chosen certain intervals in the spiral arrangements of leaves, and for the purpose I have indicated, to be sufficiently probable to justify a more careful consideration of it. Wide divergences from the most perfect realization of this purpose, such as we have among the more frequent forms in the fractions $\frac{1}{2}$ and $\frac{2}{3}$, or in the alternate and three-leaved systems, and also among the less frequent forms, indicate the existence of other conditions or purposes in these arrangements, which I propose to consider further on. I may remark here, however, that these two classes of exceptions form the most perfect realization of the distributive property, namely, those of the first series which belong to the most advanced forms of life, and those peculiar to the two other series, are probably due to widely different causes; the one having, in fact, a high degree of specialization, and the other falling short in respect to this distributive property on account of a low degree of specialization. This view, which is one of the consequences of theoretical considerations on the *origin* of these arrangements, that will be presented when we come to consider the origin of spiral arrangements in general, and of the whorl, is significantly in accordance with the observation that the forms peculiar to the two lower series are more frequent among fossil plants than among surviving ones.

[After an examination "quite independently of theory, of the properties in the spiral arrangements of all the fractions between $\frac{1}{3}$ and $\frac{2}{5}$, or rather between $\frac{1}{2}$ and $\frac{2}{5}$, and of a less denomination than 14ths," the author proceeds.]

All the fractions of the actual arrangements of nature, as well as the less simple theoretical ones of Phyllotaxy, have the property, that after the first turn of the cycle, and also in this first turn for all the fractions of the first series, or for those most commonly occurring in nature, *each leaf of the cycle is so placed over the space between older leaves nearest in direction to it as always to fall near the middle, and never beyond the middle third of the space, or by more than one sixth of the space from the middle, until the cycle is completed, when the new leaf is placed exactly over an older one.* This property depends mathematically on the character of the continued fractions, of which these fractions are the approximations, according to the theory of Phyllotaxy.

* * * * * * *

The last denominators in these continued fractions represent the ratios of the contiguous intervals introduced in the second or third turns by the third or fourth leaves. Only the first two fractions in each of these series conform to the above law. The others, like $\frac{4}{9}$ and $\frac{5}{8}$, violate the law early in the cycle; and this explains the absence of them from natural arrangements of the spiral type. The property common to the latter resembles what we have observed in the arrangements of whorls, namely, that the leaves of successive whorls are so placed that those of the upper one fall over the middle positions of the spaces between those of the lower one; but those of the next one above, or in the third whorl, are thus made to fall directly over the leaves of the first. Two whorls thus constitute a cycle, in the sense in which this name is applied to the spiral arrangements; and in respect to their distributive and cyclic characters, whorls are thus most closely related to the $\frac{1}{2}$, or alternate system. But there is, as I have said, no fundamental or genetic relationship between them and this particular form of the spiral arrangement. The relationship is rather an adaptive or analogical one. They are, so to speak, two distinct solutions of the same problem, two modes of realizing the same utilities, or securing the same advantages; like the wings of birds and bats.

One of these utilities we have now sufficiently considered, namely, that which the theoretical angle k would realize most perfectly; by which the leaves would be distributed most thoroughly and rapidly around the stem, exposed most completely to light and air, and provided with the greatest freedom for symmetrical expansion, together with a compact arrangement in the bud. Neither this property, nor an exact cyclical arrangement, ought, as I have said, to be found, or expected, in the incipient parts at the centre of the bud, any more than the perfect proportions and adaptations of the mature animal could be expected, or are found, in the embryo. Both are fully determined, no doubt, in the vital forces of the individual's growth. Our question is, what has determined such an action in these vital forces? "Their very nature, or an ultimate creative power," is the answer which the theory of types gives to this question. "The necessities of their lives, both outward and inward, or the conditions past and present of their existence," is the answer of the theory of adaptation. Science ought to be entirely neutral between these theories, and ready to receive any confirmation of either of them which can be adduced; though, from this point of view, the theory of adaptation has a decided advantage; since the theory of types can have no confirmation from observation except of a negative sort, the failure of its rival to show conclusive proofs. But we have seen that whatever can be said in favor of the view, that there is a unity of type in the intervals of spiral arrangements, is directly convertible to the advantage of the theory of adaptation; since this unity consists in the distributive property common to those arrangements.* Natural Selection, however, or the indirect agency of utility in producing adaptations, cannot, so far as we have yet seen, be appealed to for the explanation of the spiral arrangements in general; nor for the explanation of the verticil arrangements; though the character in the latter, in which they resemble the alternate system, may come within the range of this explanation through the utility I have pointed out. The only ground for the action of Natural Selection which I have yet shown is in the choice there is among possible spiral arrangements with reference to this utility; and it appears that the principle is fully competent to account for the relative frequency of these, and the entire absence of some of them from the actual forms of nature.

We now come to the special study of two other features which have appeared in these arrangements, namely, the spiral character itself and the simplicity of their cycles. The cyclic character is entirely wanting in the ideal arrangement of the

---

* There is a remarkable analogy between this relation and that of the two theories of the structure of the honey-cell. The work of the bees suggests to the geometrician a perfectly definite and regular form, which he finds to be the most economical form of compartments into which space can be divided; or he finds that the honeycomb would be the lightest, or be composed of the least material for the same capacity and number of compartments, if partitioned into such figures as the typical cell. From the definition of this figure he is able to compute its angles and proportions with a degree of precision to which the bees' work only roughly approximates at its best, and from which it often deviates widely. The theory of types regards this ideal figure as a determining cause of the structure, or as the pattern which guides the bees' instinct towards an ideally perfect economy. But a plainer order of economy, a simple housewifely one, saving at every turn, together with the conveniences and utilities which govern the work of social nest-building insects in general, would result, if carried out to perfection, in the very same form. Hence the theory of adaptation regards the honey-cells as modifications of similar but rougher structures of the same sort, determined by the further utility of simple saving in working with a costly material; and whatever evidence there is that the bees' instinct is determined toward the ideally perfect type of the honey-cell is directly convertible into proofs that it is so determined by these simple conveniences and utilities

interval k; but, as I have said, this interval cannot be proved to exist in nature; for even if it did, it would be indistinguishable even from the simple fraction $\frac{5}{8}$. This very fact, however, makes the interval $\frac{5}{8}$, a sufficiently exact realization of the distributive property, according to the degree of exactness with which actual plants are constructed. But $\frac{5}{8}$ is also a comparatively simple cycle, though there would not be sufficient evidence that its cyclic character is an essential one, or other than incidental to the scale of exactness in the structure of plants, if there did not exist several distinguishable and simpler cycles, namely, $\frac{1}{2}$, $\frac{2}{3}$, and $\frac{3}{8}$. The cyclic character of leaf arrangements is, indeed, a more noticeable feature in plants generally than the distributive one. It is obviously essential, and involves on the theory of adaptation some important utility. Whatever this may be, it is clear that it has to be gained by means directly opposed to those which secure distribution; that is, its utility depends on leaves coming together in direction, or being brought nearer to each other than they would otherwise be; instead of their being dispersed as widely and as thoroughly as possible. This utility is obviously to be sought in the internal relations of leaves to each other, or their connections through the stem, and not in their outward relations, which require exposure, expansion, and elbow-room. The apparently inconsistent means of these two ends are both realized, however, without interference, in the actual cycles of natural arrangements. Through the simplicity of these cycles leaves, not very remote on the stem, are brought nearer to each other, and into more direct internal connection than they would have but for this simplicity; while, in the more prevalent natural forms of the cycle, leaves that are nearest to each other on the stem are separated as widely as is possible under this condition. That this prevalence is due to selection, through the utility already considered, has been shown to be sufficiently probable. I propose now to connect the prevalence of simplicity in these cycles with another utility.

Leaves that are successive, or nearest each other on the stem, may be regarded as rivals, and as rendering each other no service. Those that are more remote may come into relations of dependence, one on the other. Between the leaf and the stem the relations of nutrition are reciprocal. At first, and for the development of the leaf, the stem furnishes nutriment to it. Afterwards the leaf furnishes nutriment for the further lateral expansion of the stem. The development of the stem itself, first in length, while the leaves are expanding, and afterwards in breadth and firmness through the nutrition afforded by the developed leaves, has the effect, and, we may presume, the use or function, of a still more important distribution of the leaves than that we have considered. We have hitherto attended only to the distribution effected by the character of the divergences of leaves around the stem. Their distribution along the stem, or their separation by the internodes of the stem, is a still more direct and effective mode of accomplishing at least one of the uses of the property of distribution, namely, exposure to light and air. The special accomplishment of this important end in the higher plants is secured by two different means; by the firm fibrous structure and the breadth of stems, branches, and trunks in grasses, shrubs, and trees, and by the climbing powers and prehensile apparatus of climbing plants; and in the latter we find the highest degree of specialization or development in the vegetable world. The distribution effected by the separation of leaves along the stem in great measure supersedes the value of their distribution around it, so far as the ultimate functions of leaves are concerned, and independently of their relations in development or in the bud; and this gives freer play to the means of securing whatever advantage there may be in the simpler cyclic arrangements, like the $\frac{1}{2}$ and $\frac{2}{3}$ systems. Accordingly we find, in general, the simpler cycles on the stems of those plants that have the longest internodes; and, on the other hand, the more complicated cycles are found only in cases of very short internodes or in great condensations of leaves. There is no evidence, however, that in the condensed form in which undeveloped leaves exist in the bud the cycles are any more complicated than on the stem. Nor ought we to expect such evidence; for it is a false analogy that would lead us to seek for types in the early and rude forms of embryonic life; though, if the

simpler cycles were really derived from the more complicated
ones, rather than from the utility common to all, we ought, by
the analogy of embryology, to find some traces of the process
in the bud. No doubt the types exhibited by the mature forms
of life exist in the embryo or bud, though not in a visibly
embodied form; but rather in a predetermined mode of action
in vital forces, embodied in gemmules' rather than the visible
germ. But while the distribution effected by the internodes
of the stem thus allows the simpler cycles to occur, it does
not account for their occurrence. This, moreover, must
depend on relations in mature, or else in growing leaves, to
those below them; and not on their earlier relations in the
bud; since, as we have seen, the more complicated cycles are
the best fitted for these relations, and in mature stems are only
found in great condensations of leaves; such as the bud also
presents; yet without any greater complication than the stem
has. The simplicity of the cycles in stems with long internodes has the effect that the absolute distance between two
leaves standing one over the other is not so great as it otherwise would be. There is, no doubt, a disadvantage in long
internodes, or in the separation of growing parts by long intervals from their source of nutrition; a disadvantage, which only a
better exposure to light and air for their subsequent functions
could compensate. On the theory of adaptation there would
seem to be, then, some advantage to the younger leaf in
standing directly over an older one, and not far above it; a
greater advantage than in any other position at the same
height; and this advantage could apparently be no other than
an internal nutritive one, having reference to the sources or
movements of sap and the nutrition conveyed by it. But sap
circulates with nearly equal facility around and along the
stem; and if the lower leaf were really a special source of
nutrition to the growing one above it, it could furnish nutrition
almost as readily to any other position on the stem at the
same height as to the point directly above it, or on the same
side. The new leaf is not sensibly nearer the market on account of this feature in the arrangement. But may there not
be some advantage to the older leaf in standing directly under

the younger? Next to the advantage of being near a market, or a source of supplies, is the advantage of being in the line of traffic. This, indeed, is in part what it is to be a market, rather than a mine. A leaf is not only a productive or industrial centre, but a commercial one. It effects exchanges, both giving and receiving supplies. When mature, or fully established in this capacity, it draws from the roots its raw material of water and mineral salts, and from the air its more costly material, and in exchange sends forth into the great commerce of the stem its wonderfully intricate fabrics of atoms, woven on the sunbeam, its soluble colloids. Now, although sap may flow with nearly equal facility in all directions in the stem, it probably does flow with greatest rapidity in the direct lines of the forces that impel it, the lines of osmotic force. Sap flows in the spring most freely from that side of a perforated tree which is immediately below the largest branch. This shows that even in the least active condition of the circulation, when the trunk is surcharged with sap, the forces of circulation are not simply diffusive or hydrostatic; and they must be much less so when definite outlets of this supply become established in the growing buds and leaves of the spring-time. The character of the circulation is principally determined by the hydraulic action of osmotic forces. Water *may* flow with equal facility in any part of a river-bed, and across as well as along; but it actually does flow fastest along the middle. The growing leaf has different needs from those of the mature one; hence they are not rivals, or competitors in the market, but buyer and seller, or borrower and lender. The mature leaf needs from the stem water and mineral salts; the growing leaf needs the organic materials of new tissues. The mature leaf helps to prepare the latter by concentrating it, withdrawing the water, and adding its own contribution of organic material in return. But while aiding its younger fellow in this way, it is aided in return, or its efficiency is increased, by the increased circulation produced through the forces of movement above it. In place of a glut in the market we have an active exchange. There is, undoubtedly, a tendency in these physiological causes, however feeble, to that vertical allignment of not very distant leaves, which the cyclic character of the spiral arrangements exhibits, and most markedly in the $\frac{1}{2}$ or alternate system.

We have thus assigned more or less probable utilities to two prominent features in the particular forms of the spiral and verticil arrangements of leaves; their distributive and cyclic characters. We now come to a much more obscure problem, which connects the verticil and spiral arrangements in general with their probable utilities, and through these with their origin in lower forms of vegetable life. But before entering upon the study of this as an actual physical problem, it is necessary to consider what are the real meanings of the terms "spiral" and "whorl." Are they only conventional modes of representing the phenomena of arrangement, or are they strictly descriptive of the facts in their physical connections? About the whorl there can be no doubt. The actual physical connections and separations of leaves in this type of arrangement are directly indicated by the term; but the ideal geometrical line connecting successive leaves in the so-called spiral arrangements may be a purely formal element in the description of them, and of no material account,—a mode of reducing them to order in our conceptions of them, but implying no physical relationships. There are several ways in which we can so represent the features of these arrangements. Connecting by an ideal line (which may have no physical significance) the leaves nearest to each other on the developed stem, and by the shorter way round, is one way,—the more common way of representing their arrangements. The direction in which this should be drawn, whether to the right or the left, is quite arbitrary in the $\frac{1}{2}$ or alternate system. Connecting, for other cases, the leaves in the same succession, but by the longer way round is another way. These are distinctly different spiral paths, but not the only ones by which the parts of these arrangements might be represented geometrically. By connecting them alternately, as 1 with 3, and this with 5, etc., and 2 with 4, and this with 6, etc., we should connect the leaves of the various arrangements by two spiral paths, and these either by the longer or the shorter way round. Or again, by connecting the series 1, 4, 7, etc., and 2, 5, 8, etc., and 3, 6, 9, etc., we should include all the leaves in three spiral paths; and so on. In some cases these lines would not be spiral, but the vertical allignments we have considered. For example, in the last case they would be vertical for the cycle $\frac{2}{3}$; since in this the leaves 1 and 4, or 2 and 5, are the beginnings of distinct successive cycles. If the leaves 1, 2, 3, were in this case of the same age, or at the same height on the stem, and were succeeded at an interval on the stem by 4, 5, 6, also coeval, and so on, we should have the main feature of the verticil arrangement, but not the kind of alternation that belongs to natural whorls. Between 1, 2, and 3 in the natural whorl equal intervals exist, namely, $\frac{1}{3}$; and also between 4, 5, and 6, and so on; but between 3 and 4 the interval in natural three-leaved whorls is either $\frac{1}{6}$, $\frac{1}{2}$, or $\frac{5}{6}$, according as we choose our spiral paths, or determine which member of the upper whorl shall be counted as the fourth leaf.

We perceive, therefore, that there is no continuity or principle of connection between spiral arrangements and the whorls; and, moreover, that these spiral paths are purely ideal or geometrical lines, so far as we have yet seen. Is there any good reason for supposing that the *simplest* of these, which connects successive leaves on the stem the shorter way round, is any less formal or conventional than the others; or indicates a real connection of the leaves on this path, or any closer original real connection among them? There are two significant facts bearing on this question to which I have already adverted. The first is that the natural fractions of the lower group of our table, or those peculiar to the last two series of the theory of Phyllotaxy, represent the less frequent forms of spiral arrangements, and that if the successive members of these arrangements are connected in the usual mode by this simplest path, or the shorter way round, these members are seen to have less angles of divergence than those of the more common arrangements; or are much nearer each other on this line than the others are. We should thus have the fractions $\frac{2}{7}$, $\frac{3}{11}$, $\frac{1}{4}$, $\frac{2}{9}$, $\frac{1}{5}$, all of which indicate comparatively small divergences, smaller than any among the common ones. The second fact is the observation that these arrangements are relatively more common among fossil plants than among surviving ones. These facts agree well with the supposition that this simplest spiral path is unlike the others, and is not a merely formal assumption for the representation of leaf-arrangements, but the trace of a former physical connection of the members, or even of a continuity of leafy expansion along this path; a leaf-like expansion resembling a spiral stairway. The leaves, according to this supposition, are the relics of segments made in such a spiral leaf-like expansion around the stem; remnants of it grown smaller and smaller, or more widely separated as they became more advantageously situated through the developments of the stem in length and firmness; and expanding, perhaps, in an opposite direction along the leaf-stems; or, losing their leaf-character and expansion altogether, as they became adapted to other uses in the economy of the higher vegetable life, namely, the use of the leaf-stem itself, as in the tendril, and the uses of leaf-like extensions, as in the reproductive organs of the flower.

But are there any surviving instances of such continuous spiral leaf-like expansions on vegetable stems; or, in default of these, could there be any utility in such an arrangement itself to justify the supposition of it as the basis of the development of more special forms? Before considering this question, however, I will consider what other resources of explanation hypothesis can command. The spiral arrangement might be supposed to be the result of a physiological necessity among the laws of growth, through which single leaves would be produced at regular intervals or steps of development, and placed so as to compass the utilities we have already considered, namely, those of horizontal and longitudinal distribution in successive leaves, and vertical allignment in remoter ones. This would account for the spiral arrangements, and it may be a superior mode of growth, or involve some physiological utility; but that it is not a necessity, is proved by the arrangements of the whorl, in which all the members of a group of leaves are simultaneously produced. The existence of the whorl, then, sets this hypothesis aside. Again, we might suppose on the theory of types that these two great types of arrangement are two fundamental facts in the higher vegetable life, parts of a supernatural plan; two aboriginal and absolute features in this plan. But this, as we have seen, is not to solve the problem, but to surrender it; or rather to demand its surrender, and forbid its solution. Again, the production of adventitious buds in plants, or in separated parts of plants, as in cuttings, dependent only, apparently, on a favorable situation for nutrition, is of common occurrence even in the higher plants. If we could suppose that the definite horizontal distributions of successive leaves were wholly superseded in their utility by the distributions along the stem, or that the leaves could thus be sufficiently exposed to light and air; the power of the adventitious production of buds or leaves in favorable situations might have caused an arrangement without this feature of spiral regularity. But they would still be brought into vertical allignments, if the physiological advantage of the simpler cycles, which has been pointed out, be a real and effective one; for even the so-called adventitious production of buds may reasonably be supposed to be governed by supplies of nutriment. Moreover, these vertical lines would be placed at equal intervals around the stem, on account of the advantage there would be in such a distribution, both for internal and external nutrition. But though leaves would thus be placed at convenient distances along equidistant vertical lines, there would be no consideration of utility to govern their relations to each other on different lines, so as to throw them into whorls, or into definite spiral arrangements. It might, however, be advantageous for leaves on a line between two others to be placed in intermediate positions with respect to the leaves of these two, and if the latter were placed at the same heights we should have a sector of three whorls; that is, two leaves of the highest and two of the lowest whorl, and one leaf of the intermediate whorl. But such an arrangement disregards or sacrifices in the structure of the whorl itself the advantage, if it be one, of such an alternation. It cannot be reasonable to suppose that a leaf on an intermediate line would seek distance and isolation· from those of the lines beside it, and, at the same time, seek close connection horizontally with those of its own whorl. This would be directly opposed to the accommodation of uses in spiral arrangements. The structure of whorls, and the alternation in successive ones, appear, therefore, to be of distinct origins. Whatever advantage there is in the former appears to be sacrificed by this alternation, and by the spiral arrangements; or, if it be a disadvantage, it is avoided by these. It is probably on the whole a disadvantage; since it is ill-fitted for great extensions and branchings in stems, for which the simpler spiral arrangements appear peculiarly fitted. This contrast, however, cannot be regarded as the origin of the contrasted types themselves, and the soundest conclusion appears to be, that, whatever adaptations they may have, these are only incidental, and are not concerned in their origination, either directly through physiological laws of growth, or indirectly by Natural Selection. They are properly genetic characters. This is confirmed by the fact that the particular arrangement for each plant is provided for, or already completed in the bud; that is, it is not a result of laws of development in general, but of the special nature of the plant, or the predisposition of its vital forces. In regard to the causes which I have supposed to control the so-called adventitious production of buds or leaves, it should not be supposed that these exert in actual plants any considerable influence; though the plant's particular laws of growth are probably not in opposition to them. They should only be considered as modifying agencies reacting on the formative forces; but they fail, as we have seen, to account for the spiral and verticil arrangements, and their contrasts through any utility which could modify these forces. But in concluding therefore that these general types of arrangement ought to be regarded as only genetic characters in the higher plants, and as presenting no important advantage or disadvantage, independently of the special forms which they have acquired, or in present forms of life; we are not precluded by such a conclusion from the further inquiry as to what *former* advantage there could have been in less specialized forms, before these genetic characters had lost their special significance (if any ever existed), and when they could have stood in more immediate and important relations to the conditions of the plant's existence. In this inquiry our principal guide must be hypothesis, but it will be hypothesis under the check and control of the theory of adaptation. It will not be legitimate to assume any unknown form as a past form of life, and as a basis for these arrangements, without showing that such an hypothetical form would have been a useful modification of a still simpler one, which still exists and is known. In this way we may be able to bridge over the chasm that separates the higher and lower forms of vegetable life.

Our problem then becomes, Whether, in the absence of any surviving instances of continuous spiral leaf-like expansions on vegetable stems, we can find any utility in such an arrangement that could act to modify simpler known forms, and convert them into this? If we suppose our hypothetical spiral leaf-blade to be untwisted, it becomes a single-blade frond, or a frond with one of its blades undeveloped. In considering what advantage there could be in the twist, we should revert to the general objects or functions of leaf-like expansions. They are obviously to expose a large surface to the action of light on its tissues, and to bring it into the most complete contact with the medium in which the plant lives,—with water, or, in more advanced plants, with the air. Secondly, to accomplish this with the least expenditure of material; not by an absolute, but a relative economy, which has reference to the needs of other parts, like the stem or roots. In many of the higher plants the developments of the stem serve to diminish to the utmost the amount of this material, and the needed expansion, by giving to them advantageous positions. The first of these objects is secured in the simplest and rudest manner in the *algæ*, as represented by the sea-weeds. This is a simple expansion of cellular tissue. But even here we do not find perfectly plane surfaces, facing only two ways, and allowing the water to glide smoothly and unobstructed over them. The corrugated surfaces of many of them, and in the large leaves of some land-plants, are doubtless due to unequal growths in the cellular tissues; but such a physiological explanation of this feature does not preclude the supposition of its being a fixed character in a plant, or becoming such in consequence of its utility. It certainly serves the purpose of opposing the leaf-surface to many directions, both with reference to the incidence of light, and to the movement of the surrounding medium,—to water-currents, or to breezes. *Segmentation*, again, such as is seen in the fronds of brakes or ferns, is another way of bringing the moving medium to impinge on the leaf-surface; but the feasibility of this depends on the fibrous frame-work which the leaves of land-plants have acquired for the support of their softer tissues. Such a segmentation also appears among the higher plants in compound leaves and in whorls; and, indeed, the whole foliage of trees and shrubs may, from this point of view, be regarded as the reduced segments of the blades of branching fronds, turned in all directions in search of light, and inviting the movements of air through their expanded interstices. Such is the kind of utility that may be claimed for the structure of our hypothetical spiral frond. Another utility in this structure is obvious when we consider the transition of plant-life from aquatic conditions to those of the dry land and the air; as vegetation slowly crept from its watery cradle, or was left stranded by the retiring sea. In default of strength in its material, such as a slowly acquired fibrous structure or frame-work ultimately gave to it in this transition, the *strongest form* would be the most advantageous in sustaining the weight of the no longer buoyant plant. A spiral arrangement of the blade around a comparatively firm, and, perhaps, already somewhat fibrous stem, would come nearer fulfilling this condition than any other conceivable modification of the frond.

We have, so far, in conformity to the spiral arrangement in leaves, supposed this twisted frond to be a single-bladed one, or with only one blade developed. This would be a first step in that reduction of leaf-expansion which a more advantageous situation of it would allow; and might be required, even at this early stage of atmospheric plant-life, on account of the greatly increased importance of the roots and stem. But this hypothesis is not necessary in general for the ends we have considered. A two-bladed frond might be similarly twisted and give rise to a double spiral surface like a double spiral stair-way, or like the blade of an auger; or such a surface as the two handles of the auger describe as they are revolved, and, at the same time, carried forward in the direction of the boring. The simplest segmentation of such a twisted frond, after the stem had acquired sufficient strength, and such a subsequent reduction of the segments as might be required for the nutrition of the stem, would give rise to parts, which, turned upwards to face the sky, and also separated, perhaps, by the growth of internodes in the lengthening stem, would result in what we may regard as the original form of whorls, namely, a continuous leaf-like expansion around the stem. The origin of the whorl arrangement itself would thus be distinct, as we have found that it ought to be, from the origin of the relations in the parts of whorls to one another, and to those of adjacent whorls. These would be results of a subsequent segmentation, and would be determined by the utilities which we have considered in this and in the spiral arrangements. And so both this and the spiral arrangements as general types of structure, though originating, as I have supposed, in useful relations to former conditions of existence, may be regarded in relation to later developments as useless, and merely inherited or genetic types; the bases on which subsequent utilities had to erect existing adaptations of structure. The segmentation of the single spiral frond would at first have little or no relation to these more refined utilities of arrangement, but out of all the variable and possible arrangements so produced there would be a gradual selection, and a tendency toward the prevalence of those special forms, which are at present the most common ones. The typical or unique angle of the theory of Phyllotaxy would thus appear to be the goal toward which they tend, rather than the origin of the spiral arrangements. But since a simple cyclic arrangement appears to have also an important value, we cannot concede to the typical angle the exclusive dignity of even this position.

The segmentation I have supposed in this process should not be regarded as an hypothetical element in it, since it is a well-established law of development. Distinct organs are not separately produced from the beginnings of their growth, but

make part of their progress in conjunction, or while incorporated in forms, from which they become afterwards separated;
and become then more and more special in their characters,
or different from other parts. It is this differentiation and
separation of parts out of already grown wholes which distinguishes development from mere growth. The analogy of
the phases of development in embryonic or germinal life to
development in general is liable, however, to be carried too
far; and the fact is liable to be overlooked, that these phases of
growth are special acquisitions of the higher forms of life,
which have features of adaptation peculiar to them. But the
more general features of them, and the useless, or merely
genetic phases, may safely be regarded as traces of past characters of adaptation, which a change in the mode and order
of development has not obliterated; while new adaptations
have been added, that have no relation to any past or simpler
forms of life, but only to the advantages which embryonic or
germinal modes of reproduction have secured.

If we should follow out the phases of general development in
the progress of the leaf along the line of its highest ascent in
development, from the segmentations we have supposed in the
twisted frond, we should soon arrive at the steps already familiar
in the principles of vegetable morphology. In these we have
the same law of segmentation or separation of parts, and the
same successive relations of genetic and adaptive characters.
What was produced for one purpose becomes serviceable to a
new one; and in its capacity as a merely genetic character, or
as an inherited feature, becomes the basis for the acquisition of
new adaptations. Thus the fibrous structure, at first useful in
sustaining the softer tissues of the leaf, becomes the means of
a longitudinal development of it, and its more complete exposure to light and air by the growth of the foot-stalk. This stalk
acquires next a new utility in climbing-plants to which it
becomes exclusively adapted in the tendril. The adaptive
characters of the tendril are its later acquisitions. Its genetic
characters, such as its position on the stem, and its relations to
the leaves, become useless or merely inherited characters.
The contrast of genetic and adaptive characters appears thus

to have no absolute value in the structure and lives of organisms, but only a relative one. The first are related principally to past and generally unknown adaptations; the second to present and more obvious ones.

In accordance with this law I have supposed that the general features of the two types of leaf-arrangement, for which no present utilities appear in the lives of the higher plants, were nevertheless useful features in former conditions of vegetable life. The more special features of these arrangements should not, from this point of view, be regarded as derived one from another, much less from the typical or unique form of the theory of Phyllotaxy. In one sense they may, indeed, be said to be derived from this form, at least some of them; yet not from it as an actually past form or progenitor, but rather from the utility which it represents in the abstract. I have, however, pointed out that another utility, shown in the simpler cyclic arrangements, has an equal claim to this spiritual paternity. The actual forms of the spiral arrangements in leaves should, therefore, be regarded as forms independently selected, and as selected on the two principles of utility, which we have considered, out of a very large variety of original forms. We have seen that even those forms which survive include almost all possible ones that could be distinguished; though the more prevalent ones are at present in the minority. We have also seen that the later fact, and the more frequent occurrence of inferior forms among fossil plants, are almost the only grounds on which the inductive foundation of the theory of Phyllotaxy could be regarded as well established. On these grounds, and on this foundation, I have sought by hypothesis to reconstruct the continuity of higher and lower forms in vegetable life; and through this to find the *origin* of the principal types of arrangement in leaves. The speculation lies wholly within the limits prescribed for legitimate hypothesis in science. It does not assume utilities in themselves unknown, but assumes only unobserved or unknown applications of them, and raises to the rank of essential properties relations of use, which, at first sight, appear to be only accidental ones. Attention may be claimed at the least for it as an illustration of the method by which the principle of Natural Selection is to be applied as a working hypothesis in the investigations of general physiology or physical biology.

Many features in the structure of leaves, not relating to their arrangements, fall beyond the proper province of this inquiry, but equally illustrate the relative nature of the distinction between genetic and adaptive characters. The general character common to all leaves and leaf-like organs has an obvious utility with reference to the function of nutrition. Some special modifications have the purposes of defense, as in the thorn; of mechanical support, as in the tendril; and of reproduction, as in the parts of the flower. But the vast variety of forms which leaves and the parts of flowers present do not suggest any obvious uses. On the theory of adaptation they would naturally be referred to a combination of adaptive and inherited features. A fixed proportion between the two principal tissues in a plant due to some past utility may, without being changed, become adapted to new external relations, or to new physiological conditions, through various arrangements of them in the structure of the leaf; and this would give rise to a great variety of forms. The forms of notched and sinuated leaves are referable to that process of segmentation and reduction in leaf-expansions, which we have seen to be so important a process in the derivation of the higher plants. But another principle of utility comes into play in the lives of the higher plants, similar to that which appears to be the origin of some of the more conspicuous external characters of animals, namely, what produces distinguishableness and individuation in an animal race. No doubt the laws of inheritance and Natural Selection account for much of the character of individuality in races, or for the fact that variation has a very limited range compared to the differences between species, so far as it affects any useful quality or character. But variation, not only in animals, but also in many of the higher plants, is much more limited than these causes seem capable of accounting for. It is, apparently, as limited in respect to useless though conspicuous features as in those that are of recognized value to life. Sexual Selection, through which the characters of animals are chosen by themselves, or brought into relation to their perceptive and other psychical powers, is the cause assigned for this fact in the case of animals; that is, forms are chosen for their appearance, or for the pleasure they give to the senses. But plants have no senses, except a sense of touch; and they have no other known psychical powers. Nevertheless they present many conspicuous features of beauty to the eye, and many give forth agreeable and characteristic odors. And such characters are apparently as fixed in many of the higher plants as in animals. The theory of types and the doctrine of Final Causes regard this fixedness and individuality as ends in themselves, or else as existing for the service of some higher form of life, or ultimately even for the uses of human life. But the theory of the adaptation of every feature in a form of life to its own uses is not without resources for the explanation of these characters in plants; for though the plant has no sense to appreciate, or power to select, its own features of individuality and beauty, yet the lives of many of the higher plants are essentially dependent on such power in insects; so that whatever character renders them attractive to insects, or distinguishable by their sight, may be said to be of use to plants for the ends of reproduction, and tends in this way to become a fixed or only slightly variable character. That this cause may have acted not only to determine definite shapes, colors, and odors in flowers, but also definite features in the foliage of plants, as the marks or signs of these, and that the value of such signs may have determined a greater degree of fixedness or constancy in the arrangements, as well as in the shapes of leaves, is an hypothesis that may be added to those we have already considered, concerning the utilities of these arrangements. This cause would tend to give prominence to those features in arrangement which are most conspicuous to the eye, namely, those of cyclic regularity and simplicity. Such an explanation of this cyclic character, or the simple and definite arrangements of leaves at short intervals in vertical lines on the stem, or the utility of this as a distinguishing character of the plant, is not inconsistent with the physiological utility in these arrangements, which I have pointed out ; but the two, in co-operating to the production of the same forms, would illustrate a principle in the economy of life which has a wide application,—the principle of indirect utility or correlative acquisition, dependent on ultimate laws in physical and mental natures,—through which independent utilities are realized by the same means, or the same means are made serviceable to more than one distinct end. In such ultimate, underived relations of adaptation in nature, we find principles of connection and a unity of plan which cannot be referred to any accidents of history or development.

McCOSH ON INTUITIONS.*

The philosophical and religious writings of Dr. McCosh have already secured for him a prominent position among living thinkers, and considerable influence both in Great Britain and America. The present work † exhibits so much ability, good sense, and philosophical acumen that it will doubtless increase his reputation and prove him a worthy successor of the distinguished metaphysicians who have rendered his native land famous in the contests of philosophy. Though in many respects original, professing to follow no school, and in reality independent in its spirit of all authority but that of the religious truths in behalf of which it is written, this work is nevertheless substantially a development from the Scottish school. The author regards in the same light with this school the range and province of metaphysical inquiry, and treats the doctrines of all other schools in the same spirit. He finds in the writings of Reid and Stewart, it is true, statements which would logically "land us in very serious consequences," but with the essence of their doctrines, and especially with the natural realism of Sir William Hamilton, he strongly sympathizes, though he goes somewhat beyond Hamilton in his theory of immediate consciousness.

His principal problem appears to have been to discover a theory of consciousness which shall assure us of as much as possible without carrying our assent on to the extremes to which the statements of philosophers too often logically tend. He seeks, that is, for a theory which shall assure us of the

* From The Nation, Nov. 16, 1865.

† " The Intuitions of the Mind Inductively Investigated. By the Rev. James Mc-Cosh, LL.D., Professor of Logic and Metaphysics in Queen's College, Belfast." New and revised edition. 8vo pp. 444.

reality and permanence of the external world without leading us into materialism, or into a belief of the absolute permanence of matter; which shall assure us of the reality of cause and effect and the existence of power in the world without bringing us to the "dismal consequences" to which Kant's analysis of causation appears to lead; a theory which shall guarantee us a knowledge of substance or substantive reality, without upsetting our personality and landing us in pantheism; and which, at the same time, shall be free from the psychological objections that, since the time of Locke, have been urged against certain forms of the doctrine of intuitive universal truths.

A fundamental principle of Dr. McCosh's system is that the mind always begins with the concrete, the singular, and the individual in its acquisition of knowledge, and arrives at universal truths—not, indeed, as the *results* of a process, but in the course of a process, in which the elements of universal judgments must be produced by particular experiences and special judgments. These particulars are, however, of such a nature that they warrant the universal judgment, not by the cumulative force of experience, but by the inherent force of each particular conviction, which comes from a power in the mind, and only awaits the formation of the proper formula by generalization in order to pronounce a decision of a universal character.

The author thus avoids the objections which have been so often urged against the doctrine of innate ideas. Universal judgments exist, he thinks, in the mind originally only as laws of our mental faculties, determining them to "look for" certain facts which are really universal, but are only discovered in individual cases; and the individual decisions carry in them the truth of the universal.

Having thus defined intuitive knowledge, our author proceeds to show how such knowledge can be distinguished from other kinds, and he lays down the tests which the philosophy of common sense has prescribed in the writings of the Scottish school, the tests, namely, of self-evidence, necessity, and catholicity or universality in human beliefs. He divides the cognitive acts of the mind into three species, and adopts as the generic name for them the theological term "convictions." There are the cognitive convictions, which decide immediately that an object exists, not only in relation to our faculties, but independently of them. By our cognitions we know, through sense-perception and self-consciousness, that something in particular exists, has existed, and will continue to exist. In other words, that something has present existence and present permanence. Such cognitions also decide immediately that the thing exists in space or is extended; also that it has power, or is a cause and will produce an effect. All this the intuitive powers of cognition anticipate by their innate nature, and they "look for" and discover all this in special experiences.

Such intuitions precede, both logically and chronologically, all other "convictions." In this the author dissents from Hamilton's doctrine, which supposes a faculty of faith to underlie all our cognitive acts. "Intuitive beliefs" form with him a derived class of "convictions"—not derived from our cognitions logically, but from them as furnishing the materials on which a new class of intuitive powers are brought to bear. Our faith-intuitions have no real objects presented to them. "I hold," says the author, "that knowledge, psychologically considered, appears first, and then faith. But around our original cognitions there grows and clusters a body of primitive beliefs, which goes far beyond our personal knowledge." Again he says: "Faith collects round our observational knowledge and even around the conclusions reached by inference." His examples of primitive faiths are our beliefs in the infinity of time and space, and in infinity as an attribute of the nature of the Deity. They are "beliefs gathering round space, time, and the infinite."

The third class of primitive convictions are called "primitive judgments," and have for their objects the relations of the things with which our cognitions are conversant; and they arise from a power in the mind to anticipate, to the extent of looking for, certain necessary relations among objects, such as their necessary relations in space and time, the facts, for example, that the straight line is the shortest distance between two points, and that two straight lines cannot inclose a space, and the like.

Such are the author's analysis and description of our primitive convictions, the tests of which are, first, their self-evidence; secondly, and dependent on this, their necessity; and thirdly, their catholicity. Self-evidence is the fact that the conviction exists in our own minds and exists independently of any other facts. Necessity of belief or the irresistible character of the conviction follows, according to the author, from this self-evidence. "I would not," he says, "ground the evidence on the necessity of belief, but I would ascribe the irresistible nature of the conviction to the self-evidence. As the necessity flows from the self-evidence, so it may become a test of it, and a test not difficult of application." Catholicity is also a derivative test, and, "when conjoined with necessity, may determine very readily and precisely whether a conviction be intuitive;" but all these tests "apply directly only to individual convictions. To the generalized expression of them the tests apply only mediately, and on the supposition and condition that the formulæ are the proper expression of the spontaneous perceptions." Originally these convictions are laws of the perceptive faculties guiding their action, though not determining their objects. Their objects are really discovered, and the conviction is primarily held, only in respect to particular perceptions or judgments. Generalizations are then made, but they are generalizations "of convictions in our own minds, each of which carries necessity in it." There are, therefore, according to the author, two fundamentally distinct kinds of generalization, and in this respect his doctrine is quite original. Laws or general facts may be derived from an experience, necessarily limited, of facts which are either inferences more or less perfectly drawn from intuitive perceptions, or else facts at which no power of the mind "looks" intuitively, but which find their way into the mind by the force of repeated experiences. These are laws which say nothing about the possible; they only testify of the actual. But the laws which are immediate generalizations from intuitive perceptions and judgments "are of a higher and deeper nature; they are generalizations of convictions carrying necessity with them, and a consequent universality in their very nature."

This is briefly our author's system, which he proceeds to apply to the various problems of metaphysics, such as the reality of cause and substance, and the self, and the external world. In ingenuity this theory appears to us to exceed anything which has come from the Scottish school, and in pliancy it exceeds, we think, any system which has ever been propounded. The extremes of philosophy are avoided by it with surprising agility. If any proposition be laid down as universally true from which logical consequences of a heterodox character are deducible, this system affords the means of modifying the proposition without impairing in any measure the evidence of its universality, since the infallible powers do not testify to the truth of any formula immediately, but only in so far as the formula represents the particular decisions of the mind. If, on the other hand, the "sceptic" calls in question the universality of any truth on the ground that the mind is cognizant only of the particular, or doubts the necessity of a belief on the ground that all experience is of the contingent, our author admits his grounds but denies that his conclusions follow, since universality and necessity do not come from the particulars of contingent experience as such, but from the powers of the mind looking through these into reality, and deciding absolutely only in regard to the particulars.

It is to be regretted, however, that the author does not give us a more explicit account of what he means by such expressions as "primitive particular convictions carrying necessity with them, and a consequent universality in their very nature." In all the definitions of necessity with which we are acquainted, we have nowhere found it extended beyond the facts and the logical consequences of the facts in which it is supposed to exist primitively. That the universal does not follow logically from the particular or from any number of particulars, is what the author strenuously maintains. How, then, do the particulars carry in them the necessity of the universal? for this is what we understand the author's expressions to mean. How unless it be that the particulars are known simply as instances of the universal, the truth of which we possess as an independent knowledge? But such an independent knowledge of the universal the author as strenuously denies. The universal comes to consciousness, he thinks, only through the particulars, yet not by the way of suggestion or an awakening of a dormant truth, but rather as a fact which the particular contains in itself. It is not, according to the author, from the objects of intuition on one hand, nor from the powers of intuition on the other, that the truth of a universal proposition becomes known. This is obtained by the generalization of particular decisions of the mind. In the general maxim the mind *re*-cognizes what it has previously cognized in each and every one of the particular cases. The underived necessity of the particular conviction is somehow translated into the universal truth of the general maxim.

The author probably attaches to the word "necessity" a peculiar sense, as something more than mere cogency of belief, though he nowhere defines it in any other signification. There is a real and important logical distinction involved in this word, which renders the author's theory intelligible enough, though quite a different doctrine from what he intends to set forth. There is a distinction in the logical use of the word necessity, as opposed to contingency, which relates not to the cogency of the belief with which a fact is held, but to the connection of the fact itself with other facts in our experience. When we say that "anything *must be* or *must be* so and so," we mean to express something different from the statement that "this thing *is* or *is* so and so;" yet this difference does not refer to the originality, simplicity, or cogency of our *belief* in the statement. The copulas *must be* and *cannot be* involve in them universal propositions, though they connect only individual or particular terms. They mean that the truth they predicate is unconditional—is independent of any other facts; that there exists nothing to prevent the thing from being, or being so and so; or that the particular fact does not depend on any conditions which we can suppose from the evidence of experience to be variable. From the particular proposition, " These two straight lines *cannot* inclose a space," may be deduced, through the universality implied in the copula, the universal proposition, "No two straight lines can inclose a space." For "cannot" here means that there are no conditions, or supposable variations of conditions, which will make a closed figure of these two lines. But the evidence on which such a fact rests will be equally good for any other two straight lines, since a change from these to another pair will not affect the conditions on which the truth of the particular case depends. Hence, "no pair of straight lines can inclose a space." This follows from the unconditionalness of a particular fact—not from the cogency of our belief in it. This cogency is quite another affair.

By overlooking the universal, which is implied in an unconditional, particular proposition, our author has sought for the origin of the corresponding explicit universal in the character of our particular convictions as mental acts ; whereas this character of universality really depends on the relations of particular facts to our experiences generally. We, therefore, come back to the difficulty, still unsolved, as to how we derive universality from a limited experience. Upon this Dr. McCosh lays down the usual dictum of his school. He says that "a very wide and uniform experience would justify a general expectation but not a necessary conviction ; and this experience is liable to be disturbed at any time by a new occurrence inconsistent with what has been previously known to us." But whence this liability ? On what evidence is it supposed ? Are we informed of it by an intuition or by experience ? If by the former, then we have intuitions about other generalizations than universal ones, which is contrary to our author's theory. If by the latter, then our experience is not uniform, which is contrary to his special hypothesis. As he, therefore, shuts himself off from both these sources of information on the subject, we are left no alternative but to conclude that his statement about the liability of our uniform experiences to be disturbed is wholly gratuitous and a begging of the question. Or perhaps he means that propositions which we do not feel obliged to believe, though not contradicted in our experience, should yet, from their analogy with others which are occasionally contradicted, be regarded as liable to exception. But again we demand, Whence is the force of this analogy? What right have we to draw such a conclusion? Is it not also a virtual begging of the question? For, suppose it true, what the opposite school of philosophy teach, that there exist certain universal facts, not born into the mind either as innate ideas or as laws of its faculties, but existing as the universal circumstances into which the mind is born. There could be no exceptions to the uniformity of our experience of such facts, even if there were no necessity in our convictions of them; and although, as our author's school believe, we always do have necessary convictions of such facts and of no others, the doctrine must rest, after all, on the evidence of induction—on the observation that the mark of necessity always does attend uncontradicted truths and no others. But the history of science as well as the discussions of philosophy contradict this induction. "There was a time," says Mr. Mill, "when men of the most cultivated intellects and the most emancipated from the dominion of early prejudice, would not credit the existence of antipodes." Our author, after quoting this example, observes: "I acknowledge that the tests of intuition have often been loosely stated, and that they have also been illegitimately applied, just as the laws of derivative logic have been. But they have seldom or never been put in the ambiguous form in which Mr. Mill understands them, and it is only in such a shape that they could ever be supposed to cover such beliefs as the rejection of the rotundity of the earth. . . . It is not the power of conception, in the sense either of phantasm or notion, that should be used as a test, but it is self-evidence with necessity." He then proceeds to understate the facts of the case thus: "There was a time when even educated men felt a difficulty in *conceiving* the antipodes, because it seemed contrary not to intuition but to their limited experience; but surely no one knowing anything of philosophy or of what he was speaking would have maintained, at any time, that it was self-evident that the earth could not be round." On this we have to observe, in the first place, that the difficulty of conceiving the antipodes was not, as the author appears to think, a difficulty of conceiving the rotundity of the earth, but a difficulty of conceiving men standing on the opposite side of the round earth, without having their feet stuck on, like flies to a ceiling, and this difficulty was such that these philosophers could not be made to *credit* its possibility; in other words, they had one of Dr. McCosh's intuitions on the matter. Mr. Herbert Spencer, who follows the Scottish school in positing belief as a valid and ultimate test of the truths of universals, attempts to explain away this historical example by limiting the test to what is simple and "undecomposable," and he supposes the conception of the antipodes to have been difficult or impossible to the ancients, and the fact to have been incredible, on account of the complexity of the conception. But we suspect the case to have been just the reverse of this. The antipodes were incredible to the ancients because they conceived the fact as a simple and unconditional one, and in contradiction of the equally simple and unconditional fact of their own standing on the earth. And it is because we in modern times are able to resolve both facts into the conditions on which they depend that they are seen not to be contradictory. So long as "down" was conceived as an absolute direction in the universe, dependent on nothing but its own nature, so long were the antipodes incredible and stood in contradiction of as simple, original, and necessary a belief as "that two straight lines cannot inclose a space." In short, the ancients had in this case all the tests which the Scottish school apply as ultimate in the ascertainment of truth.

But what can be more ultimate? What other tests are there? this school demand. Perhaps there are no tests of a general character, or of simple and easy application; but, without awaiting an answer, this school describe all those who oppose them as "sceptics," deniers of truth; whereas what the so-called "sceptics," "idealists," and "sensationalists" deny is only the validity of these tests as ultimate ones. What nobody doubts or calls in question, that, of course, nobody wants a test for, though it may be a useful and instructive exercise in philosophy to generalize the conditions of ultimate credibility. But such conditions are illegitimately used as an appeal from the doubts or questions of philosophy. The Scottish school, half aware of this, commonly describe the opinions and doubts from which they appeal to intuition and common sense as either insincere or as positively wicked, and our author, in particular, regards all the errors and mistakes of philosophers as coming from a perverse will, from their not yielding to their intuitive, heaven-born convictions. He describes his opponents as "opponents of intuitive truth," whereas they only oppose the theory which regards our simplest and most certain convictions as derived from a different source from that which assures us of all else that we know, namely, our experience of the world and of our own thoughts. The "sceptic" does not deny that our knowledges are produced according to laws which may be discovered in them by comparison and generalization, and his doubts and questions about metaphysical truths, such as the relation of cause and effect and the existence of the external world, are doubts and questions, not about the reality of these knowledges, but about the *kind* of reality they have, and this must be determined, he thinks, by the nature of the evidence on which they rest.

The "sceptic" does not deny that many of his beliefs are unconditional or necessary. He only denies that this quality is a proof of their simplicity or originality, and on this account he doubtless holds to them somewhat less willfully. By necessity he means unconditionalness, or that the fact is independent of all other known facts and conditions. Whatever the word necessity means more than this, comes, he thinks, from a rhetorical fervor of assertion; as if one should say, "This *must be* so," meaning that he is *determined* that it shall be so. This sort of self-determination in their convictions the Scottish school doubtless have, and they are probably correct in not ascribing it to the evidence of experience; but then they are wrong in thinking that it comes from the reason, since, in fact, its real origin is in the will.

The appeal from the "sceptic's" questions to common sense

is inept in two important particulars. In the first place, the appeal is an *ignoratio elenchi*, for the questions are not questions of facts but questions of their philosophical explanations; questions of the origin and nature of the facts as knowledges. These have nothing to do with the cogency or simplicity of our beliefs, except to explain them. When the "sceptic" asks why some beliefs are so much more cogent than others, he is accused by this school of doubting whether they really are so, and he is referred for an explanation to the very facts which he seeks to explain. But, in the second place, no discussion is legitimate which appeals to an oracle not acknowledged by both parties. The proper appeal in all disputes is to common principles explicitly announced and understood in the same sense by both disputants. It is common, indeed, in physical investigations to speak of an appeal to experiment or to observation; still, by this is meant, not an appeal from anybody's decision or opinion, but from everybody's ignorance of the facts of the case. The facts in philosophy are so notorious that this sort of appeal is not required. What is sought by the so-called "sceptic" is the *nature* of the fact, its explanation; and he is not deterred from the inquiry by the seeming simplicity of the fact, but proceeds, like the astronomer, and the physicist, and the naturalist, by framing and verifying hypotheses to reduce the simple seeming to its simpler reality. In this the idealist does not deny that there is an existence properly enough called the external world, but he wishes to ascertain the nature of this reality by studying what the notion of externality really implies; what are the circumstances attending its rise in our thoughts, and its probable growth in our experience. In this research he does not forget that all explanation ultimately rests on the inexplicable; that "there is no appeal from our faculties generally;" he only denies that the present simplicity of a fact in our thoughts is a test of its primitive simplicity in the growth of the mind. For such a test would have deterred the astronomer from questioning the Ptolemaic system and the stability of the earth, or the physicist from calling in question nature's abhorrence of a vacuum.

The oracular deliverances of consciousness, even when consulted by the most approved maxims of interrogation, cannot present a fact in the isolated, untheoretical form which criticism and scientific investigation demand. Philosophers are not the only theorizers. The vulgar, and the philosopher himself as one of them, have certain theoretical prepossessions, natural explanations and classifications of the phenomena which are habitually brought to their notice—such as the apparent movements of the heavens, and the axioms of hourly experience. How are these natural theories to be eliminated? How unless by criticism—by just such criticisms as those of the great "sceptic" Hume? But while the criticisms of Hume awoke the philosopher of Königsberg from his "dogmatic slumber," and gave rise to the greatest philosophical movement of modern times, it appeared to affect the "sceptic's" own countrymen only to plunge them into a profound dogmatic coma. The "sceptic" seemed to these philosophers to deny truth itself, and to demand a proof for everything. "There are truths," says our author, "above probation, but there are none above examination, and the truths above proof are those which bear inspection the best." This is the key to the whole Scottish method. The inspection of truths as to their credibility seems to these thinkers to be the chief business of philosophy. As if truths were on trial for their lives! As if the "sceptic" desired worse of them than their better acquaintance!

An appeal to an oracle silences but does not settle disputes. Principles to start from must be those for which no explanation is supposable. The existence of undisputed and indisputable facts is denied by no philosopher, and every true philosopher seeks for such facts; the "idealists" and the "sensationalists" as well as the rest. But idealism was ever a stumbling-block to the Scottish school, so much so that their intuitions seem to spring directly from an innate inability in the thinkers of that nation to understand this doctrine. They appear unable to distinguish between questions concerning the origin of an idea and a doubt of its reality. It is much as if a Ptolemaic astronomer should accuse a Copernican of denying or ignoring the visible changes in the aspects of the heavens.

The "sceptic" does not doubt peremptorily, but always for cause. He does not profess to doubt realities or principles, but only whether certain truths *are* principles or simple cognitions, and whether they are cognitions having the *kind* of reality they are vulgarly supposed to have. There would be a sort of grim humor in our author's discussion of "what are we to do to the sceptic?" and what we should and what we should not do for him, were it not that the discussion is too obviously a serious one. The author does not see that what we ought to do is to try to understand the "sceptic," and what we ought not to do is to misrepresent him.

"Precipitate and incorrect as Hume's conclusion was" concerning the possibility of a science of metaphysics, "yet," says Kant, "it was at least founded on investigation, and this investigation was well worthy that all the best intellects of his time should have united successfully to solve the problem, and, if possible, in the temper in which he proposed it, for from this a total reform of the science must soon have arisen. Only the unpropitious fate of his metaphysic would have it that it should be understood by none. One cannot without a certain feeling of pain see how utterly his adversaries, Reid, Oswald, Beattie, and later Priestly also, missed the point of his problem. By continually taking for granted just what he doubted, but on the other hand proving with vehemence, and, what is more, with great indecorum, what it never came into his head to doubt, they so mistook his hint towards improvement that everything remained in the old state, as though nothing had happened."—[*Prolegomena to every Future Metaphysic which can be put forth as a science.* Introduction.]

We will only add that our author has not improved upon his predecessors.

MASSON'S RECENT BRITISH PHILOSOPHY.[*]

With the true metaphysician the real motive of his pursuit is, of course, his belief in its success and in the value of the truths, as such, which he aims to establish. But, in addition to this motive, many minds discover a certain dignity and absolute worth in the pursuit itself—in the exercise of powers which, though they should fail of their end, are regarded as the noblest and the most distinctive of the tendencies native to the human mind. To this somewhat sentimental view of the value of metaphysical studies, Sir William Hamilton gave his powerful support, and his disciple, Mr. Masson, urges it in apology for his Review. [†] The "greatest and most characteristic merit of Sir William Hamilton among his contemporaries consisted," according to Mr. Masson, "in his having been, while he lived, the most ardent and impassioned devotee of the useless within Great Britain." Mr. Masson does not tell us whether Hamilton has since his death been surpassed in this excellence; but on no point in metaphysics does Mr. Masson himself take a more decided stand than on this its claim to be a very ennobling pursuit. Of a nation which should cease to care for metaphysics, he says that it "has the mark of the beast upon it, and is going the way of all brutality."

On more specific points of metaphysical doctrine, Mr. Masson's opinions are not so distinctly set forth. He manifests, however, a certain affection for transcendentalism, and a confidence that there is something in it. But his aim in this volume is not so much to set forth his own opinions as to sketch the relations of the different philosophical systems that have been

---

[*] From The Nation, November 15, 1866.

[†] "Recent British Philosophy: A Review, with criticisms; including some comments on Mr. Mill's answer to Sir William Hamilton. By David Masson." New York: 1866.

most influential in Great Britain during the past thirty years, with reference chiefly to the writings of Sir William Hamilton, Mr. Mill, and Mr. Carlyle.

For this purpose he lays down, first, a scheme for the classification of possible metaphysical opinions, following Sir William Hamilton's method, and, for the most part, adopting Hamilton's divisions and nomenclature. An admiring imitator of Hamilton's emphatic style, he divides and defines with a firmness, rather than a fineness, of discrimination. Starting with an *a priori* scheme of possible metaphysical opinions, he tries the doctrines of his three philosophers by it, and assigns them to their appropriate classes. A convenient original feature in his scheme enables him to accomplish this with considerable success. He distinguishes three forms of metaphysical belief, or three generic grounds of difference in philosophical opinion. A philosopher's opinions may belong to his "psychological theory," to his "cosmological conception," or to his "ontological faith." If his opinion is given in answer to the question, "Is any portion of our knowledge of a different origin from the rest, and of a different degree of validity in consequence of that different origin?" or "Are there any notions, principles, or elements in our minds which could never have been fabricated out of any amount of experience, but must have been bedded in the very structure of the mind itself?"—then his opinion will be the philosopher's "psychological theory," and he will be an "empiricist" or a "transcendentalist," according as he answers these questions in the negative or affirmative.

The most curious and original part of Mr. Masson's scheme is the doctrine that the philosopher's "cosmological conception" may be quite independent of his psychological theory;" that, in fact, any one may have a very distinct "cosmological conception" without any "psychological theory" at all. "A psychological theory" is a learned luxury, but every one has some sort of "cosmological conception" which is bodied forth in his sensuous image of the universe as a whole, and made up of his ideas of religion and history and the eternal verities of the world.

Philosophers are fundamentally divided, as to their "cosmological conceptions," into realists and idealists, and subdivided into "materialistic realists" and "dualistic realists;" or "natural realists," on one hand, and into "constructive idealists" and "pure idealists," on the other. These four subdivisions are flanked by two extreme classes of opinion: nihilism or non-substantialism, on one hand, and pantheism or the "absolute identity" doctrine, on the other. These extreme classes involve, however, ontological considerations, and depend on the third generic ground of difference in philosophical opinion —on the philosopher's "ontological faith."

Ontology means the science of the supernatural, of the non-phenomenal. Can there be such a science? This question admits, according to Mr. Masson, of a division into two: "Is there a supernatural, and can the supernatural be known?" By the great majority of philosophers these questions are answered in the order in which Mr. Masson puts them: the first in the affirmative and the second in the negative; though it is a puzzle to the sceptic to understand how men can confess a belief in anything of which they profess themselves utterly ignorant. But Mr. Masson offers an ingenious explanation. "Ontological faith," when it exists, depends not on evidence of any kind—the word faith connotes that—but on the existence in the philosopher of what Mr. Masson calls, euphemistically, "the ontological passion," "the rage of ontology," or "the sentiment of ontology." "What has genius been," he exclaims, "what has religious propagandism been, but a metaphysical drunkenness?" In its manifestation this passion appears to us very nearly akin to what, in the modern sense of the word, is expressed by "dogmatism." A dogmatist is one who is fond of strong assertions, who concludes with his will, and reaches his conclusion by going to it when he finds no power, natural or supernatural, by which the mountain can be forced to come to him. But Mr. Masson appears innocently unconscious of this synonym.

By the help of the "ontological passion" and his scheme of classification he discovers the relations between the opinions of his three philosophers, especially between those of Hamilton and Mill, "one of whom may be described as a

transcendental natural realist, forswearing speculative ontology, but with much of the ontological passion in his temper;
and the other as an empirical idealist, also repudiating ontology, but doing so with the ease of one in whom the ontological feeling was at any rate suppressed or languid."

The earlier chapters of Mr. Masson's book, which had gone
to press before the publication of ·Mill's "Examination of
Hamilton," anticipate two of Mr. Mill's principal criticisms.
The apparent discrepancy between Hamilton's philosophy
of the conditioned, or doctrine of relative knowledge, and his
natural realism, or doctrine of the immediate perception of
the primary qualities of matter, is explained by Mr. Masson
by referring the former to Hamilton's ontological doctrine,
and the latter to his "cosmological conception;" and the
apparent inconsistency of Hamilton's philosophy of the conditioned with his theological positions is explained, as we have
seen, by the degree to which he was possessed with the "ontological passion."

"Transcendental natural realism in Hamilton, announcing
itself as anti-ontological but with strong theological sympathies, and empirical, constructive idealism in Mill, also announcing itself as anti-ontological, but consenting to leave the
main theological questions open on pretty strict conditions—
such," it seems to Mr. Masson, "were the two philosophical
angels that began to contend formally for the soul of Britain
about thirty years ago, and that are still contending for as
much of it as has not in the mean time transported itself
beyond the reach of either." Whether any of it has done so,
and how much, and where it has gone, are matters which Mr.
Masson proceeds to discuss in his chapter on "the effects
of recent scientific conceptions on philosophy." Having in
this chapter got off the scaffolding of his classification, he
appears to us to have fallen into the most bewildering confusion. That part of the soul of Britain which appears to him
to have got beyond the reach of traditional differences in
philosophy, has done so, it seems to us, by confounding them
with the vaguer scientific speculations which, according to
Mr. Masson, have wrought this great change.

The idea that the world existed for innumerable ages without sentient life; that this life was gradually developed until it appeared in the full splendor of the human soul; that the earth and its history are but accidents in a grander cosmos, and that it and the cosmos are destined to an ultimate and universal collapse, to be refunded into a new homogeneous nebula, and to furnish elements to a new creation—this evolution from nebula, and this dissolution into nebula, repeated without end, making sentient life, the animal nature, and the human mind only phases of a continuous evolution—such ideas, our author thinks, make metaphysics stand aghast. What becomes of *a priori* and *a posteriori*, of transcendentalism and empiricism, when everything is a product and at the same time a factor; when nothing is primordial but nebula, and nebula neither matter nor mind, but the undifferentiated root of both? But Mr. Masson's faith in transcendentalism, as he understands it, is proof against this new phase of thought. He thinks that under these new scientific conceptions transcendentalism and empiricism go a neck-and-neck race back through the ages, but that transcendentalism will get ahead at the nebula.

Now, in all this Mr. Masson has confused the philosophical dogma of an *a priori* determination of knowledge with the doctrine of heredity, the doctrine, to wit, that dispositions, tendencies to action, and perhaps, also, certain elements of knowledge, are derived by birth from the characters and mental powers of progenitors. He explicitly identifies the two by affirming that the doctrine of heredity is inconsistent with empiricism in philosophy. For this confusion he is probably indebted to Mr. Spencer, to whom the world owes the introduction in philosophy of these confounding scientific conceptions. Mr. Spencer and Mr. Masson do not appear to be aware that, by "an *a priori* ground of knowledge," no reference is meant in philosophy to physical or physiological antecedency or causation, but only to the logical grounds of .belief, or to the evidence of certain general propositions. The principal question of philosophy is, whether any general truth is known by any mind except in consequence—the evidential consequence—of particular experiences, or else deductively. If it could be made out that certain general elements of knowledge are born in any mind in consequence of particular experiences in its progenitors, this would still be empiricism, and Mr. Spencer therefore professes empiricism, though he does not appear to know it. For transcendentalism maintains that certain so-called *a priori* elements of knowledge or general truths *could not* be vouched for by any amount of particular experience; and it is non-essential whether this experience be in the offspring or in its progenitors, even back to the nebula. Mr. Spencer and Mr. Masson have, therefore, got beyond the reach of "the two philosophical angels" only by getting confused by their scientific conceptions.

These nebulous conceptions have also dimmed Mr. Masson's vision of another metaphysical doctrine, that of the cosmothetic idealists, as Hamilton called them, or, as Mr. Masson prefers to call them, the constructive idealists. Either he was misled by his own terminology, or for some other reason, he has assumed that the idealism of the majority of philosophers, including Mr. Mill, presupposed the existence of a perceiving mind to constitute a cosmos. To constitute a *conceived* cosmos, or the cosmos *as known*, it is undoubtedly necessary that a mind should exist to know it, or to be aware of its effects upon mind; but that the contemplation of such a mind is necessary to the absolute existence of a cosmos can be inferred from nothing in the doctrine of idealism; and it is only inferable, so far as we can see, from the connotation of the name which Mr. Masson gives to the more common form of the doctrine—from the name *constructive* idealism. He is puzzled to conceive how, on the idealist's theory, the world could have had a progress and a history prior to its development of a perceiving mind, except, perhaps, in the mind of its Creator, who might be supposed to "have continued the necessary contemplation."

We had before supposed that the scientific conceptions, which appear to have befogged our author, had not attained to such a degree of nebulosity as to represent the universe at any time as of a nature incompatible with the existence of a perceiving mind, however unfit it may have been for the sustenance of the animal body with its perceptive organs; and we imagined that the history of the progress contemplated in these conceptions was one which was conceived as it would have appeared had it really existed and had minds existed to perceive it. But if the regress towards the nebula carry us back towards a state of things which would have been not only inhospitable but also incompatible with a distinct mental existence, then we confess that either idealism or else these scientific conceptions are much at fault. But, inasmuch as these are still conceptions, however indistinct, we cannot hesitate to give credit to idealism rather than to such self-annihilating thoughts. Thoughts of a state of things in which thought was impossible must be very transcendental indeed.

Independently of the perturbing influence of modern scientific conceptions, Mr. Masson's account of recent British philosophy is not free from confusion. In revising in his last chapter his classification of Mill's opinions as set forth in the "Examination" of Hamilton's doctrines, Mr. Masson ventures to maintain that Mr. Mill's empiricism is inconsistent with the position of the positivists, that the main theological questions should be open questions in the most advanced school of philosophy. He "can see no interpretation of Mr. Mill's fundamental principle of empiricism, according to which those questions of a supernatural, which he would keep open, ought not to be, at once and forever, *closed* questions."

A question is closed when we have a knowledge precluding the possibility of evidence to the contrary, or where we are ignorant beyond the possibility of enlightenment. An ontological knowledge of the' supernatural, or even of the natural—that is, a knowledge of anything existing by itself and independently of its effects on us—is, according to the experiential philosophy, a closed question. But a phenomenal knowledge of the supernatural is nevertheless a question still open until it be shown, beyond the possibility of rational or well-founded doubt, that the law of causation is, or is not, universal, and that absolute personal agency or free undetermined voluntary actions have, or have not, determined at any time the order or constitution of nature—difficult questions, it is true, but still open ones. Mr. Masson implicitly identifies theology with ontology—the supernatural with the non-phenomenal—and thus implicitly denies that anything can be known of the supernatural, unless it be known absolutely, or in itself. This is to stake all religious inquiry on the truth of transcendental ontology, a position which Mr. Masson, as a liberal historian of philosophy, cannot affirm as the final conclusion of his inquiry, or as warranted by any reasons he has advanced.

MANSEL'S REPLY TO MILL.*

That the two great schools of philosophy will never be able
to make much impression on one another by way of criticism
seems pretty evident from the history of the long debate the
last words of which reach us in Mr. Mansel's restatement and
defense of Sir William Hamilton's philosophy.† The only
real strength of either school appears to be in its ability to
hold and fill the minds of its disciples to the exclusion of the
other, not by logical refutations but by competitive rivalry in
meeting the intellectual demands of the thinker. Few minds
could be tempted, even were they competent to do so, to
stand in fair judgment between these contestants, and the only
feasible course of this sort ever recommended was that of
Pyrrho, who advised his disciples to stand aside rather and to
attend only to the practical questions of life. For, after all,
the intellectual demands which these philosophies are calculated to meet are creations of the philosophies themselves,
and once created they find their food only in the parent
thought. Thus, the main summary objection which the metaphysical spirit makes to the theories of the sceptical school is,
that they fail to answer the questions which the metaphysical
school has started. And the main objection of the sceptical
spirit to metaphysics is, that these questions are gratuitous,
idle, and foolish.

A compromise between the two schools was nevertheless
attempted by Sir William Hamilton in his "Philosophy of the

---

* From The Nation, January 10, 1867.

† "The Philosophy of the Conditioned; comprising some Remarks on Sir William
Hamilton's Philosophy and on Mr. J. S. Mill's Examination of that Philosophy. By
H. L. Mansel, B.D." 1866. Pp. vii. and 189. Reprinted, with additions, from the
"Contemporary Review."

Conditioned." This philosophy allows the validity of metaphysical problems; allows that the terms and positions of the orthodox philosophy mean something possibly real; but maintains at the same time that these refer to unattainable objects, and that the questions are unanswerable so far as human powers of comprehension can render the facts evident or even intelligible as such. This philosophy is in strict accordance with the teachings of Catholic theology from the earliest times, and it gives great prominence to an essential position of this theology—the antithesis of reason and faith, or the doctrine of a difference in kind between knowledge and belief. The kind of entertainment which, according to the "Philosophy of the Conditioned," it is possible for the mind to have of the ideas of metaphysics, far from being a conviction resulting from direct or intuitive evidence, is not even a conception of the facts as possibly true. A conception of the terms and of the propositions as such is, of course, not only allowed, but is an essential position of this philosophy. That which is regarded as inconceivable is the union of the terms of these propositions in reality as well as in form—in the facts which are supposed to be stated in the propositions. That such a fact can be entertained or assented to is the common ground of this philosophy and orthodox theology. "Faith" or "simple belief" is the name of this assent. But inasmuch as this assent is entirely independent of knowledge or probable evidence, an independent ground for it is required among the native powers of the mind, and this is also called "faith" or "belief." Knowledge and partial evidence may aid in fashioning our ideas of metaphysical facts, but are not regarded as the grounds of our assent to them.

To this extent the "Philosophy of the Conditioned" is nothing more than the doctrine of orthodox theology. But its essential feature is this: The faith which is ultimate and independent of knowledge is not in this philosophy a sentiment, the issue of the heart, or a conviction having its ground in aspiration, love, and devotion, but it subsists in the cold light of the intellect itself, where alone intellectual philosophy could profess to find it. It subsists as a logical necessity of thinking something to exist which is unthinkable—not merely something which we have not yet thought of—not the unknown simply, but the unknowable. Sir William Hamilton professes to demonstrate this necessity in the passage so often quoted from his review of Cousin.

"The conditioned is the mean between two extremes—two inconditionates, exclusive of each other, *neither of which can be conceived as possible*, but of which, on the principles of contradiction and excluded middle, *one must be admitted as necessary*," etc. This application of the logical laws of contradiction and excluded middle is the gist of the philosophy of the conditioned; and to this Mr. Mill, in his "Examination" of Hamilton's doctrines, has distinctly replied to the following effect: What is the evidence of the impossibility of a middle ground between contradictory propositions? Simply this: that in all that we know, and in all which we can conceive as possible, there is no such middle ground. What, then, is the evidence in regard to that which we *cannot* know and *cannot* conceive as possible? It is clear that on their proper evidence the laws of excluded middle and contradiction cannot be extended to such cases, and that such an extension of them is purely gratuitous. What hinders, either in the laws of thought or in our knowledge of things, that there should be an inconceivable middle ground between inconceivable contradictories? What hinders that both of them or that neither of them should be true, or that truth should be wholly included in what can be understood as true?

To this refutation of the main position of the philosophy of the conditioned, Mr. Mansel makes no reference in his reply, except in a very remote manner, in a passage in which he sneers at Mr. Mill's apparent ignorance of Hamilton's doctrine of the reality of space. A favorite illustration with Hamilton of his laws of the conditioned is the equal inconceivability, as he asserts, of infinite space and space absolutely bounded, one of which, on the ground of their mutual repugnance, must be admitted as real. The fitness of this illustration, to say nothing of its truth, depends on its not being confined to space as we know it, but on its extension to the really existent space, or space independent of our knowledge, if any such space exists. If no such space exists, then the illustration is wholly inapt. Mr. Mill, therefore, very naturally attributes to Hamilton the only meaning which could fit his illustration to its use, and he supposes Hamilton to refer to a "noumenon space." Mr. Mill says: "It is not merely space as cognizable by our sense, but space as it is in itself, which he [Hamilton] affirms must be either of unlimited or of limited extent." "At this sentence," exclaims Mr. Mansel, "we fairly stand aghast." "Space as it is in itself! The noumenon space! Has Mr. Mill been all this while 'examining' Sir William Hamilton's philosophy in utter ignorance that the object of that philosophy is the 'conditioned in time and *space;*' that he accepts Kant's analysis of time and space as formal necessities of thought, but pronounces no opinion whatever as to whether time and space can exist as noumena or not?" (p. 138). And so Mr. Mansel runs off on an irrelevant issue from the nearest approach he makes to the gist of the matter.

The first sixty pages of Mr. Mansel's review are devoted to a positive exposition of the metaphysical doctrine of the "unconditioned," that "highest link in the chain of thought," that "absolutely first link in a chain of phenomena" about which metaphysicians have gratuitously confused themselves for so many ages. Mr. Mansel endeavors to clear up the matter by discussing the terms employed in the doctrine, and especially the meanings attached to them by Hamilton. He then comes to the trial of Mr. Mill's "Examination," and this is his indictment: "Not only is Mr. Mill's attack on Hamilton's philosophy, with the exception of some minor details, unsuccessful; but we are compelled to add that, with regard to the three fundamental doctrines of that philosophy—the relativity of knowledge, the incognizability of the absolute and infinite, and the distinction between reason and faith—Mr. Mill has, throughout his criticism, altogether missed the meaning of the theories he is attempting to assail" (p. 63). More specifically he charges Mr. Mill with ignorance of the history of the questions discussed; with frequent perversions and even inversions of the meanings of the terms employed by Hamilton and other metaphysicians, and with an unpardonable want of familiarity with Plato and with the antiquity of the doctrines which he discovers as absurdities in Hamilton and our author.

A scholastic display of subtle learning was probably not Mr. Mill's object in entering into this debate with the metaphysicians. If metaphysical philosophy had been content to remain a purely theoretical philosophy, shut up in its own technicalities, and in the original Greek; if it had disdained to descend into the arena of practical life and to influence men's conduct, no really earnest critic, like Mr. Mill, would have opposed its pretensions. If it had not translated itself into the vernacular, and wrested words of a familiar and practical application from their familiar and practical use, and thereby sought to enslave the souls of men to a scholastic and ecclesiastical authority, no criticisms like Mr. Mill's would have disturbed its self-complacency.

That Pyrrho was wrong in his advice to abstain from such disputations, is sufficiently evinced by the influence upon practical life which the doctrines of Hamilton and Mansel were calculated to exert. "That a true psychology is the indispensable basis of morals, of politics, of the science and art of education; that the difficulties of metaphysics lie at the root of all science; that these difficulties can only be quieted by being resolved, and that until they are resolved—positively, if possible, but at any rate negatively—we are never assured that any human knowledge, even physical, stands on solid foundations;" these are reasons enough for examining the pretensions of the metaphysical philosophy; these are the sufficient grounds of the practical critic's interest in those formidable words, the infinite and the absolute, the *chevaux de bataille* of metaphysics. For these words are also common and familiar ones, and are commonly and familiarly used, as Mr. Mansel himself admits, in senses different from those assigned to them by the metaphysicians; but the conclusions drawn from their definitions in metaphysics are inevitably interpreted into a practical accordance with the common-sense meanings of the words, and hence lead to false judgments concerning the character of the evidences of religious and moral truths.

Mr. Mill's real end was, therefore, a practical one—to show that in the recognized common meanings of these words the doctrines of metaphysics make arrant nonsense, and that these words have a valid, useful, and intelligible application to the most serious practical relations of life, without any reference to their use in metaphysics. Mr. Mansel uses the word "absolute" in a sense different even from Hamilton's, and complains that Mr. Mill has not given him the benefit of his philosophically clearer and correcter definition. But we imagine that Mr. Mill was more concerned to do justice to the common-sense meaning of the word than to Mr. Mansel.

That the words "infinite" and "absolute," as defined in metaphysics, involve contradictions in their definitions, and not in the attempt to conceive the reality of the things defined, is ∙the position which Mr. Mill maintains against the philosophy of the conditioned. "The contradictions which Mr. Mansel asserts to be involved in the notions do not follow," says Mr. Mill, "from an imperfect mode of apprehending the infinite and the absolute, but lie in the definitions of them, in the meanings of the words themselves." This position Mr. Mansel flatly denies. He holds that these meanings are perfectly intelligible, and are exactly what are expressed by the definitions of the words. To test this, let us take an example. "If we could realize in thought infinite space," says an anonymous writer (a diligent student of Sir William Hamilton's writings, whom Mr. Mansel quotes with approbation), "that conception would be a perfectly definite one." The infinite, then, is not the indefinite. It is a unit, a whole. But it is without limits. It is, then, a whole without limits. But a whole implies limits. We know of no whole which has not limits. We can conceive of no whole which has not limits. Limits, in fact, belong to the∙essence of every whole of which we speak intelligibly. Does not the metaphysical idea or definition of infinity involve, therefore, a contradiction?

Of the common idea of the infinite, as involved in the concrete example, "infinite space," Mr. Mill says: "The negative part of this conception is the absence of bounds. The positive is the idea of space, and of space greater than any finite space." "This definition of *infinite space* is," says Mr. Mansel, "exactly that which Descartes gives us of *indefinite extension.*" But an indefinite extension, according to Descartes, is that which is capable of unlimited increase, and we fail to see the identity of this with Mr. Mill's definition. Moreover, according to the metaphysicians, the infinite and the finite, being contradictories, include all there is; and as the indefinite is not the infinite, it must be some finite. But Mr. Mill says that his infinite is *greater than* any finite. How, then, can it be the same as the indefinite? "Greater than any finite" excludes the finite as effectually as an absolute negation of it, but it has this positive peculiarity, that it excludes the finite in an essential and characteristic *manner.* "Greater than" is a much more specific form of denial than the "is not" by which the metaphysicians are content to distinguish the infinite from the finite. It is this specific and characteristic *mode* of exclusion which constitutes the positive part of the abstract conception of the infinite, and, according to Mr. Mansel, a positive conception, or the positive part of a conception, is that of which we can conceive the *manner* of its realization. It cannot be supposed that Mr. Mansel means by this that only those conceptions are positive of which we can have examples in intuition, for this would be to identify positive conceptions with *adequate* ones. No one asserts that the infinite can be adequately conceived except the "rationalists," to whom Mr. Mill is as much opposed as Hamilton or Mansel; but, as Mr. Mill observes, "between a conception which, though inadequate, is real and correct as far as it goes, and the impossibility of any conception, there is a wide difference."

The common notion of infinity is not, then, a mere negation. It refers to and is related to positive experience, and to valid operations of the mind in drawing conclusions from experience. It is not the same as the indefinite; it is not that to which an unlimited addition is possible, since it is defined as the greatest possible, greater than any quantities which can be measured or compared by their differences.* The metaphysical idea or definition of infinity, on the contrary, in so far as it is not merely negative, involves a contradiction, since it is asserted to be a definite whole, and, at the same time, to be without limits.

Mr. Mansel quotes Locke against Mr. Mill's position, to the effect that the supposition of an actual idea of the infinite realized in the mind involves a contradiction. But Mr. Mill does not suppose the notion to be fully realized or to be capable of complete realization. It is important only that the notion be true so far as it goes, or that it should accord with the facts and the evidences which the mind *is* capable of comprehending.

We must pass over other special points of criticism, and hasten to the chief practical ground of difference, which we conceive to have furnished the real motive of Mr. Mill's "Examination" of Hamilton's and Mansel's doctrines. Our readers will remember the paragraph in the "Examination," p. 103:

"If, instead of the 'glad tidings' that there exists a Being in whom all the excellences which the highest human mind can conceive exist in a

---

* But such quantities may still be compared by their ratios when, as in the higher mathematics, they are "the greatest possible" under certain conditions which do not, however, determine or limit their values as numbers, or as definite sums of units.

In a foot-note (p. 115), Mr. Mansel breaks a lance with Professor De Morgan, "one of the ablest mathematicians and the most persevering Hamiltono-mastix of the day." De Morgan maintains the applicability of a valid notion of infinity to mathematical magnitudes; but unfortunately assumes besides, or appears to assume, that such phrases as "points at an infinite distance," "the extremities of infinite lines," etc., are literally valid in mathematics. This assumption Mr. Mansel easily refutes. But the main position remains untouched. With the mathematician such phrases are really technical abbreviated expressions of a complex conception. Having shown validly and consistently that lines of unlimited length tend to approach continually to a given state of things, or to a given relation to one another, but in a manner which makes it impossible for them as lines, continuously drawn, *ever* to reach this state of things, the mathematician then changes the object of his contemplation. He dismisses the infinite line, and turns his attention to the state of things (the point of tangency, for example) to which his infinite lines, though always approaching, could never attain. Instead of spanning the infinite in his thought, he simply abbreviates in his language that substitution of one object for another which conducts him to the end of his research.

degree inconceivable to us, I am informed that the world is ruled by a being whose attributes are infinite ; but what they are we cannot learn, nor what are the principles of his government, except that 'the highest human morality which we are capable of conceiving' does not sanction them ; convince me of it, and I will bear my fate as I may.   But when I am told that I must believe this, and, at the same time, call this being by the names which express and affirm the highest human morality, I say, in plain terms, that I will not.   Whatever power such a being may have over me, there is one thing which he shall not do : he shall not compel me to worship him.   I will call no being good who is not what I mean when I apply that epithet to my fellow-creatures ; and if such a being can sentence me to hell for not so calling him, to hell I will go."

To this Mr. Mansel replies by discussing the meaning of the word "good."   He asks "whether Mr. Mill really supposes the word ·*good* to lose all community of meaning when it is applied, as it constantly is, to different persons among our 'fellow-creatures,' with express reference to their different duties and different qualifications for performing them ? " and he proposes to "test Mr. Mill's declamation by a parallel case":

"A wise and experienced father addresses a young and inexperienced son.   'My son,' he says, 'there may be some of my actions which do not seem to you to be wise or good, or such as you would do in my place. Remember, however, that your duties are different from mine, that your knowledge of my duties is very imperfect, and that there may be things which you cannot see to be wise and good, but which you may hereafter discover to be so.'   'Father,' says the son, 'your principles of action are not the same as mine; the highest morality which I can conceive at present does not sanction them; and as for believing that you are good in anything of which I do not plainly see the goodness'— We will not repeat Mr. Mill's alternative; we will only ask whether it is not just possible that there may be as much difference between man and God as there is between a child and his father?"

This "parallel case" is, in an important respect, a very happy one.   It suggests the real practical issue of the debate, unencumbered by theological and metaphysical obscurities; but to make it perfect, the parallel should be more exact. The real question is as to the child's obligation to respect his father's wisdom and goodness independently of any experience of them, and solely on the ground of that parent's word for them.   If, from the wisdom and the goodness which the child has seen and understood, he infers uncomprehended higher degrees of these qualities, reasoning from the known to the unknown, just as he does in all other relations of life, and just as we all do, then the child bases his faith on the sure and only ground of knowledge; and his deference to the father's judgment in all cases of doubt or conflict is the natural and direct consequence of a faith so grounded. But if, bewildered and oppressed by a metaphysical difficulty in trying to comprehend the peculiar duties of a father, he should base his faith on his ignorance of them, and believe in the goodness which he cannot comprehend, believing because of his ignorance and not on account of the little knowledge he does possess; and if, in his blind devotion, he should abdicate his own intelligence, reject his own clear judgments of right, when they are brought into apparent conflict with the parent's selfishness, or with that of servants claiming to speak by authority, then the child's devotion would not be that of an ingenuous, filial piety; it would rather be an abject slavish submission. Such we conceive to be the really parallel case, involving the real practical issue between the two philosophies. Faith is, in one, founded on knowledge by experience; in the other, it is independent of knowledge.

LEWES'S PROBLEMS OF LIFE AND MIND.*†

In one of the few passages of Aristotle's voluminous writings which contain a direct reference to himself he declares that in his logical discoveries and inventions he had no help and no precursors. He says: "The syllogism as a system and theory, with precepts founded on that theory for demonstration and dialectic, has originated with me. Mine is the first step, and therefore a small one, though worked out with much thought and hard labor; it must be looked at as a first step and judged with indulgence. You, my readers, or hearers of my lectures, if you think I have done as much as can fairly be required for an initiatory start, compared with other more advanced departments of theory, will acknowledge what I have achieved and pardon what I have left others to accomplish." "In such modest terms does Aristotle speak," says Stuart Mill, "of what he had done for a theory which in the judgment even of so distant an age as the present, he did not as he himself says, merely commence, but completed,—so far as completeness can be affirmed of a scientific doctrine." Such unconsciousness of self as identified with a great work, such an estimate of the work accomplished as compared to what was undertaken or hoped for, is characteristic of the world's greatest thinkers. Newton's indifference to the world's estimate of what had been to him merely a diversion on the shores of the great unexplored ocean of truth before him, did not rise from an underestimate of the value of his work compared to that of his precursors, since it was not with this that

---

* The latter portion of this essay was published in The Nation, June 11, 1874; the introductory part is now first printed from the author's manuscript.

† "Problems of Life and Mind. By George Henry Lewes. First series. The Foundations of a Creed. Vol. I." 1874. 8vo, pp. 434.

he habitually compared it. Self-assurance of ability in thought gained from such a comparison as a remedy to self-distrust is, however, apt to be eagerly sought by thinkers of an inferior rank. Hence, independently of any criticism of the work of these thinkers there is that in the mere personality of style which enables the world to estimate the rank of a thinker, and to recognize its greatest minds. If it were not for this quality in style wisdom could hardly be distinguished from orthodoxy by any but the wise themselves, that is, by the few ; or would be only a happy utterance of the opinions and expressed judgments of its admirers.

Among the many problems, now outgrown, which engaged the speculation of the ancient world was one which this quality of wisdom thus manifested and recognized without being fully known, forced upon the attention of philosophers. *Sophia* was the name, perhaps for this reason, given by Aristotle to the science afterwards called his metaphysics, which treats of the most abstract relations, and the first principles of the special science or philosophy separated from them though derived, according to him, from their foundations in experience, and from their special object matters. His issue with Plato was that *Sophia* is not eternal in a world of ideas, and is not born in the man except as a greater power of observation, induction, and clear thought making the most of its means and opportunities. Though his first philosophy was also called ontology, since it dealt with the relations of things merely as things, or with what was common to all objects of scientific comprehension, yet he gave no warrant for the meanings which the terms ontology and metaphysics afterwards acquired, and which they now have in relation to sources of knowledge, supposed to be distinct from proper scientific evidences. These terms have become so far identified with the doctrine of transcendentalism, the modern form of Platonism, that is, with supposed or supra-sensible grounds of valid belief, that they have been discarded by many modern thinkers as tending from their acquired meanings to associate in the mind falsely the objects of legitimate speculation in the most abstruse problems with that solution of them which is by no means accepted or acceptable to the clearest thinkers. Comte not only rejected these terms with others like Cause and Substance, from philosophy, because they had come to connote a false doctrine, but because, as he thought, they were hopelessly tainted with a disposition of the mind in the use of language to attach the notion of reality, or of being like a thing, to every familiar abstraction, and especially to such as show a marked contrast in their apparent simplicity in the familiar though merely symbolic employment of them with their really complex and ill-understood signification. As in the crudest forms of speculative imagination things and efficient causes are personified, or, more properly, are undistinguished from the more familiar natures of persons and volitions, so Comte regarded the tendency to "realize abstractions," or to consider them divided, just as things are divided, as a crude mode of thought relative to the positive stage which some modern sciences have entered. And to hasten the progress of the scientific mode of thought he proposed to discard certain terms, or to substitute others for them less liable to this infection.

Aristotle was not fully aware of this source of error, though he knew well enough what transcendentalism means. He rejected the latter error as a doctrine of evidence, though he was not free from the tendency to realize abstractions. Mr. Lewes, though for so many years a student and expounder of Comte, is much nearer to Aristotle than to his modern master in this respect.

It must not be supposed, however, that this confusion of differences in the abstract with concrete divisions in our knowledge is one purposely committed by any modern thinker of note, or is done consciously and formally as it was by some of the realist schoolmen. Nevertheless the tendency is so strong in all who are not empiricists by practice as well as in doctrine, that writers in whom we should *a priori* least expect it still give most marked indications of the tendency. It is a vice more common with the disciples and commentators of philosophy than with great original thinkers. It is what naturally happens when we become familiar with a name and with fragments, as it were, of its meaning, long before the whole signification is set before us, or where there is no definite connotation, but rather a very vague and complex one, in the name itself, as in the words civilization, gentleman, or honor, which correspond to different notions, or complex sets of notions, in different minds according to the scope of their experience. Investigators in modern science not especially distinguished for philosophical acumen yet often have the skill to exert toward the objects of their pursuit the logical function of giving valid names, or tying things together in new bundles. This skill, so far as it goes, gives to the scientific empiricist in practice a power which is shown in the higher philosophy only by the most original thinkers. Every student of science is thus within his own province of practical empiricism a positivist: though beyond this province he may be a believer in *a priori* or transcendental evidence, and will almost certainly be more or less of a realist unconsciously, if not avowedly.* Realism as a vice of thought, and transcendentalism as a doctrine of evidence, things very distinct in meaning, are closely allied in fact.

A distinction in existing terms is called an abstract one, and is often called, with a certain degree of propriety, a metaphysical distinction when it is considered in itself, and, though clearly defined, is not considered with reference to its classificatory value, or in reference to its coincidence with other distinctions which together with it serve to mark out concrete objects or distinguish them as real classes or kinds.

The classifications of natural history and chemistry afford more valuable principles of criticism on metaphysical systems

---

* He may even be such with respect to the more abstruse portions of his own science or to portions in which he is a learner or disciple rather than an investigator. The disposition to give a unity in thought to the meaning of a single name whose connotation is not fully known or is a vague and complex set of attributes or relations, is an always present temptation to speculate *a priori* or on transcendental grounds of naming: or to suppose that the empirical attributes connoted by the name are collected around a central and essential, but transcendental, condition of their co-existence, that brings them all together. The metaphysical effort is to "seize" upon this condition ; but the definiteness in thought thus gained is rather in the emphasis of the seizure than in the palpable nature of its object, and the metaphysical grasp, though often vigorous, is too often empty. Aristotle was, for instance, in Logic a positivist, and was opposed to transcendentalism in philosophy, though not free, as we have said, from realism.

than any doctrines of method among metaphysicians themselves, either ancient or modern. This modern addition to principles of method in philosophy is of the very greatest value. Every naturalist is now familiar with the fact that empirical choice is necessarily made between characters and distinctions with reference to their value in classification. A division of animals into aqueous and terrestrial, for instance, or into air-breathing and water-breathing, is not faulty merely because there are amphibious animals. Indeed, in a restricted sense, when it refers to the co-existence of lungs and gills the term amphibious is a more useful one in natural history than any terms referring simply to the animal's external relations. Such terms of distinction are not found to coincide with the numerous other and less conspicuous distinctions which together determine real kinds. A division of animals into vertebrates and invertebrates, or into warm-blooded and cold-blooded, is much more fundamental, and valuable in discriminating real kinds, yet no metaphysical insight ever excogitated this value in it. The absence of any canon of method in metaphysics for discovering the relative values of its numerous distinctions is the one great vice of its systems, and is a more characteristic mark than either the doctrine of transcendentalism in any of its forms, or the tendency to vagueness and the confusion of distinctions in abstractions with differences in things. These are indeed consequences of the fatal want of method in all ancient philosophy, and in the modern so far as it is a lineal descendant from the ancient. Though many modern writers like Mr. Herbert Spencer, M. Taine (on Intelligence) and Mr. Lewes condemn transcendentalism, their works are very properly regarded as metaphysical since they continue to pursue abstractions with as little reference to their empirically determined value in classification as ever the ancients did. Analogical generalization rather than transcendentalism is the characteristic method of the system-building modern English school of metaphysics.* The history of such

---

* While a naturalist or a chemist would be ready in conformity to widening knowledge of facts to remodel or revolutionize his divisions or even his nomenclature, metaphysical systems aim at the same end by allowing unlimited expansions to the meanings of terms. Vagueness in them is even claimed as a merit when it is perceived.

terms as "matter and form," as, from Aristotle downwards, they gradually came to be applied more and more widely or with vaguer and vaguer meanings until they ceased to have any meaning at all in their universal application, except that the one meant all the other did not mean ; the endless disputes as to how studies should be arranged in the assumed division into arts and sciences ; as to whether, for example, Logic was a science or an art ; such cases illustrate the essential character of metaphysical speculation.

Mr. Lewes has, in overlooking this fact, illustrated it anew. Dissenting from Comte's opinion that the term metaphysics is no longer of any use, and may be discarded along with the names of several allied subjects, and with terms that have a metaphysical taint and for which better terms may be substituted : holding, on the contrary, that the latter have valid meanings in experiential or positive philosophy, and that not only logic and psychology, but even metaphysics deserve a distinct place in the classification of the sciences, he discards important features of Comtism by making in metaphysics a metaphysical distinction. He divides it into valid metaphysics, amenable to the methods of science, and a branch which he calls metempirics. As a move in the tactics of philosophical debate this invention might be good. Modern transcendentalism has given formal assent to the validity and importance of modern principles of scientific method, as it had before to various precepts in philosophical method ; but for itself it openly repudiates allegiance to the special methods of scientific research, and takes refuge from criticism in assumed *a priori* grounds of knowledge, under the guidance of Kant. It has gone, it supposes, beyond the jurisdiction of the principles of method to which science is subjected. What has it to do with the rules and instruments of induction if its evidence is not inductive ? To dislodge metaphysics from this fortress by effecting a diversion and a division of its forces ; to claim for science all the rational problems of metaphysics ; to claim the name metaphysics for the rational solutions of them in which numbers can agree, and, for this purpose, to invent a name happily (or unhappily) adapted to

bear the odium of all the follies and errors for which metaphysics has been condemned; namely, the word metempirics—
ill-fated at birth—such appears to be our author's purpose.
But in this he has assumed that metaphysics is characterized
by the doctrine of transcendentalism; that it *is* the doctrine
of innate ideas.

It would be difficult, if not impossible, to assign to the name
metaphysics its meaning in modern usage, or to distinguish it
from general philosophy and the abstruser parts of the sciences
by proper definition; and especially, so far as its method is
concerned, to distinguish it from the precepts of method common to all well-conducted speculations. A lack of method, or
of many well-grounded canons of research and criticism, appears to be all that truly characterizes it, independently of an
enumeration of the special topics and doctrines to which the
name is usually given. Its method at any particular epoch in
the history of philosophy appears to have been little else than
the application of some principal doctrine in it to subsidiary
topics, the defense of which against sceptical criticisms, or
against other principles of method, has generally been the
most distinctive part it has played in the history of philosophy.
What is called the "method" of metaphysics is really an essential part of it, considered as a scientific doctrine. For example, the realism of Plato, and the forms of the doctrine held by
the Scotist and Thomist schoolmen; Plato's doctrine, that all
real knowledge is a kind of reminiscence, with the modern
doctrines of innate, transcendental, *a priori*, or intuitive elements in knowledge;. Descartes's egoistic basis of philosophical
demonstration, and the more recent developments of idealism,
are at once parts of metaphysics and principles of method in
its procedures. On the other hand, Plato's contributions to
the principles of method, in his doctrine of definition and his
examples of dialectic art; Aristotle's objections to Plato's realism, which were the foundations of scholastic nominalism, and
the ontological or universal axioms on which Aristotle based
his theory and precepts of syllogism; his defense of induction
as the basis of axioms and the ultimate ground of all truths;
and the various precepts of philosophical procedure proposed

by Descartes, Bacon, Leibnitz, and by Locke, Newton, and their modern followers, all belong to the general doctrine of method, which, so far from being peculiar to what is now called metaphysics, is really more characteristic of the modern sciences and of the Positive philosophy.

That vague and ill-defined body of doctrine which is none the less distinctly felt by all modern students of philosophy to be in a sort of antagonism to the spirit of the modern sciences and to the Positive philosophy, cannot, therefore, be clearly distinguished by a marked difference of method. Its distinction is really more fundamental, and relates to original *motives* rather than to differences of *method* in research. Yet it is true that this distinction of motives affects method very materially, and results in marked differences in modes of thought. Modern metaphysics disregards many points of method deemed essential in the Positive philosophy, not because it is ignorant of them, but because they are seen or felt to be opposed to the vital interests of the main purposes for which metaphysics is studied. When schools of philosophy differ, as they do in the fundamental division of them, in respect to the motives of their questionings or the purposes of their researches, their differences can be rationally accounted for only by recognizing their origins in differences of character in philosophers. Though it may not be strictly true that men are born either Platonists or Aristotelians, it is certain that those who take the most active part in the philosophical discussions of their day have enlisted early in life in one or the other of the two great schools, inspired predominately by one or the other of two distinct sets of philosophical motives, which we may characterize briefly as motives of defense in questioned sentiments, and motives of scientific or utilitarian inquisitiveness. The points of method or doctrine which suit either attitude of mind are those it adopts and pursues; and in modern times the notion has come in vogue, and received the sanction of metaphysics, that there are really two independent methods of equal generality, and applicable to two distinct departments of human thought.

It would be futile to classify systems of thought by this distinction in motives, since both sets of motives come into play in every thinker whose doctrines are historical, or the outgrowth of the mutual criticisms of contending sects in the past. Thinkers not uncommonly hold and even advocate, as Mr. Lewes has done, as a Positivist, for many years (in writings which therefore appear in marked contrast to his present work), doctrines derived from the school opposed to that in which they had become really enlisted, either by native character or early influences. This attitude having also the appearance of a judicial one, or manifesting a disposition to find the truth between extreme views, is often consciously assumed, though thinkers arrive at it from opposite positions, and unconsciously bring to it opposite motives of research. These motives would determine, therefore, grounds of division between thinkers who really differ less in fundamental positions, either of doctrine or method, than in *modes of thought.*

Mr. Lewes, in his plea for the higher speculative studies, is so far a metaphysician, or so far retains the effects, in his mode of thought, of the early influences of the Scottish school, that he fails to distinguish the special causes or exigencies of metaphysics from what he generously calls its "method"; though he qualifies it as "irrational." His account of this "method" is extremely vague. Comte had identified the doctrines of metaphysics with the once leading dogmas of realism; the assimilation of abstractions to things, or to self-existent and permanent beings, either material or spiritual, being the common point of departure in these scholastic speculations. But he did so because he believed these dogmas to take their rise from an erroneous but natural tendency of the mind in its earliest use of abstract terms and meanings, or from a vice of language, to which the mind is always prone, and against which the positive or scientific modes of thought and criticism are the only safeguards. With this understanding of the term he rejected metaphysics, both name and thing, from his system of rational studies; and with metaphysics he also condemned the allied studies of logic and psychology, choosing to connect what he valued in them with the general science of method, and with that of sociology. The English followers of Comte did not accept the latter reforms of positivism. Logic and psychology still hold their place in English thought, though the decline of strictly logical studies (which began long before Comte) had made itself distinctly felt in the deterioration of British philosophy, and is still very noticeable, notwithstanding the wide and beneficial effect of the publication of Mill's "Logic" thirty years ago. The rehabilitation of metaphysics, both name and thing, now proposed by Mr. Lewes, appears to him a step in the same direction. He wishes to restore what is valuable and rational in the doctrines and problems of metaphysics to the rank of a distinct science, to which he would give its ancient and honored name.

But, to do this in the interests of true science, it is necessary to exclude from metaphysics the doctrines and problems which are due to its "irrational method"; and he separates these, at least in name, by calling them "metempirics." All that we have to do, he says, is to exclude from the problems of metaphysics the metempirical elements, the questions which in their very form demand more knowledge than experience can furnish—all questions of transcendental origins and conditions—in short, all arbitrary questionings, to which gratuitous assumptions only can be given in answer, and we have left principles and problems that may be properly collected and studied under the name "metaphysics." To these he gives the taking title of " Problems of Life and Mind," a title which tacitly appeals to both of the two sets of motives, scientific inquisitiveness and the sentimental interests, which have hitherto divided the speculative world.

"Speculative minds cannot," he says, "resist the fascination of metaphysics, even when forced to admit that its inquiries are hopeless. This fact must be taken into account, since it makes refutation powerless. Indeed, one may say, generally, that no deeply-rooted tendency was ever extirpated by adverse argument. . . . Contempt, ridicule, argument are all in vain against tendencies toward metaphysical speculation. There is but one effective mode of displacing an error, and that is to replace it by a conception which, while readily adjusting itself to conceptions firmly held on other points, is seen to explain the facts more completely."

We entirely agree with Mr. Lewes that it is idle to argue against " tendencies," even tendencies to error; for this would be to argue against human nature itself. It is to specific errors that we ought to address our arguments; and we ought, by dividing the tendencies—the erroneous or misdirected from the true, to expose the false ones in their consequences, and thus conquer them. The true and false, or the well and ill directed, are naturally mixed in the speculative tendencies of the mind. To condemn all that has been or is now called metaphysics would, therefore, be on the face of it a rash procedure. But to invent a new name merely as a name for the errors or the misdirections in speculation which are involved in its questions, and for the sake only of retaining metaphysics as the name of scientific principles and problems that have been or may here-after be included in the higher philosophy, is too much in ac-cordance with older metaphysical principles of nomenclature; or, rather, is too much like the older and crude practice of met-aphysicians, to be cordially received as a scientific reform. Botanists, zoölogists, and chemists have made it evident that a distinction, however clearly defined, is not of value in classifi-cation unless it is something more than a distinction. It must coincide with and be of use as a sign of other distinctions— that is, be a mark of the things distinguished by it, in order to have real value in classification.

Mr. Lewes is so far from recognizing, in the rules of philoso-phizing followed by him, this important modern addition to scientific method, the disregard of which is a chief cause of fu-tile hair-splittings and aberrations, both in science and meta-physics, that he shows in many parts of his book a noticeable lack of familiarity with it. We do not believe that metempirics will ever become a scientific name, and we are quite sure it will not be acceptable to metaphysicians. As a literary inven-tion it is not without merits; and, indeed, the literary merits of the whole book are by far its greatest. "Metempiric" is a good retort to the reproach of the term "empiric," and, as a *ruse de guerre*, not a bad device for dividing the enemy's forces. *Divide et impera* is good strategy; and there is practically much satisfaction in a name. It is upon the associations involved in the term "metaphysics" that the larger division of modern speculative thinkers mainly subsist. To deprive them of their name would, if practicable, take away the apparent defensible-ness of their last positions, namely, that their "method" is peculiar to their problems; and that the doctrines they maintain, or defend, are safely intrenched in the transcendental mystery of the mind's birth, and are exempt from scientific criticism. "Experience," however, has also come to be a name so much respected that these thinkers, anticipating the movements which would appropriate their title to respectability, have already for some time made a counter movement, and come to hold that the evidence they contend for as ultimate still lies within the province of experience, or is not known beforehand, at least in *actual* consciousness; and to hold that it is not gathered from any but the sources of particular experiences; but that intuitive universal truths are, nevertheless, not *generalizations* of experience, and are not even to be tested and ultimately evinced as such. Induction is allowed only a limited range. Intuition is held to be another and an independent form of experience. This adoption of the word "experience" is in accordance with the time-honored practice in metaphysics of annexing troublesome neighbors, giving a vague and metaphysical expansion to the meanings of hostile words, and thus destroying their critical powers.

The sense in which induction was used by Aristotle and by the best of England's thinkers in the past, as the basis both of the intuitive and the discursive operations of thought, or as being involved in sensible perception and in reflective intuitions, or in rapid, habitual, and instinctive judgments generally, quite as essentially as in formal and consciously guarded or tested generalizations, is the sense in which these metaphysical thinkers reject induction as the real basis of all truths; and Mr. Lewes, as well as Mr. Spencer, M. Taine, and other late eclectics, weakly and confusedly go along with them—confusedly, on account of the present great deterioration of philosophical language in reference to the questions common to the present time and the old logicians, which the latter treated with a precision of philosophical language unfortunately wanting in the conceptulastic terms and phraseology of the present day. We have grounds of hope, however, that the present phase of vague speculation will soon pass away, and that a generation of thinkers will succeed, trained in so much of the refined and effective terminology and mode of thought of the nominalist logicians as Mill's "Logic" has rescued from oblivion; thinkers who will be able to understand without confusion the nature of axioms.

The fact that axioms are capable of clear, distinct, and adequate statement in language, and are not consciously based on remembered or recorded particulars of experience, but are intuitive, or habitual and rapid, interpretations of valid meanings in terms; the fact that an axiom may at first be merely one among a thousand early and spontaneous generalizations of the mind; that of these the great majority are overthrown by subsequent experience, while the one which becomes an axiom, meeting with no counter experience, but, coinciding with all subsequent experience, survives, is strengthened, and becomes habitual; that it becomes so elementary and so fundamental a habit that no other habit or power of thought can oppose it; that it has thus determined our powers of conception as well as our beliefs through experience—these facts are in strict accordance with the Aristotelian doctrine that axioms are based upon inductions, although they are not the results of a formal and consciously guarded procedure in accordance with the canons of inductive logic. In their primary signification and in this connection the terms "induction" and "inductive" refer directly to evidences, and not to any special means and processes of collating and interpreting them. Writers of the sort we have characterized continually confound these two meanings. So, also, they confound the meanings, one valid and the other not so, in the terms "intuition" and "intuitive." Mr. Lewes, after having distinctly contrasted (pp. 342-348) intuitive and discursive judgments, and characterized the former as rapid or habitual inferences, adds shortly afterwards (p. 356) that he does "not wish to be understood as adopting the view that axioms are founded on induction; on the contrary," he says, "I hold them to be founded on intuition. They are founded on experience, because intuition is empirical."

Intuition in its proper meaning of rapid, instinctive judgment, whether in the objective sensible perception of relatively concrete matters, or in the most abstract, differs equally from inductive and deductive *processes of conscious inference.* But there is no contrast or alternative between intuition and induction in reference to ultimate grounds of belief, except in the spurious metaphysical meaning of "intuition"; which Mr. Lewes has, it therefore appears, confusedly adopted, while seeming to hold his former positions as a positivist. Induction in one of its meanings, as a process of conscious generalization, and intuition, as another form of judgment, are only contrasted as *judgments;* the one consciously and the other unconsciously determined, on the occasion of making the judgment, by past particulars of experience. If Mr. Lewes had been a purist in philosophy he might, perhaps, escape from this objection, on the ground that what is meant by the phrase, "grounds of a belief," is not the unconscious but the concious causes of it; the facts or reasons from which we infer it. What is properly meant, however, by affirming particulars of experience to be the ground of belief in axioms, is not that these particulars are present individually in memory on every occasion of making such a judgment; but only that they are the proper tests of validity in an ultimate philosophical examination of axiomatic truths; and are, as they occur, the actual and conscious causes of the judgments, and of their growing certitude, and of the growing precision of meaning in the terms by which they are expressed; though individually they are not retained or recalled in memory.

So far, however, are our author's statements from being entitled to careful consideration on the ground of precision in the use of philosophical terms, that by far the greater part of what we should have to say about his book, if we had space to say it, would relate to obscurities growing out of his inattention to ambiguities and vagueness in philosophical language. Thus, he follows a bad late use of the term *a priori;* which properly, and in Kant, means a *logical* ground or cause of knowledge; and he applies the term to inherited, organized, or instinctive tendencies to the association of particulars in experience, or to "aptitudes for thought"; to which Kant properly refuses the name *a priori* (p. 410). Again, from not seeing an ambiguity in the word knowledge, he discovers (p. 405) what appears to him a contradiction in Kant's doctrine; which seems to assert that "*all* knowledge begins with experience" *a posteriori*, and yet asserts that "*some* knowledge is antecedent to and independent of experience." Our author surely cannot have failed to meet in his extensive studies with the distinction in metaphysics between the commencement or introduction, and the source (*exordium et origo*), of knowledge ; as well as the distinction of actual or present knowledge and that which we are said to possess in memory, although we are not at the time thinking of it. Yet he seems to have forgotten these distinctions. All that Kant maintains is that a knowledge like that of memory, a knowledge *in posse*, of which, as he thinks, experience cannot be the *source*, is involved, and may be recognized, in the actual judgments of experience ; but is not recognized *before* experience ; or except as a *form* given to the *matter* of experience—a doctrine vague enough, we admit, in meaning, and doubtless gratuitous in fact, but not self-contradictory. In short, Mr. Lewes's book is full of illustrations of the importance of improving metaphysics, not as a positive science, but as a dialectic art ; an art allied both to logic and to lexicography. There are, indeed, such treatises in existence, which are much less interesting than Mr. Lewes's book. Such treatises are generally, and ought to be, as dry as a dictionary, but do not the less deserve attention, as correctives of the current loose thinking on the most abstract subjects.

McCOSH ON TYNDALL.*

Among the natural consequences of the sin committed by
Professor Tyndall in the hardihood of his late Belfast address,
is the revival by it of the inextinguishable flame of metaphysical controversy. That the address was not fit, in the nature of
things—to say nothing of the conventions, the common or un-
written laws of scientific societies, which the author violated—
appears by the consequence that the most fitting reply to it
comes from Dr. McCosh.† Such popular organizations as the
British Association for the Advancement of Science were copied
from the aims and disciplines of the *élite* among modern scientific societies. These societies are, in a word, schools of Baconism, designed to embody all that was of value in the
thought and spirit of Bacon—namely, a protest against traditional authority in science, with, of course, a recommendation
of induction and of the inductive sciences for their value in the
arts of life. As to method in induction, Bacon's teaching was
of comparatively little value. His really distinguishing service
was in accomplishing a more or less complete and enduring
severance, at least in British thought, of physical science from
scholastic philosophy, and from all traditions of more ancient
thought. One of the most interesting consequences of this
movement is that the word "philosophy," and even the name
"natural philosophy," have distinctly different meanings in English and in the continental languages. The body of ancient
traditional thought was so completely routed that its name,

---

* From The Nation, April 22, 1875.

† "Ideas in Nature overlooked by Dr. Tyndall: being an Examination of Dr. Tyndall's
Belfast Address. By James McCosh, D. D., LL. D." 1875.

"The Scottish Philosophy, Biographical, Expository, Critical, from Hutcheson to
Hamilton. By James McCosh, LL. D., D. D." 1875.

Philosophy, lost its meaning, and became appropriated to the knowledge and pursuits which in ancient times divine philosophy disdained. Socrates, it is said, brought down philosophy from the clouds; and Continental thinkers have reproached the English for having degraded her to the kitchen. This recognition of the dignity of the useful and of the authority of induction, but still more the subtler perceptions of method in induction by later English thinkers, and especially in the Positivism of Locke, Newton, Herschel, and J. S. Mill, have more than anything else given the English their eminence in modern science. The restraints of the speculative spirit in scientific pursuits, determined mainly by a desire for peace with Theology and Philosophy, and accomplished by a division of provinces, have been the chief cause of the easy triumphs of inductive evidences in the modern sciences of physics, astronomy, chemistry, and even geology and biology, over an opposition which, when roused, has carried with it the strength of a desperate self-defense and all the gigantic forces of tradition. The best British thinkers, therefore, from Newton to Darwin, have respected this peace; and Dr. Tyndall has put himself out of this category by the performance that relegates him to the tender mercies of Dr. McCosh.

As spectators of the combat, we may, however, forget the rash occasion which brought our scientific hero into this arena, and extend a sympathy to him in this relation which we withheld from him as the retiring president of the British Association. In the prefaces to his published address, Tyndall charges some of his critics with " a spirit of bitterness which desires, with a fervor inexpressible in words, my eternal ill." Dr. McCosh " happens to know of some of them, that they are praying for him, in all humility and tenderness, that he and all others who have come under his influence may be kept from all evil, temporal and eternal." Such belligerent magnanimity must be very consoling to its object. To be prayed for particularly by fellow-mortals that we may be delivered from deliberately cherished, or at least seriously considered, views on the nature of things, and not alone for what we ourselves recognize as evils, may be from a sympathy with a supposed unconscious, undeveloped better-self in us; but to us, our conscious selves, it seems scarcely different, except in degree, from a sympathy and a wish for our eternal welfare which would burn us at the stake. Indeed, the attitude is not very unlike that of picking up the fagots for a spiritual cremation, of which the material symbol is now forbidden by civilized opinion and law. To use the language of kindliness and magnanimity when every page manifests an intense, though smothered, *odium theologicum*, conceals nothing, and repels more effectively than the most open hostility. Expressions of petty spite, depreciatory epithets, intimations of ill-opinion, readiness to credit evil reports of those who hold unorthodox opinions in philosophy, and misinterpretations of every sign of weakness in them— these characterize Dr. McCosh's treatment of those thinkers, included in his latest published biographies of Scottish philosophers, who differ from him in fundamental views. If his object—supposing him to have an object in this—were simply to frighten the faithful from any contact with the unholy, we can see how he might effectively keep them faithful through ignorance; but if he thinks in this way to win any one to his standard, we think he greatly mistakes the nature of the sceptic. He calls attention in his preface to the fact "that in this paper, under none of its forms, have I charged Professor Tyndall with being an atheist"; and near the close of his paper he announces that "I make no inquiry into the personal beliefs of Dr. Tyndall," though in the preface he had professed to believe that Tyndall's feelings are not fixedly bad: "At present very wavering and uncertain—*feelings*, rather than convictions founded on evidence." Dr. McCosh here makes use of the "extenuating method," the *eironeia* of Aristotle's rhetoric, though with ineffective art. His restraint from this fearful accusation is made up for by a zeal going greatly beyond due accuracy of thought and exposition, in his preparation of the case for whosoever may thereby be stimulated to prefer the charge.

We have space only for the examination of one great confusion of thought which runs through not only this paper but much of the criticism in his biographical work on the "Scottish Philosophy," wherever he treats of the opinions of the "sceptics" of his native land.

Lord Bacon is Dr. McCosh's model in philosophizing, and, however marked may be the differences, there is a striking similarity between their minds. The great point of sympathy is in Bacon's demonstrative, aggressive, and rather effusive professions of theism. This wins for Bacon the enthusiasm of such a disciple for "the comprehensiveness of his mighty mind"; and is likewise the measure with Dr. McCosh of the minds which he treats favorably in his biographies. Now, Bacon in his model inquiry which occupies so large a space in the "Novum Organum,"—the inquiry into the form of heat,—reaches the conclusion that heat is a kind of motion; meaning, of course, not the feeling of heat, but the conditions of the feeling. Dr. McCosh would be the last to charge Bacon with atheism for this verbal ellipsis. Nor do we suppose that he would be alarmed by the confusing ambiguities of the words light, sound, taste, touch, and the like, which are used by all modern philosophers to express two totally dissimilar natures, the tremors of ether and air, with the chemical and mechanical properties of bodies in contact with special organs of sense, and the sensations of light, sound, etc., of which these homonymical words are also the names; a part of the cause and its effect having the same names though wholly different in nature. Nor again do we suppose that he would take alarm at the inclusion, in such names, of the other physical conditions of a conscious product or sensation—namely, the movements or changes in living nervous tissues, which are the more immediate conditions of the production of a sensation. Mr. J. S. Mill, however, in his "Logic," takes to task a philosopher of his own school for defining an idea or notion as "a contraction, motion, or configuration of the fibres which constitute the immediate organ of sense." "Our *notions*," Mill exclaims, "a configuration of fibres! What kind of philosopher must he be who thinks that a phenomenon is *defined* to *be* the conditions on which he supposes it to depend?" What sort of philosopher must this one be, we may add, who not only makes this confusion in his imputations of opinion to scientific philosophers, ancient and modern, but intimates that the gravest defects not only of mind but of character are implied by it?

The poverty of philosophical language, rather than such fatuity, would have been the more charitable account of what is charged as materialism against these thinkers. No philosopher of note among them, we are sure, ever seriously thought that atoms by their collocations and movements *explain* (in the sense of unfolding the essential natures of) "sensation, judgment, reason; of love, passion, resolution." None ever attempted, as Dr. McCosh intimates that Tyndall has done, to "account in this way for the affection of a mother for her son, of a patriot for his country, of a Christian for his Saviour." No one ever supposed that, "aggregate them [the atoms] as you choose, and let them dance as they will," there is "any power in them to generate [in the sense of producing their like] the fancies of Shakespeare—his Hamlet, his Lady Macbeth, his King Lear—the sublimities of Milton, the penetration of Newton, or the moral grandeur of the death of Socrates." Yet Dr. McCosh calls Tyndall to account for so doing in these grave terms: "What—to employ the very mildest form of rebuke—can be the use of devising hypotheses which have not even the semblance of explaining the phenomena? In the interest of science, not to speak of religion, it is of moment at this present time to lay an arrest on such rash speculations; and to insist on the scientific men refraining from what Bacon denounces as 'anticipations of nature,' and confining themselves to facts and the co-ordination of facts."

Dr. McCosh is not quite accurate here about what his model Bacon recommends. The past errors which Bacon opposed he called "the Anticipations of Nature" by the mind, and in place of this recommended " the Interpretation of Nature," or "that which is properly deduced from things," and (it is to be presumed) may include somewhat more than a bare co-ordination of facts. But whatever Bacon meant to " denounce," it is certain that the physical sciences which have grown up since his time involved in their establishment a great deal more of "the picturing power of the mind," which Tyndall justly esteems, than Dr. McCosh is inclined to allow. But this is a comparatively trivial error. The gravamen of his charge is wholly mistaken. Tyndall publishes as an appendix to his address a lecture previously delivered, in which the doctrine thus imputed to him is disavowed. Dr. McCosh refers to this fact, but regards it as either trivial or as inconsistent with the ominous meaning of that discovery in matter of "the promise and potency of every quality of life" for the "confession" of which Tyndall "abandons all disguise." In spite of this lecture Dr. McCosh thinks that Tyndall "feels himself entitled to hold that matter, though we cannot say how, may give us all the operations of understanding and will." It is important to understand here in what sense "may give us" is to be taken. Certainly Tyndall is no disciple of Lucretius, or of the great and subtle Greek physicists, if he holds that atoms, the primordia, the elements, the seeds, or first-beginnings of things have the natures of understanding and will. That these are not the properties, but only the accidents (in the logical sense), of the movements and collocations of the elements, is the Lucretian doctrine. Moreover, "primordial elements" does not refer to remoteness in time past, but to simplicity and unchangeableness in present, past, future, or the infinitely enduring causes of change. In other words, what these philosophers sought to explain by their theory of atoms is not the natures of the passing phenomena of sense, understanding, and will, but their occurrences, and the order (such as there is) in their occurrences as actualities or events. Such phenomena were not regarded as consisting of the properties of atoms, of size, weight, movement; but only as depending for their actual manifestation on certain elemental collocations and movements. Modern physiology is in striking accordance with these vague speculations. It does not, neither did they, affirm that the properties of matter (that is, the permanent and universal natures of matter) define or determine anything except the events of phenomena. Neither were the gods excluded by these speculations from existence, or from the moral interests and regards of men, in accordance with their reputed characters. They were only excluded from the arbitrary determination of the course of events, or from any other interference than that of being in their consciousness and actions a part of this course. They, too, were dependent in their thoughts and volitions on material conditions. Whatever loss of dignity or wound to pride in men might come from such subjection to material conditions was shared, according to this philosophy, by the gods. That the conditions of the nervous tissues which we vaguely describe as health, wakefulness, and vigor are a sum of material conditions, which occurring along with other material conditions around them determine particular perceptions, thoughts, and volitions as mental events, is a modern form of the same doctrine. This does not involve, however, the kind of explanation that Dr. McCosh appears to suppose.

There are two meanings of the word " explanation," or, rather, two kinds of explanation involved in philosophy, the confounding of which, not by Dr. McCosh alone, but by nearly all the hostile critics of ancient and modern physical philosophy, has led to great confusion and injustice. To know the conditions of the occurrence of anything in such sort that we may predict this occurrence, whenever and wherever these conditions are given, though as phenomena these conditions may be in their natures wholly unlike the effects of them, is one mode of explanation. To presume this mode to be applicable to relations of any nature in which the conditions and phenomena are too complicated to be fully known or used for prediction, is to make speculative employment of it. To be able to analyze or decompose a phenomenon or effect into its constituents is another mode; whether or not we are able by combining the two modes, as in the dynamical sciences, to explain an effect as the sum of the several effects of the constituents of its cause. This most perfect kind of explanation, this combination, is reached only in dynamical science, and was never pretended to by the clear-headed Greeks who speculated so widely on the nature of things. That mental events and their combinations are fully conditioned, as events, on material ones is all that they ever pretended to believe; and in this opinion most modern physiologists agree with them. These philosophers have fared hard at the hands of the aggressive theists, their expounders and critics. Thus Bacon, as quoted by Dr. McCosh, says: " Even that school which is most accused of atheism doth the most demonstrate religion, that is, the school of Leucippus and Democritus and Epicurus. For it is a thousand times more credible that four mutable elements and one immutable fifth essence, duly and eternally placed, need no God, than that an army of infinite small portions or seeds unplaced should have produced this order and beauty without a divine marshal." Bacon here implicitly attributes to the ancient physicists that conception of their opponent Anaxagoras, which may be said to be the foundation of the philosophical theism of all subsequent times. It is common to speak of Anaxagoras as having introduced into the philosophy of nature the *nous*, or the independent agency of intelligence. It is not so commonly seen that he introduced along with this, and in anthesis to it, a still more characteristic idea, that of a primeval chaos. The anti-chaotic *nous* of Anaxagoras is not that of the physicists and the pantheists. The only chaos contemplated by the ancient atomists is the one they saw around them always existing; one which had always existed in the indeterminate confused actual order, at any time, of the universe as a whole. Its particular orders were regarded as accidents; that is, not permanent or inherent properties of the elements. This last conception, by the way, has been grossly abused, accident being interpreted to mean an absolutely undetermined event; an Anaxagorean accident, such as might have happened in that primeval chaos, which the atomists did not believe in, when " all things were in a confused heap," and before "*nous* intervened to set them in order." That " things might all have been such that there was no fitness in them, and the most unfit might have survived," is the reason Dr. McCosh gives for " discovering an ordinance of intelligence and benevolence in the very circumstance that there is a fitness, and that the fit survive." So deeply imbedded in his intelligence is this conception, this essential idea of theism, the primeval chaos, that because he can conceive an altogether undemonstrable condition of things to have been possible, he postulates as actual a cause, or a mode of action in a cause, the *nous*, which would have defeated this possibility—a very common and almost unconscious kind of *a priori* argument.

It thus appears that Dr. McCosh, not less than Professor Tyndall, " crosses the boundary of the experimental evidence," and "revels in hypotheses about world-making and world-ending." He "professes," indeed, to found his convictions in a Baconian way on "inductions," the name he gives (without adequately explaining the process) to what most other modern thinkers call, and try to explain by the name, "intuitions *a priori.*" In this Dr. McCosh has doubtless confounded the effect of repeated assertions and professions of belief with the force in producing universal beliefs of invariably repeated particular experiences—an effect enforced by that modern factitious moral obligation, "the duty of belief"; a duty which though urged upon us by modern religious teachers with respect to certain ancient speculations, as of Anaxagoras, Socrates, and Plato, was far from being felt or admitted by these great teachers. Their service to us was in teaching *how* rather than *what* to think and believe.

A singular mistake for one who has undertaken to classify modern thinkers is committed by Dr. McCosh when he makes Comte the founder of the school to which Tyndall, Spencer, Huxley, Bain, and even Mr. Darwin are assigned. Two of these thinkers—Spencer and Huxley—have publicly disavowed and disproved any obligations to Comte. It would be cruel, if it were not absurd, to make Comte and Mill responsible, as Dr. McCosh does, even in the slightest degree, for the free use of hypotheses in science made by these thinkers, and especially the use made by the cosmologists among them, by Spencer and Tyndall, of hypotheses for " crossing the boundary of the experimental evidence." Comte all his life, and Mill until late in life, resisted even the undulatory theory of light, as involving the unverifiable hypothesis of a medium, though most physicists, even in Comte's lifetime, admitted the probability of the theory which is now universally adopted. It is strange to see the use of hypotheses in physical inquiries attributed to Mill's recommendation, as it is by Dr. McCosh. As well might one attribute the invention and recommendation of reasoning to Aristotle! Mill only systematized, in his "Logic," what physicists from Galileo had been constantly doing; and no one at all conversant with mathematical and experimental researches is ignorant of the fact that the use of hypotheses, as "recommended by Mill," is indispensable in that " interpretation of nature " which Bacon recommends. But these hypotheses are, for the most part, trial-questions—interrogations of nature; they are scaffoldings which must be taken down, as they are succeeded by the tests, the verifications of observation and experiment; they form no part of the finished structure of experimental philosophy. Comte and Mill, least of all among modern thinkers, recommend their use as bridges for " crossing the boundary of the experimental evidence," whether by the Lucretian road with Tyndall, or on the Anaxagorean highway with McCosh.

SPECULATIVE DYNAMICS.* †

Whether when a body moves it is proper to say that it is *in* motion, or that the motion is *in* it, is a question often suggested by the language of even the most guarded writers on mathematical dynamics, ‡ though the strictly mathematical definitions, formulas, theorems, and problems of the science are free from any ambiguity. With what meaning the preposition " in " is used in these expressions is a further and more pertinent question. If with that meaning which the unmathematical language of these writers seems to authorize, then they have really exposed themselves and their readers to the difficulty involved in Zeno's famous paradox of motion, namely, that since a motion must be either *in* the place of the moving body or *in* some other place, and since the moving body does not move *in* its place, and does not move *in* any other place, motion is really a contradiction, and therefore, according to logic, an impossibility. The solution of the paradox, for which the science of logic had to establish a distinct principle, recognized that in such expressions the preposition " in " is not properly used in a locative sense, but only in the vaguer sense of appertaining to, or being predicable of, its object. That a body *in* motion has the attribute of motion (that is, the attribute of having a continuously-changing distance from some other body, or from some position which is regarded as at rest, or as not having this attribute);

* From The Nation, June 3, 1875.

† " The Mechanism of the Universe and its Primary Effort-exerting Powers. By Augustus Fendler." Wilmington, Del. : Printed by the " Commercial Printing Company," 1874.

‡ We follow Professors Thomson and Tait in using "dynamics" in a wide sense, including Statics, in place of " mechanics," which, though commonly used in this sense, is more properly the theory of machines and mechanical constructions than that of the abstract principles of motion and equilibrium.

and the other form of the same fact, namely, that the motion *in* the body is an attribute of the body—are equivalent or entirely accordant expressions of what is signified by the preposition " in."   Zeno's paradox is logically solved in such terms as these : motion transcends the "sphere" of the locative, or is distinct from both the positive and negative, or the contradictory locative, meanings of " in."   It is neither here nor there as a phenomenon, and yet is not an excluded middle, since the contradiction of this and some other place is a contradiction in relations, both of which are distinct from the nature of motion. Nevertheless, judging by the current language (not mathematical), and the past disputes of mathematicians on the definitions of force and motion—disputes which, after being settled within their own province, have been bequeathed to unmathematical speculators in dynamical philosophy—we should be inclined, at first sight, to allow that such speculators have the warrant of high authority for their attempts at revising the fundamental conceptions of this science.   Whether consciously or not, the mathematicians of the seventeenth century and unmathematical sciolists of later times were impelled by this old paradox to a solution of its difficulty by a metaphysical or non-phenomenal conception of the " force of motion," so called, as something locatively *in* a moving body, constituting the substantive or sustaining cause of motion ; seeing that the phenomenon itself of motion, being a continuous change of distance from a fixed position, could no more properly be *in* a body than this very distance could be locatively *in* it.

Newton from the first, and all competent mathematicians of a later time, saw that the mathematical discussion of dynamical problems had no concern with any such metaphysical conception.   The supposed cause of the uniformity of motion in a fixed direction which a body has independently of external relations, or *vires impressæ*, is not any part of dynamical science. Moreover, the causes of change in the velocities and directions of motion, or these *vires impressæ*, were conceived in a purely phenomenal or descriptive way, and measured by actually visible and tangible quantities.   It was not on account of any speculative inability in Newton to conceive a possible ulterior cause of gravity that he excluded from mathematical dynamics the search for it, and remained contented with the descriptive quantitative law of its action; but simply because such a research departed in a direction just the opposite of that which led to rigorously-demonstrated explanations of the observed phenomena of nature. If any of these phenomena could have led, "in a mathematical way," to the law of action in gravitation, Newton's genius would surely not have failed to deduce it from them. He took gravity with its law for an ultimate fact, simply because it did not follow as a consequence from any other observed laws in the same manner of mathematical deduction in which he had shown that Kepler's laws follow from it and from the three laws of motion. But even mathematicians, and especially those of Germany, whose men of science are even to this day more given to metaphysics than those of other nations, were for a long time haunted by the metaphysical spectre of a cause called the "force of motion," and supposed to be needed to keep a body agoing as well as to set it in motion or bring it to rest.

The mathematics of this science, however, deals only with the defined or measured quantitative phenomenal conditions of persistence and change in motion; and the metaphysical mathematicians were so far true to their science as to seek for a measure of this metaphysical cause of motion. A fierce dispute accordingly arose in the seventeenth century, and was continued into the eighteenth, in which the most illustrious men took part, as to whether the "force of motion" should be measured or defined by the velocity directly or by the square of the velocity. But after a bitter contention, prolonged by the rivalries of national honor among European scholars, the question was finally seen to resolve itself into whether the name *vis viva*, or "force of motion," ought properly to be given to one or to the other measure. For all mathematical and experimental purposes, these measures were all in all, and were perfectly consistent as measures of different phenomena or relations of motion, if only called by different names. And it was seen that dynamical science could get along perfectly well without any use of the confusing word "force." But the word continues still to have at least four distinct meanings in dynamical science—technical meanings related to the use of the word in mathematical reasonings, which are never, however, confounded by mathematicians. All that is really common to them is a vague reference to the production or persistence of states of motion or rest. The real gists of their meanings are in the qualifying terms annexed to them, as in the *vis impressa* of Newton or the *vis mortua* of Leibnitz, otherwise called *vis acceleratrix*, the *vis insita* or *vis inertiæ*, the *vis viva*, and the *vis motrix*. In place of these names, modern treatises often use, without the substantive word, the terms *acceleration* (retardation being a *minus* or algebraically negative acceleration); secondly, *mass* (the coefficient of velocity, or of its square, in estimating either); thirdly, the *momentum ;* and, fourthly, the *energy* of motion. But the term *energy* still has that metaphysical taint of vagueness, even with modern mathematical writers, which so long infected the word "force." It is still spoken of, both with reference to its actual and potential forms, as if it were something locatively *in* the moving body, or *in* a body capable of a defined motion; instead of being only predicably *in* the permanent internal and the special external conditions, which mathematically determine relative movements and their rates of change. It is not surprising that an unmathematical speculator in dynamics should be misled by such expressions as the following from the eminent authors, Professors Thomson and Tait, to which many parallel expressions in other authors might be added, namely, "A raised weight, a bent spring, compressed air, etc., are *stores* of energy which can be made use of at pleasure." A mathematician, knowing in what terms these antecedent conditions of motion are expressed and measured, understands them to refer only to sensible properties in these "stores," together with the restraining causes which also have sensible measures, namely, what makes them "stores," or holds the weight *up*, or the spring *bent*, or the air *compressed*. It is *in* the being held up, or bent, or compressed—*in* these antecedent circumstances, as well as in what is locatively in the bodies, that the storing of energy consists ; and this energy is also dependent in the case of the raised weight on an equally sensible and measurable outward relation, namely, distance from the ground.

The word "force," unqualified, but understood to be limited to the meaning and descriptive measure of "accelerative force," or in a strictly-defined and technical meaning, is still commonly employed in treatises on dynamics. Otherwise it is always qualified, as in the "force of *inertia*." All its uses in mathematical language, or the equivalent terms, acceleration, mass, momentum, and energy, refer to precise, unambiguous definitions in the measures of the phenomena of motion, and do not refer to any other substantive or noumenal existence than the universal inductive fact that the phenomena of all actual movements in nature can be clearly, and definitely, or intelligently analyzed into phenomena, and conditions of phenomena, of which these terms denote the measures. In modern dynamics, the mathematical measures of actual phenomena are their real essences, as scientific facts. Even the much-derided Aristotelian doctrine in explanation of the various phenomena of suction—namely, "nature's abhorrence of a vacuum"—might pass muster in science (though not now as an ultimate principle) if a determination of *how much* nature's abhorrence amounts to under defined circumstances were attached to it. The real fault of the principle and its pretended explanations would be paralleled if we should seek to explain the movements of the planets and of falling bodies by "nature's abhorrence of divorce between bodies"—which is about what the word "attraction" meant to the lively imaginations of Newton's contemporaries, as with Huygens—without estimating, as the Newtonian law of gravity does, *how much* this abhorrence amounts to under given external relations. The fact that nature has an abhorrence of a vacuum *mathematically dependent on the weight of the liquid forced into it* is not impugned by the fact, subsequently discovered, that this weight is balanced by the weight and consequent pressure of the atmosphere, any more than Kepler's three descriptive and quantitative laws were invalidated by the subsequent deduction of them from the laws of motion and of gravity. Kepler's laws served, indeed, as the most effective inductive confirmations of these laws and their universality; and Newton's law of gravity would still hold the honored place it has in science even if it should in future be shown to follow from independently demonstrated and simpler, more ultimate conditions of changes in motion. Merely speculative explanations of it have no honor at all; for its merits are in its being a precise quantitatively-descriptive law, and on this ground alone it holds its place in mathematical dynamics.

We have said that the word "force," when used without qualification, has come to mean unambiguously what, for the sake of avoiding ambiguity, Newton called *vis impressa;* so that in recent treatises the first law of motion is expressed in such terms as these: "A body under the action of no force, or of balanced forces, is either at rest or moves uniformly in a straight line." Newton's words were: "*Nisi quatenus a viribus impressis.*" Now, our author, apparently ignorant of the history of the science, and without any guidance from its mathematics, undertakes to criticise such a statement (Section VI.), simply on the ground that he has chosen, without giving any reasons for it, to give the unqualified word "force" a different meaning in what he is pleased to call an axiom (Axiom VIII., p. 12). He means by it the cause which keeps a body agoing when it moves. Of this cause modern dynamical science knows nothing, except the negative fact stated in the first law of motion, which may be given with even greater clearness without using the word "force" at all—namely, that, independently of properties through which a body is related to other bodies, or independently of such relations, its state of rest or of uniform motion in a fixed direction is unchanged. Behind this fact, except so far as it serves to define the word "force," or *vis impressa*, dynamic science does not go ; but it goes forward with this and other facts to most fruitful results in mathematical deductions, with which our author does not appear to be at all acquainted. Another fact, the second law of motion, which again may be fully expressed without the use of "force," is that the change in the component of a velocity in any direction may be measured in terms of a fixed property, namely, mass, and special outward relations, which in general are dependent simply on distances and directions.

Mathematical dynamics knows of no bodies at rest in any absolute sense. All the motions known or considered are relative motions—namely, continuous changes of distances between bodies, or between these and positions defined by other bodies. It is not known that even the centre or average position of all the masses of the universe is at rest in any absolute sense; so that the absolute motion of no body is known, and the "force" of our author is without any definite measure or utility in mathematical dynamics. The principle of relative motion leaves all measures of motion considered as absolute quite out of the problems of this science, as indeed they are quite beyond our possible knowledge.

One of the principles of mathematical dynamics which staggers the unmathematical sciolist more than any other, and was at first one of the greatest difficulties, even with mathematicians, in the Newtonian theory of gravity—a difficulty repeatedly urged, and brought out from apparently independent meditations by anti-Newtonian heretics—is the doctrine of "action at a distance." This action, the metaphysicians say, is impossible, and they devote themselves to the invention of *media* through which force and motion may be communicated, or from which it may be collected (Axiom VII., p. 11), thinking that thereby they are helping out the mathematical genius of Newton by a profounder effort of thought than he was capable of. But with metaphysical action dynamical science has nothing to do. The action at a distance, considered in this science, is simply a change in motion measurably or mathematically dependent on (or a function of) distances from bodies, distances of which nothing is asserted but that they extend indefinitely beyond the masses or the visible and tangible limits of bodies. "A body cannot act where it is not"—"With all my heart," says Carlyle, "only where is it?" If attractive force is an attribute of bodies (as it is whether or not this force depends on an intangible and invisible medium), then the presence of bodies at a distance from their visible limits must be assumed, so far at least as this attribute is concerned. The color of a body is familiarly known to be distinct from its solid extent, volume, or mass, and is not in the same place; nevertheless, as superficial, is still contiguous with its other sensible qualities. The metaphysical difficulty of believing that the attribute of attraction may be still more displaced or removed than color, is a difficulty which disappears with its cause, namely, unfamiliarity with the conception. Patient study of mathematical and experimental science has resolved many such difficulties, which are not really logical ones; for whether gravity will ever come in science to be a legitimately derived attribute or property of bodies acting through a medium, or will forever remain, as now, an ultimate phenomenal fact, there is nothing of contradiction or essential opposition to experience in its asserted action at a distance—at a distance, that is, not of course from where it acts, but from the places where other attributes of body are manifested; that is, beyond its visible and tangible limits. Most theories of a gravitative medium have been in fact atomic, and, by the interposition of voids between atoms which is thus made, have really introduced the very action at a distance which the theories were devised to do away with. Indeed, the essential principle of action at a distance is a necessary consequence of the metaphysical axiom (which we are not, however, obliged by positive evidence to accept), that pure continuous matter is incompressible, as in the supposed atoms; and though this action be only on a molecular scale, it is no more possible on this scale than on that larger one of gravitative action which mathematical dynamics is supposed to assume. But, as we have said, no such metaphysical assumption is made in this science.

No student of mathematics, competent to pass an examination in Newton's "Principia," not only on its definitions, axioms, and philosophical scholiums, but on its mathematical theorems and problems, could read with any profit, or even with any patience, Mr. Fendler's speculations. Those parts of the "Principia," or of more modern treatises, which such thinkers as our author appear to have studied, present themselves to the student who has clearly seen their embodiment in the mathematical deductions and experimental verifications of dynamical science in a wholly different light from that in which such speculative thinkers take them up. The laws or axioms and the definitions of this science are apparently considered by these thinkers as constituting in themselves a complete body of doctrine, capable of being studied and criticised quite independently of any other mathematics than what they directly involve, whereas they are really integrant parts or elements of a systematic deductive science; and whether or not they are evident at a glance through familiar inductions, or by "intuitions *a priori*" (as some thinkers will have it), they have their truest proof in the broadest possible tests of experience, through the experimental and observational verifications of their mathematical consequences. Of the nature and force of this kind of proof none but students of mathematical dynamics and experimental physics can be supposed to have any adequate conception. To attempt to criticise the elementary conceptions and first principles of the science in any other way, and especially *a priori*, or with a simple reference to *Vernunft*, is really a display of the critic's incompetency, which is not remedied by a reference of his convictions to ancestral experience, or any other modification of the *a priori* doctrine, or any treatment of mathematical axioms as philosophical truths. Several modern writers, more distinguished than our author, and especially of late Mr. G. H. Lewes and Mr. H. Spencer, have thus illustrated how *a priori* too often means no more than *ab ignorantia et indolentia*. Such writers appear to think that the mathematical deductions of the science are of secondary importance from a philosophical point of view, or are merely illustrative applications of philosophical principles to the processes of nature. But instead of the mathematical body of the science being an appendage to these principles as to an independent body of doctrines, these are themselves chosen and framed, so to speak, or determined in their forms and meanings with reference to the mathematics of a systematic deductive science.

BOOKS RELATING TO THE THEORY OF EVO-
LUTION.*

A correspondent asks for information on books relating to the development or evolution theory, especially for the book "which is not too partisan or too technical, but gives the facts and reasoning with reference to it on both sides." From a literature which has in the past fifteen years grown into an extensive department of bibliography, we ought to be able, if this were possible in any subjects of discussion, to select the book which fulfills these requisites. Yet it would be vain to seek, even in Germany, for one which surpasses in these qualities the foundation and first of the series, namely, Darwin's "Origin of Species," in which, and especially in the last edition, 1872, all the *scientific* objections that have been urged against the theory, as it is held by Darwinians, are more clearly put and fairly considered than in any treatise we could name. In no work on a subject of which the scientific evidence is essentially technical, is the fault of technicality less obtrusive; and in late editions this is still further remedied by a glossary of scientific terms. But before we can clearly characterize other books on this subject, it is necessary to make a grand division of the department into books that are strictly (like Darwin's), or predominantly, scientific and inductive; and those that treat their subject as a part, or as the foundation even (like Mr. Spencer's series), of general speculative philosophy, and in connection with theology and religion. Darwin's books have been improperly characterized as speculative. This is true of them only in the sense in which incompletely verified scientific hypotheses are called speculative; in the sense in which Newton's astronomy was,

---

* From the Nation, February 18, 1875.

until completely, or very nearly, verified; or (by a fairer instance) Newton's optics, which, in a main point, is not verified, but reversed.* It is to the *subjects* of Darwin's books, and not to his opinions or treatment, that the term speculative is applicable, if at all; and so far as it is applicable as a reproach, it applies equally, or even more, to the opinions of his opponents. His mode of treatment is strictly scientific, Newtonian, or "positive"; nowhere dealing with disputed axioms, or with deductions from axioms laid down as *a priori* valid and as if they were not disputed; nowhere considering scientific theses as either favorable or unfavorable to general philosophical or religious conclusions, except, of course, where religious teaching, in having prejudged these questions on other than scientific grounds, is presumed to have exceeded by *obiter dicta* its proper jurisdiction. With the great majority, however, of writers on this subject the names of Darwin and Spencer are closely associated; though to more than one Aristotelian master, and to many scientific students of the subjects, no two names are more widely separated by essential differences of method. Mr. Spencer has lately put forward the claim that his method is justified by Newton's precepts and practice. But, according to the judgment of the more immediate followers of Newton, the leading physicists of to-day, this claim is not substantiated.

The dispute is, however, quite aside from the reality of the distinction which, for bibliographical purposes, we here lay down. One of the requisitions of our correspondent is not fulfilled by any book of the properly speculative division. We venture to assert that in no department of speculative philosophy, either expository or historical, do treatises exist which fairly present the facts and arguments on both sides. This virtue is possible only within the limits which scientific, Newtonian, or "positive" method imposes; and within his own proper department of natural science every expert authority is a positivist, whether on other subjects he denies, or ignores, or only

---

* Speculative philosophy is properly metaphysics, and proceeds deductively from axioms, like Plato's or Kant's, or Mr. Spencer's later form of *a priori* philosophy, which he professes to found, in part, on the empirical facts of heredity, and thus give it a scientific basis.

waives the disputed axioms. The essential characteristic of properly speculative as distinguished from scientific method is, that the former seeks to expel doubt by the furcular force of the dilemma that unless one accepts as having universal validity certain axioms, which it is true are only illustrated, not verified by inductive evidences, one is not entitled to hold any beliefs at all with any certainty. Choice axioms are therefore presented, *illustrated*, and a universology is deduced from them. True scientific virtue, on the other hand, is to balance evidences, and to bring doubts to civil terms; to resist the enthusiasm of these aggressive axioms, and to be contented with the beliefs which are only the most probable, or most authentic on strictly inductive grounds. Now in the proper scientific theory of "evolution"—unhappily so called, as confounding it with a different mode of treatment, when any of the successive preceding names, "descent with modification," "derivation," "development," or "transmutation" would on this score have been better, notwithstanding a temporary disrepute in the name—the scientific evidence is in great measure technical, and a considerable part of what has accumulated in the past fifteen years is buried from the general reader in monographs of scientific publications. Essays and discourses in exposition of Darwinism or natural selection are far too numerous; the majority being better calculated to make the author shudder than to illuminate what is best got from a careful reading of his original treatise. Among brief and good essays we may mention Professor Huxley's little books on the "Origin of Species," and "Man's Place in Nature"; Mr. Wallace's collection of essays with the title of "Natural Selection" (though some of these are too speculative to come under the head of natural science); and Mr. Mivart's "Genesis of the Species," which though learned in biological science, is in many parts too speculative or un-Newtonian to be mentioned under this head. We may add a little book called the "Philosophy of Evolution," by B. T. Lowne, published in 1873, by Van Voorst, London, which received one of the Actonian prizes of the Royal Institution for 1872. This is mainly scientific, though it touches on the general philosophical or speculative bearings of the subject.

Of works more unequivocally of the speculative class, Mr. Spencer's generally, but more especially his " Biology," deserve a first place. We should not, however, in this case, as we do in Mr. Darwin's, recommend the original so much as a recently published exposition, which, under the title of " Cosmic Philosophy," is given by Mr. John Fiske. In this book, the disciple far surpasses the master in readableness and skill of exposition. Of a large subdivision of the speculative class—the books whose aim is practical and religious, and opposed to theories of evolution—no one has come to our notice which fairly presents the exact points or the scientific arguments of the theory as it is now generally held by naturalists, and few of them apparently deem it essential to their aim to do so. Finally, we may add to the scientific division of books on the subject a recent edition of Darwin's " Descent of Man," renewed by the fiery ordeal of criticism to which the first edition was subjected, and perfected, so far as scientific fairness and method can go, by the author's unbounded patience of thought and research.

GERMAN DARWINISM.*

A few months ago, in answer to the inquiries of a correspondent about books on evolution, we took occasion to point
out and emphasize a division, very fundamental and important
in our view, in books on this subject, namely, between those
which treat of it as a theorem of natural history from a Baconian or scientific point of view, either mainly or exclusively (confining themselves to scientific considerations of proof), and those
which treat of evolution as a philosophical thesis deductively,
and as a part of a system of metaphysics. Such a division
separates the names of Darwin and Spencer (which are popularly so often pronounced together) as widely as any two names
could be separated on real grounds of distinction.

Two little books have lately been published which we may
add to the short lists we gave of popular works on evolution—
one to each list. † Professor Oscar Schmidt's " Descent and
Darwinism " is essentially a scientific treatise, though of a type
which could hardly have been produced originally in the English language, or from a Baconian stand-point, and for English
students of science. Of its peculiarities we propose to speak
further on. The second book belongs to the speculative or
metaphysical branch of the subject, and consists of two essays:
one, translated from the French of Dr. Cazelles, is an account
of Mr. Spencer's philosophy, and a comparison of it with M.
Comte's; the other essay is a lecture by Dr. Youmans, given

* From the Nation, September 9, 1875.

† "The Doctrine of Descent and Darwinism. By Oscar Schmidt, Professor in the
University of Strasburg," 1875.

"Outline of the Evolution-Philosophy. By Dr. M. E. Cazelles. Translated from the
French by the Rev. O. B. Frothingham. With an Appendix by E. L. Youmans, M.
D.," 1875.

in defense of Mr. Spencer's claims to the credit of establishing the doctrine of evolution. Dr. Cazelles's essay is an interesting account of Mr. Spencer's theories by a fair-minded disciple— by as fair-minded a disciple as one could well be who is at all disposed to yield not merely to claims on one's assent for the sake of argument or system, but on one's adhesion to undemonstrated beliefs asserted to be axiomatic and irresistible. But a *system* like Mr. Spencer's is obliged to stand on such positions. To us it is inconceivable (and therefore, according to one of Mr. Spencer's criteria, opposed to truth) that any one should not resent at every step the asserted demonstrations which Mr. Spencer parades. Neither Dr. Cazelles nor Dr. Youmans begins, however, far enough back in their accounts of the origin and progress of Mr. Spencer's thoughts. These were really theological in origin, and have never departed from the theological stand-point. For it is one thing to arrive at solutions of problems different from those commonly held, or from the orthodox, and quite another thing to outgrow or be drawn by legitimate studies aside from the problems themselves. Believers in philosophies of the unknowable are very much in the state of mind towards the theological problems of their earlier years in which the converted savage is towards the powers and attributes of the idols, which his reason has come to pronounce no other in fact than common blocks or stones. Presenting evidence to this effect does not really diminish the savage's practical belief that his idols are pre-eminently ugly or awful, and preternaturally, though unapparently, unphenomenally, great. To get rid of this belief he must destroy the really harmless blocks. To have believed strongly without due evidence is a state of mind not easily convertible, when due evidence is seen to be wanting, into one to which the object is absolutely without existence, but is more commonly changed into one in which the old interest remains and the object still affects the believer as an unconditioned, unproved, undemonstrable, but not less pragmatically real existence; and this is the real starting-point of Mr. Spencer's philosophy.

Dr. Cazelles thinks that Mr. Spencer " freed his theory from all metaphysical attachments " when he came in the course of his thought to dismiss the moral or teleological implication of the word " progress," and substituted the word " evolution " as the more appropriate name for the abstraction which he sought to define as the fundamental idea of the universe; and when he also substituted in his formula of definition the word " integration " for the " individuation " which he first thought to be the true form or idea of progress. The theory was doubtless thus freed from attachment to any received form of speculation on the nature of life and being, but not at all freed from the scope and method of metaphysics—this scope being systematic omniscience, including even the unknowable. The method of metaphysics is to treat of detached abstractions—that is, abstractions without check in definition and precision, from the concrete examples and embodiments to which Plato, not less than Bacon, pointed as indispensable guides to clearness and truth. There is no profound difficulty in conceiving what progress means, if we qualify the question by the consideration of the concretes in which progress is made; not even if we extend our inquiry to the vague ranking of organisms as higher and lower. The essential error of metaphysics, or " realism," is not merely in attributing to an abstraction a truly individual, thing-like existence, or making it a " realized abstraction," but in treating it *as if* it had such an existence—in other words, *as if* it had a meaning independently of the things which ought to determine the true limits and precision of its meaning. Thus, to apply the mechanical law of the conservation of force, which, as a scientific truth, has no meaning beyond the nature and conditions of material movements (whether these are within or outside of an organism)—to apply this law analogically to all sorts of changes—to the " movements " of society, for example —is, in effect, metaphysics, and strips the law of all the merits of truth it has in the minds and judgments of physical philosophers, or of those through whose experimental and mathematical researches it came to have the clear, distinct, precise, though technical meanings in science that constitute its only real merits. The daring ignorance which in this speculation undertook to change the name of the principle, to call it " persistence of force," supposing the word " force " to refer to an incognizable substratum of causation, and not, as it really does in science, to various measurably interchangeable forms of material movement and antecedent conditions of movement (wholly phenomenal), gave the author's use of the principle the character pre-eminently of metaphysics. We remember, as its most characteristic feature, this attempt in Mr. Spencer's "First Principles" to eke out his barren "system" of abstractions by wresting and corrupting the very type of unmetaphysical scientific truth to the vagueness of a principle of the "unknowable." The principle of the "conservation of force" does refer, indeed, to what thus appeared to be hopelessly unknowable to such a mind— namely, to the experimental and mathematical measures which determine its real meaning and proof. The climax of the speculation was capped when this principle was declared to be an undemonstrable but irresistible axiom—what we cannot help believing when we have once conceived it!

In the same way, "evolution" is, with Mr. Spencer, not a theorem of inductive science, but a necessary truth deduced from axioms; and nothing can be more mistaken, therefore, than Dr. Youmans's defense of Spencer's claim to credit for substantiating a doctrine also, unfortunately, called "evolution" —the doctrine of the origin of species by "descent, with modification," which is wholly due to the labors of leading English and German naturalists—real workers in experimental science. Dr. Youmans, unfortunately for his defense, quotes (p. 125) Spencer's acknowledgment that, though in 1852, or earlier, he had conceived of the principle of "the survival of the fittest," he had not conceived of it as producing the *diversities* of living beings, or conceived of the co-operation of natural selection with indefinite variations to produce species. But this last is the whole gist of the matter, so far as mere conception is concerned; and the merit—though this is a small part of Darwin's merit in the matter—of this conception belongs so completely to him and to Mr. Wallace that the half-glimpses of the conception by earlier writers are of small account. Even Aristotle had conceived of the cause now called natural selection, in one of its modes of action; and two English writers—Dr. Wells and Mr. Patrick Matthew—in 1813 and 1831, set forth the agency of this cause in more extended but still limited forms, the latter coming very near to the views of Darwin and Wallace. So far as other elements of the doctrine of descent ought to go to any single thinker's credit, they undoubtedly belong to Lamarck, to whom, at the beginning of this century, and not to Mr. Spencer, the following introductory remark by Dr. Youmans is justly applicable—namely, that while the idea of evolution "was passing through what may be called its stage of execration, there was no hesitancy in according to him all the infamy of its paternity; but when infamy is to be changed to honor, by a kind of perverse consistency of injustice, there turns out to be a good deal less alacrity in making the revised award." In applying this remark to Mr. Spencer, as to a long-tried martyr, Dr. Youmans is himself guilty of the very injustice towards Lamarck of which he complains in behalf of Spencer; for there is nothing in Spencer's writing relating to what is really honored by men of science (namely, the scientific explanation of the origin of species) that is not to be credited either to Lamarck or to Darwin. This honor is really awarded to the scientific proofs and arguments on the subject, to which many other naturalists besides these more eminent ones, and especially those of Germany, have materially added by their contributions of observation and criticism; so that the theory as it now stands, which the sketch by Professor Schmidt sets forth very lucidly, is really a scientific theory only, and bears no necessary relation to any "system" of philosophy. It is worth noticing here that this sketch, though treating the subject historically, and canvassing the merits of various contributions to it in this century and the last, in Germany, France, and England, nowhere mentions the name or fame of Mr. Herbert Spencer.

But in Germany, where the theory first got the name of Darwinism, it is much more of an "ism," or connects itself much more intimately with general philosophical views, than in England or America, except where in these countries it has got confounded with Mr. Spencer's speculations. It is to the significance of this fact—the character of Darwinism in Germany —that we wished especially in this review to call attention, as an interesting phenomenon in the history of modern speculation, determining the true place and the essential influence of Bacon and the Baconian philosophy. German systematic historians of philosophy were never able to make out where to place Bacon's so-called philosophy, or indeed to discover that he had a philosophy, or, what has appeared to their minds as the same thing, a " system." And indeed he had no system; but by marshaling the forces of criticism known to his time, and reinforced by his own keen invention, against all systems, past and prospective, he aimed at establishing for science a position of neutrality, and at the same time of independent respectability, between the two hostile schools of the Dogmatics and the Empiricists, though leaning towards the tenets of theology just so far as these had practical force and value. He thus secured the true status for the advancement of experimental science, or of experimental philosophy, as it came to be called. He had less need of doing, and deserves less credit for what is more commonly credited to him—namely, laying down the rules of scientific pursuit, which the progress of science has itself much more fully determined. But what could be more fit as a criticism of such a " system " as Mr. Spencer's than these aphorisms from the first book of the " Novum Organum " ?

"Some men become attached to particular sciences and contemplations, either from supposing themselves the authors and inventors of them or from having bestowed the greatest pains upon such subjects, and thus become most habituated to them. If men of this description apply themselves to philosophy and contemplations of a universal nature, they wrest and corrupt them by their preconceived fancies, of which Aristotle affords us a signal instance, who made his natural philosophy completely subservient to his logic, and thus rendered it little more than useless and disputatious. The chemists, again [those of Bacon's time], have formed a fanciful philosophy from a few experiments of the furnace. Gilbert, too [a contemporary of Bacon's], having employed himself most assiduously in the consideration of the magnet, immediately established a system of philosophy to coincide with his favorite pursuit."

And again:

"In general, men take for the groundwork of their philosophy either too much from a few topics or too little from many; in either case, their philosophy is founded on too narrow a basis of experiment and natural history, and decides on too scanty grounds; for the theoretic philosopher seizes various common circumstances by experiment, without reducing them to certainty or examining and frequently considering them, and relies for the rest upon meditation and the activity of his wit."

Under the Baconian régime the physical sciences have flourished in Great Britain for more than two centuries; while "philosophy," as it is known in Germany, both orthodox and heterodox, has dwindled, except so far as it has had practical holds and bearings on one side through theology in religious teachings, or has been reinforced from time to time on both sides from the Continent. In Germany the position of the experimental sciences was far otherwise until near the beginning of this century. The sun of Baconism has not even yet shone fully on the German mind, or except as reflected from the position which the sciences have so long held in Great Britain and France, as compared to the claims of any systems of philosophy. That such a system as Oken's *Naturphilosophie*, with its vague and meaningless abstractions, was an influence at the beginning of the present century, is not, however, so surprising as perhaps it would be if Mr. Spencer's system (bearing a much greater resemblance to it than to any theories of Darwin), had not got such a footing with English-thinking readers as it appears to have. There is, however, at present in Germany an ascetic school of experimental and inductive science, which deprives itself of the aid and guidance of theoretical and deductive considerations, in order the more effectually to protect itself from their undue influence. These *Gelehrten* are not true Baconians; but their method might be appropriately named "experimentalism." Men of science in Germany have in general never considered themselves as in a respectable neutral position with reference to opposite systems of philosophy, and Professor Schmidt in his preface accordingly consents to the cry from both sides in philosophy, "Avow your colors"; and proceeds in his introduction to define his stand-point sharply on several subjects which cultivated English liberal thinkers would consider as irrelevant to the theme of his book—*e. g.*, against "dualism" in vital phenomena, against miracles and other metaphysical positions.

Nothing could be more in keeping, on the other hand, with the refinement of modern English Baconism than the manner in which Darwin presents the doctrine of descent in his "Origin of Species"; and as his scientific inquiry did not touch upon the origin of life itself—but only on the origin of its various forms and their relations to one another and to their surroundings, he even took a pleasure—a poetical, not a dogmatic one, surely—in presenting in religious language his sense of the scientific mystery of life, speaking of "life with its several powers having been originally breathed by the Creator into a few forms or into one," etc. Upon this often-quoted passage our author prosily remarks that "in this Darwin has certainly been untrue to himself, and it satisfies neither those who believe in the continuous work of creation by a personal God, nor the partisans of natural evolution." We doubt if Darwin cared to satisfy any but those who are willing to mark the boundary by a slight difference of style in speaking of the two; between what is evident or probable on experimental grounds, and what as yet baffles all approaches of experimental inquiry. It is a little incongruous that one so pre-eminently cautious and painstaking, so little speculative or metaphysical in the range of his researches, should be hailed as chief by so large a constituency of what really amounts to a philosophical school; albeit they are the brightest minds of Germany, and pre-eminently men of science. Professor Schmidt's book is in form, however, and in effect, a thorough and learned scientific treatise, though he takes grounds, as the earlier French disciples of Newton did, on matters extraneous to his scientific subject.

A FRAGMENT ON CAUSE AND EFFECT.

" Thought is a secretion of the brain " was the announcement of a distinguished naturalist and physiologist, which excited strong aversion to those studies and views of nature which could thus degrade, as it appeared to do, the dignity of so important a function of life. What was, probably, meant, however, by the saying, is the physiological truth that the brain is the organ of thought in a manner analogous to that in which a gland is the organ of secretions, or a muscle of contractions, or the heart and vascular system of circulations. Thought no more resembles a secretion, however, than this resembles a contraction, or than either of these resembles the movements and effects of circulation; not so much, indeed, as these three resemble each other ; yet, like all these three kinds of action, it is dependent, as physiological investigations show, on the intimate structure and vital activity of a special tissue, and its living arrangements and special changes in the brain. It is altogether likely that this is what was meant, and all that was meant, by the somewhat sinister and disagreeable observation that " thought is a secretion of the brain." Men of science sometimes resort to paradoxes, figures of speech, concrete ways of stating truths in science, which those who are ignorant of the science and its real ground of evidence, but imagine that they can judge of its conclusions, are almost sure to misunderstand. Irony is not a more dangerous figure than such a use of comparisons and illustrative figures of speech. Men of science are supposed, except by other men of science, to be literal and exact, and unlike poets, in all their utterances, and when, as Professor Carl Vogt did in the present instance, they seek to impress the imagination by a comparison or figure which is made at the expense of sentiment, their expositions are almost sure to be misconceived, not only by those who are ignorant of their science and its grounds of inference, but even by the more sentimental and unreflective student of the science. What these persons seem to have supposed to be meant is not that thought and its expression are allotted to the brain as a secretion is to a gland, but that thought is a function in life which, as function, is of no more worth or dignity than the functions of the kidneys or of a cutaneous gland. It is altogether probable, however, that a certain feeling of impatience or contempt for the sentimental shallowness which could so misinterpret a scientific comparison, and confound it with moral or practical considerations is a real motive prompting to the utterance of shocking paradoxes, in disregard alike of the practical effect and of scientific clearness and discrimination in the communications of truth. Native common sense is too apt to be coarse and barbarous in its manners, and too inconsiderate of weakness.

We will not venture to say that this was the case with the distinguished biologist whose words have been the cause of so much scandal. The metaphysical doctrine of materialism so often charged against or imputed to such scientific thinkers, is, in fact, a doctrine quite foreign to science, quite out of its range. It belongs, so far as it is intelligible, to the sphere of sentiment, moral feeling and practical principles. A thinker is properly called a materialist when he concludes that his appetites and passions and actions, having material objects and results for their motives, are those most worthy of serious consideration. This does not imply that he believes that natures so different as thoughts, sensations, bodies liquid and solid and their movements, are all fundamentally of the same nature, or are natures some of which are derived from certain other more fundamental ones among them: the spiritual from the material ones. It does not imply the opinion that thought is constituted of motions or liquids, does not even imply that the materialist thinker believes in, or knows anything about, the truth that actual thinking depends, phenomenally, on the tissues, structures and conditions of an organ, as intimately as the liquid secretions and the internal and external movements of a living body do.

Scientific doctrines and investigations are exclusively concerned with connections in phenomena which are susceptible of demonstration by inductive observation, and independent of diversities or resemblances in their hidden natures, or of any question about their metaphysical derivation, or dependence.

That like produces like, and that an effect must resemble its cause are shallow scholastic conceptions, hasty blunders of generalization, which science repudiates: and with them it repudiates the scholastic classification or distinction of material and spiritual which depended on these conceptions, or supposed that a cause conferred its nature on its effect, or that the conditions of a cause by the combination of their natures constituted the nature of the effect. This, in a sense,—in an identical or tautological sense—is indeed true; but from this true, though identical, sense a false and mischievous one was generalized, and still continues to corrupt and misinterpret the results of scientific observation.

In discovering anything to be the cause of something else we have added to our knowledge of the nature of the first thing. We have included in our conception of this thing the attribute of its producing, or being the cause of, the second. If now this attribute of it be the most prominent quality of it in our regard, as it is in contemplating a cause *qua* cause, the effect may, in an identical sense, be said to be constituted by its cause. In this view all the other attributes of the cause are subordinated to the attribute of producing a defined effect, or are regarded as accidental or non-essential attributes, and this is the view of the elementary relations in geometry and mathematics generally which abstraction produces, and is the source of the semblance of demonstrative certainty, and objective necessity which mathematical theorems have. But when science discovers, by induction or empirically, a new cause, the thing previously known by other attributes, to which is now added the attribute of producing a given or defined effect, has nothing in its essential or previously defining attributes at all resembling, implying or constituting its effect, and its newly discovered attribute of producing this effect remains among the added, subordinate or accidental attributes of such a cause. In its essence it does not imply, suggest or resemble its effect, and in this case the assertion that the nature of the cause determines or defines the nature of its effect, is clearly seen, so far as it is true, to be an identical proposition, meaning only that the production of the defined effect is a part, and a subordinate part, of the nature of a thing. The definition of the effect is added to that of the thing which is its cause, at least while we are contemplating this as the cause of the defined effect, and it is only by refunding to the effect what we have thus borrowed from it that we arrive at the metaphysician's mathematical conception of causation, the transference of the nature of one thing, that is, the cause, to another thing, its effect. In mathematics the elements of demonstration are so selected, by abstraction, and their definition so determined that this transference of nature is what is ostensibly done; though it is no more really done than in inferring consequents from antecedents, or effects from causes in so-called empirical science. In all cases where this appears to be the character of the connection of antecedent and consequent, or cause and effect, the transference of the nature of the cause to its effect, is only a restoration to the effect of natures borrowed from it, or into which it is resolvable by analysis. This fact is observed especially in mathematical inference, since such inference is always from a complex antecedent, or from the combination of a number of conditions, of which the aggregate is not known, named or defined by any attributes other than those which by the analysis and recombinations of mathematical demonstrations are shown to depend on the most obvious and elementary truths of our experience of measured quantities. The protasis of a geometrical theorem by the aid of geometrical constructions previously shown, or, when ultimate, simply assumed to be legitimate, is resolved into conditions which, recombined, are the apodosis or conclusion of the proposition. These conditions may be used to define the natures of both the antecedent or reason, and the consequent, and by this means their natures become identical. And both are analyzed ultimately in the course of a series of demonstrations into a few axioms, and these axiomatic truths implied in a few definitions. But not only in the mathematical, but also in the so-called em-

pirical discovery of the connections of antecedent and consequent, or cause and effect, the antecedent or cause is almost
always a combination of conditions, or a concurrence of things,
relations and events, the definition of which in their aggregate,
in merely logical consideration, may as well be the effect which
follows, provided this is sufficient for defining it, as be anything
else ; since this aggregate of conditions is not usually denoted
by a single name, the connotation of which would define its
nature. Yet for practical and scientific purposes this aggregate
is best defined by the enumeration of the conditions that compose it, to which observation adds the fact, or nature, that it
will whenever it exists be followed by a given or defined effect.
In this case the conditions which constitute the cause do not
constitute the effect. They are simply followed by the effect,
whose nature is wholly unlike that of its cause, or is like and is
implied in its cause only so far as the capacity of producing it
may be thought of identically as a part of the nature of its
cause. Thus a stone, or any body denser (1) than the air, left
unsupported (2) above (3) the surface of the earth, will fall (4)
to it, is a proposition in so-called empirical science, in which
the conditions (1) (2) (3) form an aggregate to which if we add
as a part of its nature the result (4), that is, add the unconditional *tendency* to fall inferred from facts of observation, then
the fall is a necessary consequence of the nature of its antecedent conditions, and it is like or is implied in this nature, quite
as truly as any mathematical consequence is necessary, or is
implied in mathematical protases of causes or antecedents.
But ordinarily physical philosophers are not so anxious to make
a scholastic show of demonstration as to surreptitiously add (4)
to the group of conditions (1) (2) and (3) so as to make out
their proof on the maxims that like produces like, or that effects
resemble or partake of the nature of their causes. These maxims are really no more true of abstract reasonings in the elementary demonstrations of geometry; but the aim of these
elementary reasonings justifies the procedures which give apparent countenance to their maxims.

Other and real illustrations vaguely related to these apparent
ones are given in the organic world, in the phenomena of as-

similation and reproduction. Tissues turn nutriment into substances of the same kind as their own. Offspring resemble their parents. These facts, together with the geometrical principle of Sufficient Reason appeared to be sufficient grounds with scholastic philosophers for generalizing the identity of natures in real causes and effects. But, in fact, the very opposite is true. Elementary relations of antecedence and consequence are always those of unlikeness. A simple nature or phenomenon A is invariably followed by, or joined with, another different one B. Weight in a body manifested to us primarily by pressure, or in the tension of our muscles through the statical muscular sense, is a simple nature not resembling or implying at all the downward movement which always follows it when isolated or freed from other forces or conditions that are of a nature to produce an opposite effect, namely, an elastic movement, or bearing upward, and are as unlike this effect as weight is unlike the movement of falling. So in the elements of geometry the quality straightness and that of minimum length—duration or effort in traversing a line —are antecedent and consequent, or else concomitant qualities which are essentially different in their natures, but so intimately joined in all experience and in our conceptive powers, that they seem to be different aspects of one and the same nature. Yet the fully adequate and constructive definition of straight lines as a sort, of which only one can be drawn between two given points, does not imply that this is the shortest that can be drawn, or the one soonest and easiest traversed. This constructive definition joined to the meaning of the word inclosure gives what is often regarded as an axiom, the more complex proposition, that two straight lines cannot inclose a space. Starting with these and other constructive definitions, with the most general axioms of quantity, and with postulates of construction, and combining them into more and more complex relations of magnitudes in extension, we arrive at geometrical theorems in which the protasis states the least possible that is essential as the cause, or reason, and the apodosis, or conclusion, defines succinctly the consequent, or effect; theorems in which the connections of these two terms is far from obvious, but is nevertheless necessary, at least in the abstract, or on the supposition of precise, real definition and construction. Reason and consequent imply one the other, or the nature of a cause determines that of its effect, because one is analyzed into relations already determined from fundamental propositions, and these relations serve to define, or constitute the other. It is not true in general that the effect is like its cause, or has a nature determined by that of its cause, but it is true that like causes produce like effects. Parents may be said with tolerable correctness to be the causes of their offspring resembling them, and hence in this case causes produce effects like themselves; yet it is more correct to say that the offspring resemble their parents, because both are products, though successive ones, of similar real causes and processes, some of which in nowise resemble or transfer their natures to their effects. Some implements and agents of the useful arts likewise are used to make precisely similar implements and agents, as a blacksmith's hammer to produce a similar hammer, or fire to kindle another one, or to reproduce the easily ignited substances with which fires are kindled; yet in these cases the agent that produces its like is not the whole of the cause of production. The blacksmith's forge and anvil and his arm and sight are concauses or conditions of this reproduction: and the nature of these does not re-appear in the effect, unless, as we have said, there is added to the conception of the aggregate of conditions, namely, to the conception of the iron, forge, welding-hammer, arm and sight combined, also the fact that these will produce an effect resembling one of its conditions. So in organic reproduction, the plant produces seed similar not to itself but to the seed from which it grew, and the new seed grows into a similar plant: and in this alternation in which the immediate cause really produces effects unlike itself there are many subordinate conditions and processes the similarity of which in the parent and offspring makes them similar through successive effects of similar causes, which are not of the same nature as their effect. It is only because one condition or element of the cause (the one which resembles its effect) is singled out and, in accordance with the practical usage of common language, is called the cause, on account of its prominence or conspicuousness, that it is at all proper to speak of the parent organism as the cause of the production of its offspring. The existence of the parent organism is a condition *sine qua non* of the production of its offspring, but there are other conditions equally indispensable, the natures of which in themselves are in no wise reproduced in the effects.—[1873.]

JOHN STUART MILL—A COMMEMORATIVE NOTICE.*

The name of John Stuart Mill is so intimately associated with most of the principal topics of modern philosophical discussion, and with the gravest of open questions, with so many of the weightiest subjects of unsettled theory and practice, that it would be difficult to say for which of his many works his fame is at present the greatest or is most likely to endure. Those subjects in the treatment of which the originality of his position was the least were those in which the qualities most characteristic of him, and for which his writings have been most esteemed, appear in clearest light. Unlike most other great thinkers and masters of dialectics, he did not seek to display what his own invention had contributed to the arguments, or his observation to the premises, in his discussion of philosophical and practical questions. On the contrary, he seemed to be indifferent to the appearance and reputation of originality, and actuated by a singleness of purpose and a loyalty to the views of his teachers in philosophy and science which were inconsistent with motives of personal vanity. The exercise of his admirably trained dialectical powers doubtless afforded him intrinsic delight, the joy of play, or of spontaneity of power; but it was none the less always subordinated to moral purposes which were clearly defined in his youth, and loyally pursued through an active intellectual life for nearly half a century. But his broad practical aims were never allowed, on the other hand, to pervert the integrity and honesty of his intellect. Though an advocate all his life, urging reasons for unpopular measures of reform, and defenses of an unpopular philosophy

* From the Proceedings of the American Academy of Arts and Sciences, 1873-74.

or criticisms of the prevailing one, he was not led, as advocates too frequently are, to the indiscriminate invention and use of bad and good arguments. He weighed his arguments as dispassionately as if his aim had been pure science. Rarely have strength of emotion and purpose and strength of intellect been combined in a thinker with such balance and harmony The strength of his moral emotions gave him insights or premises which had been overlooked by the previous thinkers whose views he expounded or defended. This advantage over his predecessors was conspicuous in the form he gave to the utilitarian theory of moral principles, and in what was strictly original in his " Principles of Political Economy."

In the latter, the two chief points of originality were, first, his treatment of the subject as a matter of pure abstract science, like geometry; or as an account of the means which are requisite to attain given ends in economics, or the cost needed to procure a given value, without bringing into the discussion the irrelevant practical questions, whether this cost should be incurred, or whether the end were on the whole desirable. These questions really belong to other branches of practical philosophy,—to the sciences of legislation, politics, and morals, to which the principles of political economy stand in the relation of an abstract science to sciences of applied principles and concrete matters. But, secondly, while thus limiting the province of this science, he introduced into it premises from the moral nature of man, by the omission of which previous writers had been led to conclusions in the science of a character gloomy and forbidding. The theory of population of Malthus, as elaborated by Ricardo, seemed to subject the human race to a hopeless necessity of poverty in the masses. Whether the principle of population did really necessitate this conclusion would depend, Mill taught, on more than the capacity of a soil to support a *maximum* population with the least subsistence needed for the labor of production. The principle applies without qualification to the animal world in general and to savage men; but not to progressive communities of men, in which foresight and prudence, with moral and social aspirations, are forces of more or less influence in checking increase in population, and in improving the condition of the masses. The poorest, the most wretched, are not in the same condition of want in all communities of men. The poorest savage is objectively in a worse condition than the poorest civilized man.

Mill did not oppose the views of his predecessors nor their manner of treatment, as so many other writers had done: he carried out their mode of regarding the science as a physical one, but with a thoroughness which brought to light considerations materially modifying their conclusions. The prospects of mankind are not hopeless, so long as men are capable of aspirations, foresight and hope; though they may be gloomy enough in view of the slow working of these forces. What these forces have to oppose, however, is not the resistance of an immovable necessity, but only the force of inveterate customs. To the sentimental objection that the laws of political economy are cruel, and therefore not true, Mill humorously replied that he knew of no law more cruel than that of gravity, which would put us all to death, were we not always and vigilantly on our guard against it.

With a full, perhaps a too extreme appreciation of moral forces, as elements in the problems of Political Economy, Mill still treated the science as an abstract one; as a science of conditional propositions, a science applicable to the practical problems of morals and politics, but not in itself treating of them. For example, wars are expensive, and the establishment of a new industry is also an expense which the principles of political economy can estimate; but it does so without deciding whether war or an industry ought under given circumstances to be undertaken.

Moral forces are real agents affecting the future of the human race. As causes of effects, they are calculable forces, and as means to ends are proper subjects of the abstract science of political economy. It was because Mr. Mill believed in " moral causation " (the name he gave to what had indiscriminately been called the doctrine of *necessity* in human volition), and because he himself was powerfully and predominantly actuated throughout his life by high moral considerations, that he gave such emphasis to the moral elements in political economy, and made room for hope—for a sober, rational hope—respecting the practical conclusions and applications of the science; seeing that hope can subsist with the desire that inspires it, provided the desire is instrumental in effecting what is hoped for. It was because he believed in "moral causation" that he treated political science, in general, in the manner and by the methods of physical philosophy, or as a science of causes and effects. He believed that he himself and his generation would effect much for the future of mankind. His faith was that we live in times in which broad principles of justice, persistently proclaimed, end in carrying the world with them.

His hopefulness, generosity, and courage, and a chivalric, almost romantic disposition in him, seemed to those least acquainted with him inconsistent with the utilitarian philosophy of morals, which he not only professed, but earnestly and even zealously maintained. The "greatest happiness principle" was with him a religious principle, to which every impulse in his nature, high or low, was subordinated. It was for him not only a *test* of rational rules of conduct (which is all that could be, or was, claimed for it in his philosophy of morals), but it became for him a leading motive and sanction of conduct in his theory of life. That other minds differently constituted would be most effectively influenced to the nobility of right conduct by other sanctions and motives, to which the utilitarian principle ought to be regarded as only a remote philosophical test or rational standard, was what he believed and taught. Unlike Bentham, his master in practical philosophy, he felt no contempt for the claims of sentiment, and made no intolerant demand for toleration. He sincerely welcomed intelligent and earnest opposition with a deference due to truth itself, and to a just regard for the diversities in men's minds from differences of education and natural dispositions. These diversities even appeared to him essential to the completeness of the examination which the evidences of truth demand. Opinions positively erroneous, if intelligent and honest, are not without their value, since the progress of truth is a succession of mistakes and corrections. Truth itself, unassailed by erroneous opinion, would soon degenerate into narrowness and error. The errors incident to individuality of mind and character are means, in the attrition of discussion, of keeping the truth bright and untarnished, and even of bringing its purity to light. The human mind cannot afford to forget its past aberrations. These, as well as its true discoveries, are indispensable guides; nor can it ever afford to begin from the starting-point in its search for truth, in accordance with the too confident method of more ambitious philosophers.

Such being his loyalty and generosity, it is not surprising that Mill obtained a much wider acceptance of utilitarian doctrines, and a more intelligent recognition of their real import, than previous thinkers of his school had secured. He redeemed the word "utility" from the ill-repute into which it had fallen, and connected noble conceptions and motives with its philosophical meaning. It is now no longer a synonym of the ignoble or base, or the name of that quality in conduct, or in anything which conduces to the satisfaction of desires common to all men. He made it mean clearly the quality in human customs and rules of conduct which conduces to realize conditions and dispositions which for men (though not for swine) are practicable, and are the most desirable; their desirableness being tested by the actual preference which those who possess them have for them as elements in their own happiness. This meaning of utility includes the highest motives in whose satisfaction an individual's happiness can consist, and not the baser ones alone; not even the base ones at all, so far as they obstruct the sources of a greater happiness than they can afford. It is now no longer a paradox to the intelligent student of Mill's philosophy, that he should prefer, as he has avowed, the worst evil which could be inflicted on him against his will, to the pains of a voluntary sophistication of his intellect in respect to the more serious concerns of life.

His method led him to conceal or at least subordinate to his single purpose most of what was original in his discussions of the various philosophical subjects to which he gave his attention. Yet his studies in logic, ethics, psychology, political economy and politics, and even in poetry, are full of valuable and fertile contributions of original thought; and of that kind of service to philosophy which he most valued in such writers as Dr. Brown and Archbishop Whately,—a kind of service which he believed would survive the works of more learned and ambitious thinkers. A thorough preparation for his work, to which his education was directed by his father, realized what is rare in modern times,—a complete command of the art of dialectics; an art which he believed to be of the greatest service in the honest pursuit of truth, though liable to abuse at the hand of the dishonest advocate. His education was like that of an ancient Greek philosopher,—by personal intercourse with other superior thinkers. He felt keenly in his later work, as Plato had, "how much more is to be learned by discussing with a man who can question and answer, than with a book which cannot." That he was not educated at a university, and through the influences of equals and coevals in intellectual and moral development, may account for one serious defect in his powers of observation,—a lack of sensibility to the differences of character in men and between the sexes. So far as he did recognize these mental diversities, he prized them for the sake of truth, as he would have prized the addition of a new sense to the means of extending and testing knowledge. But he did not clearly discriminate what was really a reflection, as in a mirror, or a quick anticipation of his own thoughts in other minds, from true and original observations by them. This may be accounted for in part by his philosophical habit, as has been observed, "of always keeping in view mind in the abstract, or men in the aggregate." Though he mingled in the affairs of life with other men, taking part in debates and discussions, private and public, by speech and by writing, all his life, his disposition was still essentially that of a recluse. He remained remote in his intellectual life from the minds and characters of those with whom he contended, though always loyal to those from whom his main doctrines, his education, and inspiration were derived.

A natural consequence of his private education by a philosopher (his father), and by intercourse with superior adult minds, like Bentham and the political economist Say, was that he soon arrived at maturity, and was in full possession of his remarkable powers in early youth, able and eager to exercise them upon the most abtruse and difficult subjects. Annotations to Bentham's "Rationale of Judicial Evidence" was his first publicly acknowledged literary work, performed before he was yet of age; though contributions to the science of botany and other writings were labors of his youth. While still in his youth, before the age of thirty, he advocated reforms in an article in the "Jurist" on "Corporation and Church Property," features of which became acknowledged principles of legislation in Parliament many years later. He lived to see many of the reforms proposed by Bentham enacted as public law, and to take part in Parliament in the furtherance of some of his own political ideas. His courage and hopefulness were not quixotic, but were sustained by real successes. These qualities in his character, though perhaps properly described as romantic, or as springing from an ardent, emotional temperament, were always tempered by his cooler reason and by facts. In more than one division of special study in science and philosophy he mastered facts and details at first hand, or by his own observation; thus training his judgment and powers of imagination to those habits of accuracy so essential in a true education, by which knowledge more extensive, more or less superficial, and necessarily at second hand, can alone be adequately comprehended. He was prepared for writing an important part of his great work on Logic by the study of the principles, requisites, and purposes of a rational classification in the practical pursuit of botany,—a favorite pastime with him throughout his life. The use to him of this kind of knowledge, as of all other kinds worthy to be called science, was in its bearings on other and wider branches of knowledge. He generalized the principles exhibited in the natural system of botanical classification to their application "to all cases in which mankind are called upon to bring the various parts of any extensive subject into mental co-ordination. They are as much to the point," he adds, "when objects are to be classed for purposes of art or business, as for those of science. The proper arrangement, for example, of a code of laws, depends on the same scientific conditions as the classifications of natural history; nor could there be a better preparatory discipline for that important function than the study of the principles of a natural arrangement, not only in the abstract, but in their actual applications to the class of phenomena for which they were first elaborated, and which are still the best school for learning their use." To rightly divide and define is divine, said Plato; yet it is not an excellence by which the divine is distinguished from a human perfection. It is rather a perfection which is relative to human limits and weaknesses.

The "mastery system" of studying a subject in its facts, and at first hand, was not liable with Mill to degenerate into the mere idiotic pursuit of facts, since the character of his mind was already determined by a strong philosophical bias. Even subjects like the fine arts, which are commonly and properly regarded as affording ends in themselves, or sufficient and worthy motives to study, interested Mill as affording broad principles and influences, extending beyond the immediate and present delight they inspire. In his readings of poetry he looked not merely for beauties or for sympathy, but for principles, causes, and influences; for the relations of it to the times in which it appeared. So wide was the range of his studies and his intellectual sympathies, that no writer has given wiser advice on the much debated subject of education, or advice more satisfactory to all parties, even to the advocates of special studies.

Mr. Mill was a thinker about whose personal character and circumstances of education the student naturally seeks to learn. In such a thinker, these elements of power are instinctively felt to be of prime importance. They explain Mill's later influence at the universities, where, though not personally known, his effect upon the young men of the most active minds, through his principal works, his Political Economy and his System of Logic, became a powerful one, though purely spontaneous; for it did not come in by the normal channels of the *curriculum.* It was with men of the succeeding generation (as generally happens with great innovators in science and philosophy) that his teachings were destined to be fully appreciated.

But his teachings were none of them fundamentally new; or what was new in them was, or appeared to be, subordinate to what he had avowedly borrowed from previous thinkers. He was neither the author of a new system of philosophy, nor the discoverer of a new science. He can hardly be called, in strictness, the advocate even, of any previous doctrine in philosophy or science. It was one of his short-comings that he took for granted more than most of his readers knew. His starting-point was in advance of what most of them knew, and he was thus unintelligible to many of the best minds among his coevals. Starting from what many of them did not know, he completed, carried out, and put into a scientific form in his "System of Logic," and in his "Principles of Political Economy," the views he had adopted from his earlier teachers and from his later studies.

It was through his masterly style of exposition and his skill in dialectics, and by other traits of a personal character to which active and original youth is especially alive, that he secured an unprejudiced hearing for doctrines in philosophy and practice which had almost ceased to have adherents. These doctrines had a century before, from the time of Locke (and before Hume had developed them with such alarming effect on existing beliefs), become an especially English philosophy; but had almost disappeared through the influence of the Scottish and German reactions against Hume. When his "System of Logic" was published, he stood almost alone in his opinions. The work was not written in exposition or defense of this philosophy, but in accordance with its tenets, which were thus reduced to a proximate application, or to a more determinate or concrete form. A qualified nominalism, thoroughly English, and descended from the English schoolman William of Ockham, was its philosophical basis. He welcomed and introduced to English readers the revival of this philosophy in France, by Auguste Comte, with whom he agreed in many positions,—more especially in those which were not original with Comte. His accordance with Comte can hardly be regarded as one of discipleship, since in most important practical matters Mill dissented from the views of the French philosopher. His real allegiance was to the once prevalent teachings of Locke, and to those of Berkeley, Hume, Brown, Hartley, and his father James Mill.

No modern thinker has striven more faithfully to restore and build upon those speculations of the past, which appeared to him just and true, or more modestly to exhibit and acknowledge his indebtedness to previous thinkers; yet, by the excellence of his works, this past has fallen to the inheritance of his name and fame. To give scientific form or systematic coherency to views put forth unsystematically by others, was to give soul and life to doctrines which were thus made especially his own. The teachings of Sir John Herschel's celebrated "Discourse on the Study of Natural Philosophy" were generalized by Mill into what is his most original contribution to logic, his theory of induction and of the inductive basis of all real truth. From this theory, important consequences were drawn as to the nature and function of syllogistic inference,—consequences from which the philosophical student remounts to the philosophy of experience and the teachings of Hume. From Hume and Brown, again, he derives his theory of causation, which he connects with other elements in his system, and with illustrations in science in a manner which has made the theory peculiarly his own. But it would be out of place in this notice to attempt an analysis of Mill's works. Our task is only to account for his influence.

In politics he belonged to what is called the school of "philosophical radicals," who are, as he defined them, those who in politics follow the common manner of philosophers; who trust neither to tradition nor to intuition for the warrant of political rights and duties, but base the right to power in the State on the ability to govern wisely and justly, and, seeing their country badly governed, seek for the cause of this evil, and for means to remedy it. This cause they found to be in "the Aristocratical Principle," since, in the present imperfect condition of human nature, no governing class would attend to those interests of the many which were in conflict with their own, or could be expected to give to any interests not their own any but a secondary consideration. The remedy for this evil they found in a modified democratic principle; namely, the better ability and disposition of the many to look after their own interests, than any dominant few could have, or would be likely to have,—provided the many, or their representatives, are enlightened enough to know their true interests and how to serve them. The motto of this radicalism was "Enmity to the Aristocratical Principle." From this creed sprung Mill's ardent hostility towards the South in their rebellion against our national government, and his hearty espousal of extreme anti-slavery views.

But a democracy may be tyrannical towards minorities, and, if unchecked, is likely to become so; and, what is worse, is likely to become an unprincipled tyrant, less influenced by considerations of justice or prudence than a governing class would be. This fear made Mill distrust extreme forms of democracy and government by mere majorities. Accordingly, among his later works, his "Considerations on Representative Government" undertakes to devise checks to the abuse of power by majorities. But it is evident that Mill's greatest trust was in those influences which have given to communities the ability, and thence the power and right, to govern themselves; namely, their intelligence and moral integrity, or that which reduces the necessity of government by force to the fewest functions and occasions. His famous essay on Liberty sought to establish, on grounds of moral principle, restraints of governmental force, in whatever way it might be exercised, whether in the form of public law or of public opinion; neither of which in any form of government is likely to be wiser beyond its proper sphere of duty than those it seeks to control. Government in advanced communities, capable of self-government, should not be of the parental type or degree of power. Coercion, which in itself is an evil, becomes a wrong, where persuasion, rational discussion, and conviction are capable of effecting the same ends, especially when these ends are less urgent than the need of security and self-protection in a community, for which it is the proper duty of government by force to provide. To place government in the hands of those sufficiently intelligent, whose true interests are most affected by it, and to limit its province and its functions as much as possible, leaving as much as possible to non-coercive agencies, was the simple abstract creed of Mill's political philosophy.

The essay on "Liberty" and his later essay on "The Subjection of Women" exhibit the ardent, emotional, enthusiastic, perhaps not the soundest, side of Mr. Mill's mental character and observation of human nature. Yet he cannot be said to have been without much experience in the practical art of government. He was in immediate charge of the "political department," so called, of the East India House for more than twenty years. It was during this period, and in the midst of active employments, that his Logic and Political Economy were written. Both were thought out in the vigor of life and at the summit of his powers. His mind and pen were never idle. At about the age of fifty, he published selections from his occasional short writings for reviews. These had more than a passing interest, since in them, as in all his writings, great and often new principles of criticism are lucidly set forth. In all his writings, his judgments are valued by his readers, not as judgments on occasional matters by a current or conventional standard, but as tests and illustrations of new standards of criticism, which have a general and enduring interest, especially to the examining minds of youth.

With a tact almost feminine, Mill avoided open war on abstract grounds. The principles of his philosophy were set forth in their applications, and were advocated by bringing them down in application to the common sense or instinctive, unanalyzed judgments of his readers. His conclusions in psychology and on the fundamental principles of philosophy were nowhere systematically set forth. In his Logic, they were rather assumed, and made the setting of his views of the science, than defended on general grounds; though, from his criticisms of adverse views on the principles of Logic, it was sufficiently apparent what his philosophy and psychological doctrines were.

English speaking and reading people had so completely forgotten, or had so obscurely understood the arguments of their greatest thinkers, that the inroad of German speculation had almost overwhelmed the protest of these thinkers against the *a priori* philosophy. English-speaking people are not netaphysical, and Mill respected their prejudice. But when the philosophy of Sir William Hamilton, professing to combine the Scottish and German reactions against Hume with what science had demonstrated as the necessary limits of human knowledge, was about to become the prevalent philosophy of England and America, it was not merely an opportunity, but almost a necessity, for the representative of the greatest English thinkers (himself among the greatest), to re-examine the claims of the *a priori* philosophy, and either to acknowledge the failure of his own attempt to revive the doctrines of his predecessors, or to refute and overthrow their most powerful British antagonist. Accordingly Mill's "Examination of Sir William Hamilton's Philosophy," published in 1865, when he was nearly sixty years old, but in the full vigor and maturity of his powers, was his greatest effort in polemical writing. That the reputation of Sir William Hamilton as a thinker was greatly diminished by this examination cannot be doubted. Nor can it be doubted that the pendulum of philosophical opinion has begun, through Mill's clear expositions and vigorous defense of the Experience philosophy, to move again towards what was a century and a half ago the prevalent English philosophy. That its future movements will be less extreme in either direction, and that the amplitude of its oscillations have continually diminished in the past through the progress of philosophical discussion, were beliefs with which his studies in philosophy and his generous hopefulness inspired him. Men are still born either Platonists or Aristotelians; but by their education through a more and more free and enlightened discussion, and by progress in the sciences, they are restrained more and more from going to extremes in the directions of their native biases.

In Mill's Examination of Hamilton, and in his last great work, the annotated edition of his father's "Analysis of the Phenomena of the Human Mind," many valuable subsidiary contributions are made to the sciences of logic and psychology. But in all his writings on these subjects his attention was directed to their bearings on the traditional problems and discussions of general philosophy. The modern developments of psychology, as a branch of experimental science, and in connection with physiology, deeply interested him; but they did not engage him in their pursuit, although they promise much towards the solution of unsettled questions. His mental powers were trained for a different though equally important service to science,—the service of clear and distinct thought, the understanding, first of all, of that for which closer observation and the aid of experiment are needed; the precise comprehension and pertinent putting of questions. The progress of science has not yet outgrown the need of guidance by the intellectual arts of logic and method, which are still equal in importance to those of experiment. The imagination of the scientific inquisitor of nature, the fertility of his invention, his ability to frame hypotheses or put pertinent questions, though still generally dependent on his good sense, and his practical training in experimental science, are susceptible still of furtherance and improvement by the abstract studies of logic and method. Open questions on the psychological conditions of vision are to be settled, Mill thought, only when some one so unfortunate as to be born blind is fortunate enough to be born a philosopher.

Mill has been aptly compared to Locke. Their philosophies were fundamentally the same. Both were "philosophical radicals" and political reformers. "What Locke was to the liberal movements of the seventeenth century, Mr. Mill has more than been to the liberal movement of the nineteenth century." He was born on the 20th of May, 1806, and died on the 8th of May, 1873 having nearly reached the age of sixty-seven. Previous to the brief illness from which he died, he retained unimpaired his mental vigor and industry; and though it may not be said that he lived to see the hopes of his youth fully realized, yet his efforts have met with a degree of success in later years which he did not anticipate. His followers are still few both in politics and in philosophy. So far was he from restoring the doctrines of his school as the dominant philosophy of England, that, according to his own esti-

mate, "we may still count in England twenty *a priori* or spiritualist philosophers for every partisan of the doctrine of Experience." But it was for the practical applications of this doctrine in politics and in morals, rather than for the theoretical
recognition of it in general, that he most earnestly strove; and
we should probably find in England and America to-day a
much larger proportion, among those holding meditated and
deliberate opinions on practical matters, who are in these the
disciples of Mill, than can be found among the students of abstract philosophy.

INDEX.

THE END.

1057
3